Sophistic Views of the Epic Past from the Classical to the Imperial Age

Also available from Bloomsbury

Early Greek Philosophies of Nature, Andrew Gregory
Sophist Kings, Vernon L. Provencal
Sophrosune in the Greek Novel, Rachel Bird

Sophistic Views of the Epic Past from the Classical to the Imperial Age

Edited by Paola Bassino and Nicolò Benzi

BLOOMSBURY ACADEMIC
LONDON • NEW YORK • OXFORD • NEW DELHI • SYDNEY

BLOOMSBURY ACADEMIC
Bloomsbury Publishing Plc
50 Bedford Square, London, WC1B 3DP, UK
1385 Broadway, New York, NY 10018, USA
29 Earlsfort Terrace, Dublin 2, Ireland

BLOOMSBURY, BLOOMSBURY ACADEMIC and the Diana logo are trademarks of
Bloomsbury Publishing Plc

First published in Great Britain 2022
This paperback edition published 2023

Copyright © Paola Bassino and Nicolò Benzi and contributors, 2022

Paola Bassino, Nicolò Benzi and contributors have asserted their right under the Copyright,
Designs and Patents Act, 1988, to be identified as Authors of this work.

Cover design: Terry Woodley
Cover image © *The Building of the Trojan Horse* by Giovanni Domenico Tiepolo
(1727–1804), oil on canvas, c.1760

All rights reserved. No part of this publication may be reproduced or transmitted in
any form or by any means, electronic or mechanical, including photocopying,
recording, or any information storage or retrieval system, without prior permission
in writing from the publishers.

Bloomsbury Publishing Plc does not have any control over, or responsibility for, any
third-party websites referred to or in this book. All internet addresses given in this book
were correct at the time of going to press. The author and publisher regret any
inconvenience caused if addresses have changed or sites have ceased to exist,
but can accept no responsibility for any such changes.

A catalogue record for this book is available from the British Library.

Library of Congress Cataloging-in-Publication Data

Names: Bassino, Paola, 1983– editor. | Benzi, Nicolò, editor.
Title: Sophistic views of the epic past from the classical to the imperial age /
edited by Paola Bassino and Nicolò Benzi.
Description: New York : Bloomsbury Academic, 2021. |
Includes bibliographical references and index.
Identifiers: LCCN 2021018817 (print) | LCCN 2021018818 (ebook) |
ISBN 9781350255760 (hardback) | ISBN 9781350255777 (ebook) |
ISBN 9781350255784 (epub)
Subjects: LCSH: Sophists (Greek philosophy) | Epic poetry, Greek–History and criticism.
Classification: LCC B288 .S656 2021 (print) | LCC B288 (ebook) | DDC 183/.1—dc23
LC record available at https://lccn.loc.gov/2021018817
LC ebook record available at https://lccn.loc.gov/2021018818

ISBN: HB: 978-1-3502-5576-0
PB: 978-1-3502-5580-7
ePDF: 978-1-3502-5577-7
eBook: 978-1-3502-5578-4

Typeset by RefineCatch Limited, Bungay, Suffolk

To find out more about our authors and books visit www.bloomsbury.com
and sign up for our newsletters.

Contents

Notes on Contributors   vi

Introduction   *Paola Bassino and Nicolò Benzi*   1

Part One   The First Sophistic

1. Between Homer and Gorgias: Helen's Bewitching Power
   Roberta Ioli   19

2. Palamedes, The Sophistic Hero   *Paola Bassino*   41

3. Ajax versus Odysseus   *Hugo Koning*   65

4. Mythological Role-Playing among the Sophists
   Kathryn A. Morgan   89

Part Two   The Second Sophistic

5. Homeric Exegesis and Athetesis in Lucian's Versions of the Judgement of Paris   *Nicholas Wilshere*   115

6. Helen Was Never Abducted, Paris Abducted Her Because He Was Bored: Two Ways of Rewriting Homer in Dio Chrysostom (Orr. 11 and 20)   *Sara Tirrito*   143

7. Homer's Lies and Dio's Truth? Subverting the Epic Past in Dio Chrysostom's *Trojan Oration*   *Isidor Brodersen*   165

8. A Rhetorical Trojan War: Philostratus' *Heroicus*, the Power of Language and the Construction of the Truth
   Valentin Decloquement   187

9. Reading Homer and the Epic Cycle through *Ekphrasis*: Philostratus' Epic *Imagines*   *A. Sophie Schoess*   211

Index   237

Contributors

Paola Bassino is Senior Lecturer in Classical Studies in the Department of History at the University of Winchester. She has published articles on archaic Greek epic and its reception, including on biographical representations of the ancient Greek epic poets. She is the author of *Certamen Homeri et Hesiodi: A Commentary* (Berlin 2018) and co-editor of *Conflict and Consensus in Early Greek Hexameter Poetry* (Cambridge 2017).

Nicolò Benzi is Lecturer in Classical and Archaeological Studies in the Department of Classical and Archaeological Studies at the University of Kent Honorary Research Fellow in the Department of Greek & Latin at UCL and in the Department of Classics, Ancient History, Archaeology and Egyptology at the University of Manchester. His research interests focus on the intersection between philosophy and literature, in particular in Archaic and early Classical Greece. He has published articles on early Greek philosophical poetry and its relation to epic and lyric poetry.

Isidor Brodersen is Teaching Assistant at the Ruhr University Bochum, Germany, having completed his PhD thesis on "Playing with the Past in the Second Sophistic" at the University of Duisburg-Essen in 2022. His research interests include Greek historiography, humour and laughter in antiquity, intertextuality, and reception studies.

Valentin Decloquement holds a PhD degree in Ancient Greek literature from the University of Lille (France), where he has been teaching since 2015. He wrote a dissertation, defended in 2019 and entitled 'Commenting on, criticizing and rewriting Homer in Philostratus' *Heroikos*', under the supervision of Ruth Webb and the co-supervision of Kristoffel Demoen (Ghent, Belgium). He has published articles on the Second Sophistic, rhetorical practices and Homeric criticism in the first to third centuries. He currently holds a postdoctoral fellowship funded by the Research Foundation - Flanders (FWO) at Ghent University.

Roberta Ioli (MPhil in Classics, University of Cambridge, PhD in Philosophy, University of Rome Tor Vergata) is Independent Researcher in Ancient Philosophy and cooperates with the Department of Philosophy at the University of Bologna. Her research interests mainly focus on Eleatic Philosophy, Sophistic,

Greek Epic and Tragedy. She has published on Scepticism, Presocratic Philosophy, and the connections between Greek poetry and vocality. Her most recent books are *Gorgia. Testimonianze e frammenti* (Rome 2013) and *Il felice inganno. Poesia, finzione e verità nel mondo antico* (Milan 2018).

Hugo Koning is a University Lecturer at the Classics Department of Leiden University and a teacher of Ancient Greek at Stanislascollege in Delft. His research interests focus on archaic epic, ancient reception and mythology. He is currently working with Glenn Most on a collection and translation of ancient and Byzantine exegetical texts on Hesiod's *Theogony*.

Kathryn A. Morgan is Professor of Classics at the University of California, Los Angeles. Her research interests range broadly over Greek literature of the fifth and fourth centuries BC, from Pindar, Greek lyric and Attic tragedy to Plato. Recent articles and book chapters have focused on Simonides, Platonic narratology and Platonic metaphor. Her most recent book, *Pindar and the Construction of Syracusan Monarchy in the Fifth Century B.C.* (Oxford 2015), examines Pindar's victory odes for Hieron of Syracuse and the programme of tyrannical self-representation to which they contributed.

A. Sophie Schoess is Associate Lecturer in Classics at the University of St Andrews. Her research interests include the relationship between image and text in the Classical world, and the reception of Classical myth from Late Antiquity through Modernity. Her doctoral thesis (University of Oxford, 2018) traced the reception of Ariadne's myth in literature and the visual arts from antiquity through the Renaissance. Her current research focuses on Christian interpretations and appropriations of Classical myth in Late Antiquity and the Middle Ages.

Sara Tirrito is a PhD student in Classics at the Universities of Nantes and Turin. Her research interests focus on Greek prose during the Imperial Age and in Late Antiquity, especially Rhetorical Production and Public Speaking. She worked on Aeneas of Gaza and she is currently working on Dio of Prusa's speeches 18–21. Her most recent article is 'Nota all'Ep. XXV di Enea di Gaza', *RET* 6: 83–92.

Nicholas Wilshere is Assistant Professor in Greek and Latin in the Department of Classics and Archaeology at the University of Nottingham. His research interests are Lucian, ancient humour and the reception of Homer within antiquity. He also teaches a wide variety of courses for the Leicester Adult Skills and Learning Service.

Introduction

Paola Bassino and Nicolò Benzi

This volume aims to offer new insights on the relationships between two of the main driving forces that shaped the intellectual discourse in the Greek world: the epic tradition, which for centuries influenced all aspects of the intellectual and everyday life of the Greeks, and the Sophists, who operated within – and contributed to – new, changing cultural environments. We take a diachronic perspective on the topic, including both the first and second Sophistic. By doing so, we hope to contribute to our understanding of the role that the epic tradition, on which traditional Greek values were based, played in periods of major cultural transformation.

Before delineating the main features of the relationship between Sophistic and epic, it is helpful to start with a terminological clarification, as the usage of the terms 'Sophist' and 'Sophistic' is less straightforward than it might appear at a first glance (especially in relation to the cultural milieu of fifth-century BC Greece). Who were the Sophists? The term σοφιστής functioned, in its earliest occurrences, as a near synonym for σοφός, 'wise'. It was used, with a neutral connotation, to indicate someone who could claim a share of wisdom and was applied to poets, sages, musicians, seers and other categories of experts.[1] From the fourth century BC, mainly under Plato's influence, the term assumed the more technical, and negative, meaning of 'professional educators who gave instruction to young men, and public displays of eloquence, for fees'.[2] Far from being a homogenous group of intellectuals, as the use of a common denomination might suggest, each of the Sophists pursued different interests and doctrines, ranging from politics and rhetoric to arithmetic, astronomy and music.[3] The very nature of their profession exacerbated the individualistic traits of their activity: as they were competing for pupils, the Sophists rivalled each other to prove the superiority of their skills.[4] It is possible, however, to identify some common features in their practice: to put it with Laks and Most, the Sophists 'share personal relations and similarities in their way of life, their pedagogical practices, and their general conceptual orientation'.[5] Most significantly, whatever topic they discussed, the Sophists displayed a polemic stance against traditional education and forms of wisdom, which they critically examined, questioned and even appropriated to promote their new expertise.[6]

Among the Sophists' shared interests, rhetoric appears to have held a prominent place: they not only skilfully employed it to advertise their own wide-ranging expertise, in particular in public displays (ἐπιδείξεις), but also promised to teach it to anyone who was ready to pay for it.[7] Their ability was so great, that some of them were also appointed ambassadors by their hometowns, for example Gorgias, Hippias and Prodicus.[8] The Sophists' rhetorical skills were key to their success, especially in democratic Athens, in which the acquisition and refinement of skills in public speaking became fundamental to anyone wishing to make their voice heard in the assembly or in the law court.

The Sophists' interest in rhetoric reflects their wider investigation into the nature and power of speech (λόγος) and its practical applications to the socio-political sphere.[9] Quite inevitably, such intellectual pursuit led the Sophists to engage with philosophical issues, in particular ethics, politics and, more generally, anything relating to the multiformity of human experience of reality. In terms of originality and depth, their philosophical contributions cannot be overemphasized: the νόμος-φύσις debate, agnosticism and atheism, epistemic and moral relativism, and even nihilism are among some of the most brilliant examples of their speculation.[10] In this enterprise, the Sophists came to clash with the other great innovator of Greek thought of the Classical age, Socrates. In fact, Socrates' critical stance on traditional values and his ability to scrutinize and refute other people's opinions, in particular about morals, through his skilful dialectic led many to consider him a Sophist too.[11] It was exactly this misconception that Plato tried to confute in his dialogues, in which, in order to clear Socrates of this charge, he relentlessly attacked Sophistic speculation and its possible negative influence on society.

In their process of revision and critical appropriation of tradition, the Sophists found a particularly fruitful target in the epic past, in line with the central role that epic had in Greek culture, society and education. It is possible to identify two main approaches to epic on the part of the Sophists: one akin to literary criticism, in which the epic poems, in particular the *Iliad* and the *Odyssey*, were analysed in terms of their language and narrative structure; the other consisting in the use of epic myths as subject for the Sophists' works. Starting with the first approach, we can mention Protagoras, who examined the language and internal structure of the Homeric poems;[12] similarly, Hippias seems to have investigated both the *Iliad* and the *Odyssey* from a unitarian perspective, in particular focusing on the poet's coherence.[13] Antisthenes, who devoted an impressive number of works to Homer, was interested, for example, in the meaning of Odysseus' epithet πολύτροπος, which he interpreted as indicating the hero's ability to adapt his speech to suit different audiences; he also employed what was later called the λύσις ἐκ προσώπου ('solution by reference to the character') to solve controversial points in the poems.[14] With regards to the second approach, namely the reuse of myths, to mention only the works that have been transmitted in their entirety, Gorgias wrote an *Encomium of Helen*, in which he suggests that the Greek heroine is not responsible for the Trojan War, and the *Apology of Palamedes*, a speech for the Greek hero Palamedes, accused by Odysseus of treachery; in relation to the same myth, Alcidamas, Gorgias' pupil, wrote Odysseus' accusation speech; Antisthenes then wrote two speeches for Ajax and Odysseus about their dispute over the possession of Achilles' armour. Furthermore, some ancient sources indicate that Prodicus wrote about the myth of Heracles, torn between Virtue and Vice.[15]

Modern scholarship has asked why the myths that featured in the epic tradition of the Greeks were so popular among the Sophists – and it is from that scholarship that the present volume takes its inspiration. As argued by Morgan in her pivotal study of the subject, *Myth and Philosophy from the Presocratics to Plato*, the Sophists effectively 'spoke the language of myth to access and influence the mass of society, while holding and teaching private beliefs that ran counter to these conventions'.[16] Thus they appropriated and transformed the poetic past, in order to present themselves as the heirs of traditional culture – only to attempt to replace it with their new, revolutionary models. From a similar perspective, Knudsen, in her article 'Poetic speakers, sophistic works', examines what she calls 'mytho-forensic speeches' (namely, the works by Gorgias, Alcidamas and Antisthenes mentioned above), which depict trial scenarios inspired by Greek mythology and epic; Knudsen shows how these speeches vividly display the Sophists' manipulation of the tradition, as they skilfully combine the Sophistic interest in forensic argumentation and wordplay with episodes and characters drawn from mythology and epic.[17] New opportunities for the study of the relationships and interactions between the Sophists and the poetic past have arisen with the new edition of the fragments of early Greek philosophers by Andrew Laks and Glenn Most, which encourages readers to examine the Sophists within the wider cultural context of fifth-century Greece, and the ways in which they employed tradition to channel their own innovative views on the power and limitation of speech, philosophy, and religion.[18]

This Sophistic interest in the epic past did not stop with the end of the Classical age. In their works, authors belonging to the Second Sophistic displayed an inventiveness in engaging and manipulating the epic tradition which closely resembles that of the fifth-century BC Sophists. But who were these new Sophists and what characterized their intellectual production? The term 'Second Sophistic' was coined by Flavius Philostratus who, in the *Lives of the Sophists*,[19] distinguished the practitioners of epideictic oratory, which he traced back to Aeschines in the fourth century BC, from earlier Sophists such as Gorgias, Critias and Prodicus, who used rhetoric for the discussion of philosophical themes. In particular, Philostratus focuses on eminent rhetoricians of the Imperial age, whose activity he roots in the prestigious tradition of Classical Athens.[20] The term was then revived in the nineteenth century by Rohde, who employed it to indicate a trend in the Greek rhetoric of the first two centuries AD aimed at fighting Eastern influences.[21] Even though Rohde's interpretation and the debate it sparked were dismissed at the beginning of the twentieth century, the label itself has stayed to indicate the period of Greek literature, and more generally culture, spanning the first three centuries AD.[22]

Although the term 'Second Sophistic' is employed loosely, it is possible to identify some common features shared by the writers usually numbered among the Second Sophists. Some of these features show important similarities with the First Sophistic.[23] As already mentioned, the Second Sophists were particularly skilled in rhetoric and, most significantly, used to show their ability in public ἐπιδείξεις.[24] As their fifth-century predecessors, the Second Sophists took part in the public intellectual ἀγών and displayed their learnedness in order to prove their worth and attract prospective students. Indeed, the Second Sophists played an important role in the education (παιδεία) of the elites and the formation of groups of πεπαιδευμένοι sharing similar cultural perspectives and disciplinary methodology.[25] Most significantly, despite the different historical and political circumstances in which they lived, the writers of the Second Sophistic too operated in a period of deep transformation, which saw the gradual annexation of the Greek-speaking world by the Romans. This inevitably required some negotiations: as Whitmarsh explains, 'Greek culture of the period, constrained as it was by Roman rule, had to explore issues of identity, society, family, and power'.[26]

Once again, the epic tradition provided instruments to navigate the new complex political and cultural situation. Like their Classical predecessors, writers belonging to the Second Sophistic reconfigured the value of epic poetry according to their specific circumstances. They too saw in myth an effective means to encapsulate questions central to their own intellectual agenda, which at the same time allowed them to present themselves as the heirs of traditional education. Several studies have focused on the extent and variety of the interactions with the poetic tradition on the part of the authors of that period. Poetry had a pivotal role in the Second Sophistic cultural milieu: it not only provided a virtually inexhaustible source of quotations and *exempla* that were used both for rhetorical purposes and to display the range of one's education; it was also part of some of the Sophists' literary production.[27] Homer was still considered the main authority in Greek poetry, both as a model to follow, as evidenced by a number of imitations and adaptations of the *Iliad* and the *Odyssey*, and as a polemical target, whose statements had to be tested and overtly challenged.[28] As in the First Sophistic, the Sophists of the Imperial Age showed a particular interest in mythological subjects, which provided ample material for the production of fictional rhetorical pieces that served as paradigms for persuasion (*suasoriae*) and law-court (*controversiae*) speeches.[29]

The reception of the epic tradition by the Sophists therefore offers a glimpse of the cultural dynamics in periods of major transformation in antiquity. What role did the epic tradition play in these moments of substantial change? How did the Sophists appropriate the epic past and how did this fit their intellectual agenda? How was education affected? These are the complex and interrelated questions that the contributions in this volume aim to address. While both the First and the Second Sophistic have received scholarly attention individually, there appears to be no joint study of the First and Second Sophistic's relation to the epic past. This volume aims to fill this gap, taking its impetus from the belief that the epic tradition provides an invaluable starting point to examine the connections between First and Second Sophistic beyond the widely acknowledged interest in rhetoric. In both periods, characterized as they were by lively intellectual debates and the critical assessment and revision of traditional culture, epic supplied the Sophists with an effective means to formulate and convey their messages of transformation. As will emerge from the contributions, numerous themes recur in the works of both First and Second Sophistic dealing with epic, including the use of mythical characters (both famous and more marginal ones); a deep engagement with Homeric experts, in particular aimed at detecting the hidden meanings of the Homeric poems; and the evaluation of Homer as a figure of authority and his role within the education of the elites. Thus, by identifying the modes of interaction with the epic tradition, this volume will shed further light on aspects of continuity and innovation between these two influential cultural periods of antiquity. Besides the relation between First and Second Sophistic, the volume will contribute to the wider study of the reception of epic in antiquity. In particular, we aim to highlight how, through different periods, the epic tradition remains a central and vital shared cultural patrimony for the Greeks. For epic poetry provides a common vocabulary and system of values which make it the ideal material to use in periods of major change: since it not only expresses new intellectual and educational tenets in a language that can be easily understood, but also conveys the idea of continuity with the tradition, it 'authorizes' original and potentially revolutionary ideas, and makes them appear less controversial.

The volume is structured chronologically, starting from the Classical age and engaging, in the second part, with the literature of the first two centuries AD. The first part of the volume, on the First Sophistic, discusses pivotal works such as Gorgias' *Encomium of Helen* and *Apology of Palamedes*, Alcidamas' *Odysseus or Against the Treachery of Palamedes*, and Antisthenes' pair of speeches *Ajax* and *Odysseus*, as well as a range of passages from Plato and other authors. In the first contribution, 'Between Homer and Gorgias: Helen's Bewitching Power', Roberta Ioli analyses Gorgias' appropriation of the figure of Helen in his *Encomium of Helen*. Ioli examines Homer's portrayal of Helen, with particular attention to her function as a storyteller with a mythopoietic and mimetic function. In so doing, Ioli shows the extent of Homer's influence on both Gorgias' choice of Helen as the subject of his speech and as a symbol of the power of λόγος. What emerges from Ioli's analysis, in particular, is how Gorgias turns Helen into a hypostasis of the power of poetry, thereby making her embody that very *poetics* that he himself invents and displays in the *Encomium*.

Paola Bassino's contribution, 'Palamedes, the Sophistic Hero', further explores the Sophistic manipulations of epic characters. Bassino focuses specifically on the figure of Palamedes and his enmity with Odysseus, as portrayed in Gorgias' *Apology of Palamedes* and Alcidamas' *Odysseus or on the Treachery of Palamedes*. As it appears from this contribution, the myth of Palamedes was of paramount importance to the Greek Sophistic landscape of the Classical age. It allowed the Sophists to stage a competition in speech between the two cleverest Greek heroes and set them against one another in an unprecedented show of rhetorical ability. Thus, they used it as a means to articulate their own contemporary concerns about speech and rhetoric – the power of λόγος, but also its limitations and dangers. Indeed, Palamedes ultimately failed, despite his skilful attempts to defend himself and the unsafety of the accusations. Palamedes, whose legend featured cleverness, persuasion and failure alike, was the perfect mouthpiece for the Sophists.

In 'Ajax versus Odysseus', Hugo Koning examines a fictional rhetorical contest written by Antisthenes, in which the Sophist stages the speeches delivered by Ajax and Odysseus to determine who was worthy of Achilles' arms. In this appropriation of the well-known episode of the Ὅπλων κρίσις, Koning traces Antisthenes' interest in Homeric epic and the figure of Odysseus in particular, which he examined in his work as a literary critic. Antisthenes' efforts to defend Odysseus from attacks on his heroic ethos find a vivid expression in Odysseus' response to Ajax, in which he skilfully turns against Ajax the very Homeric tradition upon which the latter's heroic fame is grounded. Thus, Odysseus instantiates and provides a paradigm for that use of mythology and poetry as a rhetorical tool which characterized the Sophists' original elaboration of the epic tradition.

In the final contribution on the First Sophistic, 'Mythological Role Playing among the Sophists', Kathryn Morgan suggests that the Sophists not only composed epideictic speeches for characters from myth, such as Helen, Odysseus, Palamedes and Ajax, but also drew implicit parallels between such figures and their own situation as speakers and educators – the Sophists were not just heirs of earlier poets and intellectuals but could also inhabit their characters. The heroes that would most appropriately lend themselves to this were those mythological figures who had a reputation for intellectual expertise and/or oratorical ability: Nestor, Palamedes, Odysseus and Prometheus. But by taking into account a wide range of witnesses (many of which come from Plato), Morgan shows how these mythological characters are 'transferable personalities' whose characterization was not predetermined: the nature of the appropriation of the heroic character could change depending on the circumstances.

The volume then moves on to discuss some of the major works of literature from the Second Sophistic dealing with the epic tradition. These include Lucian's *Judgement of the Goddesses* and Dio Chrysostom's orations 11 and 20, as well as Philostratus' *Heroicus* and *Imagines*. Nicholas Wilshere opens the second part of the volume with a contribution on 'Homeric Exegesis and Athetesis in Lucian's Versions of the Judgement of Paris'. Wilshere chooses Lucian's *Judgement of the Goddesses* as a quintessential Imperial Sophistic work, in that it combines parody, literary manipulation and learned allusions. He reveals how Lucian, in keeping with the Sophists' common showing-off attitude, displays his learning and expertise under the façade of parody by employing details from the Homeric texts and, even more significantly, allusions to interpretative issues widely debated in the Homeric scholia. The work thus provides an eloquent example of the ways in which the educated men (πεπαιδευμένοι) of the Imperial Age demonstrated their erudition not only to the wider public, but also to other fellow learned men.

The reuse of epic material in learned contexts is the subject of the two contributions on Dio Chrysostom's *Trojan Oration*, by Sara Tirrito and Isidor Brodersen. In 'Helen Was Never Abducted, Paris Abducted Her Because He Was Bored: Two Ways of Rewriting Homer in Dio Chrysostom (Orr. 11 and 20)', Tirrito examines the *Trojan Oration* and compares it and contrasts it with another oration by Dio, namely *On the Subject of Anachoretic Life*. Through her analysis, Tirrito points out that Dio manipulates the epic tradition in different ways depending on the circumstances in and about which he was writing. By analysing the inconsistencies between Dio's treatments of the Judgement of Paris in the two works, Tirrito shows how epic could easily be bent to different purposes, based on the context and the audience of the performance. In particular, she highlights once more how the encyclopaedic character of the Homeric epics turns out to be especially apt to provide the educational pretext and material for παιδεία.

In 'Homer's Lies and Dio's Truth? Subverting the Epic Past in Dio Chrysostom's *Trojan Oration*', Brodersen argues that Dio's speech, aimed at showing that Homer's account of the downfall of Troy should not be trusted as the city was never actually taken, is only apparently meant to flatter the inhabitants of Ilium to whom the speech was addressed. In fact, the *Oration* should be seen as an invitation to the audience of πεπαιδευμένοι to show their own erudition. In the speech, Dio establishes clear parallels between himself and Homer, both narrators of events of the remote Trojan past, only to emphasize that, unlike the poet, he is not addressing the masses and the common people, but rather the class of the educated few.

The final two contributions deal with Philostratus' engagement with the epic past. In 'A Rhetorical Trojan War: Philostratus' *Heroicus*, the Power of Language and the Construction of the Truth', Valentin Decloquement examines Philostratus' claim in the *Heroicus* that he is going to expose the truth about the Trojan War. In line with other Imperial authors, Philostratus seizes the opportunity the Trojan myth offers him to show his ability as rhetor. In particular, he resorts to rhetorical argumentation to refute the accounts of the war made by earlier poets, most notably Homer. In doing so, as Decloquement argues, Philostratus appropriates and re-enacts Gorgias' approach to epic, in order to illustrate and problematize the power of speech and its capacity to communicate the truth of an event which, given its remoteness in time, cannot be reached directly.

Finally, in 'Reading Homer and the Epic Cycle through *Ekphrasis*: Philostratus' Epic *Imagines*', Sophie Schoess investigates Philostratus' original engagement with the epic tradition in visual terms. Schoess shows how Philostratus' display of expertise in Homeric and epic poetry, which he uses to comment on works of art, not only adds vividness to his descriptions, but also invites his audience to draw on their own παιδεία to appreciate the multiple visual and textual connections that he establishes therein. In such a context, Philostratus' predilection for Homeric language emphasizes the continuing importance of Homer as a literary source for epic and its superiority to narratives found in other poems.

The chapters in this volume present the opportunity to make some general observations on the ways the epic past was exploited by the Sophists across different periods of antiquity. To begin with, it seems that both the First and the Second Sophistic tended to privilege the use of some myths over others. Although it might be harder to draw conclusions about the First Sophistic, because of the fragmentary status of many of its texts and witnesses, it appears quite clearly that myths like those of Helen and Palamedes were especially popular. The first, important, reason for this seems to be that both myths inspired reflection on certain themes that were relevant to intellectuals, and particularly the Sophists, throughout antiquity. As Ioli shows, Helen in Homeric epics is often associated with the power of storytelling, which she embodies both through her words and through her art of weaving. Helen is both the cause of the Trojan War, and the subject of its narrations, thus being engaged in a self-referential exercise of narration. Importantly, she can both delight and bewitch her listeners: this is what makes her a suitable character for Gorgias to explore, as she embodies the power of that very poetic rhetoric which Gorgias himself invented and championed. Ioli concludes her piece by suggesting that Helen 'is the most powerful expression of εἰκός: something that always changes its appearance, something that is always possible' – and indeed, what makes her so popular in ancient literature, from Homer and Stesichorus all the way to Gorgias and beyond, is precisely the fact that the debate over whether or not she was guilty, or even whether or not she went to Troy at all, could be potentially endless.[30] As such, writers could make up and advertise their own version of the story or add their arguments, and the ultimate result of this was, of course, that writers could challenge Homer's authority and establish their own credibility by arguing against what had been, until then, the ultimate representation of traditional truth and wisdom. This is indeed what the Second Sophistic did. Dio's *Trojan Oration* aims to confute Homer's traditional tale according to which Troy was taken by the Greeks, and suggests that the marriage between Helen and Paris was absolutely legal and approved of by all parties involved. Homer, in fact, was lying. According to some scholars, Dio merely aimed to flatter the inhabitants of New Ilion, to whom the oration was addressed, but Brodersen's chapter highlights how Dio is using the myth to display his own παιδεία, at the same time inviting the audience to display their own. But interestingly, Dio himself does not wish to present his own version as the only true one – on the contrary, as shown by Tirrito, in another oration (*On the Subject of Anachoretic Life*) Dio does not deny at all that the Trojan War took place, and that it was caused by Paris' love for Helen. The Sophists found in myths such as that of Helen flexible tools to use for different purposes, at the same time challenging the tradition and establishing their authority against it – but also against one another. Indeed, Decloquement shows that when Philostratus engages with the issue of Helen's departure and culpability, he does so in a way that echoes, and challenges, not only Homer's but also Dio's tales. The myth of Palamedes was equally suitable for Sophistic purposes. As illustrated by Bassino, the trial that pits against each other the two heroes who were more famous than any other for their wisdom and rhetorical ability articulates issues concerning persuasion and the relationship between truth and λόγος that were important to both Gorgias and Alcidamas. The key feature that makes speech so important in this myth is that it is the only way to find out the truth and resolve the issue of whether or not Palamedes deserves a punishment. In the absence of evidence, everything is left to the speakers' ability to support their own cases. Furthermore, Morgan shows that Palamedes was also one of those characters that were used and adapted by the Sophists for their 'mythological role-playing'. Plato mentioned, in a debated passage from the *Phaedrus*, an 'Eleatic Palamedes'; although the precise identity of the person behind this nickname cannot be established with certainty (and perhaps never was), Palamedes appears to be one of those heroes that were part of that 'permanently accessible database' of mythical characters that could be used flexibly and that intellectuals could draw on and manipulate. Later on, in the Imperial age, similar strategies to those used by Gorgias' Palamedes are found in Philostratus: Decloquement argues that the discussion of the Trojan War in the *Heroicus* seems to re-enact Gorgianic views: in a situation where there is no clear way to reach knowledge of the truth, human beings can only try to construct it through a skilful use of rhetoric.

In order to support their position as the new possessors, teachers and shapers of the epic traditions, the Sophists needed to engage with the other recognized authorities on the mythical past of the Greeks. In the Classical age, the rhapsodes were among those who could claim expertise on the Homeric poems, and seem to have accompanied their performances with some form of interpretation of the poems.³¹ Plato's Socrates famously, and ironically, claimed to envy the rhapsode Ion the fact that he could adorn himself and make himself look beautiful, and most importantly possessed knowledge not merely of Homer's words, but of his very thought; one cannot be a good rhapsode, he claims, if one only knows the poet's words by heart and cannot interpret them.³² The Sophists have features in common with Ion. Koning shows how Antisthenes, too, was particularly keen on establishing his voice as a Homeric critic. Antisthenes' interest in Homeric criticism is indeed testified by some ancient scholia that suggest how, among other things, he tried to defend Odysseus against possible attacks on his ethos and good judgment – so much so, Koning argues, that we might be led to think that he admired Odysseus. There are also other passages, which are not discussed in this volume, that support this view. For example, according to some extant fragments, Protagoras discussed issues of Homeric language and grammar.³³ Gorgias and Hippias were reported to have appeared in purple clothes, giving particular importance to their appearance and resembling, in this, Ion.³⁴ The writers of the Second Sophistic, too, showed and confirmed their expertise in Homeric poetry by engaging with scholarly debates on the epic poems. Wilshere illustrates various instances where Lucian, in his *Judgement of the Goddesses*, includes a nod to his more learned readers and prompts them to delve not only into the epic tradition, but also into the tradition of Homeric exegesis. Wilshere identifies in Lucian's text several references to issues discussed in the Homeric scholia, and explains how Lucian was expecting his πεπαιδευμένος reader to be able to track down these learned references in order to gain access to a fuller, richer reading experience. Thus, Lucian's text is far from being mere entertainment, but displays serious ideas about what it means to be a truly literate reader. The contribution by Sophie Schoess, furthermore, highlights how this tendency can be seen not only in Lucian, but in other writers of the Second Sophistic, too. Philostratus, in his *Imagines*, shows, imparts and expects knowledge of varied sources related to the epic tradition, both textual and visual. He draws close connections between painting, epic poetry and heroic narrative and, by drawing attention to the diverse artistic traditions that play a part in the transmission of heroic narrative, demonstrates his own skill in adapting and re-inventing them.

This volume originates from the conference *Sophistic Views of the Epic Past from the Classical to the Imperial Age*, held at the University of Winchester in September 2018. We would like to thank the institutions that have offered financial support to the event, in particular the University of Winchester, the Institute of Classical Studies, and the Society for the Promotion of Hellenic

Studies. We would also like to thank, of course, the scholars who presented their work at the event and those who attended and contributed their ideas to the discussions that followed each paper and during the final round-table. The conference brought together scholars specialized in a variety of aspects and periods of the ancient world, and creating this opportunity for scholars to reinforce existing research connections and forge new ones was the most successful and rewarding aspect of the event. We hope that this book may keep fostering the conversation and stimulate further research on the Sophistic views of the epic past.

Notes

1 For a discussion of the word σοφιστής, see Guthrie 1977: 27–34; Kerferd 1981: 24–41; Lloyd 1987: 93 n. 153; Edmunds 2006: 418–20; Bonazzi 2010: 14–16; Tell 2011: 21–38.
2 Guthrie 1977: 35.
3 Cf., for example, Plato *Protagoras* 318d–e. On this point, see Lloyd 1987: 92 n. 152.
4 On this point, see Lloyd 1987: 83–102. On intellectual competitiveness and its influence on the development of philosophy, see further Lloyd 1979: 226–67.
5 Laks/Most 2016: 3.
6 On the polemical stance as a typical Sophistic characteristic, see Bonazzi 2010: 17–18.
7 On Sophistic ἐπιδείξεις, see Kerferd 1981: 28–30 and Tell 2011: 113–34. On the Sophists' fees, see Kerferd 1981: 26–8. For a critical assessment of ancient evidence, see Tell 2011: 39–60.
8 Cf. Plato, *Hippias Maior* 281a–b; 282b; 282c.
9 Cf. Bonazzi 2010: 21 and *passim*.
10 For an overview and analysis of the Sophists' philosophical contributions, see Kerferd 1981: 68–172; Broadie 2003: 73–89; Bonazzi 2010: 23–58, 83–148.
11 See for example, Aristophanes' portrayal of Socrates in the *Clouds*. Aeschines explicitly calls Socrates 'a Sophist' (*Against Timarchus* 173). On the Sophistic traits of Socrates, see Kerferd 1981: 55–7; Edmunds 2006; Taylor 2006: 157–68; Laks/Most 2016: 6.
12 Commenting on the incipit of the *Iliad*, he criticized the use of the imperative ἄειδε and the feminine form οὐλομένην referring to μῆνιν, which he considered as naturally masculine (DK 80 A29 and Aristotle, *Sophistic Refutations* 14). In DK 80 A30, we are told that Protagoras interpreted the battle between Achilles and the Xanthus as a transition to the Theomachy.

13 At least from what emerges from the Platonic dialogue *Hippias Minor*, in which the characters of Achilles and Odysseus in the two poems are compared.
14 Cf. Nannini 2010: 75. On Antisthenes' works on Homer, see further Richardson 2006: 80–6.
15 DK 84 B1 (= Schol. Ar. *Nu.* 361); DK 84 B2 (= X. *Mem.* 2.1.21). Another example is provided by the Platonic *Hippias Maior*, in which Hippias says that he composed a speech on what occupations befit a young man, which was inspired by a conversation between Nestor and Neoptolemus (cf. *Hippias Maior* 286a–c).
16 Morgan 2000: 101.
17 Knudsen 2012.
18 On this approach, see in particular the introduction to Laks/Most 2016.
19 Philostr. *VS* 481: Ἡ μὲν δὴ ἀρχαία σοφιστικὴ καὶ τὰ φιλοσοφούμενα ὑποτιθεμένη διῄει αὐτὰ ἀποτάδην καὶ ἐς μῆκος, διελέγετο μὲν γὰρ περὶ ἀνδρείας, διελέγετο δὲ περὶ δικαιότητος, ἡρώων τε πέρι καὶ θεῶν καὶ ὅπῃ ἀπεσχημάτισται ἡ ἰδέα τοῦ κόσμου. ἡ δὲ μετ' ἐκείνην, ἣν οὐχὶ νέαν, ἀρχαία γάρ, δευτέραν δὲ μᾶλλον προσρητέον, τοὺς πένητας ὑπετυπώσατο καὶ τοὺς πλουσίους καὶ τοὺς ἀριστέας καὶ τοὺς τυράννους καὶ τὰς ἐς ὄνομα ὑποθέσεις, ἐφ' ἃς ἡ ἱστορία ἄγει. ἦρξε δὲ τῆς μὲν ἀρχαιοτέρας Γοργίας ὁ Λεοντῖνος ἐν Θετταλοῖς, τῆς δὲ δευτέρας Αἰσχίνης ὁ Ἀτρομήτου τῶν μὲν Ἀθήνησι πολιτικῶν ἐκπεσών, Καρίᾳ δὲ ἐνομιλήσας καὶ Ῥόδῳ, καὶ μετεχειρίζοντο τὰς ὑποθέσεις οἱ μὲν κατὰ τέχνην, οἱ δὲ ἀπὸ Γοργίου κατὰ τὸ δόξαν. 'Now ancient sophistic, even when it propounded philosophical themes, used to discuss them diffusely and at length; for it discoursed on courage, it discoursed on justice, on the heroes and gods, and how the universe has been fashioned into its present shape. But the sophistic that followed it, which we must not call "new," for it is old, but rather "second," sketched the types of the poor man and the rich, of princes and tyrants, and handled arguments that are concerned with definite and special themes for which history shows the way. Gorgias of Leontini founded the older type in Thessaly, and Aeschines, son of Atrometus, founded the second, after he had been exiled from political life at Athens and had taken up his abode in Caria and Rhodes; and the followers of Aeschines handled their themes according to the rules of art, while the followers of Gorgias handled theirs as they pleased.' All translations are taken from the Loeb editions.
20 On Philostratus' list and construction of the Second Sophistic, see Eshleman 2008.
21 Cf. Whitmarsh 2005: 6–8.
22 For modern scrutiny and debates on the denomination 'Second Sophistic', and its accuracy, scope and even validity, see for example Whitmarsh 2005: 3–10; Johnson/Richter 2017.
23 On the Second Sophistic general features, see Johnson/Richter 2017: 4–6.
24 On the Sophistic performance, see Whitmarsh 2005: 23–40; Schmitz 2017.
25 On παιδεία in the Second Sophistic, see Whitmarsh 2005: 13–15; Webb 2017.
26 Whitmarsh 2005: 1.

27 For a survey, see Bowie 1989: 214–54 and Baumbach 2017, in particular 495–6 for epic poetry. Maciver, following Bowie, argues that epic production, except for Scopelian's *Gigantias*, was 'virtually non-existent' (Maciver 2012: 17 n. 55). Quintus' *Posthomerica* has been at times considered as a Second Sophistic work, but the issue is debated (for an overview, see Maciver 2012: 17–18).
28 Cf. Baumbach 2017: 493–4. On Homer as a problematic historical source, see Kim 2010.
29 Cf. Whitmarsh 2005: 70–1.
30 For Stesichorus' *Palinode* see Plat. *Phaedr.* 243a: οὐκ ἔστ᾽ ἔτυμος λόγος οὗτος, / οὐδ᾽ ἔβας ἐν νηυσὶν ἐϋσσέλμοις / οὐδ᾽ ἵκεο πέργαμα Τροίας, 'That story is not true, and you did not go on the well-benched ships and you did not reach the citadel of Troy.' On the various treatments of the figure of Helen and the issue of her culpability from the archaic to the Classical age see Blondell 2013.
31 For a modern relevant study see Richardson 2006.
32 Pl. *Ion* 530bc.
33 See n. 12 p. 12
34 82 A 9 DK: Ael. *Var. Hist.* 12.32: Ἱππίαν δὲ καὶ Γοργίαν ἐν πορφυραῖς ἐσθῆσι προϊέναι διαρρεῖ λόγος, 'The story is widely reported that Hippias and Gorgias appeared in public garbed in purple attire.'

References

Baumbach, M. 2017, 'Poets and poetry', in Johnson, W. and Richter, D. (eds), *The Oxford Handbook of the Second Sophistic*, Oxford: 493–508.
Blondell, R. 2013, *Helen of Troy: Beauty, Myth, Devastation*, Oxford/New York.
Bonazzi, M. 2010, *I Sofisti*, Rome.
Bowie, E. 1989, 'Greek Sophists and Greek poetry in the Second Sophistic', *Aufstieg und Niedergang der römischen Welt (ANRW)* 2.33.1, Berlin: 209–58.
Broadie, S. 2003, 'The Sophists and Socrates', in Sedley, D. (ed.), *The Cambridge Companion to Greek and Roman Philosophy*, Cambridge: 73–97.
Edmunds, L. 2006, 'What was Socrates called?', *CQ* 56.2: 414–25.
Eshleman, K. 2008, 'Defining the circle of Sophists: Philostratus and the construction of the Second Sophistic', *CPh* 103: 395–413.
Guthrie, W. 1977, *A History of Greek Philosophy, Volume 3, Part 1: The Sophists*, Cambridge.
Johnson, W. and Richter, D. 2017, 'Periodicity and scope', in Johnson, W. and Richter, D. (eds), *The Oxford Handbook of the Second Sophistic*, Oxford: 3–10.
Kerferd, G. B. 1981, *The Sophistic Movement*, Cambridge.
Kim, L. 2010, *Homer between History and Fiction in Imperial Greek Literature*, Cambridge.
Knudsen, R. 2012, 'Poetic speakers, sophistic words', *AJPh* 133: 31–60.

Laks, A. and Most, G. 2016, *Early Greek Philosophy,* vol. 8, Cambridge MA.
Lloyd, G. E. R. 1979, *Magic, Reason and Experience*, Cambridge.
Lloyd, G. E. R. 1987, *The Revolutions of Wisdom: Studies in the Claims and Practice of Ancient Greek Science*, Berkeley.
Maciver, C. 2012, *Quintus Smyrnaeus' Posthomerica: Engaging Homer in Late Antiquity*, Leiden.
Morgan, K. 2000, *Myth and Philosophy from the Presocratics to Plato*, Cambridge.
Nannini, S. 2010, *Omero: L'Autore Necessario*, Naples.
Richardson, N. 2006, 'Homeric professors in the age of the Sophists', in Laird, A. (ed.), *Ancient Literary Criticism*, Oxford: 62–86.
Schmitz, T. A. 2017, 'Professionals of *Paideia*? The Sophists as performers', in Johnson, W. and Richter, D. (eds), *The Oxford Handbook of the Second Sophistic*, Oxford: 169–80.
Taylor, C. C. W. 2006, 'Socrates the Sophist', in Judson, R. and Karasmanis, V. (eds), *Remembering Socrates: Philosophical Essays*, Oxford: 157–68.
Tell, H. 2011, *Plato's Counterfeit Sophists*, Cambridge MA.
Webb, R. 2017, 'Schools and *Paideia*', in Johnson, W. and Richter, D. (eds), *The Oxford Handbook of the Second Sophistic*, Oxford: 139–54.
Whitmarsh, T. 2005, *The Second Sophistic*, Oxford.

Part One

The First Sophistic

1

Between Homer and Gorgias: Helen's Bewitching Power

Roberta Ioli

Introduction

Poets and philosophers have often focused on the figure of Helen: as a lively topic in antiquity, she has been considered both the shameless cause of the Trojan war, and a victim of the power of Eros, and eventually a lawful wife at the mercy of male desire. In order to save her name from disrepute, in his lost *Palinode* Stesichorus revises the Helen myth: not for Helen, but for her εἴδωλον, that is, the fleeting image identical to the real woman, a ten-year bloody war was fought.[1] While archaic poetry, in continuity with the epic tradition, focuses on Helen's weakness and subjection to love, tragedy introduces extended versions of the myth, and deals with the ethical problem of personal responsibility, as faced in Euripides' *Trojan Women*, or in his *Helen*, where the theme of the double strengthens Helen's 'ontological ambiguity'.[2] The missing link in this evolution from epic to tragedy is Sophistic. With the Sophists, especially with Gorgias, the myth becomes the record of paradigmatic characters, which are not simple models for rhetorical ostentation but can be inhabited by new intellectual and ethical values.[3]

The aim of this chapter is to investigate whether and how the Homeric Helen influenced Gorgias' *Encomium of Helen* and, even earlier, his choice of this mythical subject. On the one hand, despite his controversial relationship with epic tradition and poets (see *Hel.* 2, below), Gorgias' *Encomium* took inspiration from Homer. Of the epic Helen, he seems to echo and to appreciate a sometimes neglected aspect: her relationship not so much with pleasure and guilty desire, as with the charm of narration and the ability to understand the language of likeness. On the other hand, the Sophist was able to go beyond the tradition and to transform it into an admirable balance between poetry and rhetoric.

Thus, I would like to argue that one relevant focus of Gorgias' *Encomium* is not the mythical Helen anymore, but the power of poetic λόγοι, of which she becomes a kind of embodiment. Helen has been revitalized by Gorgias not only as a fascinating product of poetic invention, but also as inspirer of new possibilities in the art of speeches based on εἰκός.

Helen in Homer: weaver, singer, charmer

The Homeric Helen is often associated with the power of storytelling that takes place both through words and the art of weaving. In the *megaron* of Priam's palace, for example, Helen is pictured silently working on a purple robe. Her tapestry, which represents the first occurrence of a portrayed μῦθος, its muteness becoming a resonant story, evokes the narrative vividness of embroidered images.

> τὴν δ' εὗρ' ἐν μεγάρῳ· ἣ δὲ μέγαν ἱστὸν ὕφαινε
> δίπλακα πορφυρέην, πολέας δ' ἐνέπασσεν ἀέθλους
> Τρώων θ' ἱπποδάμων καὶ Ἀχαιῶν χαλκοχιτώνων,
> οὕς ἕθεν εἵνεκ' ἔπασχον ὑπ' Ἄρηος παλαμάων.

> She found Helen in the hall, where she was weaving a great purple web of double fold on which she was embroidering many battles of the horse-taming Trojans and the bronze-clad Achaeans, which for her sake they had endured at the hands of Ares.
>
> *Iliad* 3.125–8[4]

The verb ἐνέπασσεν (126) stands for the art of embroidering, with a focus on the images that, in this case, are a metaphorical model for the words, not vice versa. As Linda Clader pointed out, Helen is 'both author and subject of her work'.[5] Perhaps she is weaving not only κλέα ἀνδρῶν, that is the deeds of heroes, but also events of her own life connected with her direct responsibility in the war. She seems to anticipate, as a weaver/singer, what is going to happen in front of the Trojan walls.

Furthermore, while conversing with Hector she shows her meta-literary awareness of being, together with Paris, both cause of the tragic war and character in future narrations of it:

> οἷσιν ἐπὶ Ζεὺς θῆκε κακὸν μόρον, ὡς καὶ ὀπίσσω
> ἀνθρώποισι πελώμεθ' ἀοίδιμοι ἐσσομένοισι.

on us Zeus hath brought an evil doom, so that even in days to come we may be a song for men that are yet to be.

Iliad 6.357–8

Here there is a reference to the object of art (the evil destiny of men and women of the past), its recipient (men that are yet to be), and the means which are used (poetry, source of a memory which is a consolation as well). The episode where we see Helen as a self-referential weaver, besides combining poetry with the art of embroidering, multiplies, as in a hall of mirrors, the relationship between the narrator and the story, and represents an admirable example of *ekphrasis*, where the narrative matter ends up coinciding with the poetic construction itself.[6]

Helen's explicit consecration as a poet takes place in the *Odyssey*, when the Trojan war is over, and she is home again. Telemachus sails to Sparta looking for news concerning his father and meets the queen with her husband Menelaus. Here Helen is presented as an enchanting and attractive figure, not simply because of her beauty, but also, perhaps more importantly, due to her magical and narrative skills. She is like a healer, who can drop the right medication for a blessed amnesia into the wine. Her Egyptian φάρμακα have the power of giving a temporary oblivion from sufferings (*Od.* 4.219 ff.), just as poetry does.[7] Her tale shows many traditional features of epic poetry: first, it opens with an invocation to Zeus; then it follows the theme of τέρψις, 'pleasure' (239: τέρπεσθε), that is the invitation to enjoy that story described as ἐοικότα (239).[8] Finally, the praise that Menelaus addresses to Helen's tale as being κατὰ μοῖραν, 'harmonious' (266) – essential feature of an aedic performance – contributes to portray the woman as an expert singer.[9] As a poet, Helen recognizes her own limit: 'All the labors of steadfast Odysseus I cannot tell or recount' (*Od.* 4.240–1). While memory is the singer's primary virtue, omniscience is reserved for the gods, as mentioned at the beginning of the Catalogue of the Ships: 'For you are goddesses and are present and know all things, but we hear only a rumour (κλέος) and know nothing' (*Il.* 2.485–6).[10] Similarly, starting from the infinite repertoire of adventures affecting Odysseus, Helen is going to select deeds which are particularly suitable for her singing. The chosen story glorifies Odysseus' skill, and, at the same time, is an indirect praise for her behaviour in favour of the Greek hero.

The meaning of εἰκός/ἐοικώς has been widely discussed. In our passage in *Od.* 4 it probably has two different but interwoven meanings. On the one hand, εἰκός is a *likely* narration insofar as it is as close as possible to what has really happened. On the other, it probably refers to a content *suitable* to be sung, since it is so harmoniously structured to delight the audience.[11] Telling ἐοικότα seems like an allusion to the value of poetry, aimed not at telling what is completely true (which is an exclusive prerogative of the gods), but rather what is a likely image (εἰκών) of the truth: an image so powerful and well-constructed to give us pleasure and to increase our knowledge.

In a well-known and debated extract from Hesiod's *Theogony*, the Muses introduce themselves to the poet as the goddesses who can say not only the truth, but also 'true lies' or, literally, 'many lies similar to truth' (*Th.* 27: ψεύδεα πολλὰ [...] ἐτύμοισιν ὁμοῖα). Like the Homeric εἰκός, the likeness/verisimilitude (here suggested by ὅμοιος, or ὁμοῖος, in its epic form) is associated with the art of storytelling as its primary feature.[12] The same Hesiodic expression is attested in *Od.* 19.203, when Odysseus is addressing his last 'Cretan story' to Penelope: every time Odysseus recounts stories, mixing lies with truth, he is explicitly or implicitly assimilated to an epic singer, whose μῦθος is aimed at delighting his audience, but also at improving their awareness of the past and their perception of the future.

In her speech, Helen presents herself as devoted to the Argive cause: when Odysseus sneaked into the city in disguise, she did not reveal his identity to the Trojans. The theme of εἰκός recurs often here: Odysseus had 'the fashion of a slave' (*Od.* 4.245: οἰκῆϊ ἐοικώς) in order not to be taken, and 'he hid himself under the likeness of another' (*Od.* 4.247: ἄλλῳ δ' αὐτὸν φωτὶ κατακρύπτων ἤϊσκε). In spite of his unrecognizability, Odysseus is perfectly recognizable to Helen. She is the only one who understands and manages the language of εἰκός.[13] It is noteworthy that Helen selects an episode which can represent a forewarning of what is about to happen: by evoking the Odysseus of the past and his disguise as a beggar, she seems to predict the imminent νόστος of the hero. Furthermore, Helen is like a μάντις, a 'seer' who can interpret prodigious events and god-sent signs, such as the epiphany of a white goose gripped by an eagle, seen by Telemachus and Peisistratus (*Od.* 15.172–8).[14] By her clear understanding of the present and her anticipation of Penelope's dream (*Od.* 19.536–53), she can foresee the future, that is, the return and the vengeance of Odysseus.

Behind the ambiguity of the word εἰκός, which refers both to the deceiving appearance and the likeness to reality, we can catch a glimpse of the duplicity of Helen herself, whose intense beauty 'terribly makes her look like the immortal goddesses' (*Il.* 3.158). She moves between human and divine, appearance and reality: she is mastering deception and embodying the power of illusion as well. Moreover, Helen herself makes every story possible: in fact, in the Homeric poems, she is sometimes presented or self-presented as a fatal *casus belli* (*Il.* 2.161–2; 3.173–5; 6.344–8; 6.355–6), at other times as a victim of the will of the gods (*Il.* 3.164, *Od.* 23.223–4) and at yet other times as forced by Paris' abduction (*Il.* 2.354–6).[15]

While Helen presents herself as Odysseus' helper, in Menelaus' tale she openly challenges the Ithacan hero.[16] Actually, her voice shows a dangerous mimetic fascination: Menelaus describes her as capable of imitating the voices of the Achaean wives when, getting closer to the Trojan Horse, she responds with her deception to Odysseus' δόλος (*Od.* 4.265–89).[17] She has the extraordinary power to 'liken her voice' (279: φωνὴν ἴσκουσ') to the voices of all the Achaean women. Hence, the heroes hidden in the Horse's stomach go crazy with desire to go out and answer that voice. The focus is on Helen's ability to entice those who listen to her. The verb ἴσκειν (from the same root as εἰκός) recurs also in *Il.* 16.41, where Achilles' armour worn by Patroclus makes him look so like his friend that the scared Trojans will run away when they see him. The new semblance of Patroclus does not correspond to a change in his own identity: rather, here εἰκός aims to strengthen the Trojans' misleading impression that they are facing the most feared warrior. Finally, in the above-mentioned passage in *Od.* 19.203, Odysseus 'made the many falsehoods of his tale seem like the truth' (ἴσκε ψεύδεα πολλὰ λέγων ἐτύμοισιν ὁμοῖα): lies *are not* truths, but they *sound like* truths to Penelope who tensely listens to them. Their deceptive and mimetic power works in relation to a recipient who contributes to intensify their effect.

In these passages, ἴσκειν and εἰκός do not mean an adaptive metamorphosis, but rather help to emphasize the effects caused by strong visual or sound perceptions.[18] Many attempts have been made to solve the ἀπορία of the Homeric tale. How could Helen know, and thus imitate, all the voices? How can a single voice sound simultaneously different to different listeners? These are all questions that bypass the crucial point: this passage is not only about a mimetic reproduction, but also (and primarily) about the powerful fascination of Helen's voice that bewitches the Greek heroes. They listen to Helen, but they feel *as if* they were listening to their wives far away. Their nostalgia exalts her allure.

It may be helpful to recall the version of the episode narrated by Triphiodorus in his *The Sack of Troy*: 'three times she walked round it [the Horse] and provoked the Argives, naming all the fair-tressed wives of the Achaeans with her clear voice' (469–71). Triphiodorus talks about bewitching *evocation* of the names of the Achaean women, not about *imitation* of their voices. The effect produced on the hidden warriors is grief, poignant desire and finally a dangerous enchantment which would drive them to go out. Instead of multiplying her φωνή in the plurality of the imitated tones, Helen is modulating her divine charm in such a way as to enchant everyone, as if she were simultaneously many different women.

Her voice is artfully complex, like poetry which, even if inspired by one single story or character, talks to all of us, in a universal and, at the same time, individual modulation.

The real nature of that fascination can be revealed only by Odysseus, in a sort of symmetrical reversal of Helen's ability. Furthermore, in the Horse episode the power of her voice is much more intense because it is without body: the failed coordination between sight and sound strengthens the deception about identity. Helen's voice partly reminds us of the Sirens, whose singing seems to share her same seductive power. Like the Muses, the Sirens have a divine voice, 'harmonious', 'honeyed', but on the other hand they represent a deadly threat by promising to share their omniscience with those who listen to them (*Od.* 12.186-91). Conversely, the Muses cannot give their full wisdom even to the most beloved singer, and the disproportion between human and divine knowledge is recognized by the *Iliad*'s poet in first person (see, e.g. *Il.* 12.176). From this point of view the Sirens are anti-Muses who are in contrast with the most authentic inspiration of poetry.[19]

It is not really the song of the Sirens, but that of the Deliades, ministers of Apollo, which shows similarities with Helen's fascinating voice and evokes some relevant features of a proper aedic performance:

> πρὸς δὲ τόδε μέγα θαῦμα, ὅου κλέος οὔποτ' ὀλεῖται,
> κοῦραι Δηλιάδες Ἑκατηβελέταο θεράπναι
> αἴ τ' ἐπεὶ ἂρ πρῶτον μὲν Ἀπόλλων' ὑμνήσωσιν,
> αὖτις δ' αὖ Λητώ τε καὶ Ἄρτεμιν ἰοχέαιραν,
> 160 μνησάμεναι ἀνδρῶν τε παλαιῶν ἠδὲ γυναικῶν
> ὕμνον ἀείδουσιν, θέλγουσι δὲ φῦλ' ἀνθρώπων.
> πάντων δ' ἀνθρώπων φωνὰς καὶ κρεμβαλιαστὺν
> μιμεῖσθ' ἴσασιν· φαίη δέ κεν αὐτὸς ἕκαστος
> φθέγγεσθ'· οὕτω σφιν καλὴ συνάρηρεν ἀοιδή.

> And there is this great wonder besides, and its renown shall never perish:
> the girls of Delos, hand-maidens of the Far-shooter.
> For when they have praised Apollo first,
> and also Leto and Artemis who delights in arrows,
> 160 they sing a strain telling of men and women of past days,
> and charm the tribes of men.
> Also they can imitate the voices of all men and their clattering speech:
> each would say that he himself were singing,
> *so harmoniously overlapping* is their sweet song.
> *Hymn to Apollo* 156-64, transl. Evelyn-White, adapted[20]

When Apollo's devotees arrive in Delos, his ministers enchant the bystanders: just like in the aedic tradition, poetry is considered as a valuable memory exercise, in which the hymn to the gods is followed by the celebration of past heroes. Moreover, the Deliades show an extraordinary mimetic ability; so extraordinary that they are able to produce voices in which everybody can identify themselves. Anyone hearing this would believe himself to be the one singing or talking. The effect produced is both of charm (cf. 161: θέλγουσι) and pleasure (cf. 170: τέρπεσθε), exactly as in Phemius' or Demodocus' songs. We are introduced to a 'great wonder' (156: μέγα θαῦμα), an accomplished form of art not only for the hearing, but also for the sight due to the spectacle of ritual dances and hyporchematic performances.

The verb μιμεῖσθαι (163: literally, 'to imitate'), which here has its first technical occurrence, means the ability to give life to a true artistic representation, rather than just reproduce something. The insistence on the dramatic quality of the Deliades' performance invites us to interpret this passage as a reference to the power of their poetic singing, which achieves harmony through the balance among different rhythmic and musical components. This interpretation is suggested also by the verb συναραρίσκειν (164), which is very rarely found;[21] it probably refers to the ἁρμονία (from the same root as ἀραρίσκειν), that is, the quality of the voice that makes it similar to a musical instrument. Ἁρμονία can be interpreted as the pleasant accord of different and perfectly fitting pitches, but also – and more surprisingly – as the coexistence of many tones in one single voice emission. This resonant tuning might allow the Deliades to create more than one pitch at the same time. Just like Helen's voice, their ἁρμονία can be considered as a sort of polyphonic overtone singing, which charms the bystanders giving the impression of many different voices in one. However, unlike that Homeric episode of the Wooden Horse, the fictional frame of the Deliades' festival assures the pure pleasure of an aesthetic experience.

Helen in Gorgias: a Sophistic heroine

The Homeric Helen has a multiform nature. On the one hand she is benevolent (let us consider, for example, the gift of immortality to Menelaus for being her husband); moreover, she takes care of her guest Telemachus, by helping him temporarily forget his grief. Finally, like a poet, she is committed to delighting her listeners. On the other hand, she is the tricky enchanter described by Menelaus: her voice, one and multiple at the same time, can delight but also beguile her listeners. By considering her ambiguous and cunning nature, Barbara Cassin describes her as 'sophistic heroine par excellence'.²² But what is maintained of the Homeric Helen (weaver, singer, and charmer) in the Sophistic tradition? And what is ignored or refused?

In Gorgias' *Encomium* there is both a revival and a reversal of some aspects of Helen as an enchanter. Gorgias is particularly interested in evoking Helen as an elusive character, fleeting in her motivations and feelings. She is the subject of so many variations in epic and lyric that she can easily become a universal character in which everyone can identify themselves. Every mythical version of her story seems to have left its mark on her, so that her flowing nature makes every hypothesis plausible. Yet, in Gorgias' *Encomium* the protean Homeric Helen, capable of charming people and finally revealing their swindles, is herself charmed by persuasive speech.²³

Among the four causes which should explain Helen's leaving for Troy (divine necessity; human violence; persuasive speech; love), the λόγος is obviously the one that mostly concerns Gorgias, Sophist and rhetorician, as confirmed by the long section of the *Encomium* spent on it. The λόγος exercises its tremendous power in poetry (especially tragedy) and magic spells, but its persuasion is effective also in the speeches of physicians, philosophers, rhetoricians. In order to show it, the Sophist provides a physical theory of the λόγος, whose effects are as invincible as the deeds of a god:

> λόγος δυνάστης μέγας ἐστίν, ὃς σμικροτάτωι σώματι καὶ ἀφανεστάτωι θειότατα ἔργα ἀποτελεῖ· δύναται γὰρ καὶ φόβον παῦσαι καὶ λύπην ἀφελεῖν καὶ χαρὰν ἐνεργάσασθαι καὶ ἔλεον ἐπαυξῆσαι.
>
> Speech is a powerful ruler. Its body is very small and invisible, but its achievements are divine; for it is able to stop fear and to remove sorrow and to create joy and to augment pity.
>
> Gorgias, *Encomium of Helen* 8²⁴

Many scholars suggest that the *Encomium* should be interpreted as a defence, for the author, of his own personified rhetorical τέχνη, whose bewitching power is the same as that coming from Helen's beauty.²⁵ Helen would thus be reduced to a mere metaphor of Gorgias' rhetoric, and her body would become paradigmatic of the λόγος in its own invincible persuasion, to the point that even the less conceivable hypothesis (the innocence of the adulterous bride) finds credible support. On the one hand, I agree that the Sophist is not primarily interested in Helen's innocence (to that aim he could have followed the tradition started, for example, by Stesichorus), but rather in the performance of a powerful λόγος and its effects.[26] On the other, I believe that we can better understand Gorgias' Helen by assuming that she does not properly embody the art of rhetoric, but more specifically the essence of that *poetic* rhetoric which has been invented by Gorgias himself.[27] The *Encomium* is the first artful expression of such a prose, composed *as if* it were a poem.[28]

With this aim, I would like to provide two different kinds of argument: some arise from the evaluation of the rhythmic and stylistic features of the *Encomium*; others involve wider considerations on the status of poetry and the relationship between truth and verisimilitude. Many ancient *testimonia* confirm that Gorgias was particularly interested in tragedy.[29] All the τρόποι of sound, such as balanced antitheses, *isocola* and rhythmic effects, show his attention for the poetic charm of λόγος.[30] Aristotle criticizes his style as 'too poetic' (ποιητικῶς ... ἄγαν);[31] nevertheless, we may argue that this kind of sophisticated prose does not make the *Encomium* a mere ostentation of formal ability as an end in itself.

Gorgias' speech contains the first explicit definition of poetry: 'all poetry I consider and call as speech with metre'.[32] The two verbs in first person confirm his interest in ὀρθοέπεια and onomastic accuracy, as anything but occasional.[33] Although this definition is bare and basic, it well represents Gorgias' admiration for poetry, whose nature cannot be restricted to a mere versification: indeed, in the *Encomium* a reflection on tragic emotions is elaborated together with a physical theory of λόγος and its effects on the audience. Λόγοι are described by Gorgias as able to suppress or to generate strong emotions in listeners (see below, *Hel.* 9). Being as powerful as drugs, they can be healing and charming, or poisonous, in a way that reminds us of the Egyptian φάρμακα provided by Helen, 'many good, when mixed, and many grievous' (*Od.* 4.230):

ὥσπερ γὰρ τῶν φαρμάκων ἄλλους ἄλλα χυμοὺς ἐκ τοῦ σώματος ἐξάγει, καὶ τὰ μὲν νόσου τὰ δὲ βίου παύει, οὕτω καὶ τῶν λόγων οἱ μὲν ἐλύπησαν, οἱ δὲ ἔτερψαν, οἱ δὲ ἐφόβησαν, οἱ δὲ εἰς θάρσος κατέστησαν τοὺς ἀκούοντας, οἱ δὲ πειθοῖ τινι κακῆι τὴν ψυχὴν ἐφαρμάκευσαν καὶ ἐξεγοήτευσαν.

Just as different drugs expel different humours from the body, and some stop it from being ill but others stop it from living, so too some speeches cause sorrow, some cause pleasure, some cause fear, some give the hearers confidence, some drug and bewitch the mind with an evil persuasion.

Gorgias, Encomium of Helen 14

Words have a special power in Homer too. For example, in order to persuade Achilles to come back to the war, Phoenix introduces the myth of Meleager, persuaded by his bride Cleopatra to forget his wrath: her description of the city siege is so touching as to induce him to take up arms against enemies (*Il.* 9.523–605). The story is so vividly described that the listener feels as if he were personally involved in the mythical tale. This is a feature that good rhetoric shares with poetry, both epic and tragic: that is, the ability to put the object of the speech in front of our eyes *as though* it really happened or we were part of it.[34] In Gorgias' intention, the Homeric Helen can then become the heart of an admirable fiction: she bewitched many heroes with her body and voice, then she was bewitched by Paris' persuasive speech, and finally she carries on bewitching the audience with her many-sided nature as though she were in front of us. According to Gorgias, words are neither things nor events; nevertheless, the vivid presence of the λόγος is guaranteed by the emotions it inspires and intensifies.

The poetic inspiration of the *Encomium* seems to be confirmed also by two programmatic passages, one at the beginning and the other at the end of the speech. Its famous *incipit* is:

> Κόσμος πόλει μὲν εὐανδρία, σώματι δὲ κάλλος, ψυχῆι δὲ σοφία, πράγματι δὲ ἀρετή, λόγωι δὲ ἀλήθεια.
>
> The *harmony* of a city is excellence of its men, of a body beauty; of a *soul* wisdom; of an action virtue, of a speech truth.[35]
>
> Gorgias, Encomium of Helen 1

The truth of a speech is connected with its harmony, that is, the balance between its parts. Foreshadowing of this idea can be found in all epic tradition, whose essential requirement is the rigorous structure of the story. The periphrasis κατὰ κόσμον, which very often recurs in Homer along with κατὰ μοῖραν, refers to well-arranged and trustworthy tales, opposite to the casual and vain speech of drunk or hot-tempered people.[36] Furthermore, beauty as κόσμος is complex and multiform, like a cloth composed of twisted strands or a song with different tones. Κόσμος may be ποικίλος as well, a term with the richest semantics, referring to the variegated products of art, especially handcrafts. The analogy between different art practices (from hand-weaving to poetry itself), is mostly based on the shared idea that unity can derive from a plurality of well-combined elements.[37]

Considering the ending of the *Encomium*, many have read the term παίγνιον as delegitimizing the reliability of Gorgias' speech and reducing it to a *divertissement* or an exercise of stylistic virtuosity.[38] On the contrary, παίγνιον does not compromise Gorgias' commitment to his purpose, and actually brings us back to the specific world of art: originally, the lemma παιζ* could refer to dance accompanied by the music of a lyre.[39] Gorgias' παίγνιον probably means 'a free imaginative creation',[40] that is, the extremely serious game of art. In his essay *Der Dichter und das Phantasieren*, after introducing an analogy between the seriousness of children's games and poetry, Freud suggests that the opposite of a game is not what is serious, but what is real. This perfectly fits with Gorgias' rhetoric, capable of creating the most provocative fictions: instead of being considered as a kind of irrational manipulation or an empty pastime, his prose should be taken as an artful narration, whose effects are similar to those of poetry.

More specifically, Gorgias' παίγνιον could recall a challenging and allusive tactic. What is said hides and reveals at the same time, and the audience should complete the rebus, by giving form to the unspoken. On the one hand, Gorgias hides what is known (he intentionally omits the mythical framework), aware that it would be tedious to repeat what is well known to everybody (cf. *Hel.* 5). On the other hand, he helps to reveal a hidden and worthwhile truth: that of ethical responsibility and guilt, which comes into question when free agency is compelled by some external or internal power.[41] The enigma melts away at the end of his fascinating speech: like the Homeric Helen, the poet/rhetor too is a fortune-teller who speaks in riddles and, at the same time, reveals truths. He knows what is obscure, he alludes to what cannot be spoken of except in hints;[42] finally, he contributes to create the story while recounting it. Moreover, Gorgias' παίγνιον could indicate a specific strategy adopted by the Sophist when the myth is used as a paradigm to face ethical questions. In the Platonic *Phaedrus*, for example, Socrates contrasts a strictly dialectical proceeding with a παίζειν (παιδιᾷ, in 265c8) conceived as the playful and enjoyable deception of the myth.[43] Being a famous character, Helen is apt to renovate and challenge the creative ability of the poet/rhetor.

Finally, we know that Gorgias loved to mitigate seriousness with some laughing, and vice versa: the παίγνιον of the *Encomium* might then refer not only to the pleasure of art fiction, but also to a precise rhetorical argumentation that, by mixing or 'inverting' σπουδή and γέλως, might be a Sophist's peculiar way to floor the opponent.[44] Gorgias is introduced by Aristotle as appropriately using this strategy, which implies both the knowledge of technical procedures for the construction of the speech, and a careful evaluation of the psychological conditions of his opponents and his audience.

Although many elements overtly connect the *Encomium* with the Homeric epic (such as the relevance of the narrative structure, the intention to assure the pleasure of listening by avoiding what is well known, the focus on Helen as a personification of ποικιλία and κόσμος), Gorgias reproaches the poets of the past for erroneously blaming Helen:

[…] Ἑλένην, γυναῖκα περὶ ἧς ὁμόφωνος καὶ ὁμόψυχος γέγονεν ἥ τε τῶν ποιητῶν ἀκουσάντων πίστις ἥ τε τοῦ ὀνόματος φήμη, ὃ τῶν συμφορῶν μνήμη γέγονεν.

[…] Helen, a woman about whom both *the belief of those who have listened to poets* and the message of her name, which has become a reminder of the calamities, have been in unison and unanimity.

Gorgias, Encomium of Helen 2

This passage has often been read as a confirmation of Gorgias' undisputable hostility to poetry.[45] Nevertheless, the Sophist stands opposite not to all poetry, but only to that tradition that unjustly returned a negative image of Helen. Moreover, if we consider the Greek text, in itself rather controversial but perfectly understandable in the manuscript reading, the Sophist's polemic seems to be primarily directed towards passive listeners, that is, those who have listened to poets accusing Helen, and let themselves be convinced by them.[46] Of those traditional poets, not better identified, what emerges is the powerful ability to shape a widespread (and, in this case, unfair) opinion. In contrast, Gorgias listens to poets but is able to recreate that tradition with which he competes: on the one hand, he indirectly evokes an underestimated feature of the Homeric Helen (not her supposed adultery but her ability as storyteller); on the other, he makes Helen the perfect mouthpiece to present the power of a poetic speech grounded in likeness.

As innovator, Gorgias introduces his λογισμός as a coherent reasoning and argumentation (*Hel.* 2). Starting from agreed premises, he meticulously develops the quadrilemma of plausible causes and infers their consequences. Contrasting with rushed judgements, λογισμός works as a rational criterion apt to establish a logical truth in place of the factual one.[47] Since we could never know the truth about the mythical Helen, λογισμός assures listeners of a new truth, however grafted within that epic tradition. Moreover, Gorgias advances a new aesthetic doctrine which seems to foreshadow the Aristotelian theory of tragic emotions (cf. *Po.* 1449b24–8):

ἧς τοὺς ἀκούοντας εἰσῆλθε καὶ φρίκη περίφοβος καὶ ἔλεος πολύδακρυς καὶ πόθος φιλοπενθής, ἐπ' ἀλλοτρίων τε πραγμάτων καὶ σωμάτων εὐτυχίαις καὶ δυσπραγίαις ἴδιόν τι πάθημα διὰ τῶν λόγων ἔπαθεν ἡ ψυχή.

Into those who hear it [*scil.* poetry] comes fearful fright and tearful pity and mournful longing, and at the successes and failures of others' affairs and persons the *soul* suffers, through speeches, a suffering of its own.[48]

Gorgias, Encomium of Helen 9

Expressions recurring here (double names, compound adjectives) confirm the Aeschylean inspiration of this section of the text.[49] Fear, compassion, pain and pleasure are the effects caused by the poetic λόγος on the listeners: their intensity is guaranteed by the empathy of the audience, who feel the πάθη of others *as if* they were their own. The soul is shaped by powerful sensations and, unable to withstand their impact, activates a physiological and emotional response.[50] The transition from otherness to identity, managed by the poetry, is the most typical feature of this aesthetic experience: by its capacity of self-identification, the soul is never entirely passive, but is emotionally involved.[51]

If words and speeches are that powerful, how can we not understand the effect that λόγος must have on Helen? The principle of empathy that transforms the emotions of others into our own feelings must act even when we listen to Helen's story, but only if Helen stays at centre stage with the dignity of a poetic figure. The Homeric, enchanting Helen, who is bewitched by persuasive speech in Gorgias' *Encomium*, starts to bewitch listeners once more only if she can tell us her story again and again, at the heart of this great artistic fiction. The Sophist overcomes the tradition and reads the myth as a universal experience in which anyone can reflect and recognize himself, so that anyone can believe himself to be the one talking or acting. As Aristotle says (*Po.* 1451a36–b5), poetry should not deal with events that really happened, like history does, but with possibilities and likelihood (ἐοικότα), that is something which is universal, not particular. And εἰκός is the term deliberately used by Gorgias too, who investigates 'the causes which made it *reasonable* for Helen's departure to Troy to occur'.[52]

According to what is known about Helen's affairs, as well as to our knowledge of human nature, it is *likely* (and the less verifiable, the more fictionally reasonable) that Helen sailed to Troy. The quadrilemma of the causes is considered as exhaustive: so, whatever the cause of her departure, Helen is innocent.[53] When a factual truth is impossible to be captured, as in this case, the reference to εἰκός is introduced as an appeal to what is so likely and credible as to become a certainty to everyone.

Only another occurrence of εἰκός with the same meaning is found in the *Encomium*: 'But the woman who was violated and deprived of her country and bereaved of her family, would she not *reasonably* be pitied rather than reviled?'[54] By implying the transition from verisimilitude to necessity, Gorgias' εἰκός becomes a kind of ethical law of nature. The topic of εἰκός allows us to get closer to a hidden truth, thanks to the similarity between what is known and what is unknown, as in the ancient medicine which infers what is obscure from what is evident.[55] The power of gods, and human violence, and the persuasion of words and, finally, passionate love, are generally acknowledged by people as compelling and universal causes of human actions. Thus, by reflecting on Gorgias' Helen, we can better understand our own feelings and motivations to act. The hypothetical causes justifying her departure make such an event plausible and reasonable for listeners who are about to judge.

In the *Defense of Palamedes* too, where εἰκός recurs once, the term indicates the plausibility (or implausibility) of a reconstructive hypothesis, that is, its likelihood related to what we know about what happened (or, better, about what did not happen): 'But it is not *plausible* (εἰκός) to receive a few valuables in return for great services'.[56] While in Gorgias' *Palamedes* the power of εἰκός works as an argument from probability,[57] in the *Encomium* it seems more overtly connected with verisimilitude and analogy. Moreover, despite their persuasiveness, Palamedes' arguments are not sufficient to demonstrate the truth of his innocence and to save him, so that his apology can be read as a speech about what is not there.[58] Conversely, Gorgias' *Encomium* can be considered as a speech about what is likely to be: here the Sophist argues neither in favour of the factual truth nor of an indisputable state of things, but in favour of what is so similar to the truth as to become convincing for everybody. Let us not forget that Gorgias, together with Tisias, is introduced by Plato (*Phdr.* 267a6–7) as a theorist of εἰκός, which he would prefer to the truth. For the Sophist εἰκός is not a weak substitute for ἀλήθεια, but it can be a worthwhile and fruitful criterion to follow in absence of verifiable evidence.

Conclusion

By revitalizing the Homeric Helen and her connection with the world of εἰκός, Gorgias presents his own speech as a flexible tool, suitable for questioning the notion of factual truth and ethical responsibility. Despite his criticism of widespread and unfounded beliefs rooted in a passively accepted tradition, the fictional power of poetry seems to be an influential inspiration for Gorgias: in the Homeric epic ἐοικότα are not facts in themselves, but well-constructed speeches, likely disguises, and their consequence: that is, the emotional or psychological reactions to shared experience. Raised by poetry, emotions activate a process of understanding and self-understanding in the audience: in such a way, Gorgias creates a mirror in which anyone can reflect themselves.

His Helen is like a tragic character on the one hand, since she is still a victim of an overwhelming power, whatever the cause explaining her departure; on the other hand, she is a stock character who invites us to look over the contingency of events in order to capture the complexity of human nature. By extrapolating the mythical Helen from the Homeric background and emphasizing her nature of charmer and conjurer of likeness, the Sophist asks the audience to be part of that serious game which his Helen is; by means of his poetic fiction, the poet/rhetor can appropriately assign blame and praise according to faults and merits. In conclusion, Gorgias' Helen, who is both the mistress of a fascinating λόγος and its victim (or rather its instrument), can become the centre of a bewitching fiction again, as she is the most powerful expression of εἰκός: something that always changes its appearance, something that is always possible.

Notes

1. After the composition of a poem on Helen's adultery, Stesichorus decided to retract it and to defend her innocence (see P.Oxy. XXIX 2506 = 193 *PMGF* = fr. 90 Davies-Finglass). According to his new version of the myth, she found refuge in king Proteus' palace, while her simulacrum went to Troy with the abductor Paris. Euripides' *Helen*, and even Herodotus' extended and revised version of the myth (2.112–20), are probably influenced by Stesichorus. On the debated hypothesis that Stesichorus might have dedicated two different *Palinodes* to Helen, one against Homer and the other against Hesiod, see De Sanctis 2018: 100–1.
2. Austin 1994: 9.
3. In this regard see Morgan 2000: 7, and her contribution to this volume (Chapter 4).
4. All translations of Homer's *Iliad* and *Odyssey* are by Murray 1999 (revised by Wyatt) and Murray 1995 (revised by Dimock).
5. Clader 1976: 8. On this topic see Bergren 1983: 79; Lascoux 2006: 56–7; Nannini 2010: 153.
6. See scholium *ad Il.* 3.126–7 (I: 381, Erbse): 'the poet created a worthy archetype of his own ποίησις'. Nannini 1995: 34–5 speaks of 'vertigine temporale', and 'costante sfasamento metaepico'. On the connection between epic poetry and Helen's weaving see also Roisman 2006: 10.
7. According to Plutarch (*Quaest. Conv.* 614c5–7), Helen's φάρμακα correspond to her persuasive λόγοι, appropriate to her audience and their feelings. See Bergren 1981: 206–10, and Peponi 2012: 42–3.
8. For the different translations of εἰκός/ἐοικώς see below.
9. In the Homeric poems the periphrasis κατὰ μοῖραν is used for a reliable selection and combination of elements; it is often linked with the verb καταλέγειν (*Od.* 3.331, 8.496, 10.16, 12.35) to reinforce the idea of a detailed enumeration. As

κατὰ κόσμον, it characterizes the speech of gods, poets and wise men. Cf. Finkelberg 1998: 127–8.

10 *Recusatio* is typical of the singer when he faces a challenging and immeasurable list such as the Catalogue of the Heroines (*Od*. 11.328–9), or the names of all the Greek heroes died in the Trojan war (*Od*. 3.113–14). I disagree with Bertolín 2016: 87–8, who reads Helen's *recusatio* as confirming her distance from the truth.

11 On the semantic complexity of εἰκός see Goldhill 1991: 62 ff. and Hoffman 2008. Literally, εἰκός (derived from ἔοικα) is what 'looks like' something and is similar to it, so that it is considered 'appropriate' to such a model.

12 On the different interpretations of this passage by Hesiod see Ioli 2018: 70–5.

13 Similarly, when Telemachus arrives in Sparta without revealing his own identity, Helen is the only one who immediately recognizes him by looking at his face and noticing his resemblance to his father.

14 On Helen as a μάντις cf. Perceau 2011: 145–51.

15 These different perspectives will then be exploited and developed by the Second Sophistic (see, e.g. Tirrito's contribution in this volume).

16 The hypothesis that two different oral tales meet in *Od*. 4 is discussed by Scafoglio 2015: 133–44. Despite their antithetical features, the two tales are considered complementary by Doherty 1995a: 130; De Jong 2001: 101–2; Brillante in Bettini, Brillante 2002: 102.

17 In this regard cf. Christopoulos 2007: 105: 'la ruse de l'imitation des voix [...] constitue l'ultime possibilité pour qu'Hélène conserve sa dualité, en prolongeant l'existence de Troie'.

18 εἰκός sometimes alludes to the human, animal or natural semblance assumed by the gods. This does not presuppose a real metamorphosis, but rather a disguise of the divine so that it becomes accessible to the weak perception of men: see, e.g. the numerous disguises of Athena in *Odyssey* 13, or the appearance assumed by Poseidon, who seems identical to the seer Calchas; in fact, there are clues (the footprints and the gait) that, if carefully considered, reveal his supernatural nature and make him recognizable as a god (*Il*. 13.66–75). By considering the Homeric similes, Bryan 2012: 28–34, argues in favour of a distinction between εἰκός, which could express a subjective and emotive resemblance, and ὁμοῖος, used for a likeness that should be taken as objective.

19 In Pucci 1977: 1–9, and 1995: 209–13, the Sirens are described as Iliadic Muses, who promise Odysseus to get him back to his heroic past. See, for a different view, Doherty 1995b: 84, and Ioli 2018: 39–45.

20 Evelyn-White 1914 translates v. 164 into 'so close to truth is their sweet song'.

21 In its intransitive form, the verb ἀραρίσκειν refers in epic to a plurality of elements that stick to one another in a perfect combination, like weapons that adhere to the

body. According to Hunzinger 2015: 426, ἁρμονία is 'a perfect accord of multiple voices and different languages, such that each listener can still recognize his own individually'. See also Barker 1983: 40 n. 4. For an in-depth study of harmony in relation to μίμησις, see Halliwell 2002.

22 Cassin 1986: 15.
23 This hypothesis was touched upon in Homer as well: for example, Penelope suggests Helen might have been overcome not only by the power of the gods, but also by deceptive λόγοι (*Od.* 23.215–24).
24 The translations of Gorgias' *Encomium* are by MacDowell 1982. For the Greek text I follow Donadi 2016.
25 Cf. Verdenius 1981: 116–17; Poulakos 1983: 4; De Romilly 1988: 103; Blondell 2013: 171–6, and 2018: 129.
26 However, this does not imply that Gorgias 'makes himself the center of attention at Helen's expense' (Blondell 2013: 172).
27 See Cic. *Or.* 52.185 (= 82A32 DK): 'paria paribus adiuncta et similiter definita itemque contrariis relata contraria, quae sua sponte, etiamsi id non agas, cadunt plerumque numerose, *Gorgias primus invenit*, sed eis usus est intemperantius'.
28 As argued by Segal 1962: 127, 'the persuasiveness of a λόγος derives from its poetic composition'. Destrée 2015: 480–3 does not draw the same analogy between Gorgias' rhetoric and poetry as that which I am introducing here; still, he reads the *Encomium* as a piece of art aimed at delighting people. Many different interpretations have been proposed, such as, for example, a psychological theory of λόγος, whose magical and irrational power is acknowledged by Segal 1962: 109, De Romilly 1973: 155–62, Worman 2003: 156. In contrast, according to Mourelatos 1987, the *Encomium* is the expression of a behaviourist doctrine of λόγος, while Cassin 1986 emphasizes the demiurgic power of speech.
29 See Plu. *Glor. Ath.* 48c1–8 (= 82B23 DK). On Gorgias' 'tragic style' cf. D.H. *Lys.* 3 (= 82A4 DK), Ael. *VH* 12.32 (= 82A9 DK), Arist. *Rh.* III 3.1406b15–19 (= 82A23 DK). On the connection between tragedy and a Sophistic kind of answer see Pl. *Men.* 76e3–4 (= 82B4 DK).
30 See Philostr. *VS* I 9.2 (= 82A1 DK), *Suid.* s.v. Γοργίας (= 82A2 DK), D.S. XII 53.4 (= 82A4 DK), Syrian. *in Herm.* I 11.20 Rabe (= 82A29 DK), Cic. *Or.* 12.39 (= 82AA30 DK), Cic. *Or.* 49.165 (= 82A31 DK).
31 Arist. *Rh.* III 3.1406b10-11 (= 82B16 DK).
32 *Hel.* 9: τὴν ποίησιν ἅπασαν καὶ νομίζω καὶ ὀνομάζω λόγον ἔχοντα μέτρον.
33 According to Pollux (IX 1: 148 ed. Bethe), Gorgias was the author of an Ὀνομαστικόν: definitions must be recognized as one of his main interests. Cf. Pl. *Grg.* 502c5–7. On the originality of this definition see Schollmeyer 2020: 230–1, 234.
34 On the ἐνάργεια, 'vividness', of the epic poetry see Ford 2002.

35 MacDowell translates κόσμος into 'grace' and ψυχή into 'mind'.
36 In this regard see *Il.* 2.214, *Od.* 3.138, 8.487–98 (the last one conceived as a programmatic passage for the aedic narration).
37 Armours, bronze chariots, shields made of chromatically different metals, as well as weaving canvases are all called ποικίλα in epic. The term ποικιλία and derivatives are metaphorically used in classical poetry for the many-sided λόγοι. Cf. Nagy 1996: 39 ff.; Lascoux 2006: 43–57; Ioli 2018: 20–3, 104.
38 *Hel.* 21: 'I wished to write the speech as an encomium of Helen and an amusement for myself' (ἐβουλήθην γράψαι τὸν λόγον Ἑλένης μὲν ἐγκώμιον, ἐμὸν δὲ παίγνιον). According to Poulakos 1983: 3, and Blondell 2013: 176, the term παίγνιον undermines the seriousness of Gorgias' intention, while according to Porter 1993: 297 n. 82, the 'scandalous' παίγνιον conceals a self-refuting contradiction. In contrast, many defend the seriousness of Gorgias' speech: e.g. Bona 1974: 33; Verdenius 1981: 125; Paduano 2004: 100. An attempt to mediate can be found in Marchand, Ponchon 2016: 332–3, who suggest that the mythical fiction is pure entertainment, while the arguments are very serious. On the well-calculated relevance of the term παίγνιον and its 'retroactive' function see Schollmeyer 2020: 316.
39 See, e.g. *Od.* 23.147; *H.Ap.* 201, 206; *H.Aphr.* 120. In Plato παίγνιον sometimes refers to pantomimes, comedies (*Lg.* 816e10) and religious dances (*Lg.* 796b5).
40 Segal 1962: 119. For a similar interpretation of παίγνιον as 'a very serious game' see Decloquement's contribution to this volume (Chapter 8).
41 Gorgias is one of the first philosophers to develop a specific vocabulary about guilt, using the lexical tripartition between ἁμάρτημα, ἀδίκημα, ἀτύχημα to exculpate Helen (*Hel.* 15). In this regard, see Ioli 2007: 25–38 and 2013: 231–2.
42 That ability reminds us of Apollo, who speaks through αἰνίγματα and 'neither speaks out nor conceals but gives signs' (Heraclit. 22B93 DK). As seen above, in *Od.* 4 the Homeric Helen can expose deceptive appearances (cf. also *Iliad* 3.385–98, when she unmasks Aphrodite's disguise as an elderly spinner).
43 'We *described* the passion of love *in some sort of figurative manner* (οὐκ οἶδ' ὅπῃ ... ἀπεικάζοντες), expressing some truth, perhaps, and perhaps being led away in another direction, and after composing a somewhat plausible discourse, *we chanted a sportive and mythic hymn* (μυθικόν τινα ὕμνον προσεπαίσαμεν) in meet and pious strain to the honour of your lord and mine, Phaedrus, Love, the guardian of beautiful boys' (*Phdr.* 265b6–c3, translated by Fowler 1925). On the relevance of παίζειν in Plato's *Phaedrus* see Centrone 2011: 48–9.
44 Arist., *Rh.* III 18.1419b3 = 82B12 DK. Aristotle focuses on seriousness and laughing as technical tools to be used according to circumstances (καιρός), with the intention of refuting the adversary (cf. D.H. *Comp.* 12 = 82B13 DK). A similar strategy is attributed also to Agathon, Gorgias' disciple (see Pl. *Smp.* 197e).
45 See, e.g. Velardi 1993: 818, and Bourgeois 2017: 48.

46 Several editors emended the text to have a clear antithesis (e.g. Immish: ἥ τε τῶν ποιητῶν <πύστις ἥ τε τῶν> ἀκουσάντων πίστις). According to Condello 2008: 86–7, ῥῆσις or a similar bisillabus could be added. Others retain the *lectio* of the manuscripts but make ἀκουσάντων agree with ποιητῶν ('poets who have heard'), meaning either poets who have been inspired by the Muses (Segal 1962: 145 n. 63) or poets who have inherited an oral tradition from earlier poets (Bona 1974: 30 n. 1). I agree with MacDowell 1982: 34, in rejecting this last interpretation and following the manuscripts (see also Velardi 1993: 817–19; Ioli 2013: 220–1; Schollmeyer 2020: 176).

47 About λογισμός in Gorgias see MacDowell 1982: 21 and 29; Buchheim 1989: 5; Velardi 2001: 48–50. About the hypothesis of a 'double truth' see Buchheim 1989: 176 n. 3, and Morgan 2000: 123.

48 MacDowell translates ψυχή into 'mind'.

49 See Aesch., *Supp.* 736 for περίφοβος, and *Supp.* 449 for πολύδακρυς (but cf. also Hom. *Il.* 8.516, 17.544); lastly, φιλοπενθής, which links desire with pain, corresponds to a psychological condition which will become a *topos* in tragedy (see Eur., *Tr.* 608–9, *El.* 126–7, fr. 573N).

50 On the physical impact of strong perceptions, and their influence on the soul, see my 'Elena, Palamede e l'enigma della colpa: percezione, emozione, volontà', forthcoming.

51 It has been widely debated whether Gorgias' *Encomium* could have influenced the Aristotelian doctrine of tragedy and the notion of κάθαρσις. Pohlenz 1920: 172–3, and Segal 1962: 132, for example, see Gorgias as its forerunner. Ford 2002: 177–8 is more cautious: according to him the Sophist is interested not in the power of *poetic* λόγος, but in λόγος itself.

52 *Hel.* 5: [. . .] τὰς αἰτίας, δι' ἃς εἰκὸς ἦν γενέσθαι τὸν τῆς Ἑλένης εἰς τὴν Τροίαν στόλον. In contrast to those who suggest that the term εἰκός does not have a technical meaning in the *Encomium* (cf. Bona 1974: 32; Untersteiner 1961: 92; Gagarin 1994: 54; Spatharas 2001: 408), I would rather give it a specific value.

53 For Adkins 1972, Gorgias' argument can be valid only if each of the four causes is valid always and for everybody. Still, Gorgias often introduces the expressions 'some', 'many', 'most' (*Hel.* 11, 16, 17, 18). In contrast to Adkins, see also Tordesillas 2008. Compared to a strict reductionism, a 'soft' or 'anemic determinism' seems preferable (in this regard see Saunders 1985: 214).

54 *Hel.* 7: ἡ δὲ βιασθεῖσα καὶ τῆς πατρίδος στερηθεῖσα καὶ τῶν φίλων ὀρφανισθεῖσα πῶς οὐκ ἂν εἰκότως ἐλεηθείη μᾶλλον ἢ κακολογηθείη.

55 On εἰκός in ancient medicine see Di Piazza 2012: 14–15, and Ioli 2017: 56–9.

56 *Pal.* 9: ἀλλ' οὐκ εἰκὸς ἀντὶ μεγάλων ὑπουργημάτων ὀλίγα χρήματα λαμβάνειν.

57 In this regard see Tordesillas 1990: 248, and Bassino's contribution to this volume (Chapter 2).

58 Morgan speaks of an 'intellectually solipsistic' Palamedes, see below p. 98.

References

Adkins, A. 1972, 'Form and content in Gorgias' *Helen* and *Palamedes*: Rhetoric, philosophy, inconsistency and invalid argument in some Greek thinkers', in Anton, G. and Kustas, G. (eds), *Essays in Ancient Greek Philosophy*, vol. 2, Albany: 107–28.

Austin, N. 1994, *Helen of Troy and her Shameless Phantom*, Ithaca-London.

Barker, A. 1983, *Greek Musical Writings*, vol. 1: *The Musician and His Art*, Cambridge.

Bergren, A. 1981, 'Helen's "good drug": *Odyssey* IV 1-305', in Kresic, S. (ed.), *Contemporary Literary Hermeneutics and Interpretation of Classical Text*, Ottawa: 201–14.

Bergren, A. 1983, 'Language and the female in early Greek thought', *Arethusa* 16: 69–95.

Bertolín, R. 2016, 'The search for truth in *Odyssey* 3 and 4', in Cueva, E. and Martínez, J. (eds), *Splendide Mendax: Rethinking Fakes and Forgeries in Classical, Late Antique, and Early Christian Literature*, Gröningen: 75–91.

Bettini, M. and Brillante, C. 2002, *Il mito di Elena. Immagini e racconti dalla Grecia a oggi*, Turin.

Blondell, R. 2013, *Helen of Troy. Beauty, Myth, Devastation*, Oxford-New York.

Blondell, R. 2018, 'Helen and the divine defence: Homer, Gorgias, Euripides', *Classical Philology* 113: 113–33.

Bona, G. 1974, '*Logos* e *aletheia* nell'*Encomio di Elena* di Gorgia', *RFIC* 102: 6–33.

Bourgeois, L. 2017, 'Les stratégies de persuasion dans l'*Éloge d'Hélène* de Gorgias', *RPhA* 35, 1: 15–50.

Bryan, J. 2012, *Likeness and Likelihood in the Presocratics and Plato*, Cambridge.

Buchheim, T. (ed.) 1989, *Gorgias von Leontini, Reden, Fragmente und Testimonien, mit Übersetzung und Kommentar*, Hamburg.

Cassin, B. 1986, 'Du faux ou du mensonge à la fiction', in Cassin, B. (ed.), *Le plaisir de parler. Études de sophistique comparée*, Paris: 3–29.

Centrone, B. 2011, '*Fedro* 261e7-262c4, o l'inganno della buona retorica', in Casertano, G. (ed.), *Il* Fedro *di Platone: struttura e problematiche*, Naples: 39–55.

Christopoulos, M. 2007, 'Quelques remarques sur Hélène dans l'*Odyssée*. À la recherche des innovations mythographiques et narratives', *Gaia* 11: 101–20.

Clader, L. 1976, *Helen: The Evolution from Divine to Heroic in Greek Epic Tradition*, Leiden.

Condello, F. 2008, 'Due note all'*Encomio di Elena* gorgiano', *Eikasmos* 19: 83–93.

De Jong, I. 2001, *A Narratological Commentary on the* Odyssey, Cambridge.

De Romilly, J. 1973, 'Gorgias et le pouvoir de la poésie', *JHS* 93: 155–62.

De Romilly, J. 1988, *Les Grands Sophistes dans l'Athenes de Pericles*, Paris.

De Sanctis, D. 2018, *Il canto e la tela: le voci di Elena in Omero*, Pisa-Rome.

Destrée, P. 2015, 'Pleasure', in Destrée, P. (ed.), *A Companion to Ancient Aesthetics*, Malden MA: 472–85.

Di Piazza, S. 2012, 'Le verità regolari. L'*eikos* nella medicina ippocratica', in Piazza, F. and Di Piazza, S. (eds), *Verità verosimili. L'eikos nel pensiero greco*, Milan-Udine: 13–27.

Doherty, L. 1995a, *Siren Songs: Gender, Audiences, and Narrators in the* Odyssey, Ann Arbor.
Doherty, L. 1995b, 'Sirens, Muses, and female narrators in the *Odyssey*', in Cohen, B. (ed.), *The Distaff Side: Representing the Female in Homer's* Odyssey, New York-Oxford: 81–92.
Donadi, F. (ed.) 2016, *Helenae encomium*, Berlin.
Evelyn-White, H. G. (ed.) 1914, *Hesiod; The Homeric Hymns and Homerica*, Cambridge MA.
Finkelberg, M. 1998, *The Birth of Literary Fiction in Ancient Greece*, Oxford.
Ford, A. 2002, *The Origins of Criticism. Literary Culture and Poetic Theory in Classical Greece*, Princeton.
Fowler, H. (transl.) 1925, *Plato, Phaedrus*, Cambridge MA.
Gagarin, M. 1994, 'Probability and Persuasion: Plato and Early Greek Rhetoric', in Worthington, I. (ed.), *Persuasion: Greek Rhetoric in Action*, London: 46–68.
Goldhill, S. 1991, *The Poet's Voice: Essays on Poetics and Greek Literature*, Cambridge-New York.
Halliwell, S. 2002, *The Aesthetics of Mimesis: Ancient Texts and Modern Problems*, Princeton.
Hoffman, D. 2008, 'Concerning *eikos*: social expectation and verisimilitude in early Attic rhetoric', *Rhetorica* 26, 1: 1–29.
Hunzinger, C. 2015, 'Wonder', in Destrée, P. and Murray, P. (eds), *A Companion to Ancient Aesthetics*, Malden MA: 422–37.
Ioli, R. 2007, 'Libertà di scelta e responsabilità personale: Elena è innocente?', *Polifemo* 7: 25–38.
Ioli, R. (ed.) 2013, *Gorgia, Testimonianze e frammenti*, Rome.
Ioli, R. 2017, '*Eikos*. Simile, verosimile, probabile', *Technai. An International Journal for Ancient Science and Technology* 8: 51–65.
Ioli, R. 2018, *Il felice inganno. Poesia, finzione e verità nel mondo antico*, Milan-Udine.
Lascoux, E. 2006, 'Plaisir et variation dans l'esthétique de la voix grecque', in Lefebvre, R. and Villard, L. (eds), *Le plaisir. Réflexions antiques, approches modernes*, Rouen: 43–57.
MacDowell, M. (ed.) 1982, *Gorgias, Encomium of Helen*, Bristol.
Marchand, S. and Ponchon, P. 2016, *Gorgias de Platon suivi de Éloge d'Hélène de Gorgias*, Paris.
Morgan, K. 2000, *Myth and Philosophy from the Presocratics to Plato*, Cambridge.
Mourelatos, A. 1987, 'Gorgias on the functions of language', *Philosophical Topics* 15: 135–70.
Murray, A. T. (transl.) 1995, *Homer, The Odyssey*, revised by G. E. Dimock, Cambridge MA.
Murray, A. T. (transl.) 1999, *Homer, The Iliad*, revised by W. F. Wyatt, Cambridge MA.
Nagy, G. 1996, *Poetry as Performance: Homer and Beyond*, Cambridge.
Nannini, S. 1995, *Nuclei tematici dell'*Iliade. *Il duello in sogno*, Florence.

Nannini, S. 2010, *Omero. L'autore necessario*, Naples.
Paduano, G. (ed.) 2004, *Gorgia, Encomio di Elena*, Naples.
Peponi, A. 2012, *Frontiers of Pleasure: Models of Aesthetic Response in Archaic and Classical Greek Thought*, Oxford-New York.
Perceau, S. 2011, 'Mais devançant Ménélas, Hélène...' (*Od.*, XV 172). Se souvenir du passé: Hélène et Ménélas au chant IV de l'*Odyssée*', *Gaia* 14: 135–53.
Pohlenz, M. 1920, 'Die Anfäge der griechischen Poetik', *Nachrichten von der Gesellschaft der Wissenschaften zu Göttingen* 2: 142–78.
Porter, J. 1993, 'The seductions of Gorgias', *ClAnt* 12: 267–99.
Poulakos, J. 1983, 'Gorgias' *Encomium to Helen* and the defence of rhetoric', *Rhetorica* 1: 1–16.
Pucci, P. 1977, *Hesiod and the Language of Poetry*, Baltimore-London.
Pucci, P. 1995, *Odysseus Polutropos. Intertextual Readings in the* Odyssey *and the* Iliad, Ithaca-London.
Roisman, H. 2006, 'Helen in the *Iliad*; causa belli and victim of war: from silent weaver to public speaker', *AJPh* 127, 1: 1–36.
Saunders, T. 1985, 'Gorgias' psychology in the history of the free-will problem', *Siculorum Gymnasium* 38: 209–28.
Scafoglio, G. 2015, 'I due volti di Elena. Sopravvivenze della tradizione orale nell'*Odissea*', *Gaia* 18: 133–44.
Schollmeyer, J. (ed.) 2020, *Gorgias' Lobrede auf Helena, Literaturgeschichtliche Untersuchungen und Kommentar*, Berlin-Boston.
Segal, C. 1962, 'Gorgias and the psychology of the *Logos*', *HSPh* 66: 99–155.
Spatharas, D.G. 2001 'Patterns of Argumentation in Gorgias', *Mnemosyne* 54: 393–408.
Tordesillas, A. 1990, 'Palamède contre toutes raisons', in Mattéi, J-F. (ed.), *La naissance de la raison en Grèce*, Actes du congrès de Nice, mai 1987, Paris: 241–55.
Tordesillas, A. 2008, 'Gorgias et la question de la responsabilité d'Hélène', in Alesse, F. et al. (eds), *Anthropine sophia. Studi di filologia e storiografia filosofica in memoria di Gabriele Giannantoni*, Naples: 45–54.
Untersteiner, M. (ed.) 1961 2nd edn, *Sofisti. Testimonianze e frammenti*, vol. 2: *Gorgia, Licofrone e Prodico*, Florence.
Velardi, R. 1993, 'Gorgia e l'analisi tipologica del discorso nell'*Encomio di Elena*: discorso poetico e discorso magico', in Pretagostini, R. (ed.), *Tradizione e innovazione nella cultura greca da Omero all'età ellenistica: scritti in onore di Bruno Gentili*, vol. 2, Rome: 813–26.
Velardi, R. 2001, 'Il λογισμός di Gorgia', in Velardi, R. (ed.), *Retorica, filosofia, letteratura. Saggi di storia della retorica greca su Gorgia, Platone e Anassimene di Lampsaco*, Naples: 11–60.
Verdenius, W. 1981, 'Gorgias' doctrine of deception', in Kerferd, G. (ed.), *The Sophists and Their Legacy*, Wiesbaden: 116–28.
Worman, N. 2003, *The Cast of Character: Style in Greek Literature*, Austin.

2

Palamedes, The Sophistic Hero

Paola Bassino

Introduction

Palamedes played an important role in the story of the Trojan War: he was the one who forced Odysseus, reluctant to part from his young family, to leave Ithaca for Troy and participate in the war. Since Odysseus was then responsible for planning and leading the final sack of Troy, it seems fair to suggest that Palamedes had a share in the ultimate success of the expedition. Palamedes was also famous in antiquity for his cleverness, rhetorical ability and the multitude of inventions he had made to improve the life of human beings, from letters to numbers, war techniques and pastimes.[1] And yet, he is never mentioned in the two major epic poems, the *Iliad* and the *Odyssey*. The story of how Odysseus joined the Trojan expedition is referred to in the *Odyssey* (24.115–19) but the characters responsible for the events are Agamemnon and Menelaus – there is no mention of Palamedes, his trick, or Odysseus' subsequent revenge, perhaps because of the positive reputation that Odysseus had in the meantime acquired through the canonical epics.[2] This silence from 'Homer', however, has not cancelled the memory of this intriguing hero: authors throughout antiquity, from the Classical to the Imperial age, have exploited the potential of his myth.

This chapter discusses the two extant Sophistic works on Palamedes and his enmity with Odysseus. In Gorgias' *Apology of Palamedes*, the hero delivers his defence speech following Odysseus' accusation of treason. Gorgias' pupil Alcidamas, on the other hand, gave voice to the accuser in his *Odysseus or Against the treachery of Palamedes*. But why was this myth so popular among the Sophists? It is easy to understand why they would be interested in a character such as Odysseus, the πολύτροπος ('versatile') hero, who was indeed the protagonist of a number of philosophical speeches based on myth, including Antisthenes' *Ajax* and *Odysseus*.[3] As Morgan points out, he 'stood out as a mythological analogue for the versatility of the sophist and the late fifth-century Athenian';[4] for Worman, 'Helen and Odysseus become repositories for some of the fear and resentment that accompanied the Athenians' exposure to sophistic ideas'.[5] But Palamedes is his nemesis.[6] He too, as mentioned, was famous throughout antiquity for his ingenuity. This myth therefore allowed the Sophists to pit the two cleverest Greek heroes against each other, evaluate their wisdom, and discuss how, when and why they used it. It became a way to explore issues that were at the core of the Sophistic movement – to name but a few, the definition of wisdom (σοφία), the use of rhetoric, and the relationship between speech and reality. In this contribution, I will investigate how both Gorgias and Alcidamas use this myth, and analyse the links between their works on Palamedes and their wider literary production. Can a speech be dangerous? Is speech (λόγος) a valid means to show the truth? Is it possible at all to show, or even know, the truth in the first place? These are some of the typically Sophistic questions that the myth of Palamedes raises.

Archaic and Classical traditions on Palamedes

The earliest extant witness of the myth of Palamedes is the *Cypria*, a cyclic epic poem originally in eleven books dated by most scholars to the sixth century BC on linguistic grounds.[7] Now lost, we only have scant fragments of this poem and a fifth-century AD summary by Proclus. The poem seems to be tailored 'exactly to cover everything that happened up to the point where the *Iliad* begins'.[8] In the first appearance of Palamedes in the *Cypria*, the hero met Odysseus and tricked him into participating in the Trojan expedition:

> καὶ μαίνεσθαι προσποιησάμενον Ὀδυσσέα ἐπὶ τῶι μὴ θέλειν συστρατεύεσθαι ἐφώρασαν, Παλαμήδους ὑποθεμένου τὸν υἱὸν Τηλέμαχον ἐπὶ κόλασιν ἐξαρπάσαντες. <ἁρπάσας δὲ Τηλέμαχον ἐκ τοῦ Πηνελόπης κόλπου ὡς κτενῶν ἐξιφούλκει.>
>
> Odysseus feigned insanity, as he did not want to take part in the expedition, but they found him out by acting on a suggestion of Palamedes' and snatching his son Telemachus for a beating. [Palamedes snatched Telemachus from Penelope's bosom and drew his sword as if to kill him.]
>
> *Cypria*, Argumentum 5b

The death of Palamedes, it seems, was at the very end of the poem, and is only briefly mentioned in the last paragraph of Proclus' summary; more details are given by Pausanias:

ἔπειτά ἐστι Παλαμήδους θάνατος·

Then comes the death of Palamedes;

Cypria, Argumentum 12

Παλαμήδην δὲ ἀποπνιγῆναι προελθόντα ἐπὶ ἰχθύων θήραν, Διομήδην δὲ τὸν ἀποκτείναντα εἶναι καὶ Ὀδυσσέα, ἐπιλεξάμενος ἐν ἔπεσιν οἶδα τοῖς Κυπρίοις.

That Palamedes was drowned on a fishing expedition, and that Diomedes was the one who killed him with Odysseus, I know from reading it in the epic *Cypria*.

Pausanias, *Description of Greece* 10.31.2

Furthermore, the *Cypria* refers to Palamedes' involvement in an episode of famine in the Greek camp.[9] Other hexameter poetry informs us about traditions regarding Palamedes that were in circulation from the archaic period: Hesiod mentions Palamedes' father Nauplius, and Stesichorus attributes to Palamedes the invention of the alphabet.[10]

In the earliest extant sources, Palamedes was already ascribed some of those features that would prove popular in later traditions. Information about his parentage, his talent as an inventor, his resourcefulness and, most importantly, Odysseus' resentment against him, were all well attested by the Classical age. Sixth- and fifth-century authors, especially those active in the new fields of philosophy and theatre, made use of the myth of Palamedes, at times adapting some of its features, in order to investigate contemporary new concerns about the use and the power of language typical of democratic Athens. According to the *Cypria*, Palamedes was drowned by Odysseus – but in the new socio-political and cultural context, the hostility between the two heroes was seen as an opportunity to stage a competition in speech between two of the best orators featuring in the epic tradition. To this end, Classical authors created the new version of the myth according to which Odysseus put forward a charge of treason against Palamedes, as a result of which Palamedes was tried and put to death.

The three major tragedians wrote about this mythical trial, its causes, and its aftermath. Fragments of Aeschylus' *Palamedes* include a self-defence speech in which the hero emphasized his inventions and his activity as a benefactor of Greece, and Nauplius' reaction to the unjust execution of his son.[11] Sophocles composed a trilogy or tetralogy on the myth, which seems to have included one or two plays on Nauplius,[12] *The madness of Odysseus*[13] and *Palamedes*. Extant fragments from the *Palamedes* mention, as well as the inventions of the hero, also the famine he drew away.[14] Euripides' *Philoctetes* (431 BC) contains the earliest extant reference to Odysseus' accusation:[15]

ΟΔ. προδοσίαν ἐπενεγκὼν τοῦ στρατοῦ τοῖς Πριαμίδαις.
ΦΙ. ἦν δὲ κατ' ἀλήθειαν οὕτως ἔχον ἢ πέπονθε κατεψευσμένος;
ΟΔ. πῶς δ' ἂν δικαίως γένοιτο τῶν ὑπ' ἐκείνου γιγνομένων ὁτιοῦν;

Odysseus: He charged him with betraying the army to the sons of Priam.
Philoctetes: Was there truth in that, or did he suffer from a false accusation?
Od. How could anything whatever of that man's actions be just?

Euripides, *Philoctetes* fr. 789d (8)

A tragedy entitled *Palamedes* was performed in 415 BC as part of a trilogy that featured *Alexander* and *Trojan Women*, and was closed by the satyr drama *Sisyphus*.[16] This play is particularly fascinating because it seems to put the emphasis on a theme that recurs in many fifth-century versions of the myth: the connection between wisdom and speech. The following fragment points out that the ability to make a fine speech is not necessarily a sign of true wisdom:

ὅστις λέγει μὲν εὖ, τὰ δ' ἔργ' ἐφ' οἷς λέγει
αἰσχρ' ἐστί, τούτου τὸ σοφὸν οὐκ αἰνῶ ποτέ.

One who makes a fine speech when the actions upon which he speaks are shameful – I never praise this man's wisdom.

Euripides, *Palamedes* fr. 583

As Nightingale claims, Euripides' *Palamedes* 'brings two different kinds of wisdom into conflict – Odysseus' calculating cleverness and Palamedes' beneficial inventiveness and cultured intelligence'.[17] But it seems interesting that these verses cannot be attributed with certainty to either Palamedes or Odysseus: both claimed to be speaking according to the truth and to justice, and accused the other of making a fine but untruthful speech. It is therefore possible that the fragment presents Palamedes in the act of warning the judges about Odysseus' false accusation and deceitful rhetorical skills; but it is equally possible that it presents Odysseus accusing Palamedes of using speech deceitfully, as a persuasive strategy within his own deceitful speech. This brings to mind the charges put forward by the accuser of another man famous for his wisdom and put to death unjustly, namely Socrates – and indeed, according to ancient sources, Euripides' audience perceived the similarities between the two characters and their fate:[18]

λέγεται . . . ὅτι Εὐριπίδου βουλομένου εἰπεῖν περὶ αὐτοῦ (τοῦ Σωκράτους) καὶ δεδιότος ἀναπλάσασθαι Παλαμήδην, ἵνα διὰ τούτου σχοίη καιρὸν τοῦ αἰνίξασθαι εἰς τὸν Σωκράτη καὶ εἰς τοὺς Ἀθηναίους· 'ἐκάνετε, ἐκάνετε τῶν Ἑλλήνων τὸν ἄριστον', ὅ ἐστιν ἐφονεύσατε. καὶ νοῆσαν τὸ θέατρον ἅπαν ἐδάκρυσε, διότι περὶ Σωκράτους ᾐνίττετο.

It is said ... that when Euripides wanted to speak about him (Socrates) and was afraid to do so, he portrayed Palamedes, so as to have the opportunity through him of alluding darkly to Socrates and the Athenians: 'You have killed, you have killed the best of the Greeks' – that is, you have murdered him. The entire theatre understood this and wept, because of the allusion to Socrates.

Introduction to Isocrates' Busiris 24–30

Of course, the anecdote does not work chronologically: Euripides, who died in c. 406 BC, could not have made a reference to Socrates' execution in 399 BC; but the story shows how strong and long-lasting the perceived parallel between Palamedes and Socrates was. Famously, Plato picked up on this parallel too; his Socrates says:

ἐγὼ μὲν γὰρ πολλάκις ἐθέλω τεθνάναι εἰ ταῦτ' ἔστιν ἀληθῆ. ἐπεὶ ἔμοιγε καὶ αὐτῷ θαυμαστὴ ἂν εἴη ἡ διατριβὴ αὐτόθι, ὁπότε ἐντύχοιμι Παλαμήδει καὶ Αἴαντι τῷ Τελαμῶνος καὶ εἴ τις ἄλλος τῶν παλαιῶν διὰ κρίσιν ἄδικον τέθνηκεν, ἀντιπαραβάλλοντι τὰ ἐμαυτοῦ πάθη πρὸς τὰ ἐκείνων – ὡς ἐγὼ οἶμαι, οὐκ ἂν ἀηδὲς εἴη.

You see I'm willing to die many times over if this is the truth, since for myself spending time there would be wonderful, when I could meet Palamedes and Aias, Telamon's son, and any others of olden times who died as a result of an unjust judgment, and compare my experiences with theirs – in my view it would not be unpleasant.

Plato, Apology of Socrates 41b

The mention of Palamedes among the people Socrates would like to meet in the underworld is particularly relevant: not only were the two charged, tried and put to death unjustly – but being accused of using speech deceptively, they themselves fell victims of deceptive speakers. From the very beginning of the *Apology*, Socrates puts the emphasis on one particular point of the accusation: that he was a 'clever speaker'; and yet, he claims, his accusers are cleverer than he was, as they made an untrue but persuasive speech.

[17a] Ὅτι μὲν ὑμεῖς, ὦ ἄνδρες Ἀθηναῖοι, πεπόνθατε ὑπὸ τῶν ἐμῶν κατηγόρων, οὐκ οἶδα· ἐγὼ δ' οὖν καὶ αὐτὸς ὑπ' αὐτῶν ὀλίγου ἐμαυτοῦ ἐπελαθόμην, οὕτω πιθανῶς ἔλεγον. καίτοι ἀληθές γε ὡς ἔπος εἰπεῖν οὐδὲν εἰρήκασιν. μάλιστα δὲ αὐτῶν ἓν ἐθαύμασα τῶν πολλῶν ὧν ἐψεύσαντο, τοῦτο ἐν ᾧ ἔλεγον ὡς χρῆν ὑμᾶς εὐλαβεῖσθαι μὴ ὑπ' ἐμοῦ ἐξαπατηθῆτε [17b] ὡς δεινοῦ ὄντος λέγειν.

In what respect you, men of Athens, have been affected by my accusers I do not know; however that may be, thanks to them even I myself almost forgot who I was, they spoke so plausibly. Yet almost nothing of what they said is true. One of their many lies in particular surprised me, the one where they were saying that you ought to be on your guard not to be fooled by me because I'm a clever speaker.

Plato, *Apology of Socrates* 17a–b

This scene reminds the reader of the trial involving Odysseus and Palamedes, in which the contenders, in the absence of objective evidence, claim to be using speech to demonstrate the truth, at the same time each accusing the other of using it deceptively. There are many other echoes and parallels between the trial of Socrates and that of Palamedes, and several scholars have studied the relationships between Gorgias' and Plato's *Apologies* in detail.[19] These points of contact between Socrates' and Palamedes' claims are not limited to the use of similar rhetorical strategies: as McCoy suggests, 'Plato's defense of Socrates is intended to be reminiscent of Gorgias' *Palamedes* in particular', and takes up elements of Sophistic rhetoric to use them 'in service of a higher moral purpose'.[20]

The myth of Palamedes and Odysseus was successful in the Classical age because it raises a series of interrelated issues concerning the use of speech which, in a democratic context where speaking and persuading were synonyms for political power, were more pressing than ever. It is only to be expected that the Sophists, concerned as they were with such issues, would find in this myth appealing material.

Gorgias' *Apology of Palamedes*

Gorgias engages mainly with one aspect of the myth of Palamedes, namely the paradoxical message it seems to give about the power of speech. The hero is a skilful speaker and, indeed, as we shall see, performs a compelling speech, one that seems almost impossible to confute; however, that speech will fail to convince the judges that Palamedes is innocent, and the hero will be condemned to die. The story of Palamedes, perhaps more than any other story provided by the epic tradition, allows Gorgias to reflect on the power of λόγος on the one hand, but also, on the other, on its limitations. Importantly, the ideas about λόγος that seem to emerge from the *Apology of Palamedes* are closely related to Gorgias' wider ontological and epistemological views. As Morgan claims, Palamedes brings up two problems dear to Sophistic hearts: how can one transfer knowledge of something from one person to another through speech, and how can one say what is not?[21] These issues are investigated by Gorgias in his other works, the *On the Non-Being* and the *Encomium of Helen*, and Gorgias uses and shapes the myth of Palamedes in order to provide answers to these questions.

As well as the rhetorical tropes for which he is famous, in this speech Gorgias uses techniques borrowed from the context of the Athenian legal practice, and, as highlighted by Knudsen, from Homeric epic.[22] The *Apology of Palamedes* argues for the hero's innocence by using three main rhetorical strategies: arguments from probability (εἰκός), a speaker's appeal to his own character (ἦθος) and appeal to emotions (πάθος).[23] More specifically, the defence speech starts by proposing a twofold argument from probability, which aims to show that Palamedes could not have committed the crime, and even if he could, would not have done so. After that, the hero addresses Odysseus, and argues that his accuser did not base his accusation upon knowledge of the facts, but upon mere opinion; and finally he addresses the judges and presents himself as a benefactor to Greece, before concluding his speech by encouraging the jury to make their decision according to justice.

Arguments from probability, therefore, hold a prominent place in Gorgias' defence of Palamedes. However, they alone are not sufficient to show the truth: first-hand knowledge of the facts is necessary. This necessity is reiterated in several passages of the work and, in turn, the effects of the lack of direct knowledge are felt throughout the defence – increasingly towards the end, as Palamedes seems to be aware that death is approaching despite his efforts.[24]

Right at the beginning of the defence, Gorgias introduces a crucial distinction between knowledge and opinion:

[3] εἰ μὲν οὖν ὁ κατήγορος Ὀδυσσεὺς ἢ σαφῶς ἐπιστάμενος προδιδόντα με τὴν Ἑλλάδα τοῖς βαρβάροις ἢ δοξάζων γ᾽ ἀμῇ οὕτω ταῦτα ἔχειν ἐποιεῖτο τὴν κατηγορίαν δι᾽ εὔνοιαν τῆς Ἑλλάδος, ἄριστος ἂν ἦν ὁ ἀνήρ.

[3] If then it is because of his goodwill toward Greece that my accuser, Odysseus, has made the accusation – either knowing clearly that I was betraying Greece to the barbarians, or supposing somehow that this was how things were – then he would be the best of men.

Gorgias, *Apology of Palamedes* 3

In this passage, opinion per se is not presented in a negative light. In a sense, for Palamedes, it is understandable that Odysseus relied upon it, as any human being would: he would still be the best of men if he was basing his accusation on opinion, provided that in turn his opinion was based on goodwill towards Greece. But this does not mean that opinion, even when one relies upon it in good faith, is as valuable as truth itself:

[4] αἰτία γὰρ ἀνεπίδεικτος ἔκπληξιν ἐμφανῆ ἐμποιεῖ, διὰ δὲ τὴν ἔκπληξιν ἀπορεῖν ἀνάγκη τῷ λόγῳ, ἂν μή τι παρ' αὐτῆς τῆς ἀληθείας καὶ τῆς παρούσης ἀνάγκης μάθω, διδασκάλων ἐπικινδυνοτέρων ἢ ποριμωτέρων τυχών. [5] ὅτι μὲν οὖν οὐ σαφῶς <εἰδὼς> ὁ κατήγορος κατηγορεῖ μου, σαφῶς οἶδα· σύνοιδα γὰρ ἐμαυτῷ σαφῶς οὐδὲν τοιοῦτον πεποιηκώς·

[4] For an unproven accusation produces a manifest consternation, and from this consternation it follows necessarily that I am at a loss for speech, if I do not learn from the truth itself and from the present constraint, though finding therein teachers who provide more risks than resources. [5] Well, that the accuser has accused me without knowing clearly – this I know clearly. For I am clearly aware that I have done nothing of this sort.

Gorgias, Apology of Palamedes 4

Λόγος alone cannot achieve truth. On the other hand, it depends on truth – in fact, Palamedes claims he would even be 'necessarily at a loss for speech' (ἀπορεῖν ἀνάγκη τῷ λόγῳ) if he did not have knowledge of the truth, which he does because the events concern him directly. In another passage, Palamedes reiterates the importance of direct knowledge of the events:

[15] ὡς δ' ἀληθῆ λέγω, μάρτυρα πιστὸν παρέξομαι τὸν παροιχόμενον βίον· τῷ δὲ μάρτυρι μάρτυρες ὑμεῖς ἦτε· σύνεστε γάρ μοι, διὸ σύνιστε ταῦτα.

[15] To the fact that I am telling the truth, I shall offer my past life as a trustworthy witness; and you, be witnesses in support of this witness. For you are together (*suneste*) with me, and for this reason you know (*suniste*) this.

Gorgias, Apology of Palamedes 15

Here, to prove to the judges that they should believe what he is saying, Palamedes points out that they actually 'know' the truth already, because they 'are together' with him and therefore could witness the hero's past life for themselves. Once again, λόγος is the means by which Palamedes tries to *tell* the truth, namely that he is innocent, but it is not enough to *prove* it to the judges – if the judges did not know it already, Palamedes' λόγος alone would not be enough to demonstrate it. The play on σύνεστε / σύνιστε reinforces the idea that knowledge is connected to direct participation to the events.[25]

Palamedes, then, goes back to the contrast between knowledge and opinion made at the beginning of the speech (par. 3). Palamedes has proved that Odysseus cannot possess knowledge of the events – it remains that he based his accusation on opinion.

[24] ὅτι μὲν οὖν οὐκ οἶσθα ἃ κατηγορεῖς, φανερόν· τὸ δὴ λοιπὸν <οὐκ> εἰδότα σε δοξάζειν. εἶτα, ὦ πάντων ἀνθρώπων τολμηρότατε, δόξῃ πιστεύσας, ἀπιστοτάτῳ πράγματι, τὴν ἀλήθειαν οὐκ εἰδώς, τολμᾷς ἄνδρα περὶ θανάτου διώκειν;

[24] Therefore, the fact that you do not have knowledge of what you are accusing me of is evident. It remains that, <not> knowing, you have an opinion. Then is it trusting (*pisteusas*) in opinion, that most untrustworthy (*apistotatos*) of things, and not knowing the truth, that you, most audacious (*tolmêrotate*) of all humans, have the audacity (*tolmais*) to accuse a man of a capital crime?

Gorgias, *Apology of Palamedes* 24

At this stage in the speech, opinion – which was originally connotated positively, at least when accompanied by good intentions (par. 3) – is radically redefined as untrustworthy. Furthermore, according to Palamedes, Odysseus' speech is contradictory: it also shows a fatal gap in its understanding of σοφία, 'wisdom', 'craftiness':

[25] κατηγόρησας δέ μου διὰ τῶν εἰρημένων λόγων δύο τὰ ἐναντιώτατα, σοφίαν καὶ μανίαν, ὥπερ οὐχ οἷόν τε τὸν αὐτὸν ἄνθρωπον ἔχειν. ὅπου μὲν γάρ με φῂς εἶναι τεχνήεντά τε καὶ δεινὸν καὶ πόριμον, σοφίαν μου κατηγορεῖς, ὅπου δὲ λέγεις ὡς προὐδίδουν τὴν Ἑλλάδα, μανίαν·

[25] You have accused me, in the speeches I have mentioned, of two things that are completely contrary to one another, craftiness (σοφία) and madness, of which it is not possible for the same man to possess both. For you accuse me of craftiness when you say that I am skilled, clever, and resourceful, but of madness when you say that I betrayed Greece.[26]

Gorgias, *Apology of Palamedes* 25

Palamedes claims that true wisdom cannot be used to damage others, and therefore he would never have used it to betray Greece. This is a crucial feature of the character of Palamedes as presented by Gorgias, and indeed the next stage of the argument is based precisely on the idea that Palamedes has used his cleverness to benefit Greece:

[30] φήσαιμι δ' ἄν, καὶ φήσας οὐκ ἂν ψευσαίμην οὐδ' ἂν ἐλεγχθείην, οὐ μόνον ἀναμάρτητος ἀλλὰ καὶ μέγας εὐεργέτης ὑμῶν καὶ τῶν Ἑλλήνων καὶ τῶν ἁπάντων ἀνθρώπων, οὔκουν τῶν νῦν ὄντων ἀλλὰ τῶν μελλόντων, εἶναι.

[30] I would assert – and in asserting this neither would I be telling a lie nor would I be refuted – that not only am I free from fault but also that I am a great

benefactor for you, both for the Greeks and for all humans, not for those now alive but for those yet to come.

Gorgias, *Apology of Palamedes* 30

We are now approaching the end of the speech, and Palamedes, as he claimed, has been using λόγος to try to show the truth because that is the only means he has, in the absence of evidence. But will it be sufficient? Once again, he emphasizes that he wants to make his case based on truth, especially since his audience includes the 'very first of the Greeks':

[33] παρὰ δ' ὑμῖν τοῖς πρώτοις οὖσι τῶν Ἑλλήνων καὶ δοκοῦσιν, τῶν Ἑλλήνων καὶ δοκοῦσιν, οὐ φίλων βοηθείαις οὐδὲ λιταῖς οὐδὲ οἴκτοις δεῖ πείθειν ὑμᾶς, ἀλλὰ τῷ σαφεστάτῳ δικαίῳ, διδάξαντα τἀληθές, οὐκ ἀπατήσαντά με δεῖ διαφυγεῖν τὴν αἰτίαν ταύτην.

[33] But in the presence of you, who both are and are reputed to be the very first of the Greeks, I do not need to persuade you by means of the assistance of friends, entreaties, or laments, but to be acquitted of this accusation by the most evident justice, by teaching you the truth, not by deceiving you.

Gorgias, *Apology of Palamedes* 33

And finally, he makes a strong statement concerning what he thinks he might, realistically, achieve:

[34] ὑμᾶς δὲ χρὴ μὴ τοῖς λόγοις μᾶλλον ἢ τοῖς ἔργοις προσέχειν τὸν νοῦν...
[35] εἰ μὲν οὖν ἦν διὰ τῶν λόγων τὴν ἀλήθειαν τῶν ἔργων καθαράν τε γενέσθαι τοῖς ἀκούουσι <καὶ> φανεράν, εὔπορος ἂν εἴη κρίσις ἤδη ἀπὸ τῶν εἰρημένων· ἐπειδὴ δὲ οὐχ οὕτως ἔχει, τὸ μὲν σῶμα τοὐμὸν φυλάξατε, τὸν δὲ πλείω χρόνον ἐπιμείνατε, μετὰ δὲ τῆς ἀληθείας τὴν κρίσιν ποιήσατε.

[34] As for you, you should not pay attention to speeches more than to deeds...
[35] Well, if it were possible for the truth about actions to become pure <and> clear for listeners by means of speeches, it would already be easy to form a judgment on the basis of what I have said. But since matters are not like this, protect my body, wait for a longer time, form your judgment in conformity with the truth.

Gorgias, *Apology of Palamedes* 34

Palamedes knows that he is innocent and tries to convince his audience in the only way he can: through a well-crafted speech. However, as claimed before, λόγος is not sufficient to show the truth. Now this idea comes up in all its strength, with Palamedes admitting that his speech is the best possible; indeed, it would have worked, if speech had been a sufficient means of showing the truth

– but it is not. Therefore, he can only ask the judges to wait a little longer before they make their decision.[27]

The myth tells us that Palamedes will die. As he feared and expected, his λόγος, excellent though it was, could not show the truth in the absence of other, concrete evidence, and especially of direct knowledge of the facts. The message Gorgias gives is clear: with Morgan, we can claim that the *Apology of Palamedes* 'is far from a textbook rhetorical exercise designed to be copied blindly and emulated as a model. There is every reason not to conclude that Gorgias' work has an entirely positive thrust'.[28] Gorgias has not used Palamedes simply to create an example of good speech – for this, he would probably have chosen a character whose speech was successful. Instead, Gorgias wanted to emphasize both the power and the limitations of human λόγος.

If we take a 'holistic' approach to Gorgias' works,[29] we can find further support for this analysis: indeed, there are passages from his extant corpus in which the Sophist seems to give similar warnings about λόγος. The *Encomium of Helen* presents, at its very beginning, a connection between speech and truth – in fact, truth is the very ornament of λόγος, its quintessential feature:

> [1] κόσμος πόλει μὲν εὐανδρία, σώματι δὲ κάλλος, ψυχῇ δὲ σοφία, πράγματι δὲ ἀρετή, λόγῳ δὲ ἀλήθεια.
>
> [1] An ornament (κόσμος) for a city is manliness; for a body, beauty; for a soul, wisdom; for an action, excellence; for a speech (λόγος), truth.
>
> Gorgias, *Encomium of Helen* 1

In the next paragraph, when Gorgias moves on to illustrate the main argument of his speech, Helen's innocence, he claims that, in order to make his speech *correctly*, he aims to show the truth:

> [2] τοῦ δ' αὐτοῦ ἀνδρὸς λέξαι τε τὸ δέον ὀρθῶς καὶ ἐλέγξαι τοὺς μεμφομένους Ἑλένην... ἐγὼ δὲ βούλομαι... δεῖξαι τἀληθές.
>
> [2] It belongs to the same man both to say (λέξαι) correctly what is necessary and to refute (ἐλέγξαι) those who blame Helen... As for me, I wish... to show (δεῖξαι) the truth.
>
> Gorgias, *Encomium of Helen* 2

For Gorgias, rhetoric appears to be more than just an art of persuasion that relies and works on human opinion, something that can deceive the audience, if necessary – speech needs to be correct, true and beneficial to the community.[30]

The limitations of human knowledge and communication are also at the core of Gorgias' treatise *On the Non-Being*:

[65] ἐν γὰρ τῷ ἐπιγραφομένῳ Περὶ τοῦ μὴ ὄντος ἢ Περὶ φύσεως τρία κατὰ τὸ ἑξῆς κεφάλαια κατασκευάζει, ἓν μὲν καὶ πρῶτον ὅτι οὐδὲν ἔστιν, δεύτερον ὅτι εἰ καὶ ἔστιν, ἀκατάληπτον ἀνθρώπῳ, τρίτον ὅτι εἰ καὶ καταληπτόν, ἀλλὰ τοί γε ἀνέξοιστον καὶ ἀνερμήνευτον τῷ πέλας.

[65] In his text entitled *On Nonbeing* or *On Nature*, he [i.e. Gorgias] maintains three main points in sequence: one, the first one, that nothing is; second, that even if [scil. something] is, it cannot be apprehended by a human; third, that even if it can be apprehended, nonetheless it can certainly not be expressed and explained to someone else.

Gorgias, *On the Non-Being* D26 bB3 = Sextus Empiricus, *Against the Logicians* 7.65[31]

This reasoning seems to summarize the thought of Palamedes, particularly his concerns about the limitations of human λόγος: his speech aims to show the truth, but the truth, even if it exists, cannot be communicated to another human being effectively through speech. Palamedes, with his speech that fails for lack of concrete evidence, despite being carefully and logically crafted, is therefore the perfect mouthpiece for Gorgias to present his rhetorical theories.

Alcidamas' *Odysseus or On the Treachery of Palamedes*

Like Gorgias, Alcidamas too explores his own rhetorical theories and contrasting types of wisdom through the myth of Palamedes.[32] In his version of the story, the evidence for Palamedes' betrayal would have been an arrow with an incriminating message written on it, but that very arrow was shot back by mistake by Teucer. With it, the evidence was lost, and Odysseus – just like Gorgias' Palamedes – had to make his case based solely on his rhetorical ability.

Alcidamas was one of the key figures in the debate about λόγος that developed in the fifth and fourth centuries BC. While Isocrates, another pupil of Gorgias, claimed the superiority of written over purely oral speeches, Alcidamas suggested that a good orator must be able to allow for at least some degree of improvisation in his performance. Λόγος should consider the circumstances, the audience and their reactions – and the orator needs to be able to modify, lengthen or shorten his speech *impromptu* to achieve the best result, which is not possible when performing a written speech. In this picture, the concept of 'critical moment', καιρός, is crucial: as noted by McCoy, 'Alcidamas uses the vocabulary of philosophy, rhetoric, and sophistry in order to build up a normative picture of philosophy as a practice centered upon a person's capacity to speak well with attention to καιρός'.[33] The focus of the present analysis of the *Odysseus* is precisely the normative picture Alcidamas is building up through the myth of Palamedes: as we did with Gorgias, we can take a holistic approach to Alcidamas' corpus, and find points of contact between the way he engages with the legend of Palamedes and the rhetorical teachings he supports in other works. Indeed, it seems that Alcidamas himself encouraged his readers to look at his work that way, from the very beginning:

[1] πολλάκις ἤδη ἐνεθυμήθην καὶ ἐθαύμασα, ὦ ἄνδρες Ἕλληνες, τὰς γνώμας τῶν λεγόντων, τί ποτε ἄρα βουλόμενοι ῥᾳδίως δεῦρο παριόντες συμβουλεύουσιν ὑμῖν, ἀφ' ὧν ὠφέλεια μὲν οὐδεμία ἐστὶ τῷ κοινῷ, λοιδορίαι δὲ πλεῖσται γίγνονται ἐν ἀλλήλοις, εἰκῇ τε λόγους ἀναλίσκουσιν ἀκαίρους, περὶ ὧν ἂν τύχωσι. [2] λέγουσι δὲ τὴν αὐτῶν δόξαν ἕκαστος βουλόμενοί τι λαβεῖν, οἳ δὲ καὶ μισθὸν πραττόμενοι συναγορεύουσι, παρ' ὁποτέρων ἂν νομίζωσι πλείω λήψεσθαι.

[1] Often in the past, men of Greece, I have pondered and been astonished at the intentions of those who address us, wondering what on earth their purpose is in readily coming forward here and giving advice to you when they offer no help to the common cause, and very many mutual insults are produced, and they waste untimely words at random on whatever subject they happen to choose. [2] They speak, each of them wanting to get some advantage in selfish glory, and some even charge a fee for consulting with those from whom they think they can get a greater return.

Alcidamas, Odysseus 1–2

At the beginning of Odysseus' speech, Alcidamas plunges the reader straight into a world where past and present are blended by putting Palamedes in a very contemporary setting, one that echoes not only deliberation scenes depicted in the Homeric epics,[34] but also rhetorical practice contemporary to Alcidamas. The idea of stepping to centre stage (δεῦρο παριόντες, 'readily coming forward') reminds Alcidamas' audience of the public performances of rhapsodes or orators. Furthermore, the claim that 'some even charge a fee' may well bring to mind contemporary Sophists, rather than epic heroes. Therefore, in this very first section, Alcidamas seems to be putting forward his views about what an orator should do: speaking or acting not 'at random' or lightly, seizing the moment, adapting the speech to the circumstances – which a speaker can only achieve, Alcidamas warns, with a degree of improvisation, and without following a script.

These people are said to 'waste untimely words at random' (εἰκῇ τε λόγους ἀναλίσκουσιν ἀκαίρους) – a very pointed statement, as καιρός is a prominent concept in the treatise *On the Sophists*.[35] It is important because extemporaneous speech gives 'freedom, independence, and increased power of the able speaker in relation to the political community'.[36] See for example the following passage:

[9] ἡγοῦμαι δὲ καὶ τῷ βίῳ τῶν ἀνθρώπων τὸ μὲν λέγειν ἀεί τε καὶ διὰ παντὸς χρήσιμον εἶναι, τοῦ δὲ γράφειν ὀλιγάκις εὔκαιρον τὴν δύναμιν αὐτῷ καθίστασθαι.

[9] I think that in the life of men also making speeches is both constantly and in every circumstance useful, but writing ability is seldom apt for the critical moment.

Alcidamas, *On Sophists* 9

Adapting to the critical moment means to be able to lengthen the speech or certain parts of it when circumstances require it, which Alcidamas calls μακρολογία – Odysseus seems to do just that when he sets out to offer a long digression on Palamedes' family:[37]

[12] τά τε πράγματα τὰ περιεστηκότα καὶ τὴν στρατείαν πᾶσαν ἐπιδείξω αἴτιον γεγονότα ἡμῖν τόν τε πατέρα αὐτοῦ καὶ τοῦτον αὐτόν. ἀνάγκη δὲ καὶ διὰ μακροτέρων λόγων ῥηθῆναι τὰ γενόμενα.

[12] And I shall demonstrate that his father and he himself are responsible for our present circumstances and for the whole expedition. It is necessary that what has happened should be explained at greater length.

Alcidamas, *Odysseus* 12

The *Odysseus* also contains references to writing, which plays an important part in the version of the events proposed by the accuser. In this case, too, Alcidamas seems to be exploiting the myth to make a reference to one of the main tenets of the stylistic theory, namely the superiority of oral to written speech. Writing is indeed depicted in a very negative light, as it is the means through which Palamedes communicated with Alexander in order to arrange the crime:

[6] ... δείκνυσί μοι τὸν οἰστὸν ὑπὸ τοῖς πτεροῖς γράμματα ἔχοντα. [7] ... ἡ δὲ γραφὴ ἐδήλου τάδε· 'Ἀλέξανδρος Παλαμήδει. ὅσα συνέθου Τηλέφῳ, πάντα σοι ἔσται, ὅ τε πατὴρ Κασάνδραν γυναῖκα δίδωσί σοι, καθάπερ ἐπέστειλας· ἀλλὰ τὰ ἀπὸ σοῦ πραττέσθω διὰ τάχους.'

[6] ... he showed me the arrow which had some writing under the feathers. [7] ... The writing said this: 'Alexandros to Palamedes. All that you agreed with

Telephos will be yours and her father gives Cassandra to you as wife just as you ordered in your message. But let your side of things be done speedily.'

Alcidamas, *Odysseus* 6-7

References to writing are also found in paragraphs 9-10, where Odysseus claims there was a trident as a symbol (σημεῖον) embossed on Palamedes' shield so that he could be recognized, and suggests there was a message written on a javelin stating when he would commit the treachery.[38]

Furthermore, again much like Gorgias, Alcidamas takes this myth as an opportunity to think about the positive and negative effects of speech. He does so, I argue, through a well-measured usage of words such as φιλόσοφος, δεινός and σοφιστής, whose definition and connotation were flexible and almost ambivalent for a long time in antiquity.[39] In the *Odysseus*, Palamedes is straightaway defined as φιλόσοφός τε καὶ δεινός – but it does not seem immediately clear whether this is good or not:

[4] ὁ δὲ ἀνήρ ἐστι φιλόσοφός τε καὶ δεινός, οὗ μέλλω κατηγορεῖν, ὥστε εἰκότως τὸν νοῦν προσέχειν <δεῖν> ὑμᾶς καὶ μὴ ἀμελῆσαι περὶ τῶν νυνὶ λεγομένων.

[4] The man I am going to accuse is both educated and clever, so it is right that you might give me your attention and not be careless over what is now being said.

Alcidamas, *Odysseus* 4

This may mean that Palamedes' case deserves careful consideration, since his intellectual talents have earned him a good reputation among the Greeks, and as such he cannot be condemned without the most thorough investigation. But it could also be a warning to the judges not to let Palamedes deceive them through his skilful, but dangerous, speech. Indeed, Odysseus argues that Palamedes has used his cleverness also to do wrong. This is made clear in paragraph 12, where he claims:

[12] ἆρά γε ἐνθυμεῖσθε, ὦ ἄνδρες Ἕλληνες, ὅτι ταῦτα τοῦ σοφιστοῦ τῆς διανοίας καὶ τοῦ φρονήματος αὐτοῦ . . ., τυγχάνει φιλοσοφῶν, ἐφ' οἷς ἥκιστα ἐχρῆν αὐτὸν ταῦτα πράττειν.

[12] Do you consider, men of Greece, that these things <. . .> the intent and thinking of this expert who happens to be using his ingenuity in those matters in which he should least of all have acted?

Alcidamas, *Odysseus* 12

The same ambiguity in the use of those words can be perceived in several other passages of the work. An example is in par. 21, where Palamedes is called τὸν σοφιστήν, and in par. 22 where Odysseus goes on to illustrate 'in what matters he tried to be clever' (ἃ καὶ φιλοσοφεῖν ἐπικεχείρηκεν). Later on, when introducing Palamedes' inventions, Odysseus argues that Palamedes either did not make the inventions he claimed for himself, thus showing himself to be a liar, or only made detrimental inventions, and of course betrayed Greece.

Interestingly, Odysseus also uses one of those words, namely δεινός, in the context of an example of use of 'cleverness' that would have a positive impact on human life:

[26] νομίσματα δὲ οὐ Φοίνικες ἐξηῦρον, λογιώτατοι καὶ δεινότατοι ὄντες τῶν βαρβάρων;

[26] Did not the Phoenicians, being the most logical and clever of the barbarians, discover coinage?

Alcidamas, Odysseus 26

Cleverness is therefore a double-edged sword. It can be employed for good actions and inventions, but also for extremely damaging ones; and in the same way, it can be used to support a just or a wrong case, to tell the truth or to lie. That Palamedes possesses a high degree of cleverness is not in doubt – but Odysseus needs to encourage the judges to think about how his opponent uses it, and to warn them not to fall victim to that clever man and his deceitful speech.

[29] εἰ δὲ κατελεήσαντες αὐτὸν διὰ τὸν δεινότητα τῶν λόγων ἀφήσετε, θαυμαστὴ παρανομία γενήσεται ἐν τῷ στρατεύματι.

[29] And if, having felt sorry for him, you let him off because of the cleverness of his arguments, an astonishing lack of discipline in the army will ensue.

Alcidamas, Odysseus 29

Odysseus, on the other hand, wants to appear as the champion of true speech, and sets himself the challenge to succeed in what Gorgias' Palamedes failed: arguing for his case in the absence of evidence. The ambiguities of Palamedes' character and speech, conveniently, do not seem to apply to him.

[13] γνώσεσθε δὲ προϊόντος τοῦ λόγου, τὰς ἀληθείας ἀκούσαντες τῶν γενομένων.

[13] And, as my speech goes on, you will realize this as you hear the truth of what happened.

Alcidamas, Odysseus 13

The myth of Palamedes seems to have been used and shaped by Alcidamas in ways that reflect his beliefs concerning the nature of rhetoric and its aims. Some elements come up from this speech that are at the forefront of Alcidamas' stylistic theory as described in his own work *On Sophists*. Among these there are the ability of the speaker to adapt the speech to the circumstances, to seize the critical moment, and to lengthen or shorten the speech as needed; skills that are crucial to Alcidamas and which set him as a rhetorical theorist in sharp contrast to supporters of the written speech such as Isocrates. Furthermore, once again, in Alcidamas the myth of Palamedes is used to reflect on the dangers of rhetoric: Odysseus emphasizes repeatedly that cleverness can be used in different ways, not only to do good but also to commit unjust deeds and persuade the audience of false claims. At the same time, though, if Palamedes is innocent, Odysseus himself is actually committing the very crime of which he accuses Palamedes, namely using speech to support an unjust cause – Odysseus is thus proving himself right in his main point: rhetoric is dangerous.

Conclusion

Both Gorgias and Alcidamas articulate their own concerns about rhetoric through the legend of Palamedes. If we wonder why the Sophists chose to engage so actively with the story of Palamedes, the answer seems to be because it allowed them to stage a competition between the two cleverest Greeks, and set one of them up against the other in an unprecedented show of rhetorical ability. Furthermore, Palamedes is absent from the Homeric epics, which means that his legend could be adapted more freely: it was therefore possible to suggest that he was not drowned in a fishing expedition, as stated in the *Cypria*, but that he was tried and condemned. But, most importantly, Palamedes ultimately fails, despite probably being innocent. Palamedes, whose legend featured cleverness, persuasion and failure alike, was the perfect mouthpiece through whom the Sophists could articulate their own concerns about speech and rhetoric – the power of λόγος, but also its limitations and dangers.

Notes

1 A short but comprehensive introduction to the myth of Palamedes is found in Woodford 1994. All texts and translations in this article are taken from the Loeb editions, except for Alcidamas, which is taken from Muir 2001.
2 Danek 1998: 139, 237.

3 Koning in this volume (Chapter 3) offers a comprehensive analysis of this work and shows its importance in the Sophistic cultural landscape.
4 Morgan 2000: 115.
5 Worman 2002: 149–50.
6 Knudsen 2012: 36.
7 See most recently West 2013: 55–128 and Currie 2015: 281–305 for general information on the poem, discussion of authorship and dating, as well as commentaries on (some of) the fragments.
8 West 2013: 57. More specifically, it can be divided into five sections, as per West 2013: 59–60: '1. The wedding of Peleus and Thetis following Zeus' consultation with Themis, with the goddesses' quarrel and the Judgment of Paris. 2. Paris' journey to Sparta and abduction of Helen, to Menelaos' return from Crete. 3. The recruitment of an army, the first gathering at Aulis, and the mistaken invasion of Teuthrania. 4. The second gathering at Aulis and the taking of Tenedos. 5. The landing in the Troad and all that happened there.'
9 Fr. 26 West = Schol. *Lyc.* 570.
10 Hes., fr. 234 [297 MW] Ps. Apollod. *Bibl.* 2.[23]1.5 (p. 57.13 Wagner); Stesich. 213 Schol. Vat. in D. T. 6 (p. 183 Hilgard).
11 See for example fr. 181a: ἔπειτα πάσης Ἑλλάδος καὶ ξυμμάχων / βίον διῴκησ' ὄντα πρὶν πεφυρμένον / θηρσίν θ' ὅμοιον. 'Then I organized the life of all the Greeks and their allies, which previously had been as chaotic as that of beasts.' Full discussion of Aeschylus' play in Sommerstein 2009: 182–9.
12 Lloyd-Jones 1996: 218–25; see esp. frr. 429 and esp. 432 on Palamedes' inventions.
13 Lloyd-Jones 1996: 240–2.
14 Lloyd-Jones 1996: 248–51. See fr. 479: οὐ λιμὸν οὗτος τῶνδ' ἀπῶσε, σὺν θεῷ / εἰπεῖν, χρόνου τε διατριβὰς σοφωτάτας / ἐφηῦρε φλοίσβου μετὰ κόπον καθημένοις, / πεσσοὺς κύβους τε, τερπνὸν ἀργίας ἄκος. 'Was it not he who drove famine away from them, be it said with reverence towards the god, and he who discovered the cleverest ways of passing time for them when they were resting after their struggle with the waves, draughts and dice, a pleasant remedy against idleness?'
15 Collard/Cropp 2009: 368–403.
16 Collard/Cropp 2009: 46–59. See also Scodel 1980: 43–63.
17 Nightingale 1995: 153. The theme of wisdom and its ambiguous connection with speech is indeed present throughout the play: see, for example, frr. 581, 584, 585 and 588.
18 Euripides mentions Palamedes in other plays too: see *Iphigenia at Aulis* 192–8, *Orestes* 432–4 (see also the ancient scholia to this passage, that preserve the fullest account of Palamedes' story); Aristophanes makes fun of Euripides' *Palamedes* in his *Women at the Thesmophoriae* (768–84) and calls it a 'flop' (848); in the *Frogs*, Palamedes is used as a byword for wisdom and genius (1451: εὖ γ', ὦ Παλάμηδες, ὦ

σοφωτάτη φύσις, 'By Palamedes, that's good; you're a genius!'; finally, we know of a play entitled *Palamedes* written by Astydamas and Eupolis mentions Palamedes as an inventor (fr. 385).

19 See, for example, Coulter 1964, Biesecker-Mast 1994, Barrett 2001, Tanner 2017: 8–12, and most recently the edition with commentary of both Plato's and Xenophon's *Apology of Socrates* by Denyer 2019: 6–7, 141–2. It is also interesting to look at the mention of Odysseus in Plato's *Apology* 41b–c among the figures Socrates wishes to cross-examine in the Underworld: as suggested by Barrett (2001: 8), Socrates, like Palamedes, 'will expose not simply those who believe (unjustifiably) that they are wise; he will unmask famously deceptive masters of speech'. On this mention of Odysseus see also Montiglio 2011: 55. Palamedes is mentioned by Plato also in *Phaedrus* 261cd, where interestingly Palamedes is mentioned as an author of a treatise on rhetoric (see Dušanić 1992, Nightingale 1995:149–154, Werner 2012: 187–8). Morgan in this volume (Chapter 4) discusses this passage and shows its importance in relation to the Sophists' mythological role-playing. See also *Epistle* 1, 311ab, *Republic* 7.522d and *Laws* 677d. The parallel between Socrates and Palamedes is also exploited by Xenophon: see his *Apology of Socrates* 26: παραμυθεῖται δέ τί με καὶ Παλαμήδης ὁ παραπλησίως ἐμοὶ τελευτήσας· ἔτι γὰρ καὶ νῦν πολὺ καλλίους ὕμνους παρέχεται Ὀδυσσέως τοῦ ἀδίκως ἀποκτείναντος αὐτόν. 'And I take further comfort from the case of Palamedes, who died in circumstances similar to mine; for even now he affords us a far finer theme for songs than does Odysseus, the man who unjustly caused his death.' Other mentions of Palamedes in Xenophon's works are in *Memorabilia* 4.33 and *On Hunting* 11–12.
20 McCoy 2008: 23–55, quotes from pp. 32 and 40.
21 Morgan 2000: 120.
22 For example, Knudsen 2012: 41–2 mentions the episode of the embassy to Achilles in *Iliad* book 9 as a parallel.
23 Knudsen 2012: 37–8. See also Spatharas 2001: 58: 'each stage in the discussion of the actions preparing an alleged betrayal is presented as logically following the preceding one'.
24 See also Spatharas 2001: 49 on this point. On the εἰκός see also Roberta Ioli's contribution to this volume (Chapter 1).
25 See also Ioli 2013: 14, 22, 256 and 259, with the emphasis on the importance of experience as a means to reach knowledge in Gorgias' thought. The judges have not taken part to the events discussed at the trial, so they can only listen to contraposed speeches – which, however, can convey only themselves, and not the truth of the facts. But they did witness Palamedes' blameless life.
26 See Ioli 2013: 31 and 253 on the two types of 'wisdom' represented by Palamedes and Odysseus respectively, with the two corresponding types of rhetoric.
27 See also Ioli 2013: 260 on the 'divario incolmabile tra fatti e discorsi destinato a sfociare nell'incomunicabilità del vero' in relation to this passage.

28 Morgan 2000: 121.
29 McComiskey 1997: 4: 'The three primary extant fragments of Gorgias of Leontini – *On Non-Existence* (or *On Nature*), the *Encomium of Helen*, and the *Defense of Palamedes* – are not disparate or contradictory statements, as is often assumed, but are intricately interrelated and internally consistent contributions to a complex theory and art (*techne*) of rhetoric.' See also Ioli 2013: 12 on the connection between Gorgias' *On the Non-Being* and his two extant orations, and 262–4 on the connection between *On the Non-Being* and the final section of the *Defense of Palamedes* in particular.
30 See Valiavitcharska 2006, who emphasizes the connection between truthful and correct speech (ἀληθής and ὀρθὸς λόγος) and shows that correct speech goes beyond the effectiveness of language and into the domain of ethical correctness and responsibility.
31 The passage chosen for the quotation above summarizes clearly and concisely the main points of the *On the Non-Being*. However, Gorgias' argumentation is very complex and nuanced, as shown by what follows in Sextus Empiricus' text (7.65-87) and by the anonymous text *De Melisso Xenophane Gorgia* (979a12-980b21). See Ioli 2013: 157–94, where the two sources are commented on in detail and compared with each other.
32 It is necessary to start with some considerations on the authorship of the *Odysseus*, as it has sometimes been suggested that the work is not by Alcidamas. The debate developed around linguistic issues, and the fact that in the ancient sources there is no mention of the *Odysseus* among Alcidamas' works – there is an ambiguous passage in Plato's *Phaedrus*, but the earliest evidence of the attribution to Alcidamas is on the medieval manuscripts that transmit the work (Auer 1913; McDowell 1961; Avezzù 1982; Dušanić 1992; Muir 2001; Worman 2002: 183; López Cruces/Campos Daroca/Márquez Guerrero 2005: 21–4; O'Sullivan 2008; Knudsen 2012: 32 n. 3). I believe that this piece is genuinely by Alcidamas. First, '*Odysseus* provides a natural thematic counterpart to Gorgias' *Defense of Palamedes*. Alcidamas may, in fact, have composed this speech as a rejoinder to Gorgias' speech, considering that he was one of Gorgias' pupils' (Knudsen 2012: 43). Furthermore, O'Sullivan 2008, in his attempt to deny Alcidamas' authorship of the work on linguistic basis, does not take into account P.Mich. 2754 – but this is a crucial piece of evidence that shows how difficult it is to find any definitive answer about Alcidamas' authorship of a work solely based on style and language (for discussion see Bassino 2018: 67–75).
33 McCoy 2009: 46–7. On the debate written–oral speech, Alcidamas-Isocrates, see also O'Sullivan 1992: 23–62.
34 A recent study on the influence of Homeric epics on Classical rhetoric is Knudsen 2014.
35 On the concept of καιρός in Alcidamas, see Vallozza 1985 with further bibliography at p. 119 n. 2. At p. 119 n. 3 she lists the occurrences of the word in the *On Sophists*.

Muir 2001: 78 also notes another relevant passage: in *Odysseus* 17 the word καιρός 'has its full meaning of "this critical moment"'.

36 McCoy 2009: 48.
37 Muir 2001: 74.
38 Mention of writing is anachronistic in a Homeric setting, but it may be relevant that also in the only, debated, reference to it in the *Iliad* or the *Odyssey*, writing holds similarly negative associations. I refer to the episode of Bellerophon, *Iliad* 6.168–70 (πέμπε δέ μιν Λυκίηνδε, πόρεν δ' ὅ γε σήματα λυγρά, / γράψας ἐν πίνακι πτυκτῷ θυμοφθόρα πολλά, / δεῖξαι δ' ἠνώγειν ᾧ πενθερῷ, ὄφρ' ἀπόλοιτο, 'but he sent him to Lycia, and gave him fatal tokens, scratching in a folded tablet signs many and deadly and ordered him to show these to his father-in-law, so that he might perish'), on which Graziosi/Haubold 2010: 124–5, with further bibliography on the passage and the issues it opens up in relation to orality and writing in the composition of the Homeric poems.
39 See for example McCoy 2009: 51 n. 8: 'What is clear is that a number of ancient figures in the late fifth and early fourth century rely upon a certain degree of ambiguity in terms such as sophist, rhetoric, and philosophy in order to extol or to criticize particular activities.' Nightingale 1995: 15 claims that φιλοσοφία before Plato occurred with the meaning of '"intellectual cultivation" in a broad and unspecified sense'. On φιλοσοφία see also Laks 2018: 41–4. On σοφία and σοφιστής see Lloyd 1987, esp. chapter 2; at pp. 92–3, Lloyd points out that 'the category of sophist, in Plato himself, as well as elsewhere, is far from far-hedged, and there were important overlaps not only between sophists and natural philosophers but also and more especially between sophists and medical writers or lecturers. There is permeability in those categories, as well as permeability in the audiences the individuals concerned took as their targets'. References to relevant primary sources are provided in n. 152. On σοφιστής, see Laks 2018: 48. More specifically on Alcidamas' use of these words, see also McCoy 2009: 52 and Mazzara 2005: 54–8.

References

Auer, H. 1913, *De Alcidamantis declamatione quae inscribitur ΟΔΥΣΣΕΥΣ ΚΑΤΑ ΠΑΛΑΜΗΔΟΥΣ ΠΡΟΔΟΣΙΑΣ* (dissertation), Münster.
Avezzù, G. (ed.) 1982, *Alcidamante. Orazioni e frammenti*, Rome.
Barrett, J. 2001, 'Plato's *Apology*: Philosophy, rhetoric, and the world of myth', *CW* 95, 1: 3–30.
Bassino, P. 2018, *Certamen Homeri et Hesiodi: A Commentary*, Berlin-New York.
Biesecker-Mast, G. J. 1994, 'Forensic rhetoric and the constitution of the subject: Innocence, truth, and wisdom in Gorgias' Palamedes and Plato's Apology', *Rhetoric Society Quarterly* 24, 3/4: 148–66.

Collard, C. and Cropp, M. 2009, *Euripides. Fragments: Oedipus-Chrysippus. Other Fragments*. Edited and translated by Christopher Collard, Martin Cropp, Cambridge, MA.

Coulter, J. 1964, 'The relation of the *Apology of Socrates* to Gorgias's *Defense of Palamedes* and Plato's critique of Gorgianic rhetoric', *HSCP* 68: 269–303.

Currie, B. 2015, 'Cypria', in Fantuzzi, M. and Tsagalis, C. (eds), *The Greek Epic Cycle and Its Ancient Reception*, Cambridge: 281–305.

Danek, G. 1998, *Epos und Zitat. Studien zu den Quellen der Odyssee*, Vienna.

Denyer, N. 2019, *Plato: The Apology of Socrates and Xenophon: The Apology of Socrates*, Cambridge.

Dušanić, S. 1992, 'Alcidamas of Elaea in Plato's *Phaedrus*', *CQ* 42, 2: 347–57.

Graziosi, B. and Haubold, J. (eds) 2010, *Homer: Iliad Book VI*, Cambridge.

Ioli, R. 2013, *Gorgia. Testimonianze e frammenti. Introduzione, traduzione e commento di Roberta Ioli*, Rome.

Knudsen, R. A. 2012, 'Poetic speakers, Sophistic words', *AJPh* 133, 1: 31–60.

Knudsen, R. A. 2014, *Homeric Speech and the Origins of Rhetoric*, Baltimore.

Laks, A. 2018, *The Concept of Presocratic Philosophy: Its Origin, Development, and Significance*, Glenn W. Most (tr.), Princeton.

Lloyd, G. E. R. 1987, *The Revolutions of Wisdom: Studies in the Claims and Practice of Ancient Greek Science*, Berkeley.

Lloyd-Jones, H. 1996, *Sophocles. Fragments*. Edited and translated by Hugh Lloyd-Jones, Cambridge, MA.

López Cruces, J. L., Campos Daroca, F. J., and Márquez Guerrero, M. Á. (eds) 2005, *Testimonios y fragmentos / Alcidamante de Elea: Retórica a Alejandro / Anaxímenes de Lámpsaco*, Madrid.

Mazzara, G. 2005, 'La rhétorique éléatico-gorgienne d'Alcidamas chez Diogène Laërce (IX, 54) et les quatre fonctions fondamentales du λόγος', *AntCl* 74: 51–67.

McComiskey, B. 1997, 'Gorgias and the art of rhetoric: Toward a holistic reading of the extant Gorgianic fragments', *Rhetoric Society Quarterly* 27, 4: 5–24.

McCoy, M. B. 2008, *Plato on the Rhetoric of Philosophers and Sophists*, Cambridge.

McCoy, M. B. 2009, 'Alcidamas, Isocrates, and Plato on speech, writing, and philosophical rhetoric', *Ancient Philosophy* 29, 1: 45–66.

McDowell, D. 1961, 'Gorgias, Alkidamas, and the Cripps and Palatine manuscripts', *CQ* 11, 1: 113–24.

Montiglio, S. 2011, *From Villain to Hero: Odysseus in Ancient Thought*, Ann Arbor.

Morgan, K. A. 2000, *Myth and Philosophy from the Pre-Socratics to Plato*, Cambridge.

Muir, J. (ed.), 2001, *Alcidamas. The Works and Fragments*, London.

Nightingale, A. W. 1995, *Genres in Dialogue: Plato and the Construct of Philosophy*, Cambridge.

O'Sullivan, N. 1992, *Alcidamas, Aristophanes and the Beginnings of Greek Stylistic Theory*, Stuttgart.

O'Sullivan, N. 2008, 'The authenticity of [Alcidamas] Odysseus: Two new linguistic considerations', *CQ* 58, 2: 638–47.

Scodel, R. 1980, *The Trojan Trilogy of Euripides*, Gottingen.

Sommerstein, A. 2009, *Aeschylus. Fragments. Edited and translated by Alan H. Sommerstein*, Cambridge, MA.

Spatharas, D. 2001, *Gorgias: an edition of the extant texts and fragments with commentary and introduction*. PhD thesis, University of Glasgow.

Tanner, S. M. 2017, *Plato's Laughter: Socrates as Satyr and Comical Hero*, Albany, NY.

Valiavitcharska, V. 2006, 'Correct λόγος and truth in Gorgias' *Encomium of Helen*', *Rhetorica* 24, 2: 147–61.

Vallozza, M. 1985, 'Καιρός nella teoria retorica di Alcidamante e di Isocrate, ovvero nell'oratoria orale e scritta', *QUCC* 21, 3: 119–23.

Werner, D. S. 2012, *Myth and Philosophy in Plato's Phaedrus*, Cambridge.

West, M. L. 2013, *The Epic Cycle: A Commentary on the Lost Troy Epics*, Oxford-New York.

Woodford, S. 1994, 'Palamedes seeks revenge', *JHS* 114: 164–9.

Worman, N. 2002, *The Cast of Character: Style in Greek Literature*, Austin.

3

Ajax versus Odysseus

Hugo Koning

Introduction

Antisthenes of Athens (*c.* 446–360 BC) is generally counted among the Sophists, and is reported to have started his philosophical career as a pupil of Gorgias, whose influence on Antisthenes' language is visible in his work. Later in his life, perhaps in his forties, Antisthenes 'converted' and became one of Socrates' closest followers and one of Plato's most important intellectual competitors, developing his own philosophy so as to become the father of Cynicism. With the Sophists, and the Socratics, he shared a lifelong fascination for language, truth, reality and knowledge, and was similarly absorbed by investigations into ethical matters like virtue, φιλία, and good government.

All these areas of interest come together in the speeches by Ajax and Odysseus, which are the subject of this contribution. The speeches are supposed to have been delivered by the heroes to determine who was worthy of the arms of Achilles, a mythical episode known as the ὅπλων κρίσις or Judgement of the Arms. The speeches were written by Antisthenes perhaps around 380 BC,[1] and are the only complete texts by his hand that have come down to us.[2] Antisthenes was a prolific author, as may be gleaned from the impressive bibliography provided by Diogenes Laertius, but there is very little left of his writings. The speeches have therefore become of paramount importance in Antisthenean scholarship, providing scholars with the intriguing challenge of mapping and understanding the relationship between the speeches and the fragments. The challenge of making sense of the speeches is even further complicated by the fact that the speeches are written *in persona* and supposed to be delivered in turn, a situation that is unique (at least so far as we know).[3]

The speeches by Ajax and Odysseus make abundantly clear that Antisthenes was greatly interested in Homer, epic and myth in general, just like other intellectuals of his day. As is well known, philosophers and Sophists often used traditional tales, and especially Homeric poetry, to evaluate the heroes as ethical models, question the poets as educators, and to facilitate the discussion of philosophical matters in a *lingua franca* accessible to all Greeks.[4] As the Sophists already understood, Panhellenic myths were regarded as 'good to think with'.[5]

Antisthenes' interest in Homer also manifested itself in his work as a Homeric critic, preserved in several scholia.[6] In his critical work, he seems to have been particularly bent on defending Odysseus against possible attacks on his ethos and good judgement. For instance, Antisthenes explained Odysseus' choice to renounce Calypso's offer of immortality,[7] his supposedly foolish insult to the Cyclops[8] and, most notably, his epithet πολύτροπος ('of many ways'). Decades of bad press had turned this adjective into the best single word summary of Odysseus' shiftiness, hypocrisy and mendacity. Antisthenes, however, if we can trust Porphyry, reinterpreted the term to denote the ability to converse with people in many different ways, or the wisdom to adapt the tale to the audience.[9]

Antisthenes' work as a literary critic may lead us to think that he admired Odysseus. We will soon see how his hero is holding up against Ajax in his speech. First, we will take a brief look at the sources for the Judgement of the Arms and earlier reception of the Homeric characters Ajax and Odysseus.

The next-best of the Achaeans

The mythical episode of the adjudication of Achilles' arms to Odysseus is not in Homer, but the tale is as old as the *Odyssey*.[10] When Odysseus visits the Underworld, he tries to make amends with Ajax's shade, standing there 'alone' among the ghosts eager to hear news from the upper world, but the hero famously backs away from Odysseus' approach, not saying anything. Far from admitting the judgement was wrong, Odysseus does regret winning the prize. He blames the gods for what happened, and describes Ajax as 'who in beauty and in deeds of war was above all the other Danaans, next to the flawless son of Achilles'.[11] Characteristically, Odysseus adds that 'he might yet have spoken to me for all his wrath',[12] were it not for his desire to see other ghosts.

The Judgement was certainly part of the Epic Cycle, probably featuring at the end of the *Aethiopis* and at the start of the *Little Iliad*. The references differ as to the people involved, the role played by Athena and the identity of the judges. Two sources explicitly mention that the κρίσις was (or turned into) a judgement on who was the 'best' warrior, Odysseus or Ajax,[13] and one source signals difficulties concerning the criteria, saying that the 'best' warrior was understood as 'the one who had hurt the enemies the most'.[14] There is no evaluation on the quality of the judgement here, although some sources state that its outcome was divinely ordained, seeing that Athena 'wanted' Odysseus to win.[15] It is clear from the fragments, as is re-stated in Antisthenes' speeches, that the reason for Ajax and Odysseus being eligible for Achilles' arms was not because they were considered most worthy,[16] but because they were the two heroes involved in retrieving Achilles' body and arms from the battlefield.[17]

The last explicit references to the Judgement before Antisthenes are made by Pindar, in his *Nemean Odes* 7 and 8. These are remarkable for their explicitness and partiality. Consider these lines:

20 ...ἐγὼ δὲ πλέον' ἔλπομαι
    λόγον Ὀδυσσέος ἢ πάθαν
    διὰ τὸν ἁδυεπῆ γενέσθ' Ὅμηρον
    ἐπεὶ ψεύδεσί οἱ ποτανᾷ <τε> μαχανᾷ
    σεμνὸν ἔπεστί τι· σοφία
    δὲ κλέπτει παράγοισα μύθοις. τυφλὸν δ' ἔχει
    ἦτορ ὅμιλος ἀνδρῶν ὁ πλεῖστος. εἰ γὰρ ἦν
25 ἓν τὰν ἀλάθειαν ἰδέμεν, οὔ κεν ὅπλων χολωθείς
    ὁ καρτερὸς Αἴας ἔπαξε διὰ φρενῶν
    λευρὸν ξίφος· ὃν κράτιστον Ἀχιλέος ἄτερ μάχᾳ...

20 I believe that Odysseus' story
    has become greater than his actual suffering
    because of Homer's sweet verse,
    for upon his fictions and soaring craft
    rests great majesty, and his skill
25 deceives with misleading tales. The great majority
    of men have a blind heart, for if they could have seen
    the truth, mighty Aias, in anger over the arms,
    would not have planted in his chest
    the smooth sword. Except for Achilles, in battle he was the best...

Pindar, *Nemean* 7. 20–7, transl. W. H. Race

These words, and perhaps even more bitter ones in *Nemean* 8, take an unprecedently clear stand on the Judgement: Odysseus stole the prize with deceiving words,[18] since Ajax was the better warrior who could not withstand Odysseus' lying tales.[19] Obviously, Pindar, as befits a singer of athletic victories, uses the excellence in physical combat as a criterion.

The context in both odes is that of assigning praise and blame, a familiar theme in Pindar. The poet often tells us it is his solemn duty to stick to Muse-inspired truth as he describes the athletes' exploits faithfully and gives praise where it is due. Odysseus is portrayed as an anti-Pindar, not only because he lies about himself, but also, and most importantly, because he slanders Ajax, like a blame poet kicking another man down to polish up his own image.

Apart from the clear stand on the Judgement of the Arms, the fragment from *Nemean 7* is interesting for the ambiguity concerning Pindar's target. When he states that he believes 'Odysseus' story' has been inflated, he could be talking about Homer's tale about Odysseus or Odysseus' tale about himself, i.e. the story about his adventures that he tells the Phaeacians in books 9 to 12 of the *Odyssey*. It is deliberately unclear to whom the 'fictions', the 'soaring craft' and the 'misleading tales' belong.[20] The syntax would suggest Homer, but the rest of the passages indicates he might have been talking about Odysseus. There is a careful blend of narrator and protagonist, and 'the great majority of men' seem to be both the people present at the Judgement and the audiences of Homer.[21]

We know that Aeschylus had written a *Judgement of the Arms*, and even though only a couple of lines remain, it is most likely that Ajax's honesty was contrasted with Odysseus' fraudulence and mendacity: Ajax suggests that Sisyphus was Odysseus' father, and states that 'the words of truth are simple'.[22] Finally, we have quite a few vase paintings depicting the Judgement.[23] On some of these, Agamemnon presents the arms to Odysseus; on others, Athena is looking towards Odysseus, foreshadowing the outcome. Remarkably, some vases present the conflict as far more physical than our other sources suggest, with Ajax and Odysseus trying to leap at each other, both restrained by their friends. It seems that the popularity of the vase scene peaked around 500–480 BC, perhaps as a response to Aeschylus' play.

Antisthenes may not have been familiar with all the sources described above, and he undoubtedly knew of other versions unknown to us. But at least we can understand the basic outlines of the mythical episode before Antisthenes started to work on it.[24] Before we have a look at the speeches, however, we will first briefly turn to other instances of reception of the characters of Ajax and Odysseus that may have influenced him.

Odysseus and Ajax in the Greek imagination

The episode of the Judgement of the Arms was a creative force in the Greek imagination of Odysseus and Ajax, but presumably less so for Odysseus than for Ajax. Odysseus was a major character from the earliest beginnings of Greek literature, and, as Stanford has made clear, he was sufficiently polyvalent to be interpreted, imitated, evaluated and appropriated in all kinds of ways.[25] Kirk noted some sixty years ago that 'even within the *Odyssey* itself his character is inconsistent', playing incompatible roles at the same time;[26] similarly, Strauss Clay found a 'doubleness' in Odysseus, traceable to his very name: as the 'Man of Wrath', he is both victim and victimizer.[27] What Ioli has said about Helen seems to go for Odysseus as well: he is a 'universal character'.[28]

In Antisthenes' days, however, the hero's polyvalence may have eroded somewhat as 'general opinion seems to have been against Odysseus'.[29] Despite some relatively good press by Alcman and Archilochus, who probably regarded him as a sturdy warrior, by Theognis, who praised his ruthlessness against the suitors, and by Plato and Xenophon, who were impressed by Odysseus' self-control, it was Odysseus' versatility and mental flexibility that, especially in the age of the Sophistic movement, made him vulnerable to charges of hypocrisy, egotism, cruelty and mendacity, a potential that was fully exploited in the popular medium of tragedy. In several of Euripides' plays, Odysseus is portrayed as a morally repellent, all words-and-no-deeds, might-is-right politician propelled by pragmatism.[30]

In Sophocles' *Philoctetes*, much of the 'amoral opportunism' of Odysseus in Euripides' plays is foreshadowed.[31] Interestingly enough, in Sophocles' *Ajax*, the portrayal of Odysseus is more nuanced. Although he is initially called an 'enemy' of Ajax, he does sympathize with the hero, refuses to gloat over his fate and ensures his burial in the end. Jebb speaks of 'wise moderation' and 'generous action', which is just an example from more words of praise in modern scholarship.[32]

Even though Sophocles may have presented an Odysseus that did not conform with or perhaps even ran counter to the 'general opinion', his portrayal of Ajax fits the trend, established by Homer and continued with such force by Pindar, that Ajax was the greatest Greek warrior after Achilles. Sophoclean heroes are generally regarded as 'larger than life' characters who stick to their (often traditional and shame-induced) principles and suffer the ultimate consequence. Aristotle's famous dictum that Sophocles portrayed his protagonists as people 'the way they should be' is mostly agreed upon in modern times, and many believe that Ajax is the most Sophoclean of Sophoclean heroes: an 'extraordinary figure'[33] that has a firm determination, is unswayed by advice, stands alone, prefers dying to surrendering and does not accept human frailty and limitations. It is part of the model of the Sophoclean hero to have strongly Homeric overtones: the heroic ethos is determined by competitive values, a desire for honor and stubborn defiance.[34] It is clear from Antisthenes' speech of Ajax that he has made use of this traditional characterization.

The traumatic Judgement of the Arms is a crucial part of the traditional story of Ajax and his heroic suicide. And even though Odysseus is not a hateful character in the *Ajax*, and is not structurally opposed to Ajax, his role is still that of a foil, a non-Ajax. As Burton notes, there seems to be 'a conflict between two worlds, the world of the Homeric warrior and a more compassionate and humane world to which Odysseus belongs, and in which Ajax is an alien'.[35] This new world is that of the fifth-century community of the *polis*, the world of Antisthenes and his audience.

The speeches: Ajax

The speeches of Ajax and Odysseus have been the subject of much scholarship, and scholars disagree both on some of its key issues and on many smaller-scale aspects. What is generally agreed upon, however, is that the speeches' main theme is excellence (or, more specifically, bravery) and the criteria to determine and measure it. The speeches deal with a mythical contest, the result of which was marvelled at and criticized but could not, of course, be altered in a new version. Much like Hesiod's victory in the *Contest of Homer and Hesiod*, the decision to award the arms to Odysseus was widely regarded as mistaken,[36] and that was presumably what attracted Antisthenes. It provided him with the rhetorical and philosophical challenge of beating the odds: as Odysseus faced the best warrior after Achilles, Antisthenes had to spin the bad reputation of Odysseus. Furthermore, also much like the situation in the *Contest*, the competitors are widely different: the archaic 'man of action' versus the modern 'consummate rhetorician'.[37] This is a contest that is far less symmetrical than the mythical contest between Palamedes and Odysseus, which pits 'the two cleverest Greek heroes against each other'.[38] As we shall see, however, truth and knowledge are central criteria in the Judgement of the Arms as well.

Ajax's speech is the shorter of the two, about two-thirds of that of his opponent. It is not structured as a typical rhetorical exercise,[39] the language is blunt, strained, even tortuous sometimes, and the logic of his reasoning is not always obvious. He makes three positive arguments to back his claim to the arms, but none of them carry the force they could have had in the hands of a more trained rhetorician.[40] A larger part of his speech is devoted to disqualifying Odysseus, calling him a shameless rogue who would do anything for profit, a coward working in disguise and under the cover of darkness.[41] The arms surely do not belong to him, because Odysseus would not dare use them: 'for no coward would use distinguished weapons, knowing that the weapons reveal his cowardice' (§3).[42] These attacks on Odysseus, much like the arguments in defence of himself, are clumsily framed and provide convenient starting points for Odysseus later on. By far the strongest part of Ajax's speech, however, is concerned with his belief that words are unable to give a fair sense of reality or clarify one's character. War is decided by deeds and not words (§7), so the contest should likewise be decided by deeds; but since words 'have no strength against deed' (§7), and since the judges have not been witness to the deeds, they have no idea what they are talking about. For all that matters, Ajax may just as well stay silent (§1)! Five out of nine paragraphs deal with the idleness of words and the incompetence of the judges; it is very obvious that Ajax resists the very form of the contest.

Ajax's views on the referentiality of language are extremely interesting from an epistemological point of view, and scholars have paid a great deal of attention to them.[43] They are less relevant in the present chapter however, although it is worthwhile to note that some of Ajax's ideas seem to coincide with those of Antisthenes himself. For instance: he agrees with Antisthenes that virtue is a matter of deeds, and almost quotes Antisthenes when he claims that 'it is not possible to refute' the enemy.[44] Ajax's Antisthenean views on the correctness of names and on the limited referentiality of words have long led scholars to believe that Ajax was meant to be understood as the better speaker.

It appears that the Ajax of Antisthenes, although, of course, ultimately based on Homer, is derived from the post-Homeric, *krisis*-informed tradition rather than from the *Iliad*. His aversion to trickery and devotion to reputation are not typical for Ajax in Homer but rather generally heroic, and his sullen, tortured attitude, the stubbornly self-damaging behaviour and rhetorical clumsiness are in fact rather a far cry from the character in the *Iliad*[45] – but they do fit the tradition visible in Sophocles' *Ajax*. Also, the main argument behind the attack on Odysseus' character, the theft of the Palladium (§3 and 6), is not in Homer but is part of the Cycle (as is Ajax's claim that Odysseus did not come willingly to Troy in §9).

It is true that Ajax, referring to his silence twice (§1 and 7), combined with his refusal to address Odysseus directly, may contain a reference to the silent treatment of Odysseus in the Underworld. Apart from that, however, it is striking that one of the most remarkable characteristics of Ajax in the *Iliad*, the use of his unique and wall-like shield, is explicitly dismissed in his own words, and in a very significant part of the speech at that. Ajax's last line is that the Judgement 'is about a man who came to Troy not willingly but unwillingly, and about myself, who has been stationed in battle always first and alone and without fortification' (§9). It is odd that Ajax describes himself as ἄνευ τείχους, 'without fortification', for the shield and the hero are inextricably linked in the *Iliad*. There is a Homeric formula for Ajax approaching on the battle field, 'carrying his shield that was like a city wall'.[46] Homer explains how remarkable it is for its size and weight, consisting of seven layers of ox-hide and one layer of bronze.[47] It is arguably Ajax's most recognizable feature, earning him the title of 'bulwark of the Achaeans', offering protection even to others than himself.[48]

Ajax, the hero so obviously driven by the values of the traditionally heroic shame-culture, is here to be seen as unaware of his reputation. Most interestingly, he is unaware of his image in Homeric poetry – this ignorance is, of course, logical in terms of the dramatic setting, but contrasts sharply with the position of Odysseus, as we will later see. It is remarkable that Ajax, in what he presumably believes is a fitting finale to his speech and ultimate testament to his character, in fact throws his iconic shield away, so to speak, and becomes immediately vulnerable to Odysseus.

The speeches: Odysseus

Odysseus' speech is a return address, no set speech but a true response. He tackles the arguments raised by Ajax and adds a few of his own.[49] Some scholars believe that this approach is meant to be understood as proper philosophical (or Socratic) dialectic, not Sophistical eristic.[50] Understandably, Odysseus does not share Ajax's obsession with the problematic ontological status of words. He does state that the jurors (just as Ajax himself) are ignorant of some of his exploits, but this is not considered a problem: he can just tell them about it. Although Odysseus is more careful than Ajax to claim truth for himself,[51] he does suggest that the judges and Ajax can acquire knowledge through his words. Whereas Ajax stated (in Antisthenean terms) that 'it is impossible to refute the enemy in argument, but only to win by fighting or to serve as a slave, in silence' (§7), the last line of Odysseus' speech seems to suggest that not only weapons, but true discourse can 'silence' the other speaker as well. This is perhaps one of the points of Odysseus' reference to Homer's comparison of Ajax to 'asses and oxen (…) who give over to others the power of bonding and harnessing themselves' (§14).[52]

Prince rightly states that the speeches, among other things, 'are advertisements for Antisthenes' teaching program on the correctness of names,'[53] and this is especially apparent in Odysseus' speech. A large part of Odysseus' counter-argumentation is based on redefinition of concepts and notions that Ajax put forward. Ajax's accusation of temple robbing, for instance, is neutralized by Odysseus' claim that the Palladium was robbed from the Greeks by Alexander in the first place – so Odysseus did not rob it but 'saved' it instead. Similarly, Odysseus denies that fighting openly is a necessary contingent of excellence (§6), and slams Ajax's claims of bravery in multiple ways. He reduces Ajax's main achievement (and main argument for gaining the arms) of carrying Achilles' corpse to the Greek camp to a matter of strength not bravery (§11), and further in the speech again separates strength from bravery: it is 'wisdom in war' that defines courage (§13). It turns out, Odysseus argues, that it is Ajax who is the true coward, an inversion that is driven home by turning the tables on Ajax's argument that Odysseus would not dare to wear Achilles' arms because they would reveal his cowardice. Odysseus, referring to a non-Homeric tradition we know from Pindar and Sophocles,[54] says Ajax is 'the biggest coward of all' and 'the most afraid of death' because he has 'weapons that are unbreakable and invincible' (§7). Ajax's supposed bravery relies on external objects, whereas Odysseus can fight with any weapon and under any circumstance (§9 and 10). Ajax's main character flaw, fuelling the misconceptions that lead to his cowardice, is ignorance, 'the greatest evil to those who have it' (§13). The core of that ignorance is apparently the inability to distinguish clearly between means and ends, to keep one's eye on the goal. 'We did not come here in order to fight the Trojans, but so that we could recover Helen and capture Troy,' says Odysseus (§2). Ajax, however, seems content just to be engaged in fighting and killing: he does not achieve anything more than that (§2), fights 'for nothing' (§6) and would achieve nothing at all if he were to encounter an enemy equally dressed in unbreakable armour (§7).[55] It is clear that Odysseus believes Ajax is missing the bigger picture. He seems tragically and unknowingly trapped in a traditional sense of heroism and courage.

Odysseus, by contrast, is fully aware of these traditional cultural patterns and transcends the heroic code so that he can see an alternative set of moral values. As Prince states: 'Odysseus appropriates and manipulates social categories.'[56] He has the wish and courage to break from shame-driven behaviour, and, moreover, is able to explain and justify his own interpretation of virtue. Many scholars believe that this own code of virtue is essentially Cynic and (thus) Antisthenean, giving rise to the modern general consensus that we are meant to see Odysseus as the rightful winner of the debate (and the arms).[57]

Still, the degree of Antisthenes' connection to Cynicism is debated. Nevertheless, it does seem possible to find three clearly Cynic aspects of Odysseus' thinking in his speech, although it appears all three of them should be qualified in one way or another. The first and most obvious one, described in the 'most proto-Cynic section of Odysseus' speech',[58] is the hero's indifference to appearances. He does not care to be caught in actions or attire that are typically shameful,[59] and does not care if useful and beneficial actions remain unseen. This attitude alone makes Odysseus invulnerable to Ajax's outrage (though not necessarily in the eyes of the audience). Paradoxically, the Cynic indifference to public appreciation and recognition also qualifies the need for Odysseus to win the contest, and, by consequence, the arms of Achilles. Odysseus, so it seems, does not need a win for himself, but rather speaks in the interest of truth and the education of mankind (including Ajax).[60]

The second Cynic characteristic is the stress on φιλανθρωπία, the Cynic's self-effacement to serve humanity as a whole. Odysseus is not worried about himself but instead cares for all Greeks (§8), and repeats that his missions were undertaken for the common good. According to Montiglio, this universal scope includes even the Trojans, leaving aside the 'nationalistic thrust' of Gorgias' *Palamedes*. Diogenes supposedly said, 'other dogs bite their enemies, I, my friends – so that I may save them'.[61] Such benevolence may inform Odysseus' aversity to the strategy of 'fighting (and presumably killing) Trojans', ascribed to Ajax. As a counterargument to this view, we may point to the fact that if Odysseus is a pure Cynic, he is 'biting' only Ajax here, and it is not clear at all that Odysseus is ultimately bent on saving him.

And, third, there is the personal quality that makes it possible to go so far as to oppose Ajax's traditional notions: the value of thinking, especially independent thinking, as a basis for human behaviour. Ignorance is described as the worst of evils, whereas individual responsibility,[62] and especially intellectual autarchy, are seen as essential to Odysseus' notion of virtue. By contrast, Odysseus tries to frame Ajax as a 'herd thinker'. As Prince noted, Ajax is of course an individual as well, but only so in a physical sense. She rightly sees that Odysseus assesses the return of Achilles' body an achievement of strength alone, something that could also have been done by two lesser men: 'The physical power of Ajax can be balanced by mere multiplication of bodies and therefore had no real unity or principle of individuation.'[63]

Odysseus' 'transcendence', his ability to see and thus go beyond a cultural paradigm, is also apparent in his knowledge of the literary tradition. Whereas Ajax's remarks are in line with the tradition, Odysseus is able to speak about that tradition, exhibiting knowledge that goes beyond the dramatic restrictions of his persona. We first notice this when we are half-way into his speech, and Odysseus hints twice at Ajax's future suicide (§5 and 6, see for the full text below). This 'prediction' by Odysseus is based on the tradition of the Cycle, even, perhaps, directly referring to Sophocles' play.[64]

Scholars have so far understood the prediction rather generally in (proto-) Cynic terms. They notice that Odysseus in both cases blames 'anger' for Ajax's suicide, pointing out that anger (as are other vehement passions) is regarded as a dangerous emotion by the Cynics.[65] Furthermore, this 'anger', the direct cause of Ajax falling onto his sword, is probably to be seen as ultimately fuelled by ignorance, a character flaw Odysseus mentions multiple times in this particular passage. Several scholars believe the references to Ajax's future are meant as a warning; as such, the references would fit a bigger attempt by Odysseus to actually teach Ajax something about true courage and excellence – according to this reading, Ajax can learn and change his views, avoiding his premature death altogether.[66]

While I think the Cynic overtones are clear in this passage, I believe the references to Ajax's suicide can be understood more fully if we see them as part of a larger strategy on Odysseus' (or Antisthenes') part to turn the tables on Ajax, to redefine his own beliefs and so defeat him. Odysseus' use of Homer, so far not discussed, is crucial to this strategy. As we will see below, there are more references to Homer in Odysseus' speech than we have hitherto seen, and I believe the role of the poet is even more important to Antisthenes' Odysseus than we have so far acknowledged.

Harnessing Homer

In this final section, I will discuss the Homeric references in Odysseus' speech in four subsequent passages: §5–6 (centring on Ajax's suicide), §7–8 (on Ajax's shield), §10 (on proper heroic fighting) and the grand finale in §14.

I will start with §5–6, which have already been introduced above. In order to fully explain the Homeric subtext here, and especially its relation to §10, it is useful to quote the passage in full:

[5] κἀγὼ μὲν οὐκ ὀνειδίζω σοι τὴν ἀμαθίαν· ἄκων γὰρ αὐτὸ καὶ σὺ καὶ <οἱ> ἄλλοι πεπόνθατε ἅπαντες· ἀλλ' ὅτι διὰ τὰ ὀνείδη τὰ ἐμὰ σῳζόμενος οὐχ οἷός τε εἶ πείθεσθαι, ἀλλὰ καὶ προσαπειλεῖς ὡς κακὸν δράσων τι τούσδε, ἐὰν ἐμοὶ τὰ ὅπλα ψηφίσωνται. καὶ πολλάκις γε ἀπειλήσεις καὶ πολλά, πρὶν καὶ σμικρόν τι ἐργάσασθαι· ἀλλ' εἴπερ ἐκ τῶν εἰκότων τι χρὴ τεκμαίρεσθαι, ὑπὸ τῆς κακῆς ὀργῆς οἴομαί σε κακόν τι σαυτὸν ἐργάσεσθαι. [6] καὶ ἐμοὶ μέν, ὅτι τοὺς πολεμίους κακῶς ἐποίησα, δειλίαν ὀνειδίζεις· σὺ δὲ ὅτι φανερῶς ἐμόχθεις καὶ μάτην ἠλίθιος ἦσθα. <ἢ> ὅτι μετὰ πάντων τοῦτο ἔδρασας, οἴει βελτίων εἶναι; ἔπειτα περὶ ἀρετῆς πρὸς ἐμὲ λέγεις; ὃς πρῶτον μὲν οὐκ οἶσθα οὐδ' ὅπως ἔδει μάχεσθαι, ἀλλ' ὥσπερ ὗς ἄγριος ὀργῇ φερόμενος τάχ' ἄν ποτε ἀποκτενεῖς σεαυτὸν κακῷ περιπεσών τῳ.

(5) Well, I do not blame you for your ignorance, for you and all the others have suffered this unwittingly, but because you cannot be persuaded that through these blameworthy acts of mine you were saved, but you even threaten that you will do something bad to these people if they vote the arms to me. Well, you will boast much and often before you will accomplish even a small thing. But if there is any conclusion that should be drawn from the evidence of probability, I think you are going to do something harmful to yourself under the influence of your mean-spirited anger. (6) And because I treated our enemies badly, you blame me for cowardice. Well, you, because you toiled openly, and for nothing, you were a fool. Or do you think you are better because you did what you did along with the others? And then you speak to me about excellence? You who first of all do not even know how one should fight, but like a wild boar carried by your anger you will perhaps kill yourself one day, having met with something evil.

Antisthenes, *Odysseus* 5–6

This is an important though perhaps somewhat incoherent piece of Odysseus' speech, which makes more sense if we analyse the Homeric subtext. Starting with the description of Ajax as a 'wild boar' (ὥσπερ ὗς ἄγριος): this is not a general reference to the Homeric warrior, so regularly compared to a some awesome beast from the wild, but a specific reference to *Iliad* 7.256–7, where Ajax and Hector, engaged in a duel, are compared to 'raw meat-eating lions or wild boars, whose strength is not feeble'.

Once the subtext of the duel is established, some other elements of Odysseus' speech fall into place. One is the remark that 'you toiled openly, and for nothing' – for the duel between Ajax and Hector takes place in all openness,[67] and ends without a winner (even though Ajax seems to have the upper hand), underscoring Odysseus' point about the Greeks having come to Troy not to fight the Trojans, but to capture Troy.[68] Another is his remark that Ajax 'boasts much' without accomplishing much, since it is before the inconclusive fight with Hector that Ajax indeed utters a boast or threat, and Odysseus uses the same verb as Homer does in *Il.* 7.225 (ἀπειλέω). It is rather remarkable that the bT-scholia link the Homeric phrase 'threateningly, he addressed him' to Ajax's anger: 'he is a fool and shows his anger because he is agitated ... through the word order, Homer shows that his anger comes before his words'.[69] Though this is presumably the over-subtle interpretation of Porphyry, there may be an older critical tradition connecting Ajax to anger in the passage of the duel.[70]

That Antisthenes is tapping into Homeric criticism here may be confirmed by another passage with Homeric references, §10. The passage in question reads:

οὐδ' ἡνίκα κάμνω μαχόμενος, ὥσπερ σύ, τὰ ὅπλα ἑτέροις παραδίδωμι, ἀλλ' ὁπόταν ἀναπαύωνται οἱ πολέμιοι, τότε αὐτοῖς τῆς νυκτὸς ἐπιτίθεμαι, ἔχων τοιαῦτα ὅπλα ἃ ἐκείνους βλάψει μάλιστα. καὶ οὐδὲ νὺξ πώποτέ με ἀφείλετο, ὥσπερ σὲ πολλάκις μαχόμενον ἄσμενον πέπαυκεν·

And when I get exhausted in a fight, I do not hand off my weapons to other people, as you do, but whenever the enemies stop, just then I attack them by night, having the sort of weapons that will do them most harm. Nor has night ever hindered me, as it has many times made you happy to stop fighting.

Antisthenes, *Odysseus* 10

Odysseus is referring here to another meeting between Ajax and Hector, at the end of book 13, where the warriors exchange insults just before Homer calls for an intermezzo, picking up their battle again somewhere in the middle of book 14. Just before they meet, Homer tells us that Ajax is in the company of 'many mighty men, his comrades, who would take from him his shield whenever weariness and sweat came upon his limbs' (*Il.* 13.709–11).[71] Odysseus is obviously talking about this Homeric passage when he mentions Ajax's habit of 'handing off' his weapons when he gets tired; conversely, his comments on Ajax's night-time inactivity refer back to his breaking off the duel with Hector in *Iliad* 7. Nightfall made the warriors stop, as it was customary to end hostilities when the dark came on – and this, of course, is one of the customs Odysseus transcends.

What the two Iliadic passages referred to by Odysseus in §5–6 and §10 have in common, apart from the fact that they both pit Ajax against Hector (and thus perhaps underscoring his ineffectiveness, because we know Hector is eventually killed by Achilles), is that they are connected in Homeric criticism. The scholiasts note, for instance, that Hector credits Ajax with 'wisdom' (πινυτή) in *Iliad* 7.289, but calls him 'witless in speech' (ἁμαρτοεπής) and a 'braggart' (βουγάϊος, note again the boasting) in *Iliad* 13.824. Both these qualifications are nuanced,[72] but they do contain a hint that Ajax's expertise at warfare was a matter of ancient discussion. This hint is strengthened by the fact that both Hector and Ajax, in their speeches in books 7 and 13, claim to be knowledgeable about war: Hector claims to 'know' all there is to know about the art,[73] whereas Ajax states that 'we are in no way ignorant of battle'.[74] The scholiast too says these statements are to be understood as opposed to each other.

These considerations lead me to suppose that Odysseus refers to these two passages precisely because they were (among the) the *loci classici* for debating Ajax's martial expertise. Odysseus, of course, argues that Ajax 'knows nothing about the things you have done well by', and that 'you first of all do not even know how one should fight'. His words, backed up by a carefully selected Homeric subtext, are meant to counter Ajax's own claims that he alone knows about his heroic achievements and is solely qualified to evaluate them. So Odysseus uses Homer's words against Ajax, re-evaluating the hero's (self-)image by referring to the very text that had laid the foundations for it.

Between these two passages on Ajax's skill and bravery, there is the passage concerning the hero's shield. As we have already seen, the closing remarks of Ajax's speech focus on his fighting 'without fortification', a statement that is obviously at odds with his depiction in the *Iliad*, where his huge shield is part of his persona,[75] and perhaps even more so with his post-Homeric image, where his armour even renders him invulnerable. Odysseus taps into both traditions, mentioning, 'you have weapons that are unbreakable and invincible, on account of which they say you are invincible' (§7), and referring to the famous shield of 'seven bull's hides' that we find in Homer (§7).

Many scholars have noticed how Odysseus picks on Ajax's closing remark as an opportunity to turn the tables on him, but we should first note how Odysseus' use of Ajax's shield fits the general pattern of his attack. The tradition of Ajax's invulnerability makes him, in Odysseus' eyes, 'the biggest coward of all' and 'most afraid of death', referring back to Odysseus' earlier claim that Ajax is an ineffective fighter, ignorant when it comes to fighting, and unfit to speak on excellence (§6). Furthermore, Odysseus lays the groundwork here for an implicit attack in §10. As Prince notes, we see how 'the qualities of Ajax's external equipment are transferred (…) to Ajax himself';[76] Odysseus implies that Ajax is virtually identical to his shield. So what happens if he 'hands off his weapons to other people' (§10)? Nothing of real warrior-substance remains, it is implied. He is just a tired man 'snoring' (§10), letting Odysseus do the fighting. The passage on the shield fits Odysseus' strategy visible in paragraphs 5–6 and 10, aptly described by Rankin: 'Odysseus overthrows not only Aias' interpretation of his own actions, but also the value of the actions themselves.'[77]

Odysseus thus uses the traditional armour of Ajax to annihilate his traditional image of the 'bulwark of the Achaeans': when Ajax uses the shield, he is a coward, and when he doesn't, he is but a shade of a warrior. The message, of course, is clear: this person is not worthy of Achilles' arms. Odysseus, by contrast, portrays himself as the true master of weapons. His knowledge of courage and excellence ensures that he can fight with any weapon, at any time, and in any circumstance. His martial prowess is based on his knowledge of fighting, an internal type of excellence, which means that he is able to claim that whatever he can use is fit as a weapon. As Prince noted: 'it is clear that on a poetic level Odysseus has appropriated the term ὅπλα ('weapons'), and therefore that he has won these ὅπλα of Achilles, the trophy and symbol of victory, as well'.[78]

We can see Prince's point most clearly when we now turn to Odysseus' inversion of Ajax's claim of fighting 'without fortification'. Odysseus says that Ajax in fact 'walks around wearing a fortress of seven bull's hides on himself' (§7). This is immediately contrasted with Odysseus going 'unarmed not toward the fortresses of the enemies but inside the very fortresses' (§8). Odysseus' covert operations, earning him the title of 'temple robber' in the eyes of Ajax, actually trump Ajax's claims to courage in multiple respects: Odysseus is apparently courageous enough to not need any armour at all, and manages to penetrate the enemy's walls, something that a moving fortress like Ajax could never do.[79]

The purpose of Odysseus' sneaking around in Troy is not to 'fight the Trojans', even though he does 'take out the waking watchmen of the enemies' (§8), but to acquire information.[80] He does not need spies but relies on himself, enabling him to 'know both affairs here and affairs among the enemy', his 'most explicit claim to omniscience'.[81] In his own words, he is 'both the general and the watchman' (§8). The goal, Odysseus explains, is to use this knowledge to protect 'both you and all the others' (§8), a claim that is repeated in §10. Paradoxically, it is the unarmed hero Odysseus, the true bulwark of the Achaeans, who is protecting all the Greeks. Meanwhile, Ajax is 'sleeping securely' (§10), not even noticing Odysseus' true excellence – and so Ajax has to own the ignorance he attributes to the jury, not knowing anything because he was not there to bear witness to Odysseus' actions, relying instead on hearsay. As in the case of the passages discussed above, but more obviously so, Odysseus proves to transcend the actual dramatic setting, acquiring a meta-literary level that Ajax cannot rise to, and using it to invert the image of Ajax to his own benefit.

Odysseus' speech: Conclusion

Odysseus' powers of transcendence reach their peak in his conclusion (§14), which is also the last part of this chapter. It is useful to quote this paragraph in full:

οἶμαι δέ, ἄν ποτέ τις ἄρα σοφὸς ποιητὴς περὶ ἀρετῆς γένηται, ἐμὲ μὲν ποιήσει πολύτλαντα καὶ πολύμητιν καὶ πολυμήχανον καὶ πτολίπορθον καὶ μόνον τὴν Τροίαν ἑλόντα, σὲ δέ, ὡς ἐγῷμαι, τὴν φύσιν ἀπεικάζων τοῖς τε νωθέσιν ὄνοις καὶ βουσὶ τοῖς φορβάσιν, ἄλλοις παρέχουσι δεσμεύειν καὶ ζευγνύναι αὐτούς.

But I think, if some poet who is wise about excellence ever comes along, he will portray me having suffered many challenges, with many wits and many resources, a sacker of cities and the lone destroyer of Troy, and he will portray you, I think, by comparing you in your nature to dull asses and oxen that graze in the pasture, who give over to others the power of bonding and harnessing themselves.

Antisthenes, Odysseus 14

Odysseus' references to the tradition here are remarkable because he is not just echoing familiar cruxes of Homeric scholarship or using Homer's words; he goes a significant step further and actually mentions Homer,[82] foreshadowing his and Ajax's portrayal in the Homeric poems.

The explicit references have been the subject of some scholarly debate. Suffice it to say here that Odysseus mentions the epithets that are both ubiquitous in Homer,[83] and most fitting for his portrayal of himself in this speech: πολύτλας ('having suffered many challenges') conforms to his image of self-abasement and extreme actions, πολύμητις ('with many wits') refers to his superb knowledge of warfare in general and tactical information in particular, and πολυμήχανος ('with many resources') to his ability to use any weapon and fight in any circumstance.[84] That he is a 'sacker of cities' and the 'lone destroyer of Troy' refers back to his statement that he, in contrast to Ajax, manages to keep his eyes on the prize, and instead of aimlessly fighting with Trojans 'destroys' Troy.

The parting shot of Odysseus' speech is aimed at Ajax, whom the wise poet will compare to 'dull asses (νωθέσιν ὄνοις) and oxen (βουσὶ) that graze in the pasture'. These are references to *Il.* 11.558–65 and 13.703, where Ajax is indeed compared to a 'dull ass' (ὄνος ... νωθής) and, together with the Lesser Ajax, to 'oxen' (βόε). Odysseus' words here are rhetorically efficient on several levels. First of all, his final words are to be contrasted with Ajax's final words: where Ajax stated something about himself that was 'Homerically' incorrect (claiming to be 'without fortification'), Odysseus strikes back with references that are, indeed, Homeric.[85] Moreover, the Homeric similes are deployed to reinforce Odysseus' point that Ajax, for all his supposed uniqueness, is in fact a herd animal that is unable to govern itself. Ajax is short-sighted and controlled by his circumstances, whereas Odysseus is the 'general and watchman' who protects and cares for others. Ajax may be the strongest, but he 'gives over to others'[86] the power be 'bound' and 'harnessed'.[87] Naturally, we should also understand this jibe at a meta-level, as Odysseus has through his speech 'bound' Ajax.

Through these references, Antisthenes does more than just let Odysseus 'predict' or 'foreshadow' the words of Homer – Odysseus is actually made to 'prompt' the poet, as it were, and so frame the tradition. This is obvious from the cattle imagery just described. As scholars have noted, the similes of the ass and the oxen are actually meant in a positive way: in the Homeric text, they illustrate the steadfastness, endurance and reliability of Ajax. There is no hint of stupidity and helplessness.[88] Antisthenes, of course, knows this. It is part of his rhetorical game to try to let Odysseus force this particular interpretation of the similes upon the audience before the images are even created by Homer himself. This may also explain Odysseus' use of the words 'in your nature' (τὴν φύσιν): the similes, however they are used, lay bare the essence of Ajax.[89]

The most interesting thing about Odysseus formulating the similes for Homer (and also offering the right interpretation) in the final paragraph of his speech, is that Antisthenes thus makes use of a critical tradition as old as Pindar: that the voices of Odysseus and Homer are thought to be similar, or even that they blend so as to become indistinguishable. In §5 and §6, we saw that Odysseus already knows how Ajax's story will end; in §8, he claims a near-'omniscience' by 'knowing both affairs here and affairs among enemy'; and in the last paragraph, he refers to Homer as the 'wise poet about excellence' while he has implicitly claimed knowledge of excellence throughout the speech; and finally, he is suggesting the right epithets for himself and the right similes for his opponent.

In Pindar, Odysseus' Homeric quality derives from his image as the smooth-talking deceiver, and it is described as dangerous. In Antisthenes, by contrast, Odysseus' appropriation of Homer's powers is an expression of his Cynic ability to transcend social codes and manipulate cultural categories. Antisthenes demonstrates this by turning Odysseus into a meta-literary voice. In Odysseus' speech, the hero proves he is the master of his own narrative.

Notes

1. Some scholars have argued for a relatively early date, stressing the similarities with Gorgias' speeches on Helen and Palamedes (which were collected in the same manuscripts as Antisthenes' speeches), but the comparison is both inaccurate and irrelevant. I believe, with Prince and others, that the speeches are manifestations of Antisthenes' philosophical maturity.
2. Most modern scholars (Decleva Caizzi, Focardi, Patzer, Rankin, Romeyer-Derhey and Prince) follow the lead of Lulofs 1900 in setting aside the arguments of e.g. Radermachter, Von Arnim and Wilamowitz and believing the speeches are authentic (see e.g. Patzer 1970: 203–8 and Giannantoni 1990: 216–18 and 257–60, who nonetheless expresses caution about over-confidence in this matter).
3. This is thus perhaps the most extreme example of the 'role-playing' discussed by Morgan in this volume. Gorgias' defence of Helen is a third person speech (like that of Isocrates on Helen), and in Gorgias' *Palamedes* and Alcidamas' *Odysseus* there is no 'mirror' speech.
4. See e.g. Morgan 2000, esp. ch. 1 and 2.
5. Cf. Morgan (Chapter 4 in this volume): 'mythological analogy is a kind of heuristic' (p. 100).
6. See Prince 2015: 584–677 for a collection, translation and interpretation of all the fragments concerning Antisthenes' work as a Homeric critic.
7. He believed Odysseus was right to say no to Calypso and eternal life because the goddess was in love and so could not be trusted (see t. 188 Prince).
8. Antisthenes interpreted Odysseus' insult that 'not even the Earthshaker will heal your eye' as a correct statement; for not Poseidon, but Apollo is the god of healing (cf. t. 190 Prince, who comments that this reading 'shows the lengths to which Antisthenes went to defend the virtue of Odysseus').
9. T187 Prince, on which e.g. Prince 2015: 231, Malherbe 1983: 153, Montiglio 2011: 22, Romeyer-Derbhey 1996: 259–62.
10. See Goulet-Cazé 1992 for a collection (and French translation) of pre-Antisthenean sources on the Judgement.
11. *Od.* 11.550–1. The whole episode is *Od.* 11. 543–67. All translations from the *Odyssey* and the *Iliad* are taken from Murray's Loeb edition.
12. *Od.* 11.565.
13. Sch. *Od.* 11.547 (ἄριστον), sch. Ar. *Eq.* 1056 (περὶ τῶν ἀριστείων).
14. Sch. *Od.* 11.547.
15. Procl. *Chr.* 2 t. V. p. 106.19–23 Allen, sch. Ar. *Eq.* 1056. In the scholium on Aristophanes' *Knights*, Athena interferes during the Judgement and has one of the jurors rebuke an argument in favour of Ajax as 'a lie that is not in line with reality' (οὐ κατὰ κόσμον ... ψεῦδος).

16 As is the case, for instance, in Ovid's version of the myth, where all heroes except Ajax and Odysseus are afraid of laying claim to the arms (Ov. *Met.* 13.620–8).
17 Obviously, it could have been part of the original narrators' design to have Ajax and Odysseus bring back the body so they could pit brawn versus brains in the conflict over the arms.
18 Cf. Pi. *N.* 8: 'words are dessert to the envious, and envy fastens always on the good, but has no quarrel with lesser men' (21–2); 'yes, hateful deception existed even long ago, the companion of flattering tales, guileful contriver, evil-working disgrace, which represses what is illustrious, but holds up for obscure men a glory that is rotten' (32–4).
19 Cf. *N.* 8: 'Truly, oblivion overwhelms a man whose tongue is speechless, but heart bold, in a grievous quarrel; and the greatest prize has been offered up to shifty falsehood' (24–5); 'In truth, unequal indeed were the wounds they tore in the warm flesh of their foes with succoring spears when they were hard pressed, both in fighting over Achilles newly slain and in the murderous days of their other labors' (28–32).
20 See on this matter Pratt 1993: 127–8 and Most 1985: 148–56, who claims (rightly, in my view) that Pindar refers to Odysseus and Homer at the same time in the first part of the passage.
21 Cf. Prince 2015, who also comments on the interplay of the dramatic and the actual audience (e.g. p. 222).
22 See *TrGF* 3, F175–6.
23 See on this Williams 1980.
24 The episode remained popular in antiquity; see Prince 2015: 199 for a brief overview and bibliography.
25 See Stanford 1963.
26 Kirk 1962: 364.
27 Strauss Clay 1983: 54–64.
28 See Ioli in this volume (Chapter 1) p. 26.
29 Stanford 1963: 100.
30 See Stanford 1963: ch. 7.
31 Cf. Schein 2013: 20–3; the citation is from p. 23.
32 Jebb 1907: xli.
33 As stated by Knox (cited by Finglass 2011: 44).
34 See Finglass 2011: 42–6 for a brief history and a critical discussion of the model of the Sophoclean hero as a commonplace of Sophoclean criticism.
35 Burton 1980: 11.
36 In the *Contest*, Homer and Hesiod try their poetical skills against each other in several rounds, as the audience grows ever more desirous to see Homer crowned. In the end, the sole judge Paneides ('All-Knower') grants the victory to Hesiod, because

he sang of peace instead of war. In this piece, it is the criteria of poetic excellence that are at stake, the subject of the poem turning out to be decisive.

37 Both characterizations come from Knudsen 2012 (49 and 51).
38 See the contribution of Bassino in this volume (Chapter 2). The quote is from p. 42.
39 Cf. e.g. Patzer 1970: 211, Sier 1996; Prince 2015: 199 does liken Ajax's speech to forensic oratory.
40 These are: 1) he rescued the body of Achilles (§2), being more important than the arms (a point that is insufficiently prominent); 2) he is worthy of the arms because he would give them to Achilles' friends (§3; this may be so, but we know from the Cycle that Odysseus did not keep the arms either and in fact gave them to Achilles' son Neoptolemus) and 3) Ajax 'has been stationed in battle always first and alone and without fortification' (§9; this is the most powerful claim to excellence and bravery, but it is very poorly handled, being the final sentence of the speech).
41 Ajax is thinking primarily of Odysseus' theft of the Palladium from the temple of Athena in Troy, but may also generally refer to Odysseus' scheming, disguising and night-time sneaking around.
42 This is the first hint of a topos in both speeches, that a person's weapons are to be understood as a 'sign' or σημεῖον revealing the being of that person (cf. Prince 2015: 208). All texts and translations from the speeches are taken from Prince 2015.
43 Cf. esp. Sier 1996, Romeyer-Dherbey 1996, Prince 2006 and Prince 2015. See also Bassino in this volume (Chapter 2) on the limitations of λόγος.
44 Par. 7, t. 152–6 Prince. The exact meaning of this presumably rather famous saying of Antisthenes is disputed; nevertheless, it is clear that Ajax in referring to Antisthenes' dictum is not using it as it was meant by Antisthenes. It is not unlikely that there are more references in Ajax's speech that we do not know about.
45 Cf. Trapp 1961.
46 *Il.* 7.219, 11.485 and 17.128 (the Greek word is πύργος).
47 *Il.* 7.219–23.
48 Cebriones recognizes Ajax by his shield in *Il.* 11.526–7. The title 'bulwark of the Achaeans' occurs thrice in the *Iliad* (3.229, 6.5 and 7.211, and he is even compared to a 'tower' in the Underworld episode, *Od.* 11.556); Ajax protects Teucer behind his shield in *Il.* 8.268–72.
49 Cf. Sier 1996: 64.
50 Cf. Antisthenes t. 187 Prince, where Odysseus is implied as one of the wise men δεινοῖ διαλέγεσθαι ('good at dialectic/discourse'), a phrase probably meant to be distinguished from δεινὸς λέγειν ('good at speaking'), a reproach often leveled at the Sophists (cf. Montiglio 2011: 23).
51 Prince 1999: 59 notes (as do others) that Ajax repeatedly says he 'knows' (οἶδα) things, whereas Odysseus is more cautious and uses the word 'think' (οἴομαι) more often.

52 The terms 'bonding' and 'harnessing' 'imply ethical slavery' (Prince 2015: 232); for more on this expression see below.
53 Prince 2015: 197.
54 Pi. *I.* 6.45, S. *Aj.* 576, Pl. *Smp.* 291e (from Prince 2015: 224).
55 Knudsen 2012 notes that this argument also 'implicitly invites the audience to question Ajax's need for Achilles' armor' (53).
56 Prince 2006: 84.
57 Some scholars are more careful. Rankin 1986: 154 believes that 'both contending parties represent different facets of the Antisthenan hero'. Likewise, Sier 1996: 70 warns that there is 'einige Sicherheit' that Odysseus' picture of Ajax does not reflect Antisthenes' opinion of the hero. Prince 1999: 61 also believes that it is an overstatement to see Odysseus as 'an allegory of Cynic virtue'.
58 Prince 2015: 226.
59 Höistad 1948: 97 even speaks of the 'self-abasement of the typical cynic'.
60 Cf. Montiglio 2011: 24, claiming Odysseus is concerned with 'defending truths beneficial to all'.
61 Montiglio 2011: 30.
62 Cf. Odysseus' comparing himself to a captain on a ship, an image that may refer to his role in the *Odyssey* (so Prince 2015: 226) but also stresses the 'responsibilità del singolo' (Decleva Caizzi 1966: 91, who rightly connects this to the concept of philanthropy).
63 Prince 2015: 228. Cf. Ioli's comment on Helen's claim (in Gorgias' *Encomium of Helen*) that she, because of her unique ποικιλία and κόσμος 'with a single body, brought together many bodies of men'.
64 Cf. Prince 2015: 223.
65 Cf. Prince 2015: 222, referring to Graver's analysis of the Stoic view of anger (Graver 2007: 122–32). According to Graver, anger is particularly dangerous because of its sweeping power, carrying the angry person away. This is also what Odysseus says will happen to Ajax in §6 ('like a wild boar carried (φερόμενος) by your anger you will perhaps kill yourself one day').
66 Cf. e.g. Romeyer-Dherbey 1996: 265–6.
67 As Hector in fact suggests in *Il.* 7.243.
68 Cf. *Il.* 7.273–82; the warriors stop because of nightfall (on which see further below). It may be this kind of fighting that Odysseus has in mind when he pictures Ajax as fighting wholly to no effect with an opponent who is equally strong (or well-equipped) in §7.
69 'νωθὴς μέν εστι, κινηθεὶς δὲ ὀργὴν ἐνδείκνυται, ἀφ' ἧς αὐτῷ καὶ ἡ κίνησις· [...] τὴν ὀργὴν δὲ καὶ πρὸ τῶν λόγων τῷ σχήματι ἐπεδείξατο.'
70 See Wilshere's contribution to this volume (Chapter 5) for the practice of referencing the critical tradition during the Second Sophistic.

71 '... πολλοί τε καὶ ἐσθλοὶ / λαοὶ ἔπονθ᾽ ἕταροι, οἵ οἱ σάκος ἐξεδέχοντο, / ὁππότε μιν κάματός τε καὶ ἱδρὼς γούναθ᾽ ἵκοντο.'
72 Hector's praise for Ajax may be genuine but could also be motivated by Hector's relief to have escaped a better man; on the other hand, his mocking words could just be inspired by 'good luck' on the battlefield (schol. 7.284bT); 'such is man', the scholiast on 13.824 notes: 'when he is caught in a dangerous situation, he humbles himself; when he has slipped away, he is rebellious'.
73 The claim to knowledge is very marked, using οἶδα ('I know') five times: 'Full well I know battles and slayings of men. I know well how to wield to right, and well how to wield to left my shield of seasoned hide (...); and I know how to charge into the battle of chariots drawn by swift mares; and I know how in close fight to tread the measure of furious Ares' (*Il.* 17.237–41).
74 *Il.* 17.811.
75 See p. 72 above.
76 Prince 2015: 224.
77 Rankin 1986: 170 (on the matter of the retrieval of Achilles' body).
78 Prince 1999: 63.
79 For Ajax as a 'defensive' fighter in the *Iliad* see e.g. Trapp 1961: 273, Prince 2015: 226.
80 See Prince 2015: 225 on the possibility that Odysseus might be speaking metaphorically here, penetrating 'the minds of his opposition'. The wakeful Trojan watchmen may represent intellectually active people, with whom the pre-philosophical, 'snoring' Ajax can be contrasted. Cf. Malherbe 1983 on Antisthenes' application of the image of the fortified city to the sage's soul in fragment 134 Prince.
81 Prince 2015: 225, cf. n. 47 above.
82 Homer was the 'wise poet about excellence' not just in Antisthenes' view (see Prince 2015: 230); this qualification reflects the common opinion of the Greeks.
83 Prince 2015: 231 provides the numbers: πολύτλας is said of Odysseus forty-three times in the Homeric poems, πολύμητις eighty-six times and πολυμήχανος twenty-two times.
84 Interestingly, his best-known epithet πολύτροπος is missing, perhaps to stay away from controversial connotations of this term (cf. Prince 2015: 231).
85 The 'dull ass' is an exact reference, although Odysseus uses a plural instead of a singular (on which see Prince 2015: 231, who believes the plural 'might be a way of undercutting the singularity Ajax claimed for himself in his own final words'). It strikes me as odd that Odysseus says of the oxen that they 'graze in the pasture', for the epithet he uses (φορβάσιν) does not appear in Homer.
86 The phrasing may be meant to recall Ajax's 'handing off' his weapons to others when he is tired, cf. p. 77 and note 71 above. The verb is not the same, but both contexts mention the fighter getting tired (ἡνίκα κάμνω (§10), ὁππότε μιν κάματος τε καὶ ἱδρὼς γούναθ᾽ ἵκοιτο (*Il.* 13.711).

87 Homer in fact says in *Il.* 13.706 that the oxen are 'yoked'. Cf. Lévystone 2005: 189: 'Ajax est de ceux qui acceptent d'être transformés en esclaves de l'opinion car il craint le jugement des autres, et c'est aussi en cela qu'il est lâche'.
88 So also the scholia, which say that the comparisons are meant to indicate Ajax's superiority, steadfastness and eagerness.
89 Cf. Prince 2015 t. 51 and t.150A.4 on the importance of similes for Antisthenes, who may have believed they demonstrated the essence of things.

References

Burton, R. 1980, *The Chorus in Sophocles' Tragedies*, Oxford.
Decleva Caizzi, F. 1966, *Antisthenis Fragmenta*, Milan.
Finglass, P. 2011, *Sophocles. Ajax*, Cambridge.
Giannantoni, G. 1990, *Socratis et Socraticorum reliquiae*, vol. 4, Naples.
Goulet-Cazé, M. 1992, 'L'Ajax et l'Ulysse d'Antisthène', in Goulet-Cazé, M. et al. (eds), Σοφίης Μαιήτορες, *Chercheurs de sagesse: Hommage à Jean Pepin*, Paris: 5–36.
Graver, M. 2007, *Stoicism and Emotion*, Chicago.
Höistad, R. 1948, *Cynic Hero and Cynic King*, Uppsala.
Jebb, R. 1907, *Sophocles: The Plays and Fragments*, vol. 7, Cambridge.
Kirk, G. 1962, *The Songs of Homer*, Cambridge.
Knudsen, R.A. 2012, 'Poetic speakers, sophistic words', *AJPh* 133: 31–60.
Lévystone, D. 2005, 'La figure d'Ulysse chez les Socratiques: Socrate polutropos', *Phronesis* 50: 182–213.
Lulofs, H. 1900, *De Antisthenis studiis rhetoricis*, Amsterdam.
Malherbe, A. 1983, 'Antisthenes and Odysseus, and Paul at war', *Harvard Theological Review* 76: 143–73.
Montiglio, S. 2011, *From Villain to Hero: Odysseus in Ancient Thought*, Ann Arbor.
Morgan, K. A. 2000, *Myth and Philosophy from the Pre-Socratics to Plato*, Cambridge.
Most, G. 1985, *The Measures of Praise: Structure and Function in Pindar's Second Pythian and Seventh Nemean Odes*, Göttingen.
Patzer, A. 1970, *Antisthenes der Sokratiker: Das literarische Werk und die Philosophie, argestellt am Katalog der Schriften*, Heidelberg.
Pratt, L. 1993, *Lying and Poetry from Homer to Pindar*, Ann Arbor.
Prince, S. 1999, 'Ajax, Odysseus, and the act of self-representation', *AncPhil* 19: 55–64.
Prince, S. 2006, 'Socrates, Antisthenes, and the Cynics', in Ahbel-Rappe, S. and Kamtekar, R. (eds), *A Companion to Socrates*, Malden: 75–92.
Prince, S. 2015, *Antisthenes of Athens: Texts, Translations and Commentary*, Ann Arbor.
Race, H. 1997, *Pindar*, vol. 2, Cambridge MA.
Rankin, H. 1986, *Anthisthenes Sokratikos*, Amsterdam.
Romeyer Dherbey, G. 1996, 'Tra Aiace e Ulisse: Antistene', *Elenchos* 17: 251–74.

Schein, S. L. 2013, *Sophocles. Philoctetes*, Cambridge.
Sier, K. 1996, 'Aias' und Odysseus' Streit um die Waffen des Achilleus', in Mueller-Goldingen, C. and Sier, K. (eds), *AHNAIKA: Festschrift für Carl Werner Müller*, Stuttgart: 53–80.
Stanford, W. 1963 (second edition), *The Ulysses Theme*, Oxford.
Strauss Clay, J. 1983, *The Wrath of Athena. Gods and Men in the Odyssey*, Princeton.
Trapp, R. 1961, 'Ajax in the *Iliad*', *CJ* 56: 271–5.
Williams, D. 1980, 'Ajax, Odysseus, and the arms of Achilles', *Antike Kunst* 23: 137–44.

4

Mythological Role-Playing among the Sophists

Kathryn A. Morgan

Introduction

In a famous passage of Plato's *Protagoras*, the sophist Protagoras gives a brief cultural history of his art. In his opinion, many of the famous poets of the past (Homer, Hesiod, Simonides), as well as Orpheus and Musaeus, and various musicians and physical trainers down to the present day, were all sophists, but because they feared the hostility and jealousy that arise when an intellectual expert arrives in a city and persuades young people to consort with him for educational purposes, they dissembled. They used their arts as screens to hide the truth. Protagoras, however, admits that he is a sophist and an educator (*Prt.* 316c–317b). This narrative makes Protagoras and the sophists at home in a long tradition of poetic didactic activity, casting them as the direct descendants of the early epic poets. The sophists were also, as is well-known, critics and interpreters of Homer at a linguistic, narratological and ethical level.[1] They could also, however, be cast as inheritors or renovators of traditions of rhetorical excellence that stretched back into the mythological past. This was certainly so by the Roman period. Philodemus finds it necessary to debunk people who thought that there was an art of rhetoric in mythological times, and other sources listed in Radermacher show that there was lively debate on the practice of rhetoric among the heroes.[2] Pausanias (2.31.3), for example, reports that Pittheus was supposed to have taught the art of rhetoric, and an ancient *prolegomenon* to Hermogenes' *On Issues* reports that 'some say the first to give a forensic speech was the Athenian general Menestheus'.[3]

It is difficult to specify when this sort of association began. It seems plausible that it dates back to the time of the sophists and the later fifth century (one thinks, e.g., of Odysseus the demagogue in Euripides' *Hecuba*). The passages of Plato that will be discussed in this chapter make it clear that the relationship was well enough established for Plato to have Socrates make fun of it, and we also have, from the fifth and early fourth centuries, some examples of set speeches composed for mythological characters (Palamedes, Odysseus and Ajax) by Gorgias, Alcidamas and Antisthenes. Interest in these set speeches has grown in recent years. Nancy Worman made them a part of her wide-ranging analysis of literary representations of linguistic style in Archaic and Classical literature, arguing that particular heroes came to be viewed as representatives of particular types of style.[4] Rachel Knudsen has focused on Gorgias' *Defence of Palamedes*, Alcidamas' *Odysseus* and Antisthenes' paired speeches on Ajax and Odysseus as an oratorical appropriation of the poetic tradition whose goal was to sweeten the tedium of learning rhetorical tropes.[5]

My own contribution to this scholarly reconsideration had been to analyse these speeches in the context of other sophistic appropriations of the mythological tradition, arguing that the mythological context allowed their composers to create a kind of dramatic irony centred on the tension between an audience's knowledge of how a story ended and the type of argumentation used in the speeches.[6] In what follows I would like to return to this material and reconsider it from a perspective that I originally treated only briefly: the potential for conflation between a sophist and a mythological figure. The sophists are not just heirs of earlier poets and intellectuals, but can inhabit their characters. Poets had long made use of analogies between mythological and contemporary individuals (one thinks of epinician lyric), but in the second half of the fifth century this process took on a special character consonant with contemporary interests in education, rhetoric and the performance of wisdom more generally. Not only did sophists compose epideictic speeches in praise of mythological characters (like Gorgias' *Encomium of Helen*), but they drew implicit parallels between such characters and their own situation as speakers and educators. Unsurprisingly, the crucial players in their performances were mythological characters who had a reputation for intellectual expertise and/or oratorical ability: Nestor, Palamedes, Odysseus and Prometheus. These parallels should be examined in terms of sophistic engagement with notions of intellectual and cultural innovation, but also in connection with issues surrounding the flexibility of persona. The heroes of the mythological tradition offered rich resources of exemplary ethical and intellectual achievement and failure. Playing with a mythological persona was a self-reflexive way of meditating upon cultural identity and exploring diverse instantiations of σοφία.

Plato, with his profound interest in the effects of mimetic performance of mythological characters, explored the subject of mythological role-playing with great subtlety, and my analysis here will make extensive use of Plato's portrayal of various sophists and Socrates in his dialogues. This leaves me open to the objection that I am overreading the evidence or identifying a Platonic rather than a sophistic phenomenon. Each reader will have to judge my guilt or innocence of this charge, yet a case can be made for the assertion that Plato's treatments of mythological role-playing are best seen as plays upon a fairly widespread sophistic practice. One might also, moreover, connect the practice of mythological role-playing with a more colloquial, even comic, practice of nicknaming or identifying a contemporary with a famous mythological or historical predecessor. A comic fragment of the fifth century asserts that 'Cleon is a Prometheus after the event' (Κλέων Προμηθεύς ἐστι μετὰ τὰ πράγματα, Eupolis fr. 456 Kock = *PCG* vol. 8 [*Adespota*] 461; trans. Olson 2014), a characterization that Olson interprets as 'a cynical comment about Cleon's misleading *ex eventu* self-presentation'. He aptly compares Aristophanes' line about Meton at *Birds* 1009: 'The guy's a Thales!'[7] Not all nicknames, of course, were mythological or historical. Protagoras was apparently called *Logos* (schol. ad Pl. *Resp.* 600c; in the Suda his nickname is reported as '*Logos* for hire', Λόγος ἔμμισθος), and Pericles was famously 'the Olympian' (Plut. *Per.* 8.2–3). In the material I will be considering here this practice of nicknaming converges with sophistic appropriation of the mythological past. Plato in turn mocks this phenomenon in various dialogues.

Nestor

Hippias' *Trojan Dialogue* can be reconstructed from Plato's *Hippias Major* (286a–b = DK 86A9). Hippias boasts that he has made a great impression in Sparta discoursing on the noble pursuits that a young man should follow (286a: περί γε ἐπιτηδευμάτων καλῶν ... ηὐδοκίμησα διεξιὼν ἃ χρὴ τὸν νέον ἐπιτηδεύειν).[8] He has composed an *epideixis* on the subject, and this is its premise: Neoptolemus at the fall of Troy asks Nestor what he should do in order to achieve a great reputation. Nestor then speaks, recommending numerous excellent practices. This is the performance Hippias has just given in Sparta and in three days' time he will do the same in Athens. It is clear from Plato's wording that his character Hippias draws no distinction between Nestor's and his own teachings. He has gained a great reputation (ηὐδοκίμησα) narrating excellent pursuits – interestingly this looks forward to Neoptolemus' desire to have the greatest reputation (εὐδοκιμώτατος) – and it is Nestor who speaks for Hippias in the *epideixis*. My previous analysis of this material focused on the potential incongruity of having Neoptolemus ask about reputable conduct in the young, the problem being that a powerful and even prevalent version of Neoptolemus had him killing Priam on the very altar of Zeus, a paradigm of horrifying and sacrilegious behaviour. Is this the kind of young man who wants to gain a great reputation? Did Hippias construct this context to undermine the content of the moral lessons that Nestor was teaching, as an assertion of his superiority to the tradition and his cleverness, and perhaps to signify that he could be relied upon to straighten out the most intransigent pupil?[9]

I now suspect that something rather more subtle was going on. There were, after all, many Neoptolemuses: the murderer we see on vase paintings and probably in the Cyclic epics, the sacrilegious hero destroyed at Delphi by Apollo or the noble Aeacid youth we see in Pindar's *Nemean 7*, who dies by accident in the sanctuary. It is true that he is, for the most part, mad, bad and dangerous to know, but if Pindar could rehabilitate him anything is possible (indeed, in Euripides' *Andromache* Neoptolemus heads off to Delphi to make amends to Apollo for having insulted him). Perhaps one version of the point is that if Neoptolemus had been lucky enough to have someone like Nestor, or indeed Hippias, as his teacher, things might have gone very differently. There is another possibility as well. It seems clear that sophistic educators were sometimes accused of corrupting the young. Plato's Gorgias (speaking of oratory) explains at some length that the teacher should not be blamed for the crimes or mistakes of the student. The teacher teaches a skill to be used justly and should therefore not be exiled or hated if his students act unjustly (*Grg.* 456c–457c). If, when we consider the Neoptolemus of the *Trojan Dialogue*, we envision his murderous version, we are presented with a situation where a respected teacher produces an unjust pupil despite his own best efforts. The implications are defensive: powerful people do not always listen to the wise advisor. Nestor and Hippias may be virtuous teachers, but an out-of-control pupil (a Critias or an Alcibiades!) may still occur. The flexibility and variety of mythological tradition allow us to meditate upon the role of educator and advisor and their success or failure in the educational enterprise.

In the *Hippias Minor*, as Ruby Blondell has shown, Plato uses Hippias to exemplify the cultural continuity between epic poetry and sophistry.[10] As the dialogue begins, Hippias has just finished an *epideixis* on Homer at the House of Eudicus; this *epideixis* seems to have been the *Trojan Dialogue*.[11] Socrates asks him who is the better, Achilles or Odysseus. Hippias replies that Homer made Achilles the best of those who went to Troy, Nestor the wisest (σοφώτατον) and Odysseus the most versatile (πολυτροπώτατον), and when pressed it turns out that for Hippias πολύτροπος means 'false' (364c–365c). At this point, of course, they are off to the elenctic races and a discussion of whether the true man is the same as the false. The details of this need not concern us, but it is worth noting that before commencing further discussion, Socrates establishes that Hippias' opinion is the same as Homer's on these matters (365c–d) and that Hippias is answering his questions on both his own and Homer's behalf. At this point, Hippias is aligned with Homer. Yet we must also ask why Hippias adds Nestor to the traditional pairing of Achilles and Odysseus? Clearly, as Blondell suggests, because Hippias wants to set up the 'wisest' Nestor as a model for himself.[12] Given that he uses Nestor as his mouthpiece in the *Trojan Dialogue* this identification is not surprising, and there is one other way in which Nestor is a good match for a sophist wanting to give an *epideixis*: his tendency to give long (and to some annoying) speeches. This characteristic is guaranteed to rub Socrates up the wrong way. In dialogue after dialogue he tries to stop his sophistic interlocutor speechifying, and *Hippias Minor* is no exception. At 373a as Socrates attempts to make Hippias continue to answer his questions, he declares that Hippias will not heal him of his ignorance if he gives a long λόγος (an epideictic display) but only if he gives short answers.

Socrates, then, is keen to pre-empt Hippias' Nestorian persona. Yet he is also keen to make another identification: Hippias' inconsistent argumentation and habit of shifting his ground remind Socrates of Odysseus, and he says so at 370e 'You are deceiving me, dearest Hippias, and are yourself playing the part of (μιμῇ) Odysseus'. Socrates' descriptions in the dialogue of Hippias' accomplishments and versatility make him seem quite Odysseus-like.[13] Hippias, on the other hand, paints Socrates as a wrongdoer in argument (369b–b, 373b). There is, moreover, another potential identification at stake. As Richard Hunter has observed, 'in Hippias' mind, so we are to understand, it is also clear that he himself is the Achilles'. He declares towards the beginning of the dialogue that he has never met anyone better than himself in competing at Olympia, and casts Socrates as the tricky Odysseus.[14] One of the questions at stake in the dialogue, then, is who is more like – not Nestor but – Odysseus (standing for the false and deceptive speaker). Later writers also could see Hippias as Odyssean. Hunter notes that in his speech *On the Philosopher* Dio Chrysostom sets up Hippias and Odysseus as expert in many different fields (71.2–3) and speculates that this may reflect Hippian self-promotion.[15] If this is right, it is worth remarking that Hippias seems to have been perfectly comfortable switching mythological *personae* as the need arose. Hippias oscillates between Nestor, Achilles and Odysseus.

Hippias was not the only fifth-century intellectual who could be identified with Nestor. This nickname was also applied to Antiphon in the Suda and the *Lives of the Ten Orators* (for the purposes of this discussion, I treat Antiphon the sophist and Antiphon of Rhamnous as the same person).[16] The *Life of Antiphon* transmitted with his preserved speeches records that Antiphon became so proficient in speaking and writing that he was dubbed 'Nestor' because of the pleasantness of his speech (εἰς τοσοῦτον προῆλθε δεινότητος, ὥστε Νέστωρ ἐπεκαλεῖτο διὰ τὴν ἐν τῷ λέγειν ἡδονήν). This identification is repeated in Philostratus who reports that Antiphon was addressed as Nestor because of his ability to persuade his hearers on any subject.

> πιθανώτατος δὲ ὁ Ἀντιφῶν γενόμενος καὶ προσρηθεὶς Νέστωρ ἐπὶ τῶι περὶ παντὸς εἰπὼν ἂν πεῖσαι νηπενθεῖς ἀκροάσεις ἐπήγγειλεν, ὡς οὐδὲν οὕτω δεινὸν ἐρούντων ἄχος, ὃ μὴ ἐξελεῖν τῆς γνώμης.

> Antiphon, being very persuasive, and nicknamed 'Nestor' because of his ability to persuade when speaking on any subject, announced pain-removing lectures, in the belief that people would tell no grief so terrible that he could not remove it from their mind.[17]
>
> Philostratus, *Lives of the Sophists* 1.498

Our various sources differ on whether Antiphon was called Nestor because of his intelligence, his persuasiveness, or the pleasure of his speech; it is clear that the reason had to be reconstructed but that the appellation was well-attested. Nestor's fame as a wise advisor and fluent speaker meant that this was a convenient identity for anyone with pretensions to oratorical and intellectual expertise.

This suspicion is confirmed by a passage in Plato's *Phaedrus*, which implies that Gorgias might also be called Nestor. During their discussion of rhetoric, Socrates defines rhetoric as the art that influences people both in public and in private. Phaedrus objects that he thinks rhetoric applies only to public speaking. Socrates responds:

> ΣΩ. Ἀλλ' ἢ τὰς Νέστορος καὶ Ὀδυσσέως τέχνας μόνον περὶ λόγων ἀκήκοας, ἃς ἐν Ἰλίῳ σχολάζοντες συνεγραψάτην, τῶν δὲ Παλαμήδους ἀνήκοος γέγονας;
>
> ΦΑΙ. Καὶ ναὶ μὰ Δί' ἔγωγε τῶν Νέστορος, εἰ μὴ Γοργίαν Νέστορά τινα κατασκευάζεις, ἤ τινα Θρασύμαχόν τε καὶ Θεόδωρον Ὀδυσσέα.

> Socrates: What! Have you only heard about the arts of speech of Nestor and Odysseus which they composed during their spare time at Troy, but you haven't heard of the one Palamedes wrote?

Phaedrus: By Zeus, I haven't even heard of Nestor's, unless you are making Gorgias out to be a Nestor, or Thrasymachus and Theodorus an Odysseus.

Plato, *Phaedrus* 261b

This fascinating exchange is often cited in handbooks on rhetoric to show that rhetorical treatises of some sort were composed by Gorgias, Thrasymachus and Theodorus. The scholion to the passage concluded that Socrates compares Gorgias to Nestor because he lived a long time.[18] What is more interesting, though, is how easily Socrates slips into playing the game whereby contemporary sophists take on the mantle of mythological heroes famed for their intellectual and rhetorical ability – and how easily Phaedrus picks up on the conceit.[19] Note the τινα when he suggests that Socrates is making Gorgias out to be *a* Nestor. This sets up 'Nestor' as a transferable personality. Similarly, either Thrasymachus or Theodorus could be *an* Odysseus. There is no fixed series of identifications, but a repertory of possible connections that could be deployed.

Palamedes

The passage of the *Phaedrus* just quoted mentions three heroes famed for their intellectual and oratorical abilities: Nestor, Odysseus and Palamedes. A little later Socrates returns to the 'Eleatic Palamedes':

> Τὸν οὖν Ἐλεατικὸν Παλαμήδην λέγοντα οὐκ ἴσμεν τέχνῃ, ὥστε φαίνεσθαι τοῖς ἀκούουσι τὰ αὐτὰ ὅμοια καὶ ἀνόμοια, καὶ ἓν καὶ πολλά, μένοντά τε αὖ καὶ φερόμενα;
>
> Don't we know that the Eleatic Palamedes speaks with art so that the same things appear to his listeners as like and unlike, one and many, staying still or in motion.
>
> Plato, *Phaedrus* 261d

Starting with the scholia, most interpreters have seen here a reference to Zeno of Elea, whose paradoxical arguments on the one and the many are celebrated in Plato's dialogue *Parmenides*.[20] Slobodan Dušanić sees rather a combination of Zeno and Alcidamas, based on Quintilian's statement in Book 3 of the *Institutio oratoria* that an art of speech was composed by 'Alcidamas of Elaia' (*Elaites*), 'whom Plato calls Palamedes'; Plato has associated Zeno with Alcidamas, Dušanić argues, because of Zeno's influence on Alcidamas.[21] It is difficult to assess how strongly the figure of Alcidamas would have suggested itself to an ancient audience. Dušanić is probably right that the *Phaedrus* is the best candidate for being the source of Quintilian's identification, and a speech by Odysseus prosecuting Palamedes for treason was attributed to Alcidamas,[22] but the precise identity of the figure standing behind Palamedes must have been as much guesswork in antiquity as it is now. By speaking of the *Eleatic* Palamedes, moreover, Socrates suggests that there might be other modern versions of Palamedes as well, once again assuming that a contemporary intellectual can find his counterpart among the heroes. In this second *Phaedrus* passage we are not in the situation where a sophistic speaker of an *epideixis* or composer of a *techne* channels a hero. Socrates has taken the further step of generalizing the principle, as though the eloquent heroes of myth exist as a permanently accessible database. We are not, I think, dealing with established allegorical connections between particular heroes and sophists, but with a more general network of associative possibilities.[23]

Such a reconstruction coheres with what we know about early 'arts of speech'. Whatever else they may have been, they included both collections of exemplary devices such as are mentioned by Socrates at *Phaedrus* 266d–267d, as well as sample speeches that served as storehouses of forensic argumentation.[24] Gorgias' *Defence of Palamedes* is an example of the latter (like the paired speeches of Ajax and Odysseus by Antisthenes and Alcidamas' speech for Odysseus). When Gorgias performed the *Defence of Palamedes* he was taking on the persona of the hero, and the same applies to other such speeches. Every speaker of this *Defence* would do so, could choose – or be said – to be Palamedes. This type of projection is maybe one of the things that lies behind a curious etymology of the word 'hero' in Plato's *Cratylus*:

> ἢ ὅτι σοφοὶ ἦσαν καὶ ῥήτορες [καὶ] δεινοὶ καὶ διαλεκτικοί, ἐρωτᾶν ἱκανοὶ ὄντες· τὸ γὰρ "εἴρειν" λέγειν ἐστίν. ὅπερ οὖν ἄρτι λέγομεν, ἐν τῇ Ἀττικῇ φωνῇ λεγόμενοι οἱ ἥρωες ῥήτορές τινες καὶ ἐρωτητικοὶ συμβαίνουσιν, ὥστε ῥητόρων καὶ σοφιστῶν γένος γίγνεται τὸ ἡρωικὸν φῦλον.
>
> ... or [they were called heroes] because they were wise and clever speakers and dialecticians, capable of asking questions, since the verb *eirein* is to speak. So then, as I was just saying, when heroes are spoken of in the Attic dialect they turn out to be orators and askers of questions, so that the tribe of heroes becomes the race of speakers and sophists.
>
> Plato, *Cratylus* 398d–e

We have here the same combination of public oratory and private dialectic we saw combined in the *Phaedrus* passage cited above, but what makes Socrates' tongue-in-cheek etymology at all plausible is a cultural background where heroes could be portrayed as orators and intellectuals. It is a small step from here to those later authors who projected the origins of rhetoric back into the heroic age.

Let us now return to Palamedes, whom we have already met as the mythological counterpart of Zeno, and who is the speaker of the epideictic *Defence of Palamedes*. The hero does not appear in Homeric epic, but did make an appearance in the *Cypria*, where he became the enemy of Odysseus by seeing through his pretence of madness. Odysseus later caused his death, either by drowning him (the *Cypria*) or by framing him for treason: he buried gold in Palamedes' tent, and using a forged letter accused him of betraying the Greeks to the Trojans. This scenario seems to have been a favourite with the fifth-century tragedians. Aeschylus, Sophocles and Euripides all wrote tragedies on this topic, and Palamedes turns up as a nickname in comedy as well. When Dionysus praises Euripides' cleverness in *Frogs* he calls him 'Palamedes': 'O well said, Palamedes, you wise creature' (1451: εὖ γ', ὦ Παλάμηδες, ὦ σοφωτάτη φύσις).[25] Several scholars have argued that the theme of differing kinds of σοφία was prominent in Euripides' version of the Palamedes myth.[26] As James Barrett puts it, 'Palamedes ... is a wise σοφός with an ethical commitment to telling the truth; Odysseus ... is a clever σοφός with no such commitment'.[27] His fate, and the focus on it by the tragedians, reflects the nightmare scenario for fifth-century Athenians: finding oneself on trial for one's life in a lawcourt and opposed by an expert and unscrupulous opponent.

Gorgias' defence obviously participates in this late-fifth-century interest, although we cannot be sure whether Euripides' *Palamedes* responds to Gorgias.[28] This is not the place to engage in detailed analysis of the speech, which is composed largely of arguments from probability (how could Palamedes, a Greek, talk to a barbarian who had no Greek?, etc.) and character.[29] Paola Bassino's chapter in this volume (Chapter 2) engages in greater detail with these issues, focusing on the power and limitations of speech, and the contrast between knowledge and opinion; my purpose here is to highlight the convergence of mythological character and a sophistic intellect. I have argued previously that the speech reflects Gorgianic concerns surrounding the possibility of communication as expressed in his treatise *On What Is Not* (DK 82B3).[30] Here Gorgias argued that nothing exists, that even if something did exist it could not be apprehended by us, and even if it were apprehended it could not be communicated. Palamedes knows his own innocence but asks how he can communicate this to the jury unless he can discover something in the truth itself and the present necessity – both dangerous teachers (4). Palamedes is in a tricky situation; he cannot point to any external proof of his innocence and he is trying to prove the non-existence of what is not. Moreover, he is trying to do this by means of λόγος. Λόγος, however, as Gorgias says in the treatise *On What Is Not*, although we reveal things by means of it, is not substance (84). What we reveal to the person we are talking to, by λόγος, is λόγος. Now, the *Palamedes* is by no means a mere illustration of *On What Is Not*, but when we read it with this in mind we are struck by how intellectually solipsistic the *Palamedes* is. It is a speech that creates its effects by stressing what is not there: no opportunity, no common language between Palamedes and the Trojans, no witness in a military camp where everybody sees everything all the time. Even Odysseus, in this scenario, has no proof. We hear nothing of the gold and incriminating letter that Odysseus is supposed to have used to convict Palamedes, nor indeed of any person Odysseus might bring forth as a witness. Palamedes asks him repeatedly at the end of the speech to provide such witnesses. Ironically of course it was not witnesses who convicted Palamedes in myth, but objects – a letter in particular, a reproduction of a λόγος.[31] The *Defence* is a λόγος (speech) that delivers λόγοι, words, and λόγος, reasoning. It focuses insistently on mental constructs and thus is, among other things, a representation of Gorgianic thought. It is not just a collection of linked εἰκός arguments, but presents the dynamic interaction of heroic and sophistic intellects. The mythological situation has been contrived to isolate the speaker from normal forms of evidence and proof, and contrived to showcase Gorgianic logic, conceived both as an art of reasoning and an art of speech. Gorgias may also be mounting a subtle defence against those who are hostile towards him as a teacher of rhetoric. When Gorgias speaks Palamedes, he takes on the persona of an unjustly accused wise man in a hostile world, who can use only reason to save himself.

We have already seen that Plato was not slow to pick up on the potential of Palamedes. During the discussion of rhetoric in the *Phaedrus* referred to above, the hero figured as the originator of an art of speech composed at the time of the Trojan War. Andrea Nightingale has further suggested that he may lurk underneath the character of Theuth when Socrates discusses the dangerous powers of writing later in the dialogue (*Phdr.* 274c ff.). Socrates narrates how the Egyptian god Theuth invents a number of skills and games that are often associated with Palamedes: number and calculation, geometry and astronomy, dice and checkers, and writing. When he asks his superior, Thamus, to approve his inventions, Thamus objects that writing will not, as Theuth asserts, be an aid to memory but to forgetfulness (274c–275b).[32] Nightingale explores how the myth of Theuth appropriates and rewrites its Palamedean prototype; in the present context I would like to focus on Phaedrus' bemused comment that Socrates finds it perhaps too easy to make up Egyptian stories and stories from wherever, together with Socrates' reply that it should not matter where the stories come from, just whether they are true (275b–c). Perhaps one of the things that confuses Phaedrus here is the transfer of Greek myths of cultural invention to an Egyptian context. If the argument of this chapter is persuasive, their previous discussion has progressed along fairly conventional lines, connecting rhetorical education with the Greek heroic past, just as various sophistic practitioners had done. It is a Socratic twist to deconstruct this fantasy of cultural continuity by the insertion of invented Egyptian material.

Plato had previously played on the notion of a connection between Palamedes and a historical intellectual in his *Apology*, where Palamedes appears as a counterpart to Socrates. The fundamental parallel is clear: once again a 'wise' man – though in the case of Socrates, 'wise' in a special sense – is on trial for his life and has to try to prove a negative: he does not introduce new gods; he does not corrupt the young. James Coulter laid out a number of similarities in the way rhetorical τόποι are used in the *Apology* and the *Defence of Palamedes*, some of which involve very similar Greek wording. His conclusion was that Plato played on Gorgias' speech in order to critique Gorgianic rhetoric. Palamedes, the argument goes, is deploying arguments from probability, whereas Socrates is laying out his divine mission. Palamedes defers to the rhetorical needs of the moment and privileges δόξα, whereas Socrates is uncompromising and sticks to the straightforward truth.[33] Yet this cannot be the whole story. There are indications in the *Apology* that Socrates might be identifying with Palamedes; he would thus provide another example of mythological role-playing. At 41a–b Socrates tells the jurors that it would be interesting to talk in the other world to mythological judges and to poets like Homer and Musaeus. It would be particularly wonderful to talk to heroes who had died as a result of unjust trials:

ἔμοιγε καὶ αὐτῷ θαυμαστὴ ἂν εἴη ἡ διατριβὴ αὐτόθι, ὁπότε ἐντύχοιμι Παλαμήδει καὶ Αἴαντι τῷ Τελαμῶνος καὶ εἴ τις ἄλλος τῶν παλαιῶν διὰ κρίσιν ἄδικον τέθνηκεν, ἀντιπαραβάλλοντι τὰ ἐμαυτοῦ πάθη πρὸς τὰ ἐκείνων – ὡς ἐγὼ οἶμαι, οὐκ ἂν ἀηδὲς εἴη.

Life there would be amazing for me, when I came across Palamedes and Ajax the son of Telamon and any other of the ancients who died because of an unjust judgement, comparing my experiences with theirs – in my opinion it wouldn't be unpleasant.

Plato, *Apology of Socrates* 41a–b

He also relishes the prospect of cross-examining Sisyphus and Odysseus. For Coulter, this implies that Socrates will cross-examine Palamedes and find him wanting. There is, however, more to this vignette. As James Barrett points out in an excellent article, Palamedes in the *Apology* need not be a reflection only of Gorgias, even if there are Gorgianic resonances in the *Apology*. For the tragedians, as we have seen, Palamedes could be used to present real wisdom as opposed to an Odyssean sly cleverness. Barrett usefully brings the *Apology* into juxtaposition with the group of speeches written for mythological figures by Gorgias, Antisthenes and Alcidamas and shows how Plato sets Socrates in a mythological context.[34] One might add that it is probably no accident that the two heroes mentioned by Socrates in the *Apology* sentence quoted above are speakers in this epideictic tradition. While Palamedes may be used to stand for beneficial wisdom, Ajax can represent the honest speaker bereft of rhetorical finesse (precisely the way Socrates portrays himself at the beginning of the dialogue).

We should, however, note a difference between the mythological contextualizing of Socrates in the *Apology* and the other examples examined so far. Socrates never ventriloquizes Palamedes, but always keeps a critical distance. As has been widely observed, Socrates' activities in Hades will match closely his elenctic activities during life. Christopher Rowe's analysis of this passage reinforces this point; he observes that 'Socrates' future in Hades is also his future in Plato's dialogues' where he will examine poets and politicians of the present and past.[35] If I am correct that the sophists could take on the personae of mythological characters, we can see how his imagined interaction with heroes in the underworld might also stand in for his examination of various sophists.[36] Although Socrates may take on the mantle of Palamedes he is interested not so much in identification as in comparison (ἀντιπαραβάλλοντι) and examination. This is an important point. The reader of a Platonic dialogue, like Socrates, must engage in careful comparison when investigating mythological analogies. Until this takes place one cannot be sure of the suitability of the analogy. Socrates is placed in a situation where he can speak with the 'original' Palamedes; he will not simply appropriate him but investigate him. We may compare here Socrates' procedure at the beginning of the *Phaedrus*, where he reveals his interest in considering whether he is a 'more complex beast than Typhon and more inflamed, or a more gentle and simpler creature, sharing naturally in a divine and un-Typhonic portion' (*Phdr.* 230a). Mythological analogy is a kind of heuristic.

It is in keeping with this investigative model that we are invited to compare Socrates to another mythological hero in the *Apology*. At 28b–d Socrates says that he is indifferent to death if only he can do what is right, and quotes Achilles' similar sentiment from *Iliad* 18.95–6, where the hero wishes to die once he has extracted justice from Hector for the death of Patroclus. Plato now seems to be interested in comparing Socrates to Achilles (an analogy that pops up again in the *Crito*). For Barrett, the importance of this connection lies in Achilles being a mythological figure who, like Palamedes, was often placed in opposition to Odysseus, and this seems convincing.[37] It is not insignificant that among the mythological characters listed at *Apology* 41b we find Ajax, Palamedes and Odysseus. Achilles and Odysseus, we recall (along with Nestor), figure as models in Hippias' Homeric criticism, and Plato's *Hippias* dialogues play with the notion that Hippias or Socrates might be Odysseus or Achilles. Odysseus and Palamedes (and Nestor!) modelled differing kinds of σοφία that could be matched up with differing rhetorical and intellectual strategies, while Achilles and Ajax could stand for a simpler and even hostile approach to rhetoric. The group of 'rhetorical' heroes (Odysseus, Palamedes, Nestor) was particularly suitable for sophistic appropriation, but none of these mythological characters was so fixed that the particular intellectual flavour of the characterization was predetermined (even if a positive or negative ethical valence could be pronounced). Hugo Koning's chapter in this volume on the speeches of Ajax and Odysseus by Antisthenes (Chapter 3) shows that we might read Odysseus' speech in that pair along similar lines. Following an approach laid out by Susan Prince, Koning sees Odysseus as a vehicle for Antisthenes' own approach to language and to excellence.[38] The projection of Antisthenes onto Odysseus is never explicit, but as was the case with Gorgias and Palamedes, there is a suggestive convergence. The audience of these speeches and Platonic dialogues must ask: Is Gorgias Palamedes? Is Socrates Palamedes? Is Socrates Odysseus? Is Hippias (or Antisthenes) Odysseus? A Socratic (or Eleatic) Palamedes, or Odysseus, or indeed Achilles, will have his own special characteristics. This is so even when a Socratic Palamedes plays with the rhetorical τόποι of his Gorgianic counterpart.

Adrastus

At *Phaedrus* 269a, Socrates is discussing with Phaedrus the distinction between knowing lists of rhetorical devices and knowing how to use them. He appeals to mellifluous Adrastus – or Pericles – as rhetorical experts:

ΣΩ. Τί δὲ τὸν μελίγηρυν Ἄδραστον οἰόμεθα ἢ καὶ Περικλέα, εἰ ἀκούσειαν ὧν νυνδὴ ἡμεῖς διῇμεν τῶν παγκάλων τεχνημάτων – βραχυλογιῶν τε καὶ εἰκονολογιῶν ...

Socrates: What do we think about Adrastus with his honey-sweet voice, or indeed Pericles – if they should hear what we were just now discussing about those absolutely wonderful devices: brachylogies, imagery ...

Plato, *Phaedrus* 269a

What is the significance of Adrastus here? Ast thought that Plato meant Antiphon, though few have agreed with him. The consensus is that Plato is engaging in hendiadys, and that he means 'that Adrastus, Pericles'.[39] Why Adrastus? Dušanić thought it was because Adrastus was connected with funeral orations, and this is likely enough. A critic of Pericles might observe that Adrastus was a leader who induced his city to wage a disastrous war that ended in defeat.[40] Certainly Tyrtaeus, whom Plato may be channelling here, mentioned Adrastus as renowned for his power of speech, speaking of his 'honey-sweet voice' (Tyrt. 9.8: γλῶσσαν δ᾽ Ἀδρήστου μειλιχόγηρυν). Adrastus, then, is another mythological orator to add to our collection. We are not in a position to know whether anybody other than Socrates called Pericles 'Adrastus', but the success of the quip is based on the relative transparency of this form of comparison.

Prometheus

For one final Platonic example, we may return to the *Protagoras*. As discussed at the beginning of this chapter, this is a dialogue much concerned with cultural trajectory, with Protagoras tracing the prehistory of the sophistic art back into the mists of antiquity. Cultural trajectory, the march of education and civilization, is also the subject of Protagoras' Great Speech, which aims to prove by means of a myth (descended ultimately from Hesiod) that all men are innately endowed with the capacity for political excellence (*Prt.* 320c–323a). The myth sets Prometheus against Epimetheus. The latter is charged with handing out protective characteristics to living creatures but forgets to give man anything; true to his name (Afterthought), he only thinks of things after the event. Prometheus therefore steals fire and technological skill from the gods and gives them to man. Humanity, however, has difficulty forming social relationships, and is therefore in danger of destruction, so Zeus has Hermes give men justice and respect. This myth may reflect Protagorean discourse on the history of civilization, or it may be Plato's invention, or some combination of the two.[41] Prometheus was often seen as a culture hero in the fifth century; witness the *Prometheus Bound*, where he is explicitly set up as a sophist and teaches mankind most of the arts of civilization.

It is significant that in Protagoras' myth, political skill, which is what Protagoras himself teaches, come not from Prometheus but from Zeus. Earlier in the dialogue Protagoras criticizes his fellow sophists for teaching the young specialist studies such as geometry and music, casting them back into the τέχναι they have just escaped (ἐμβάλλουσιν εἰς τέχνας) whereas he teaches household and civic management (318d–e), which Socrates glosses as the political art (τὴν πολιτικὴν τέχνην, 319a). We might say, then, that Protagoras distinguishes himself from his sophistic competitors because they teach narrow intellectual technologies that will line up with Promethean technological wisdom, whereas he teaches the political art which, as will be revealed in his myth, comes from Zeus. This makes Protagoras into a Zeus-like figure and casts his competitors as subordinate (and inevitably discomfited?) figures. Such a contrast may well reflect the self-positioning of the historical Protagoras. At the most basic level we might interpret Protagoras in the dialogue as an educator whose job is to activate people's Zeus-given political skills. If we read with mythological role-playing in mind, we may further suspect that the association between Protagoras and Zeus is an even stronger one. Protagoras was, of course, an associate of that other 'Olympian', Pericles.

Given the role of Prometheus in Protagoras' myth, it is no surprise that the figures of Prometheus and Epimetheus, who come off rather poorly in his narrative, occur elsewhere in the dialogue. This network of references is a Platonic construction, to be sure, but it functions successfully because Plato capitalizes on the larger phenomenon of mythological role-playing. Protagoras may aspire to an Olympian persona, but it is Socrates' task to pull him back down to earth. Plato represents Socrates and the sophist jockeying for position around the question of which of them should be seen as Prometheus and which Epimetheus, just as in the *Hippias Minor* Socrates and Hippias spar over the roles of Odysseus and Nestor.

In fact, our first vision of Protagoras at the house of Callias casts the sophist as a different mythological character entirely. Shortly after his arrival Socrates sees Protagoras walking in the colonnade surrounded by admirers. He comments that Protagoras has gathered his followers from the cities through which he has travelled, 'bewitching them with his voice like Orpheus, and they follow after his voice bewitched' (315ab: κηλῶν τῇ φωνῇ ὥσπερ Ὀρφεύς, οἱ δὲ κατὰ τὴν φωνὴν ἕπονται κεκηλημένοι). Allusions to Odysseus' journey to Hades soon follow (315b–d), making it clear that Socrates' visit is a conceptually katabatic one. Orpheus is one of the proto-sophists soon to be mentioned by Protagoras (316d), and as was the case with the *Apology*, we find the underworld a useful space in which to compare and examine famous heroes and their latter-day counterparts.

When Socrates approaches Protagoras he asks whether their conversation concerning the education of Socrates's friend Hippocrates should be public or private. Protagoras replies to him, 'It is right of you to show forethought on my behalf, Socrates.' (ὀρθῶς, ἔφη, προμηθῇ, ὦ Σώκρατες, ὑπὲρ ἐμοῦ) 'When a stranger comes to a great city and persuades the best of the young men to leave their normal associations and associate with him on the grounds that they will become better, he should take care' (316d). The verb Protagoras uses of Socrates' forethought (προμηθῇ) is of course cognate with the Titan Prometheus. Protagoras graciously says that Socrates is foresightful but attributes the greatest foresight to himself: he admits that he is a sophist and teacher but has also taken certain unspecified precautions to ensure that no harm comes to him (317b–c). At this point in the dialogue the use of Promethean vocabulary is not marked. It is planted as a seed for future elaboration, and only begins to exercise its full resonance with the myth and in the subsequent discussion.

At the end of the dialogue, Socrates suggests to Protagoras that they should now try again to define excellence:

ἐγὼ οὖν, ὦ Πρωταγόρα, πάντα ταῦτα καθορῶν ἄνω κάτω ταραττόμενα δεινῶς, πᾶσαν προθυμίαν ἔχω καταφανῆ αὐτὰ γενέσθαι, καὶ βουλοίμην ἂν ταῦτα διεξελθόντας ἡμᾶς ἐξελθεῖν καὶ ἐπὶ τὴν ἀρετὴν ὅτι ἔστιν, καὶ πάλιν ἐπισκέψασθαι περὶ αὐτοῦ εἴτε διδακτὸν εἴτε μὴ διδακτόν, μὴ πολλάκις ἡμᾶς ὁ Ἐπιμηθεὺς ἐκεῖνος καὶ ἐν τῇ σκέψει σφήλῃ ἐξαπατήσας, ὥσπερ καὶ ἐν τῇ διανομῇ ἠμέλησεν ἡμῶν, ὡς φῂς σύ. ἤρεσεν οὖν μοι καὶ ἐν τῷ μύθῳ ὁ Προμηθεὺς μᾶλλον τοῦ Ἐπιμηθέως· ᾧ χρώμενος ἐγὼ καὶ προμηθούμενος ὑπὲρ τοῦ βίου τοῦ ἐμαυτοῦ παντὸς πάντα ταῦτα πραγματεύομαι.

So, Protagoras, seeing all of our discussion thrown up and down into terrible confusion, I am extremely eager that things become clear, and I could wish that, now we have gone through all this, we could also arrive at the question of what excellence is and then investigate again whether it can be taught or not, so that that Epimetheus doesn't keep on deceiving and tripping us up in our investigation too – just as, so you say, he neglected us in his distribution. I liked Prometheus more than Epimetheus in the myth, too. I busy myself about all this using him as my model and exercising forethought for my whole life.

Plato, *Protagoras* 361c–d

As has been observed, to talk about the teachability of excellence before having defined what it is, is a classic example of afterthought.[42] The mythological identification is explicit, and Prometheus and Epimetheus seem to be standing for certain types of argumentation.[43] When Socrates exercises foresight (προμηθούμενος) on behalf of his life, he is again using Promethean vocabulary, and the use of this verb in direct proximity to a reference to the mythological Prometheus confirms that the mythological resonance is no accident. This reference to Prometheus closes the structural ring opened by Protagoras at the start of the dialogue (316d). Moreover, the exercise of forethought on behalf of one's life should remind us of the skill that Socrates earlier argued was essential to a successful life, the art of measurement. Before we embark on any course of action, we need to sum up the pleasures and pains involved (the 'hedonistic calculus'), and act accordingly (356e–357e). Indeed, elsewhere in Plato, the word for forethought, προμηθία, is used for the supervision of the soul by its rational part.[44] Prometheus, then, is a figure for this kind of activity in the soul. The calculation can be merely prudential, as it is in the case of Protagoras, or can aim at what is really best for the soul, as Socrates thinks it should.[45] What kind of Prometheus do we want to be? A slippery trickster or a culture hero? We cannot doubt that Plato wants us to see Socrates in the latter role, although it is also worth remarking that Socrates' opponents, such as Callicles in the *Gorgias*, view him as a diabolical trickster. Not only is Socrates a better Prometheus than Protagoras, he is, for Plato, the right *kind* of Prometheus.

The Promethean resonances of Protagoras and Socrates clearly emerge from the wider practice of mythological role-playing, a practice that Plato elaborates and manipulates for his own purposes. He has Socrates undermine the arrogance with which the sophists appropriate famous figures of myth when his questioning reveals that a respondent is not so much of a Nestor or Prometheus as he thinks he is. He shows Socrates flirting with mythological personae himself, although he maintains a critical distance and does not allow identification to become complete. Yet there is often a faint whiff of the comic about the Socratic version of this practice. Socrates does not take his mythological forays too seriously, presumably because it would distract from the serious business of self-examination. His goal is not to define himself against or with a tradition, even if the audience of the dialogues may be prone to situate him within it. The comic fragment where Cleon is called 'a Prometheus after the event', or the passage from *Frogs* where Euripides is addressed as Palamedes, shows both that intellectual pretension in the fifth century was easily expressed in terms of identification with the mythological intellectuals, and that the trope could verge upon the trite.

Coda: The Second Sophistic

Mythological role-playing was an important aspect of intellectual display during the Second Sophistic. '[S]ophists were judged by their audience and peers on their ability to convincingly perform fictionalised discourses of what certain historical or pseudo-historical characters might have said in a given situation ... Sophistic declamation is thus the performance of a double identity.'[46] These performances, as well as the *progymnasmata* of rhetorical education wherein, e.g., a student staged himself as Ajax having lost the contest for the arms of Achilles, were the descendants of Classical performances.[47] Yet mythological impersonation as a rhetorical exercise could also broaden into the self-reflective phenomenon laid out in this chapter. Dio Chrysostom compares himself to Odysseus, Hermes, and 'often plays Nestor since Homer's Nestor was the wise advisor *par excellence*'. Dio's Nestor, moreover, has the characteristics of a Cynic philosopher.[48] Philostratus' *Life of Apollonius of Tyana* represents the fictionalized sage as being connected to Palamedes. In India, he meets a young boy who is a reincarnation of the hero (*VA* 3.22).[49] When he visits Troy, Apollonius goes to the hero's tomb to ask him to forget his anger against the Greeks and restores his cult site. Most interesting is that the sage greets Palamedes as 'the source of language, of the Muses, of myself' (*VA* 4.13, trans. Jones: δι' ὃν λόγοι, δι' ὃν Μοῦσαι, δι' ὃν ἐγώ).[50] Wannes Gyselinck and Kristoffel Demoen interpret Palamedes as a 'patron saint of the sophists', and suggest that, prior to his visit to the tomb, Apollonius 'casts himself successively as a new Nestor, Phoenix, Priam and Odysseus'.[51] We cannot linger here on the metafictional dynamics uncovered in this passage by Gyselinck and Demoen, but it does seem clear that Philostratus, like his Classical predecessors, is using intellectual genealogy and mythological role-playing to explore cultural identity and the nature of σοφία.

Lucian's composition *To One Who Said 'You're a Prometheus in Words'* will serve as a conclusion to this brief foray into the Second Sophistic and an apt commentary on mythological analogy. The premise is that someone has called Lucian a Prometheus, and Lucian wonders what he can have meant. Is the label meant to be praise or irony? Are Lucian's words like clay? Are they very wise and well-wrought? Was something else intended?

Καίτοι, φαίη τις ἂν παραμυθούμενος, οὐ ταῦτα εἴκασέ σε τῷ Προμηθεῖ, ἀλλὰ τὸ καινουργὸν τοῦτο ἐπαινῶν καὶ μὴ πρός τι ἄλλο ἀρχέτυπον μεμιμημένον ... ὁ μὲν ταῦτα ἂν εἴποι, πρός γε τὸ εὐφημότατον ἐξηγούμενος τὸ εἰρημένον, καὶ ἴσως οὗτος ὁ νοῦς ἦν τῷ λελεγμένῳ.

Yet someone might console me by saying 'It was not in these respects that he compared you to Prometheus. No, he was praising your originality in following no exemplar'... That is what he might say, putting at least a gracious interpretation on your words, and perhaps that was what you meant.[52]

Lucian, *To One Who Said 'You're a Prometheus in Words'* 3

Indeed, it is to this piece that we are indebted for the preservation of the comic fragment that calls Cleon 'a Prometheus after the event', as Lucian wonders whether the intention of the comparison is to undermine (2). As he concludes, his focus is on the novelty of combining (philosophical) dialogue and comedy. Perhaps he is a Prometheus because he gives his audience 'bones covered in fat, comic jests under philosophic solemnity'. In any case, he cannot now change his approach, since 'to change one's plan is the work of Epimetheus, not Prometheus' (7: τό γε μεταβουλεύεσθαι Ἐπιμηθέως ἔργον, οὐ Προμηθέως ἐστίν). The exemplarity of mythological characters is a complex phenomenon, and Lucian is at his most Socratic as he investigates what the basis of such a comparison might be. Karen ní Mheallaigh's stimulating exploration of Lucian as a theorist of fiction concludes that Prometheus is 'a metaliterary icon for Lucian himself', both in this work and elsewhere (in the dialogue *Prometheus*, 'Lucian depicts the Titan as a mirror image of himself', delivering a sophistic lecture to Hermes and Hephaestus).[53] This is surely correct, and we are now in a better position to see how the creation of such icons in the Second Sophistic was a sophisticated transformation of earlier rhetorical practice.

Conclusion

Sophistic interaction with the epic and mythological past occurred on a number of fronts, starting from the fundamental Greek habit of bringing poetic allusion and citation into cultivated speech. The sophists of the fifth century BC developed this practice into teaching their pupils skills of linguistic analysis and interpretation of the poetic tradition, but also used mythological characters as vehicles for their teaching. Speeches such as the *Defence of Palamedes* or the *Trojan Dialogue* combine transmission of useful content (noble occupations, arguments from probability) with, in the case of Gorgias at least, a specific intellectual voice. The nature of the appropriation of the heroic character could change depending on the circumstances and it thus became possible to identify sophists with mythological characters, such as Nestor with Hippias, Gorgias and Antiphon. Plato inherits this set of approaches and appropriates them for his own, repeatedly interweaving in his dialogues questions about the extent to which his characters (Socrates but also others) create their own versions of mythical prototypes. Ast once observed (with reference to *Phdr.* 261b) that 'the Sophists, in order that they might win greater authority for their skills, were accustomed to boast that they existed already in the heroic age'.[54] This is a point worth remembering when it comes to sophistic use of the past. The sophists were viewed with suspicion in some quarters, and the fiction that they were inheritors of the rhetorical and ethical traditions of the heroes could help to domesticate them in their own cultural environment. There was a general tendency in Greek culture for innovators to appeal to the past, but such appeals can 'reveal, rather than obscure, the fact of innovation'.[55] Sophistic practitioners of wisdom took on the mantle of mythology to demonstrate their mastery over tradition and to refashion it to reflect on the demands of a new intellectual environment.[56]

Notes

1 Richardson 1975; Ford 2002: 152–7, 194–208.
2 Radermacher 1951: 4–6.
3 *Prolegomena* in Hermogenis Περὶ στάσεων W. 7.5–6: λέγουσι δέ τινες δικανικὸν λόγον εἰρηκέναι πρῶτον Μενεσθέα τὸν στρατηγὸν τῶν Ἀθηναίων. . . . An intrusive gloss adds (interestingly) ἄλλοι δὲ λέγουσιν Ἀντιφῶντα τοῦτον τὸν ῥήτορα; the effect of the intrusion is to pair mythological and sophistic rhetoric.
4 Worman 2002: 149–92.
5 Knudsen 2012: 33–5.
6 Morgan 2000: 105–30.
7 Olson 2014: 257–8.
8 Reported also in Philostr. *VS* 1.11.1 in almost the same words.
9 Morgan 2000: 109–11.
10 Blondell 2002: 113–64. The following analysis is much indebted to her discussion.
11 Blondell 2002: 128–9; Hunter 2016: 86 n. 5.

12 Blondell 2002: 133–5 ('Hippias takes onto his own shoulders the epic mantle of sage paternalism').
13 Cf. Blondell 2002: 147.
14 Hunter 2016: 98–9.
15 Hunter 2016: 99 n. 38.
16 [Plut.] *X orat.* 832e; Suda *s.v.* 'Anthiphon' = T3 Pendrick 2002.
17 Trans. Pendrick 2002 T6(d).
18 Schol. *Phdr.* 261b.
19 Ast 1810: 352 aptly remarks on the irony of Socrates attributing the composition of rhetorical treatises at Troy to the *leisure* time of the heroes there ('Haec Platonis ironiam manifestam reddunt'). Cf. Worman 2002: 183.
20 Thompson 1868: 97; Rowe 1988: 196; Yunis 2011: 185.
21 Dušanić 1992a.
22 For an argument that the attribution is mistaken, see O'Sullivan 2008.
23 Cf. Horky 2013: 213–15, 229. Horky's interest is in Plato's response to mathematical Pythagoranism, but speaking of Plato's references to mythological and historical predecessors, he writes of 'the surplus of meaning that marks the heurematographical myths of Plato' (229) and comments that 'we are both stimulated to seek the identities of these figures in such mythological presentations and frustrated by our failure to determine it' (215).
24 Cf. Knudsen 2012: 33–5.
25 Eupolis fr. 385 K.-A. speaks of a 'Palamedean discovery'.
26 Scodel 1980: 43, 93, 105; Nightingale 1995: 152–3; Barrett 2001: 10, 13–14.
27 Barrett 2001: 12.
28 Scodel 1980: 90 n. 26 judges that Euripides used Gorgias' *Defence of Palamedes* as a source.
29 Worman 2002: 171–82; Knudsen 2012: 37–43.
30 Morgan 2000: 119–22.
31 Cf. Scodel 1980: 116–17 and 129, on Euripides' *Palamedes*) and Nightingale 1995: 152 for the irony whereby the father of writing (Palamedes) is killed by his own child.
32 Nightingale 1995: 149–54.
33 Coulter 1964. See also the list of parallels in Barrett 2001: 26–30.
34 Barrett 2001: 6–7, 15. ('In aligning Socrates with the mythical Palamedes in opposition to (the likes of) Odysseus, the *Apology* hints at the value of mythic models for understanding Socrates' predicament in court.')
35 Rowe 2007: 83–4.
36 I thank the anonymous referee for this point.
37 Barrett 2001: 15–19.
38 Prince 2015: 197, 220. As both Prince (2015: 200–1) and Koning observe, some interpreters have identified Ajax, rather than Odysseus, with Antisthenes' positions.

Prince leaves open the possibility that Antisthenes 'presents two aspects of ethical character, each to be endorsed up to a point'.
39 Ast 1810: 372 (followed by Thompson 1868: 118–9). For the close association with Pericles, see Rowe 1988: 203.
40 Dušanić 1992b: 29. His interest in in political allegory, which is not the focus of my current discussion. See Shey 1976: 10–13 for a reading of the comparison as critical. Philodemus may also have listed Adrastus as an eloquent hero (Phld. *Rh.* II p. 76 fr. III p. 77 fr. IV).
41 Morgan 2000: 134–6.
42 Coby 1987: 175–6.
43 Coby 1987: 175–6. For further consideration of the complexities of the role-playing here, see Morgan 2000: 149–53.
44 *Grg.* 501b: Socrates distinguishes those that have forethought for what is good for the soul, and those that do not; *Rep.* 441e: the rational part of the soul has forethought on behalf of the whole. Cf. fr. 145 K.–A. of the comic poet Plato (from *Sophistai*), which, depending on how one reconstructs it, may refer to Prometheus as people's mind (νοῦς): προμηθία γάρ ἐστιν ἀνθρώποις ὁ νοῦς; or καὶ γὰρ Προμηθεύς ἐστιν ἀνθρώποις ὁ νοῦς (Kock).
45 In the *Philebus* 16c–17a Socrates asserts that 'some Prometheus' brought down to humans (along with fire) the knowledge that all existing things comes from the one and the man, and contain within them the finite and the infinite. All the inventions of τέχνη have come to pass through this (πάντα γὰρ ὅσα τέχνης ἐχόμενα ἀνηυρέθη πώποτε διὰ ταύτης φανερὰ γέγονε). This fascinating passage merges the traditional invention of τέχναι by Prometheus with foundational philosophical methodology. Horky 2013: 202, 224–50 explores in detail what figure might stand behind Prometheus here (Philolaus, Pythagoras, Archytas, Hippasus).
46 Gyselink and Demoen 2009: 95–6.
47 Cf. Knudsen 2012: 32.
48 Saïd 2000: 167.
49 Downie 2016: 72–6 (on the reincarnated Palamedes as representing in 'a vivid manifestation of one of the blind spots of Greek memory').
50 Downie 2016: 76–9, focusing again on the correcting of Greek cultural memory.
51 Gyselinck and Demoen 2009: 115–6.
52 Trans. Kilburn 1959.
53 Ní Mheallaigh 2014: 6–7.
54 Ast 1810: 352. 'Et ironia simul est in hac Sophistarum cum antiquis heroibus comparatione, quod Sophistae, ut artibus suis maiorem conciliarent auctoritatem, jam heroica eas aetate floruisse gloriari solebant.'
55 D'Angour 2011: 30.
56 I would like to thank Joshua Billings, David Blank and Bryant Kirkland for helpful discussion of this chapter.

References

Ast, F. 1810, *Platonis Phaedrus*, Leipzig.
Barrett, J. 2001, 'Plato's *Apology*: Philosophy, rhetoric, and the world of myth', *CW* 95: 3–30.
Blondell, R. 2002, *The Play of Character in Plato's Dialogues*, Cambridge.
Coby, P. 1987, *Socrates and the Sophistic Enlightenment*, Lewisburg.
Coulter, J. A. 1964, 'The relation of the *Apology* of Socrates to Gorgias' *Defense of Palamedes* and Plato's critique of Gorgianic rhetoric', *HSCPh* 68: 269–303.
D'Angour, A. 2011, *The Greeks and the New: Novelty in Ancient Greek Imagination and Experience*, Cambridge.
Downie, J. 2016, 'Palamedes and the wisdom of India in Philostratus' *Life of Apollonius of Tyana*', *Mouseion* 13: 65–83.
Dušanić, S. 1992a, 'Alcidamas of Elaea in Plato's *Phaedrus*', *CQ* 42: 347–57.
Dušanić, S. 1992b, 'Athenian politics in Plato's *Phaedrus*', *Aevum* 66: 23–39.
Ford, A. 2002, *The Origins of Criticism. Literary Culture and Poetic Theory in Classical Greece*, Princeton.
Gyselinck, W. and Demoen, K. 2009, 'Author and narrator: Fiction and metafiction in Philostratus *Vita Apollonii*', in Demoen, K. and Praet, D. (eds), *Theios Sophistes. Essays on Flavius Philostratus' Vita Apollonii*, Leiden: 95–127.
Horky, P. 2013, *Plato and Pythagoreanism*, Oxford.
Hunter, R. 2016, 'The *Hippias Minor* and the traditions of Homeric criticism', *CCJ* 62: 85–107.
Jones, C. (ed.) 2005, *Philostratus. Apollonius of Tyana*, Cambridge MA.
Kilburn, K. (ed.) 1959, *Lucian*, vol. 6, Cambridge MA.
Knudsen, R. A. 2012, 'Poetic speakers, sophistic words', *AJPh* 133: 31–60.
Morgan, K. 2000, *Myth and Philosophy from the Presocratics to Plato*, Cambridge.
Ní Mheallaigh, K. 2014, *Reading Fiction with Lucian: Fakes, Freaks and Hyperreality*, Cambridge.
Nightingale, A. 1995, *Genres in Dialogue. Plato and the Construct of Philosophy*, Cambridge.
Olson, S. 2014, *Eupolis frr. 326-497. Fragmenta Comica* 8.3, Heidelberg.
O'Sullivan, N. 2008, 'The authenticity of [Alcidamas] *Odysseus*: two new linguistic considerations', *CQ* 58: 638–47.
Pendrick, G. 2002, *Antiphon the Sophist: The Fragments*, Cambridge.
Prince, S. 2015, *Antisthenes of Athens: Texts, Translations, and Commentary*, Ann Arbor.
Radermacher, L. 1951, *Artium Scriptores*, Vienna.
Richardson, N. 1975, 'Homeric professors in the age of the Sophists', *PCPhS* 21: 65–81.
Rowe, C. 1988, *Plato. Phaedrus*, Oxford.
Rowe, C. 2007, *Plato and the Art of Philosophical Writing*, Cambridge.
Saïd, S. 2000, 'Dio's use of mythology', in Swain, S. (ed.), *Dio Chrysostom: Politics, Letters, and Philosophy*, Oxford: 161–86.

Scodel, R. 1980, *The Trojan Trilogy of Euripides*, Göttingen.
Shey, H. 1976, 'Tyrtaeus and the art of propaganda', *Arethusa* 9: 5–28.
Thompson, W. 1868, *The Phaedrus of Plato*, London.
Worman, N. 2002, *The Cast of Character: Style in Greek Literature*, Austin.
Yunis, H. 2011, *Plato. Phaedrus*, Cambridge.

Part Two

The Second Sophistic

# Homeric Exegesis and Athetesis in Lucian's Versions of the Judgement of Paris

Nicholas Wilshere

Lucian (c. AD 120–190), from Samosata in Roman Syria, is one of the more notable omissions from Philostratus' canon of sophists, although his diverse writings include numerous sophistic declamations. Indeed, the interest in 'princes and tyrants' that Philostratus specifically identifies as a characteristic of the 'second' Sophistic is to the fore both in Lucian's pair of *Phalaris* speeches and in his *Tyrannicide*.[1] But other typically sophistic concerns are found throughout this author's work: we can observe in particular the numerous occasions when he puts speeches in the mouths of mythological characters, not simply as a rhetorical exercise but as a means to serious satirical ends that connect the authority of literary tradition with the more subversive aims of Cynic philosophy.[2]

Throughout Lucian's work we also find a sophistic emphasis on the skills of reading and interpretation that make one truly literate, especially (as I show in this chapter) through polemic concerning the correct interpretation of the Homeric text. Notably, in *Against the Ignorant Book Collector* Lucian writes a sustained attack on a collector of *de luxe* editions who has enough skill to read aloud from them fluently but does not have the requisite level of education to pass muster in the analysis of the texts – something which sets him apart from the educated group of which Lucian considers himself a part.[3]

It is clear from the short piece *Prometheus es* that Lucian took special pride in his invention of a new literary genre through combination of the established forms of dialogue and comedy. Many of Lucian's shorter dialogues take the form of gently humorous conversations between mythological characters which dramatize events 'off-stage' or on the margins of stories that are well known from treatments in earlier authors, in particular Homer.[4] This requires the author to have a thorough understanding of the Homeric characters, but also makes demands of the reader, who must be able to pick up the context and significance of the episodes being dramatized. As Kim has written, 'the pleasure of the dialogues arises from their "filling in" and commenting on Homeric episodes rather than from any attempt at parody or burlesque'.[5]

As it is one of the longest examples of this type, the dialogue *Judgement of the Goddesses* (Θεῶν Κρίσις, *Dearum Iudicium*) provides a fine illustration of the various ways in which Lucian responds to epic material as he combines humour with sophistic self-presentation. In this chapter I demonstrate how Lucian not only entertains his audience through the imaginative, parodic re-presentation of a familiar epic story, but also shows off the thoroughness of his learning through knowing allusions to other episodes in the story of Troy, details from the Homeric text and, in particular, debates about interpretative questions that appear in the Homeric scholia.[6] I also consider briefly how this dialogue connects with two other places where Lucian alludes to the Judgement of Paris, and conclude with a discussion of the ways in which his approach to this story from the world of epic illustrates the different levels of knowledge and engagement that authors of the period anticipated in their audiences.

The text begins with Zeus dispatching Hermes, together with the three goddesses Hera, Athena and Aphrodite, to Gargaron in the foothills of Mount Ida. In a sensible attempt to avoid becoming involved in any acrimony, he says that he has no intention of awarding the golden apple himself, so Paris must make the decision (1–2). Lucian then presents the four gods' conversation on the journey (3–6); when they arrive they locate Paris, to whom Hermes explains the situation (7–8) before they negotiate the contest's ground-rules (9); the goddesses then disrobe (10) and present themselves naked, each trying to persuade Paris by offering their bribes (11–15). The dialogue ends when Paris agrees to award the fateful apple to Aphrodite after extracting a promise from her that he will marry Helen (16).

In its general outlines the dialogue seems to be based on the version of the story told in the *Cypria*:[7]

παραγενομένη δὲ Ἔρις εὐωχουμένων τῶν θεῶν ἐν τοῖς Πηλέως γάμοις νεῖκος περὶ κάλλους ἐνίστησιν Ἀθηνᾷ, Ἥρᾳ καὶ Ἀφροδίτῃ· αἳ πρὸς Ἀλέξανδρον ἐν Ἴδῃ κατὰ Διὸς προσταγὴν ὑφ' Ἑρμοῦ πρὸς τὴν κρίσιν ἄγονται. <αἳ δὲ ἐπαγγέλλονται δῶρα δώσειν Ἀλεξάνδρῳ· Ἥρα μὲν οὖν ἔφη προκριθεῖσα δώσειν βασιλείαν πάντων, Ἀθηνᾶ δὲ πολέμου νίκην, Ἀφροδίτη δὲ γάμον Ἑλένης.> καὶ προκρίνει τὴν Ἀφροδίτην ἐπαρθεὶς τοῖς Ἑλένης γάμοις Ἀλέξανδρος.

As the gods are feasting at the wedding of Peleus, Strife appears and causes a dispute about beauty among Athena, Hera, and Aphrodite. On Zeus' instruction

Hermes conducts them to Alexander on Ida for adjudication. <They promise Alexander gifts: Hera said that if she were preferred she would give him kingship over all, Athena promised victory in war, and Aphrodite union with Helen.> Alexander, excited by the prospect of union with Helen, chooses Aphrodite. (transl. West)

Cypria, Argumentum 1

Lucian's dialogue reproduces this version of events, although he has no parallel to the process of Aphrodite's beautification that appears in a pair of fragments that evidently describe the preparations for the contest.[8] In Lucian's version the focus is much more on the satirical potential of the goddesses' objections to each other's adornments, as part of the short-tempered bickering with which Lucian characterizes them. In any case, there is no need for such adornments since Paris cannot resist the temptation to see the goddesses naked. Their disingenuous questions to Hermes about Paris' marital status (3–4) create a similarly satirical feel.

When Lucian's Aphrodite first speaks, she is responding to Zeus' opening speech, which appointed Paris as judge. She says: 'As far as I am concerned, Zeus, even if you were to appoint Momus himself as our judge, I would go confidently to the exhibition. For what could he find fault with in me?' (2: ἐγὼ μέν, ὦ Ζεῦ, εἰ καὶ τὸν Μῶμον αὐτὸν ἐπιστήσειας ἡμῖν δικαστήν, θαρροῦσα βαδιοῦμαι πρὸς τὴν ἐπίδειξιν· τί γὰρ ἂν καὶ μωμήσαιτό μου;). The most obvious reason for her to mention Momus here is that he is the personification of fault-finding, as her use of the verb μωμήσαιτο emphasizes, so he is the most extreme possible example of a judge who is hard to please.

But the mention of Momus at the opening of the text signals its parodic, satirical nature: Lucian elsewhere uses Momus as shorthand for a certain type of humour, positioning both himself and Nigrinus as 'like Momus'.[9] Lucian's Momus is also an advisor to the gods: at *Zeus the Tragedian* 19, Zeus encourages Momus to advise, as his παρρησία will be beneficial, and he speaks at length in *Parliament of the Gods*. Most significantly, readers who know the full background to the Judgement of Paris will recall that, in one version, Momus had an important role in changing Zeus' plans for reducing the world's population, in such a way as to create the circumstances that allowed the familiar story of Paris and Helen to happen.[10] Here, then, readers with different levels of knowledge can read Aphrodite's words as a simple figure of speech, as a comment particularly appropriate to a divine debate, or as a more subtle allusion to another part of the story.

The fragmentary state of our knowledge about the *Cypria* makes further comparison difficult, although it seems likely that Lucian's dialogue is fundamentally a parody of the *Cypria* version.[11] More promising is a study of the aspects of this text that show intertextual relations with Homer. The *Judgement of the Goddesses* is about something that happened long before the main action of the Homeric epics, so one should not be surprised that there are few obvious direct references to events in Homer. Indeed, the Loeb edition is conspicuously short of footnotes highlighting Homeric references here, compared with most of Lucian's other texts.[12] But this gives a misleading impression; in fact, the allusions are rather harder to find because they require a πεπαιδευμένος' knowledge of Homeric scholarship. To illustrate this, let us turn first to the most likely place to track down such exegetical material.

The Judgement of Paris makes only a brief appearance in Homer, who evidently assumes that his audience already know the story, since he merely alludes to it when explaining the antipathy of Athena and Hera towards Troy:

ὣς ὁ μὲν Ἕκτορα δῖον ἀείκιζεν μενεαίνων
τὸν δ' ἐλεαίρεσκον μάκαρες θεοὶ εἰσορόωντες,
κλέψαι δ' ὀτρύνεσκον ἐΰσκοπον Ἀργεϊφόντην.
25 ἔνθ' ἄλλοις μὲν πᾶσιν ἐήνδανεν, οὐδέ ποθ' Ἥρῃ
οὐδὲ Ποσειδάων' οὐδὲ γλαυκώπιδι κούρῃ,
ἀλλ' ἔχον ὥς σφιν πρῶτον ἀπήχθετο Ἴλιος ἱρὴ
καὶ Πρίαμος καὶ λαὸς Ἀλεξάνδρου ἕνεκ' ἄτης,
ὃς νείκεσσε θεὰς ὅτε οἱ μέσσαυλον ἵκοντο,
30 τὴν δ' ἤνησ' ἥ οἱ πόρε μαχλοσύνην ἀλεγεινήν.

So in his rage did [Achilles] mistreat godlike Hector. But the blessed gods felt pity as they looked on him, and they roused keen-sighted Argeiphontes to steal him away. Then were all the other gods pleased, but never Hera, nor Poseidon, nor the bright-eyed maiden, but they remained just as when sacred Ilios and Priam and his people first became hateful to them, because of the rashness of Alexander, who insulted the goddesses when they came to his farmstead, and favoured her who granted his grievous lust.

Iliad 24.22–30

This was a controversial passage, with debate among ancient scholars concerning the necessity for, and extent of, athetesis.[13] The scholia offer assorted arguments in favour of Aristarchus' view that at least some of the lines should be athetized. For example, evidence is presented to show that Homer cannot have known this story at all:

Σ A *Il.* 24.25–30: τήν τε περὶ τοῦ κάλλους ἔριν οὐκ οἶδεν· πολλαχῇ γὰρ ἂν ἐμνήσθη.

And [Homer] does not know the contest about beauty; for he would have mentioned it in many places.

Σ bT *Il.* 24.23: πῶς δ' ἂν τὰς ναῦς "ἀρχεκάκους" εἶπε καὶ οὐ τὴν κρίσιν;

And how would he call the ships 'the start of trouble' [5.63] and not the judgement?[14]

But the opening of the b-scholia's essay on the Catalogue of Ships provides a glimpse of another view, where the Judgement of Paris is adduced as evidence of Homer's propensity to allude fleetingly to parts of the story lying outside the main narrative – in other words, this scholar viewed the lines in *Il.* 24 as genuinely Homeric.[15]

Since this passage was a site of such controversy, it is unsurprising that Lucian quickly includes a nod to his more learned readers when he begins the dialogue by having Zeus explain that he would be hated by the losers in the competition if he were to judge it himself. He includes a clear reminiscence of the text of Homer, with Zeus employing the verb ἀπεχθάνεσθαι which pointedly recalls ἀπήχθετο in *Il.* 24.27: 'Besides, it is inevitable that if I were to give the beauty-prize to one, I would be completely hated by the majority of you' (ἄλλως τε καὶ ἀνάγκη, μιᾷ τὸ καλλιστεῖον ἀποδόντα πάντως ἀπεχθάνεσθαι ταῖς πλείοσιν). Zeus correctly identifies the nature of the goddesses' reaction, even down to the vocabulary that describes it. This is a first hint both that Lucian is asking his audience to recall the Homeric background to the story, and that he will have in mind specifically this much-debated passage.

This type of allusion is easily missed if we think only in terms of direct quotation. As my earlier mention of the Loeb edition suggested, those modern scholars who have undertaken analyses of Homeric quotations, allusions and reminiscences throughout Lucian found little of interest in this text. In his statistical tables Householder records the number of 'direct quotations' from Homer as zero,[16] while Bouquiaux-Simon identified quotations of the two epithets γλαυκῶπις and βοῶπις (10).[17] Although epithets have their own special entries at the end of her index of Homeric passages, she is still only seeking verbatim direct quotation, or at least very close paraphrase. These two scholars' approaches led to their shared failure to identify Zeus' allusion to Homer through the choice of a differently inflected verb form.

I shall return to these epithets shortly, but before they appear in Lucian's text, Paris decides to undress the goddesses, with an eagerness which recalls not only a detail of the Book 24 passage but also a question of audience-response:

ΠΑΡΙΣ: ἐκεῖνο δὲ πρότερον εἰδέναι βούλομαι, πότερ' ἐξαρκέσει σκοπεῖν αὐτὰς ὡς ἔχουσιν, ἢ καὶ ἀποδῦσαι δεήσει πρὸς τὸ ἀκριβὲς τῆς ἐξετάσεως;

ΕΡΜΗΣ: τοῦτο μὲν σὸν ἂν εἴη τοῦ δικαστοῦ, καὶ πρόσταττε ὅπη καὶ θέλεις.

Π.: ὅπη καὶ θέλω; γυμνὰς ἰδεῖν βούλομαι.

Ε.: ἀπόδυτε, ὦ αὗται· σὺ δ' ἐπισκόπει· ἐγὼ δὲ ἀπεστράφην.

Paris: But first here's something I want to know: will it be sufficient for me to look at them as they are, or will they need to undress for precision of examination?

Hermes: This should be your decision, as you're the judge. Give an order in the manner you wish.

P.: In the manner I wish? I want to see them naked.

H.: Undress, you ladies. Make your inspection, Paris; I have turned away.

Lucian, Judgement of the Goddesses 9

Here Paris is showing that μαχλοσύνη of which he is accused in *Il.* 24.30, and which the scholia gloss as 'madness for women' (γυναικομανία, Σ A *Il.* 24.25–30) and 'things concerning prostitution, hair and beauty' (τὰ πρὸς πορνείαν, τὴν κόμην καὶ τὸ εἶδος, Σ bT *Il.* 24.30*b*). Aristarchus seems to have had particular objection to the usage of this word (Σ A *Il.* 24.30*a*): 'Aristarchus athetizes the line because of the word "lust"' (ἀθετεῖ γὰρ Ἀρίσταρχος διὰ τὴν "μαχλοσύνην" τὸν στίχον).

But Paris is also succumbing to a temptation that the scholia are alert to. They say that when Hera is preparing for the *Dios apatē*, Homer very properly avoids any hint of nudity:

καίτοι δὲ τῶν περὶ ταῦτα δεινῶν γυμνὰς γραφόντων ἢ πλασσόντων τὰς γυναῖκας καὶ πρὸς ἀπάτην, ὁ ποιητὴς παραλιπὼν γυμνουμένην αὐτὴν δεῖξαι, ἵνα μὴ εἰς αἰσχρὰν ἐνέργειαν τὴν τῶν ἀκροωμένων διάνοιαν προκαλέσηται, κοσμηθεῖσαν ἐνεφάνισε, καὶ λόγοις πλειόνων χρωμάτων αὐτὴν διετύπωσε.

Although those who are skilled in these things draw or sculpt women naked so as to beguile, the poet, forbearing to show [Hera] naked, lest he prompt the audience's thoughts into shameful activity, has shown her adorned, and with words has fashioned her [to be] of many colours.

Scholia bT Iliad 14.187

Without the restraining hand of such a wise poet, Paris' thoughts are indeed prompting themselves into 'shameful activity' when confronted by the temptation of seeing three naked goddesses.

However, when Sistakou examines this passage in the context of erotic epigrams on the Judgement of Paris she concludes that Lucian's version is actually quite restrained: 'Lucian in his parodic *The Judgment of the Goddesses* vulgarizes the Paris' episode, mainly by insisting on the nakedness of the three candidates, ... but is never straightforwardly obscene.'[18] In particular it does not contain anything like the detailed description of buttocks that Sistakou notes in an epigram of Rufinus:

πυγὰς αὐτὸς ἔκρινα τριῶν· εἵλοντο γὰρ αὐταὶ
  δείξασαι γυμνὴν ἀστεροπὴν μελέων.
καί ῥ' ἡ μὲν τροχαλοῖς σφραγιζομένη γελασίνοις
  λευκῇ ἀπὸ γλουτῶν ἤνθεεν εὐαφίῃ
τῆς δὲ διαιρομένης φοινίσσετο χιονέη σὰρξ
  πορφυρέοιο ῥόδου μᾶλλον ἐρυθροτέρη
ἡ δὲ γαληνιόωσα χαράσσετο κύματι κωφῷ,
  αὐτομάτη τρυφερῷ χρωτὶ σαλευομένη.
εἰ ταύτας ὁ κριτὴς ὁ θεῶν ἐθεήσατο πυγάς,
  οὐκέτ' ἂν οὐδ' ἐσιδεῖν ἤθελε τὰς προτέρας.

I judged the buttocks of three; they themselves chose me, showing me the naked lightning of their limbs. The first marked with round dimples, were white and soft to touch. The flesh of the second, when stretched apart, from snow-white shaded into red – a purple red brighter than the colour of the crimson rose. The third, calm and tranquil, was furrowed by the soundless wave of the delicate skin, as it wavered by itself. If Paris who judged the goddesses had seen such buttocks, he would not have wished to look again on the former ones.

Anthologia Palatina 5.35, trans. Paton, rev. Sistakou

It is significant that by the time of both these later authors, the idea that the beauty contest took place in the nude was evidently well-established, both in literature and art.[19] This might well prompt a reader of Homer to reinterpret the very brevity of Homer's allusion to the Judgement as a further attempt to restrain his own audience's erotic imagination. In Lucian, Paris displays μαχλοσύνη – which Aristarchus felt constituted an argument against the Homeric lines – while Hermes' reaction shows the god observing exactly the kind of propriety that the text of Homer models.

As the goddesses are in the process of undressing for inspection by Paris, the two epithets appear. Aphrodite says:[20]

καλῶς, ὦ Πάρι· καὶ πρώτη γε ἀποδύσομαι, ὅπως μάθῃς ὅτι μὴ μόνας ἔχω <u>τὰς ὠλένας λευκὰς</u> μηδὲ τῷ <u>βοῶπις</u> εἶναι μέγα φρονῶ, ἐπ' ἴσης δέ εἰμι πᾶσα καὶ ὁμοίως καλή.

Very well, Paris. I'll undress first, so you can learn that it's not just <u>white arms</u> that I have, and that I'm not just proud of being <u>'ox-eyed'</u>, but I'm totally and completely beautiful all over.

Lucian, Judgement of the Goddesses 10

Aphrodite teases Hera by suggesting that the Homeric epithets 'white-armed' and 'ox-eyed' are a kind of damning with faint praise by Homer, who draws attention to them because they are the only parts of Hera that are attractive, whereas Aphrodite is beautiful all over. She then goes on to suggest that Athena's famously γλαυκός eyes are terrifying: as I show below, it is clear from elsewhere in Lucian that by his time the word had acquired negative connotations. She says: 'Or are you afraid that the <u>brightness of your eyes</u> might cause you to be criticised, if it's seen without the terrifying object [i.e. your helmet]?' (ἢ δέδιας μὴ σοι ἐλέγχηται <u>τὸ γλαυκὸν τῶν ὀμμάτων</u> ἄνευ τοῦ φοβεροῦ βλεπόμενον;).

In two of these three examples Aphrodite does not quote the Homeric epithet directly, but stays close enough to the Homeric vocabulary that it is easy for even a fairly inexperienced reader of Homer to see how Homer is being used. Similarly, when Momus calls Anubis 'dog-face' (κυνοπρόσωπε) at *Parliament of the Gods* 10, this is a form of abuse familiar from Homer although the precise phrasing (κυνῶπις, *Il.* 1.159, 3.180, 18.396 etc.) is again varied.[21]

But once more there is a deeper significance, since Aphrodite is weaponizing this vocabulary in a fashion that seems inspired by Achilles' allegedly mocking use of an epithet. When Achilles responds to Ajax and the embassy from Agamemnon, the scholia raise and answer an interpretative question: why does Achilles use an epithet ('godlike Hector', Ἕκτορα δῖον) that seems to express approval of his enemy Hector? The answer is that this is part of the characterization of Achilles, who is deliberately using the word, because he wants to annoy his audience.[22] Lucian's reasonably obvious reminiscence on the verbal level therefore signals a further awareness of the way that such details were interpreted, which his more learned readers can observe with satisfaction.

This conversation is already showing Lucianic characters as unmistakably Homeric, with the jealous, suspicious immortals acting just as one would expect from their appearances together in Homer. Indeed, it seems from this text that Lucian would agree with Reinhardt's argument that there are allusions to the origins of their enmity in the less-than-cordial meeting of the three goddesses at *Il.* 21.415–34, and similarly the passage (5.422–5) in which Athena (in cahoots with Hera) makes fun of Aphrodite's wound:[23]

> ἦ μάλα δή τινα Κύπρις Ἀχαιϊάδων ἀνιεῖσα
> Τρωσὶν ἅμα σπέσθαι, τοὺς νῦν ἔκπαγλα φίλησε,
> τῶν τινα καρρέζουσα Ἀχαιϊάδων ἐϋπέπλων
> 425 πρὸς χρυσῇ περόνῃ καταμύξατο χεῖρα ἀραιήν.

Yes, Cypris has definitely been urging one of the Achaean women to follow after the Trojans, whom she loves exceedingly; as she was stroking one of these fair-dressed Achaean women she has scratched her slender hand on a golden brooch.

Iliad 5.422–5

In Lucian this mutual suspicion has already been felt when Athena objects to Hermes' private discussion with Aphrodite as they are travelling from Olympus:

> ΑΘΗΝΑ: παραπρεσβεύεις, ὦ οὗτος, ἰδίᾳ πάλαι ταύτῃ κοινολογούμενος.
>
> ΕΡΜΗΣ: οὐδέν, ὦ Ἀθηνᾶ, δεινὸν οὐδὲ καθ' ὑμῶν, ἀλλ' ἤρετό με εἰ ἄγαμος ὁ Πάρις ἐστίν.

Athena: Hey, you! You're being a biased negotiator, talking with her for a long while in private.

Hermes: It's nothing to get indignant at, Athena, nothing against you two. She was asking me if Paris is unmarried.

Lucian, *Judgement of the Goddesses* 4

Lucian's audience knows perfectly well that Aphrodite's questions have an ulterior motive, as will become explicit at the end of the dialogue; here Hermes is being either diplomatic or naive.[24] The *Homeric Hymn to Apollo* (97–106) shows that such underhand tactics are a real concern, since Hera is there tricked by Iris through secret bribery of Eileithyia.

Earlier, at the first opportunity (2), Hera had teased Aphrodite for having been discovered in a compromising position with Ares, alluding to *Od.* 8.267–369 – 'We're not afraid either, Aphrodite, not even if the judgement is turned over to your friend Ares' (οὐδ' ἡμεῖς, ὦ Ἀφροδίτη, δέδιμεν, οὐδ' ἂν ὁ Ἄρης ὁ σὸς ἐπιτραπῇ τὴν δίαιταν)[25] – and again with her visits to Anchises at *Il.* 2.819–21 and in the *Homeric Hymn to Aphrodite*:

ΗΡΑ: ὥρα σοι, ὦ Ἀφροδίτη, προϊέναι καὶ ἡγεῖσθαι ἡμῖν τῆς ὁδοῦ· σὺ γὰρ ὡς τὸ εἰκὸς ἔμπειρος εἶ τοῦ χωρίου πολλάκις, ὡς λόγος, κατελθοῦσα πρὸς Ἀγχίσην.

ΑΦΡΟΔΙΤΗ: οὐ σφόδρα, ὦ Ἥρα, τούτοις ἄχθομαι τοῖς σκώμμασιν.

Hera: You ought to go in front and lead the way for us, Aphrodite; you're probably familiar with the region, since (as the story goes) you often used to come down to visit Anchises.

Aphrodite: I'm not particularly vexed by these jibes, Hera.

Lucian, Judgement of the Goddesses 5

Aphrodite's reply clearly signals the humour (σκώμματα being 'jokes, jests'), but what is happening here is more than a simple joke. The characters amusingly demonstrate the least appetising features of Homer's immortals (so that this dialogue is to some extent indebted to those thinkers, going back at least to Xenophanes,[26] who criticized Homer for the gods' anthropomorphic immorality); and this humour is clear without the reader's recognition of verbatim quotations or specific allusions. As Householder acknowledged, one of the reasons why Lucian consistently alludes to Homer throughout his *oeuvre* – in particular, to well-known passages – is that Homer, alongside Euripides, is so widely familiar to his readership: 'anyone with any education at all had read Homer'.[27] So the reader who knows in a very general way that these goddesses are always sniping at each other in Homer will see a similarity in their characters here. Furthermore, the goddesses' use of epithets as part of their squabble shows that Lucian expects the reader to pick up on the vocabulary of their standard descriptions in Homer, first by a mild paraphrase (ἔχω τὰς ὠλένας λευκάς, rather than e.g. λευκώλενός εἰμι), and then by literal quotation (βοῶπις).

The connection with Achilles' use of epithets is a more subtle one, but contributes an extra level of satisfaction for the reader who identifies it. Hera also deploys a weaponised 'Alexandrian footnote' ('as the story goes', ὡς λόγος), which alludes in particular to the main part of the *Homeric Hymn to Aphrodite*. The attempt to shame Aphrodite proves the truth of Aphrodite's own prediction in the *Hymn* (247–55), where she says to Anchises that their relationship will cause her to suffer 'great shame among the immortal gods' (μέγ' ὄνειδος ἐν ἀθανάτοισι θεοῖσιν, 247).[28] Hera's πολλάκις could either be a malicious exaggeration, or may mean 'many times [in literature]', since the hymn actually describes only a one-night (or rather one-afternoon) stand.[29]

The goddesses' argument continues with an allusion to the girdle used by Hera in the *Iliad*'s *Dios apatē* episode:[30]

ΑΘΗΝΑ: μὴ πρότερον ἀποδύσῃς αὐτήν, ὦ Πάρι, πρὶν ἂν τὸν κεστὸν ἀπόθηται – φαρμακὶς γάρ ἐστιν – μή σε καταγοητεύσῃ δι' αὐτοῦ. καίτοι γε ἐχρῆν μηδὲ οὕτω κεκαλλωπισμένην παρεῖναι μηδὲ τοσαῦτα ἐντετριμμένην χρώματα καθάπερ ὡς ἀληθῶς ἑταίραν τινά, ἀλλὰ γυμνὸν τὸ κάλλος ἐπιδεικνύειν.

ΠΑΡΙΣ: εὖ λέγουσι τὸ περὶ τοῦ κεστοῦ, καὶ ἀπόθου.

ΑΦΡΟΔΙΤΗ: τί οὖν οὐχὶ καὶ σύ, ὦ Ἀθηνᾶ, τὴν κόρυν ἀφελοῦσα ψιλὴν τὴν κεγαλὴν ἐπιδεικνύεις, ἀλλ' ἐπισείεις τὸν λόφον καὶ τὸν δικαστὴν φοβεῖς; ἢ δέδιας μή σοι ἐλέγχηται τὸ γλαυκὸν τῶν ὀμμάτων ἄνευ τοῦ φοβεροῦ βλεπόμενον;

ΑΘ.: ἰδού σοι ἡ κόρυς αὕτη ἀφῄρηται.

ΑΦ.: ἰδοὺ καί σοι ὁ κεστός.

Athena: Don't let [Aphrodite] undress, Paris, until she takes off the girdle – because she's an enchantress and otherwise she might cast a spell on you with it.[31] And indeed she shouldn't come before you beautified like that and daubed with all those colours, just as if she were really a courtesan. But she should show her beauty without dressing it up.

Paris: They've got a good point about the girdle. Take it off.

Aphrodite: So why don't you take off your helmet, Athena, and show your head bare, rather than shaking your plume and terrifying the judge? Or are you afraid that the brightness of your eyes might cause you to be criticised, if it's seen without the terrifying object?

Ath.: Look, there's the helmet for you. I've taken it off.

Aph.: And look, there's the girdle for you.

Lucian, *Judgement of the Goddesses* 10

The alert reader will recall that the Homeric passage implicates not just Hera (who uses the girdle) but Aphrodite (who provides it for her), so that Athena is cleverly using a single passage to attack both of her rivals at once.

Athena claims that Hera is wearing make-up, which is probably a lie, since the reply of Paris ignores it while acknowledging that the girdle is a valid point of contention; more subtly, there is no indication that Aphrodite uses any make-up in the *Cypria* fragments, or in *Homeric Hymn* 6 (in which she is adorned by the Horai, and where *Il.* 14.187 is repeated verbatim). However, Lucian does use the word χρώματα, emphasizing the importance of colour in these beautification-scenes – as highlighted in the scholium on *Il.* 14.187 discussed above. So Athena may be accidentally-on-purpose forgetting that the colours in these Homeric passages are flowers and clothes, rather than the make-up implied by ἐντετριμμένην, a word used specifically for cosmetics.[32]

Aphrodite herself then responds by attacking Athena for wearing her helmet and thereby frightening Paris; she tells her to remove it. Here the whole situation, including the detail that it is specifically the helmet's *plume* that is frightening, is a strong evocation of the famous scene in which Hector's helmet, with its λόφος, frightens the baby Astyanax.[33] This makes Aphrodite's objection at once a comic misappropriation of the text of Homer and a poignant anticipation of the death of Hector which will result from Paris' imminent decision – just the kind of narrative foreshadowing picked up in the final example in Σ b *Il.* 2.494 cited above.

Next Aphrodite alleges that the reason for Athena wishing to conceal her eyes with the helmet, even though it is frightening, is that they are even more terrifying. The word she uses is γλαυκός, another allusion to an epithet – γλαυκῶπις – which appears in the phrase γλαυκώπιδι κούρῃ at *Il.* 24.26, one of Aristarchus' athetized lines. She is deliberately understanding the word in a negative way: 'The word with which Homer describes the eyes of Athena had an uncomplimentary sense in Lucian's time,' writes Harmon.[34] Lucian and Aphrodite are exploiting this semantic uncertainty, raised by the gloss at Σ D *Il.* 1.206: 'beautiful, or else with eyes that are gleaming and striking/terrifying' (καλή, ἢ γλαυκοὺς καὶ καταπληκτικοὺς τοὺς ὦπας ἔχουσα). A second scholium makes this plainer (Σ D *Il.* 2.166): 'gleaming-eyed, beautiful, terrifying, or astonishing to see' (γλαυκόφθαλμος, καλή, φοβερά, ἢ καταπληκτικὴ τὴν πρόσοψιν).[35]

There is a further irony in Lucian's focus on this epithet in particular, since Σ T *Il.* 24.23 uses Homer's descriptions of the goddesses' eyes as a (not entirely convincing) way of arguing that they could not have quarrelled:

πῶς δὲ οὐκ ἄτοπον Ἀθηνᾶν, περὶ ἧς φησι "δεινὼ δὲ οἱ ὄσσε φάανθεν", ἐρίζειν Ἀφροδίτῃ, περὶ ἧς φησι "καὶ ὄμματα μαρμαίροντα", ὡς εἰ καὶ Ἡρακλῆς ἀγωνίζοιτο πρὸς Ἄδωνιν;

And how is it not absurd that Athena, about whom he says 'terrible did her eyes shine' [1.200], should quarrel with Aphrodite, about whom he says 'and her gleaming eyes' [3.397], as if Heracles were to compete with Adonis?

The goddesses' combative use of epithets is thrown into relief by the conspicuous lack of guile or malicious intent when, in the presence of Hermes, Paris (presumably unconsciously) alludes to Hermes' own regular epithet ἀργειφόντης 'the slayer of Argus', which, like γλαυκῶπις, appears in the group of athetized lines (*Il.* 24.24). Paris says: 'I am sad that I can't look at [the goddesses' beauty] with my whole body, as Argus did' (8: ἄχθομαι, ὅτι μὴ καὶ αὐτὸς ὥσπερ ὁ Ἄργος ὅλῳ βλέπειν δύναμαι τῷ σώματι). In a significant contrast to the goddesses, Paris fails to use this epithet's potential for attacks on Hera or Hermes, both of which would be possible since Hermes killed Argus at Zeus' behest in order to frustrate Hera's plans.[36] But of course this does not necessarily imply any lack of education or knowledge about the story; rather, being (at this point at least) an unbiased judge and a mere terrified mortal, Paris has no reason to attack them.

But these examples nonetheless suggest Paris' rustic simplicity, as does his wide-eyed incredulity at the very concept of stealing someone else's wife:

ΑΦΡΟΔΙΤΗ: εἰ δὴ θέλοις, ἐγώ σοι καταπράξομαι τὸν γάμον.

ΠΑΡΙΣ: πῶς φής; τὸν τῆς γεγαμημένης;

Α.: νέος εἶ σὺ καὶ ἀγροῖκος, ἐγὼ δὲ οἶδα ὡς χρὴ τὰ τοιαῦτα δρᾶν.

Aphrodite: If you'd like I shall arrange the marriage for you.

Paris: What do you mean? Marriage with a married woman?

A.: You're young and rustic, but I know how this sort of thing ought to be done.

Lucian, *Judgement of the Goddesses* 14

This leads on to another scholarly debate, since Paris' rusticity is yet another issue raised in connection with the Book 24 passage. Lucian not only makes Paris a simple, uneducated rustic, but emphasizes this repeatedly, with references in the following places:

1: Zeus says Paris is 'royal' (βασιλικός) and related to Ganymede, but otherwise 'a simple mountain-dweller' (ἀφελὴς καὶ ὄρειος).
3: Hermes says Paris has a wife who is 'a countrywoman and terribly mountainy' (ἀγροῖκος . . . καὶ δεινῶς ὄρειος).
4: He is referred to as 'herdsman' βουκόλος by Athena (and is addressed thus by Hermes in 7).
5: Paris first appears by a cave, running out from rocks, holding a crook, chasing his herd.[37]
7–8: Paris protests that he can judge between she-goats but not 'women who aren't the sort to roam mountains, being so beautiful'; he says he is 'a countryman' (ἀγροῖκος) and 'herdsman' (βουκόλος), and that one of the 'townfolk' (ἀστικοί) would judge better.
13: Aphrodite says that Paris should not be satisfied with living in the countryside with a wife who is 'some rustic peasant woman' (ἀγροῖκόν τινα καὶ χωρῖτιν).
14: Aphrodite too calls him 'countryman' (ἀγροῖκος).

Among the various arguments in support of Aristarchus' athetesis of the lines referring to Judgement of Paris is one based on an inconsistency between this passage and the earlier words of Paris' older brother Hector (3.39–57) which appear to indicate that Paris was brought up as an effete, lyre-playing ἀστικός rather than a rugged countryman:

> καὶ ἡ μέσαυλος σημαίνουσα τὴν ἐν ὄρει οἴκησιν, Ὁμήρου παραδεδωκότος ἐν ἄστει τεθράφθαι τὸν Ἀλέξανδρον καὶ μουσικὴν πεπαιδεῦσθαι· "οὐκ ἄν τοι χραίσμῃ κίθαρις τά τε δῶρ' Ἀφροδίτης, ἥ τε κόμη τό τε εἶδος", ἅ ἐστιν οὐδαμῶς ἀγροίκῳ ἁρμόζοντα.
>
> And μέσαυλος ('inner courtyard' / 'farmstead' [24.29]) means his residence on the mountain, although Homer has told us that Alexander was brought up in the city and learned μουσική: 'Your lyre-playing and the gifts of Aphrodite will be of no help to you, nor your hairdo and your appearance' [3.54–5], things which are not at all in harmony with being a rustic.
>
> Scholia bT *Iliad* 24.23–30

This helps to explain why Lucian makes Hermes allude to Ganymede (already named by Zeus in the opening speech) as a pipe-player, immediately before addressing Paris, who has no musical instrument:

> καὶ ὁπότε γε ἤδη ἐν τῷ ἀετῷ ἦν, συμπαριπτάμην αὐτῷ καὶ συνεκούφιζον τὸν καλόν, καὶ εἴ γε μέμνημαι, ἀπὸ ταυτησὶ τῆς πέτρας αὐτὸν ἀνήρπασεν. <u>ὁ μὲν γὰρ ἔτυχε τότε συρίζων πρὸς τὸ ποίμνιον</u>, καταπτάμενος δὲ ὄπισθεν αὐτοῦ ὁ Ζεὺς κούφως μάλα τοῖς ὄνυξι περιβαλὼν καὶ τῷ στόματι τὴν ἐπὶ τῇ κεφαλῇ τιάραν ἔχων ἀνέφερε τὸν παῖδα τεταραγμένον καὶ τῷ τραχήλῳ ἀπεστραμμένῳ εἰς αὐτὸν ἀποβλέποντα. <u>τότε οὖν ἐγὼ τὴν σύριγγα λαβών</u>, ἀποβεβλήκει γὰρ αὐτὴν ὑπὸ τοῦ δέους – ἀλλὰ γὰρ ὁ διαιτητὴς οὑτοσὶ πλησίον, ὥστε προσείπωμεν αὐτόν. χαῖρε, ὦ βουκόλε.
>
> And in fact when [Zeus] was in the eagle I flew with him, by his side, and helped lift the handsome chap. And if my memory serves, it was from this rock here that Zeus took him up. <u>For at that moment he happened to be piping to his herd</u>, and Zeus, flying down behind him, very lightly enfolded him with his talons, held in his beak the cap on the boy's head, and carried him upwards, agitated and looking at him with neck turned back. <u>So then I took the panpipe</u>, for he had dropped it because of his fear – but here's your umpire close by, so we can speak to him. Hello, herdsman![38]
>
> Lucian, *Judgement of the Goddesses* 6

Here Paris is not playing the allegedly urban and anti-heroic lyre – but neither is he playing the bucolic pipe.[39] Lucian therefore seems not to be taking a position on whether Paris is educated in μουσική, but is quietly showing his awareness of the debate through the contrast with Ganymede. Similarly, when Hermes says

(3) that Paris pays little attention to his countrywoman-wife (unnamed but presumably Oenone), the reader might wonder whether this hints that he is not entirely at home in the countryside.

An unequivocal allusion to Homeric exegesis comes when Lucian answers the question 'Can Homeric heroes read?'[40] This issue is debated in the scholia, where different answers are given in relation to the story of Bellerophon. In this episode, with the phrase 'baneful signs' (σήματα λυγρά), Homer has appeared to imply that a message was communicated in writing. The scholia offer numerous explanations of the phrase, suggesting that the 'signs' are letters of the alphabet (Σ b *Il.* 6.168–9), or not writing at all but a kind of wordless comic-strip (Σ A *Il.* 6.169), or, more vaguely, 'certain signs and symbols' (σημεῖα τινὰ καὶ συμβόλαια, Σ D *Il.* 6.169) since 'the heroes do not know letters' (τοὺς γὰρ ἥρωας μὴ ἐπίστασθαι γράμματα). By contrast with the D-scholia's straightforward claim, we read in the T-scholia a strong assertion that the otherwise knowledgeable Homeric heroes must be able to read, so the 'signs' must be some form of writing:

> ἄτοπον γὰρ τοὺς πᾶσαν τέχνην εὑρόντας οὐκ εἰδέναι γράμματα. τινὲς δὲ ὡς παρ' Αἰγυπτίοις ἱερὰ ζῴδια, δι' ὧν δηλοῦται τὰ πράγματα.
>
> For it is absurd if those who discovered every skill do not know letters. But some say that they are like the holy images of the Egyptians, through which things are made known.
>
> Scholium T *Iliad* 6.168

Lucian's answer comes when he makes Hermes ask Paris to read the writing on the golden apple:

> ΕΡΜΗΣ: τοῦ δὲ ἀγῶνος τὸ ἆθλον εἴσῃ ἀναγνοὺς τὸ μῆλον.
> ΠΑΡΙΣ: φέρ' ἴδω τί καὶ βούλεται. "ἡ καλή," φησίν, "λαβέτω."
>
> Hermes: You'll know the prize of the contest if you read the apple.
> Paris: Come, let me see what meaning it has. 'Let the beautiful one take me', it says.
>
> Lucian, *Judgement of the Goddesses* 7

There is no need for Hermes to do this: in his opening speech, Zeus has already explained to Hermes what the contest is about, so this information could have been passed on orally together with the other information that he gives to Paris. Instead, Hermes carefully engineers a situation where Paris successfully reads the writing, thereby solving the problem we find raised in the scholia.[41] Even Paris, whose uneducated rusticity Lucian has been at such pains to emphasize, knows how to read – *a fortiori*, the other Homeric heroes must also have this skill.

But the words that he reads from the apple are not quite what we are most familiar with in modern tellings of the story. It reads not 'For the fairest', or 'Let the fairest take me', but 'Let the fair one take me' (ἡ καλὴ λαβέτω). The superlative would seem to make better sense, since the winner of the contest will necessarily have to be the most beautiful of the three goddesses. They are each καλή, so the question to be decided is about their degree of κάλλος.

A reason for this apparent oddity can again be found in ancient discussions of Homer, this time concerning a problem relating to superlatives and how to interpret them. The potential for confusion is well illustrated by a nineteenth-century joke:

> 'My dearest Maria,' wrote a recently-married husband to his wife. She wrote back, 'Dearest, let me correct either your grammar or your morals. You address me, "My dearest Maria." Am I to suppose you have other dear Marias?'[42]

Superlatives can be used in either an absolute, 'elative' sense or a relative, true 'superlative', sense; Maria's husband used 'dearest' as an elative ('very dear') in a context where Maria can interpret it as a superlative ('most dear [of all]'), implying favourable comparison with other Marias.

A number of scholia show ancient readers wrestling with just this problem, which occurs when Homer appears to contradict himself by calling multiple characters 'the most beautiful'.[43] But the scholia suggest that careful reading can solve the problem:

> Σ A *Il.* 13.365*a*: ὅτι νῦν μὲν τὴν Κασσάνδραν "εἶδος ἀρίστην", ἐν ἄλλοις δὲ τὴν Λαοδίκην, καὶ οὐ μάχεται.
>
> Here [Homer calls] Cassandra 'best / very good in appearance', but in other places [he says the same about] Laodice [*Il.* 6.252], and does not contradict himself.
>
> Σ bT *Il.* 13.365*b*: αὕτη τῶν ἀγάμων ἀρίστη, τῶν δὲ γαμηθεισῶν Λαοδίκη.
>
> She is the best of the unmarried women, but Laodice [is best] of the married ones.[44]

One further example has special relevance to the *Judgement of the Goddesses*, since it both involves a form of the word καλός and is important in another of Lucian's mini-dialogues. In the *Iliad* Homer refers to Nireus as κάλλιστος:

> Νιρεύς, ὃς κάλλιστος ἀνὴρ ὑπὸ Ἴλιον ἦλθε
> τῶν ἄλλων Δαναῶν μετ' ἀμύμονα Πηλεΐωνα

675 ἀλλ' ἀλαπαδνὸς ἔην, παῦρος δέ οἱ εἵπετο λαός

Nireus, the most beautiful man who came beneath Troy, of all the other Danaans after the unimpeachable son of Peleus. But he was feeble, and only a few troops followed him.

Iliad 2.673–5

The addition of line 674 narrows down the interpretation: he is only κάλλιστος i) of all the Danaans, ii) except for Achilles. A scholium reports Zenodotus' concerns about this description:

ἐκ τῶν τριῶν τοὺς δύο ἠθέτηκε Ζηνόδοτος, τὸν δὲ μέσον οὐδὲ ἔγραφεν, τοῦ Ὁμήρου φιλοτιμουμένου ἐν πᾶσι τὸν Ἀχιλλέα προτεροῦντα στῆσαι.

Of the three lines Zenodotus athetised two [673, 675], and did not write the middle line [674], since Homer aspires to set up Achilles as superior in all respects.

Scholium A *Iliad* 2.673–5

Lucian alludes to these lines in a gruesome parody of the Judgement of Paris (*Dialogues of the Dead* 30 Macl. = 25 vulg.), when the dead Nireus and Thersites appear together along with Menippus, whom they have called in as judge for a beauty contest, on the face of it a ludicrous event since Homer calls Nireus κάλλιστος and Thersites 'very ugly' (*Il.* 2.216: αἴσχιστος).[45] It is therefore a surprise that the result is a draw; but, in Menippus' words, 'Neither you [sc. Nireus] nor the other is handsome; for in Hades there is equality of honour and everyone is alike' (οὔτε σὺ οὔτε ἄλλος εὔμορφος· ἰσοτιμία γὰρ ἐν Ἅδου καὶ ὅμοιοι ἅπαντες).

Thersites has only one speech of any substance, in which he expresses his delight that Menippus cannot immediately tell who is who. In particular, he makes a snide suggestion that 'that blind Homer' (Ὅμηρος ἐκεῖνος ὁ τυφλός) was in no position to make a pronouncement on Nireus' handsomeness, which explains why it is not so outstanding as Homer had suggested.

Nireus confidently cites his own description in Homer, quoting line 673 verbatim:

ΘΕΡΣΙΤΗΣ: ὅρα δὲ σύ, ὦ Μένιππε, ὅντινα καὶ εὐμορφότερον ἡγῇ.

ΝΙΡΕΥΣ: ἐμέ γε τὸν Ἀγλαΐας καὶ Χάροπος, "ὃς κάλλιστος ἀνὴρ ὑπὸ Ἴλιον ἦλθον".

Thersites: But you, Menippus, have a look to see which you consider the more handsome.

Nireus: Me, the son of Charops and Aglaea, 'the most beautiful man who came beneath Troy'!

Menippus ignores this, pointing out that they have not come ὑπὸ Ἴλιον now; all that matters is whether Nireus is the handsomest man who has come beneath the earth (ὑπὸ γῆν). In fact, by the criteria of the fleshless Underworld, Thersites is preferable because Nireus' skull is fragile and not manly. This line of argument draws on another part of the Homeric description, with Menippus using the same word to describe the skull as Homer uses to describe Nireus (ἀλαπαδνός, 675).

Lucian's Nireus is effectively entering a debate with Zenodotus here – but hardly as an impartial observer. He approves of 673, which credits him with being κάλλιστος, but would excise 675, which makes him ἀλαπαδνός. He would be happy to follow Zenodotus in removing completely line 674, which puts him as second after Achilles. He therefore partly agrees and partly disagrees with Zenodotus.

That other dialogue clearly shows Lucian's awareness of difficulties about Homer's beauty-related superlatives. The lack of a superlative on the golden apple should therefore be read as an allusion to this, an interpretation supported by one further piece of evidence.

At the beginning of the text, Zeus gives instructions to Hermes, including a speech that he is to report verbatim, Homeric-fashion. But Hermes makes some slight changes when he actually gives Paris these instructions (7); the parts of Zeus' speech that Hermes actually delivers are underlined:

Ἑρμῆ, λαβὼν τουτὶ τὸ μῆλον ἄπιθι εἰς τὴν Φρυγίαν παρὰ τὸν Πριάμου παῖδα τὸν βουκόλον – νέμει δὲ τῆς Ἴδης ἐν τῷ Γαργάρῳ – καὶ λέγε πρὸς αὐτόν, ὅτι "σέ, ὦ Πάρι, κελεύει ὁ Ζεύς, ἐπειδὴ καλός τε αὐτὸς εἶ καὶ σοφὸς τὰ ἐρωτικά, δικάσαι ταῖς θεαῖς, ἥτις αὐτῶν ἡ **καλλίστη** ἐστίν· τοῦ δὲ ἀγῶνος τὸ ἆθλον ἡ νικῶσα λαβέτω τὸ μῆλον."

Hermes, take this apple, go off to Phrygia, to Priam's son the herdsman – he's using the pasture on Gargaron in the foothills of Ida – and say to him, 'Zeus orders you, Paris, since you are beautiful yourself and wise in matters of love, to judge for the goddesses which of them is the most beautiful. And as the prize for the contest, let the winner take the apple.'

ΕΡΜΗΣ: κελεύει δέ σε δικαστὴν γενέσθαι τοῦ κάλλους αὐτῶν· "ἐπεὶ γάρ," φησι, "καλός τε αὐτὸς εἶ καὶ σοφὸς τὰ ἐρωτικά, σοι τὴν γνῶσιν ἐπιτρέπω." τοῦ δὲ ἀγῶνος τὸ ἆθλον εἴσῃ ἀναγνοὺς τὸ μῆλον.

ΠΑΡΙΣ: φέρ' ἴδω τί καὶ βούλεται. "ἡ **καλή**," φησίν, "λαβέτω."

Hermes: [Zeus] orders you to be the judge of their beauty; he says 'since you are beautiful yourself and wise in matters of love, I entrust the decision to you.' You'll know the prize of the contest if you read the apple.

Paris: Come, let me see what meaning it has. 'Let the beautiful one take me,' it says.

As we have already seen, Lucian has made Paris read the apple to demonstrate that Homeric heroes can read. But what is Hermes' motivation for not passing on Zeus' words? If he is aware of the Homeric problems about superlative beauty, just as the goddesses are aware of their Homeric epithets,[46] Hermes is staying scrupulously impartial and encouraging Paris to make the interpretation himself, just as he will leave to him the decision about nudity.[47]

But there is a surprise, since Paris actually reads out the positive form of the adjective: ἡ καλὴ λαβέτω. Even as Lucian demonstrates Paris' literacy, he causes the reader to wonder about the level of this literacy; if he has bungled the reading of a fairly straightforward text, Paris is not such a good reader after all. Indeed, he is an even worse reader than the Ignorant Book Collector, who could at least read fluently, despite his lack of deeper knowledge. Here, then, Lucian is again hedging his bets: this Homeric hero *can* read, but not especially well.[48]

A reader familiar with Lucian's other dialogues will recall that exactly the same wording, with the positive form of the adjective, is used in his other reference to the apple (*Dialogues of the Sea-gods* 7.1 Macl. = 5.1 vulg.), when Panope says: 'Eris threw into the feast an all-beautiful apple, completely golden, Galene. On it was written "Let the beautiful one take me".' (ἡ Ἔρις δὲ . . . ἐνέβαλεν ἐς τὸ συμπόσιον μῆλόν τι πάγκαλον, χρυσοῦν ὅλον, ὦ Γαλήνη· ἐπεγέγραπτο δὲ "ἡ καλὴ λαβέτω"). Bartley's interpretation here is that the wording implies that Aphrodite – the very personification of 'beauty' if anyone is – will inevitably win the contest.[49] If this is the case, then Paris' poor reading could even be something of a Freudian slip, as he has unconsciously awarded the apple to Aphrodite already. In just the same way Panope (who may have only heard, not read, the text) has prejudged the judgement: 'No one other than Aphrodite will win, if she competes' (οὐκ ἄλλη κρατήσει τῆς Ἀφροδίτης ἀγωνιζομένης). By contrast, Zeus is able to preserve an Olympian detachment, having recused himself from the decision, and this allows him to read the apple without such bias.[50]

I have argued that in more than ten places the text of Lucian's dialogue prompts its readers to delve into the traditions of Greek poetry and, in particular, the tradition of Homeric exegesis in order to gain access to a fuller, richer reading experience. This experience ranges from a simple awareness of the outlines of the story being parodied, through the humorous (mis)use of epic-style vocabulary and allusions to other Homeric episodes, to full-blown and longstanding academic debate about controversial interpretative issues. The text's apparent flippancy conceals its cunning deployment of serious ideas about what it means to be a truly literate reader.

In his preface to *True Histories*, Lucian initiates the reader into his approach to parody and allusion in that work, saying that it will be amenable to readers for several reasons, but for one in particular:

> καὶ τῶν ἱστορουμένων ἕκαστον οὐκ ἀκωμῳδήτως ᾔνικται πρός τινας τῶν παλαιῶν ποιητῶν τε καὶ συγγραφέων καὶ φιλοσόφων πολλὰ τεράστια καὶ μυθώδη συγγεγραφότων.
>
> Each of the matters I relate hints, in a way which is not un-comic, at one or other of the ancient poets, historians and philosophers who have written many prodigious and mythical things.[51]
>
> Lucian, *True Histories* 1.2

This explicit invitation to the reader can be applied to Lucian's whole oeuvre: the reader is constantly, though usually more implicitly, invited to spot 'hints' (as suggested here by the verb ᾔνικται). The reader's reward for successfully doing so is an added element of amusement (οὐκ ἀκωμῳδήτως).

The level of knowledge required for Lucian's intertextual play in this dialogue argues strongly against older views about this author's 'short cuts to culture',[52] since, although some allusions do appear on the surface to be simply rehashings of the most famous and hackneyed scenes from Homer, they are merely the point of departure for novel approaches to old questions. Part of the fun of reading this dialogue is working out just what questions Lucian is asking of the Homeric text.

My analysis therefore illustrates how well the *Judgement of the Goddesses* fits into Korenjak's tripartite typology of Imperial Greek audiences, which he divides into 'Der ungebildete Hörer', 'Der gebildete Hörer' and 'Die Experten: Sophisten und Rhetorikschüler'.[53] In this he follows the lead of Lucian himself, who contrasts audiences comprising the scholars (πεπαιδευμένοι) who are private readers and will keep referring back to the text, and the crowd (πληθύς) who hear the text just once at the first performance.[54]

In his discussion of ancient and modern parody, Dentith singles out this dialogue for special mention as an example of Lucian's use of a parodic mode as a means of displaying his learning:

> Parody here [i.e. 'in a period known as the Second Sophistic'] becomes almost a manner of learning; certainly this was a period which was very conscious of its

belatedness in relation to a past golden age.... What is perhaps remarkable is that the old Greek pantheon has survived long enough to give the demystifying spirit of parody some continued leverage.[55]

With the abundance of Homeric allusions that I have identified, some of them obvious, some much more concealed, this dialogue is an excellent example of the lengths to which the 'educated men' – the πεπαιδευμένοι – of Lucian's age would go to signal their learning. Furthermore, they show this off not only to the general public but also to those fellow-πεπαιδευμένοι who were in a position to appreciate an allusion and to understand that within it there could be lurking a further polemical allusion to well-established debate about details of the text. What makes this possible is not simply the survival of the Homeric pantheon, but also the survival of Homer's poems themselves as artefacts considered worthy of exhaustive study, which therefore continue to be susceptible to meaningful parody even for Imperial sophistic authors.

Lucian's use of the dialogue form has allowed him to create disarmingly informal conversations between Homeric characters, which contrast with the formal *suasoriae* and *controversiae* more often put in their mouths.[56] Furthermore, by focusing on the backstory to Helen's abduction, he takes a sidelong approach to a character who was of special interest to the sophists. It is no accident that at the end of the dialogue Paris feels himself being overcome by Aphrodite's power of bewitchment as he thinks about Helen, whose bewitching words were of such interest to Gorgias.

As the *Judgement of the Goddesses* demonstrates, Lucian's versions of Homeric characters are acutely aware of their own presentation in epic, even down to the details of each other's epithets. But this literary knowledge is wielded as a weapon, just as Lucian's own obsessive interest in minuscule details of language gives rise to his lengthy and vitriolic attack on an unfortunate fellow-sophist in *Pseudologistes*. The Homeric expertise of Lucian's gods brings out the contrast with the naive and uneducated Paris who is out of his depth and easily manipulated when he finds himself suddenly thrust into the world of epic and forced to find the best way to interpret the written word. By contrast, Lucian's own readers are encouraged to feel at home in Lucian's text: by approaching it in the manner of a set of riddles they can not only find rewarding additional readings beneath the surface but also reinforce their sense of belonging to the sophistic in-group from which an Ignorant Book Collector, whose focus is solely on a superficial kind of reading, is excluded.[57]

Notes

1 *VS* 481. Translations are my own unless otherwise noted.
2 Anderson 1986: 87–8 discusses the explanations that have been advanced for Lucian's exclusion by Philostratus. Eunapius (*Vit. Soph.* 454) does at least mention Lucian, as 'a man serious about raising a laugh' (ἀνὴρ σπουδαῖος ἐς τὸ γελασθῆναι), recalling Strabo's description (16.2.29) of the Cynic Menippus as 'the serio-comic' (ὁ σπουδογέλοιος).
3 What Lucian specifically identifies here (*Ind.* 2–3) is an ability to discuss the texts' good and bad features (τὴν ἀρετὴν καὶ κακίαν ἑκάστου τῶν ἐγγεγραμμένων), in particular those relating to the correct usage of words and expressions. He asks, 'Do you say that you are knowledgeable, even though you have not learned the same things that we have?' (φῄς, καὶ ταῦτα μὴ μαθὼν ἡμῖν, εἰδέναι;).
4 For example, two dialogues show the responses of Ajax and Achilles in the Underworld immediately following Odysseus' visit in *Od.* 11 (respectively, *Dial. mort.* 23 Macl. = 29 vulg. and 26 Macl. = 15 vulg.).
5 Kim 2010: 160. As will be clear from what follows, the *Judgement of the Goddesses* contains a greater element of parody than many of the other mythological dialogues.
6 This attention to minute detail of the Homeric text can be seen even in the extravagantly mendacious and iconoclastic *True Histories*, where we find 'authorial anxiety about altering Homer's story-world' (Ní Mheallaigh 2014: 244); compare Richter's observation that 'all good mimesis, and this is central for Lucian, begins with careful study' (2017: 341, discussing *Against the Ignorant Book Collector* 2).
7 Proclus, *Chrestomathy*, supplemented from Apollod., epit. 3. For the various alternative versions of the Judgement story, see Gantz 1993: 567–71; for Dio's response to it, see Tirrito's contribution in this volume (Chapter 6).
8 *Cypria*, *PEG* frr. 4–5 = 5–6 West, on which see Brillet-Dubois 2011: 110.
9 At *Dionysus* 8, Lucian describes the text as a joke at his own expense 'in the style of Momus' (κατὰ τὸν Μῶμον); at *Nigrinus* 32, Nigrinus' satirical observation imitates Momus' manner of expression (ἀτεχνῶς τοῦ Μώμου τὸν λόγον μιμησάμενος). Other passing mentions: *Icaromenippus* 31, *Hermotimus* 20.
10 Σ D *Il.* 1.5: 'Zeus at first immediately brought about the Theban War, through which he destroyed a great many, and afterwards again, with Momus as his advisor – what Homer calls "the plan of Zeus" – since he was able to destroy everyone with thunderbolts or floods. Momus prevented this and proposed two ideas to him, the marriage of Thetis to a mortal and the birth of a beautiful daughter; from these two things a war happened between the Greeks and barbarians, as a result of which it came about that the earth was lightened, since many were taken away. The story is told by Stasinus, the poet of the *Cypria*.' (τὸν δὲ Δία πρῶτον μὲν εὐθὺς ποιῆσαι τὸν Θηβαϊκὸν πόλεμον, δι' οὗ πολλοὺς πάνυ ἀπώλεσεν, ὕστερον δὲ πάλιν, συμβούλῳ

τῷ Μώμῳ χρησάμενος, ἣν "Διὸς βουλὴν" Ὅμηρός φησιν, ἐπειδὴ οἷός τε ἦν κεραυνοῖς ἢ κατακλυσμοῖς πάντας διαφθείρειν· ὅπερ τοῦ Μώμου κωλύσαντος, ὑποθεμένου δὲ αὐτῷ γνώμας δύο τὴν Θέτιδος θνητογαμίαν καὶ θυγατρὸς καλῆς γένναν, ἐξ ὧν ἀμφοτέρων πόλεμος Ἕλλησί τε καὶ βαρβάροις ἐγένετο, ἀφ' οὗ συνέβη κουφισθῆναι τὴν γῆν πολλῶν ἀναιρεθέντων. ἡ δὲ ἱστορία παρὰ Στασίνῳ τῷ τὰ Κύπρια πεποιηκότι.)

11 Wright 2007 demonstrates that the causes of the Trojan War – especially the Judgement of Paris – were of special interest to the comedians. Parodic versions also appeared in art: see Kossatz-Diessmann 1994: 186 (nos. 108–13).

12 Harmon 1921: 384–409.

13 Athetesis involved the marking of lines as in some way 'suspicious', for example because of their absence in some manuscripts, because of apparent inconsistency with another passage, or because they presented gods or heroes behaving in ways deemed inappropriate. In Aristarchus' view, such factors suggested non-Homeric authorship. On this and other aspects of Aristarchus' critical procedure, see Schironi 2018, especially 3.6.B and, on the Judgement of Paris in particular, 663–5. Opinions differed on the number of lines requiring athetesis in this case, ranging from eight (23–30) to seven (24–30) to six (25–30). See the discussion in Erbse 1977: 519–22 and, for the full list of arguments, Richardson 1993: 276–8. For a modern analysis of the passage's role within the *Iliad* see Mackie 2013.

14 See too Σ bT *Il.* 24.23, which suggests that Zeus would not have asked Hera the question 'In what way now do Priam and Priam's sons do so many evil things against you that you rage unceasingly?' at 4.31–2, since the answer would be obvious if the Judgement was the reason for Hera's hatred. Σ T *Il.* 24.23 points out that Helen not only fails to take several obvious opportunities to mention the Judgement but even implies that Paris acted entirely on his own initiative.

15 Σ b *Il.* 2.494: 'Marvellous is the poet, since he does not leave out anything at all of the subject-matter, but narrates everything by turning back at the appropriate moment, [such as] the quarrel of the goddesses, the rape of Helen, the death of Achilles.' (θαυμάσιος ὁ ποιητὴς μηδ' ὁτιοῦν παραλιμπάνων τῆς ὑποθέσεως, πάντα δ' ἐξ ἀναστροφῆς κατὰ τὸν ἐπιβάλλοντα καιρὸν διηγούμενος, τὴν τῶν θεῶν ἔριν, τὴν τῆς Ἑλένης ἁρπαγήν, τὸν Ἀχιλλέως θάνατον.)

16 Householder 1941: Table II.I.C.

17 Bouquiaux-Simon 1968: Table 3 (with 13–14). She lists this dialogue in the traditional way as number 20 of the *Dialogues of the Gods*.

18 Sistakou 2011: 199 n. 21.

19 Kossatz-Diessmann 1994: 176 writes 'That the goddesses appear before Paris naked, in order to put their beauty on show, is an accepted version in the Hellenistic period.' ('Daß die Göttinnen nackt vor Paris auftreten, um ihre Schönheit zur Schau zu stellen, ist wohl eine im Hellenismus aufgekommene Version').

20 The manuscripts attribute this speech to Hera, misled by the epithets; the true attribution was restored by Hemsterhuis. See MacLeod 1991: 254.
21 Here there is an additional joke, since Anubis really does have a dog's face. On the Homeric insult see Graver 1995. For another example of a sophistic character's awareness of his own Homeric epithets, see the conclusion to Koning's contribution in this volume (Chapter 3).
22 Σ bT *Il.* 9.651: 'The epithet is not Homer's, but Achilles has used it as he is annoying the Achaeans.' (οὐχ Ὁμηρικὸν τὸ ἐπίθετον, ἀλλ' ὁ Ἀχιλλεὺς πεποίηκεν αὐτὸ λυπῶν τοὺς Ἀχαιούς.)
23 Reinhardt 1938.
24 Much of the dialogue's humour comes from its making explicit what is implicit in Homer, namely that outright cheating was involved. Gumpert 2001: 64 notes that later tellings 'tend to emphasize the way in which the contest was fixed'.
25 This episode is the subject of Lucian's *Dialogues of the Gods* 21 Macl. = 17 vulg.
26 DK 21 B11–B12.
27 Householder 1941: 64. The words of Cadau 2015: 82 apply just as much to Lucian as to her subject, Colluthus: 'the choice of such a well-known story ... guaranteed high expectations in the readers in terms of content, characterisation and ethical interpretation'.
28 On Aphrodite being 'shamed' in the hymn see Furley 2011: 220–1.
29 The story also appears at Hes. *Th.* 1008–10.
30 *Il.* 14.214–20.
31 The fear is justified, since the girdle 'steals even wise men's reason' (217).
32 LSJ s.v. ἐντρίβω. A possible further intertext here is Callim., *Hymn* 5.13–22, where Aphrodite's toilette contrasts with Athena's (and Hera's) lack of concern for such things, even at the Judgement of Paris (ὅκα τὰν Ἴδα Φρὺξ ἐδίκαζεν ἔριν), because she is always beautiful. This point is made, in connection with Colluthus' version of the story, by Cadau 2015: 124.
33 *Il.* 6.466–96, esp. 469.
34 Harmon 1921: 399 n. 3, citing parallels in *Dialogues of the Courtesans* 2.1.1 and *Dialogues of the Gods* 13 Macl. = 8 vulg. Stewart 2006: 327: 'The poetic interpretation of *glaukos* implies reverberations of "odd, uncertain, uncanny".' This Lucianic moment is a good example of the 'synchronic intertextuality' identified by Machacek 2007: 525.
35 Lucian might possibly intend a reference to poor sight through glaucoma or cataracts, which ancient doctors did not clearly distinguish: Boudon-Millot 2012: 562 n. 47.
36 Apollod. 2.1.3.
37 Zeus' mention of Gargaron (1), and Hermes' direction of Hera's gaze towards Paris, 'not at the top of the mountain, but on the side' (5: μὴ πρὸς ἄκρῳ τῷ ὄρει, παρὰ δὲ

τὴν πλευράν) could also be a polemical correction of an alternative view: contrast Strabo 13.1.51, where the Judgement happened on the mountain Alexandreia, and Ov. *Her.* 16.53–4, where Paris says that it happened in 'a place in the middle of the valleys of wooded Ida' (*locus in mediis nemorosae vallibus Idae*).

38 Hermes follows the version in the *Homeric Hymn to Aphrodite* 202–17, rather than *Il.* 20.232–5, where 'the gods' rather than Zeus take Ganymede.

39 See *Homeric Hymn to Aphrodite* 80 with Faulkner 2008: 160–1 on the (non-)heroic implications of Anchises' lyre-playing on Ida; Paris' pipe-playing is prominent in other texts such as Eur. *IA* 573–89 and Colluthus 108–26, and his lyre makes appearances in art (Kossatz-Diessmann 1994: 186).

40 On reading and writing in Homer see also Bassino in this volume (Chapter 2).

41 This elegant answer to the problem recalls the ease with which even the most burning Homeric questions are easily solved when Lucian meets and questions the poet himself in *True Histories*, to the extent that he does not even need to ask whether Homer is blind, since it is obvious that he is not (2.20).

42 *The Illinois Farmer*, June 1863: 186.

43 On this specific phenomenon see Nünlist 2009: 301–2, and the whole of chapter 15 more generally on the ancient interpretation of Homer's use of epithets.

44 Similarly Σ A *Il.* 20.233a on a description of Ganymede: 'He uses "most beautiful" as would be appropriate for his eulogy. For he calls others "most beautiful" too.' (ὅτι, ὡς ἂν ἁρμόζῃ πρὸς τὸ ἐγκώμιον, τίθησι τὸ "κάλλιστος"· καὶ γὰρ ἄλλους καλλίστους λέγει.)

45 On this dialogue see too Kim 2010: 159–60, who observes 'not only that Nireus and Thersites are Homeric characters, defined and embodied by Homer's verses, but also that they are fully conscious of that fact'.

46 In Colluthus, Hermes describes the apple: 'Come here and decide the more excellent beauty of face; to the fairer lady give this apple, a delightful fruit.' (δεῦρο διακρίνων προφερέστερον εἶδος ὀπωπῆς / φαιδροτέρῃ τόδε μῆλον, ἐπήρατον ἔρνος, ὀπάσσαις, 130–1.) Hermes' use of these unexpected comparatives perhaps plays with the same problem as Lucian's text does.

47 The combination of verbatim repetition and tactful omission in Hermes' speech has Homeric precedent; it is reminiscent of Odysseus' omission of the intemperate lines *Il.* 9.158–61 in his otherwise literal report of Agamemnon's speech to Achilles – cf. 9.299–306.

48 It is likely that Lucian's point would be clearer if we had the *Cypria* and could read the text of the apple there – if indeed it was quoted.

49 Bartley 2009: 105.

50 I am grateful to the anonymous reader for a very helpful suggestion about the interpretation of this passage.

51 On parody and allusion throughout *True Histories* see Georgiadou/Larmour 1988: 22–44.

52 e.g. Anderson 1976, from the title of which I take the quoted phrase.
53 'The uncultured listener', 'The cultured listener', and 'The experts: sophists and students of rhetoric'. Korenjak 2000: 52–65.
54 *Apologia* 3; Korenjak 2000: 53. On Lucian's evident fascination with the oral and written mediums through which his work was disseminated, see Ní Mheallaigh 2014: 144–51. In a modern context, Gray 2006 presents an analysis of the different levels of humour that are designed to appeal to a wide range of audiences in the animated television series *The Simpsons*, which combines slapstick humour with satirical jokes and specific, detailed parodies of cultural artefacts. See especially ch. 5, 'Parody and/as interpretive community'; in Part III Gray reports on responses to the show's parody and humour by 35 viewers 'in the chaotic realm of the audience' (120), each bringing their own 'DIY cultural citizenship' consisting of their personal experience of media texts.
55 Dentith 2000: 49.
56 On these, see the earlier chapters in this volume.
57 This chapter is an expanded version of material from my doctoral thesis. I am grateful to the AHRC for funding that research; to my supervisors Judith Mossman and Patrick Finglass, at the University of Nottingham, for guidance; and to my examiners Oliver Thomas and Tim Whitmarsh, for detailed comments. Earlier versions were read at the Classical Association Annual Conference in 2014, at Nottingham's research seminar and at the Winchester conference. My thanks to those audiences for thought-provoking questions and suggestions.

References

Anderson, G. 1976, 'Lucian's classics: Some short cuts to culture', *BICS* 23: 59–68.
Anderson, G. 1986, *Philostratus: Biography and Belles Lettres in the Third Century A.D.*, London.
Bartley, A. 2009, *Lucian's* Dialogi Marini, Newcastle upon Tyne.
Boudon-Millot, V. 2012, 'Vision and vision disorders: Galen's physiology of sight' in Horstmanshoff, M., King, H. and Zittel, C. (eds), *Blood, Sweat and Tears: The Changing Concepts of Physiology from Antiquity into Early Modern Europe*, Leiden: 551–67.
Bouquiaux-Simon, O. 1968, *Les lectures homériques de Lucien*, Brussels.
Brillet-Dubois, P. 2011, 'An erotic aresteia: The *Homeric Hymn to Aphrodite* and its relation to the Iliadic tradition' in Faulkner, A. (ed.), *The Homeric Hymns: Interpretative Essays*, Oxford: 105–32.
Cadau, C. 2015, *Studies in Colluthus'* Abduction of Helen, Leiden.
Dentith, S. 2000, *Parody*, Abingdon.
Erbse, H. 1969–88, *Scholia Graeca in Homeri Iliadem*, 7 vols, Berlin.

Erbse, H. 1977, *Scholia Graeca in Homeri Iliadem*, vol. 5, Berlin.
Faulkner, A. 2008, *The Homeric Hymn to Aphrodite: Introduction, Text, and Commentary*, Oxford.
Furley, W. 2011, 'Homeric and un-Homeric hexameter hymns: A question of type', Faulkner, A. (ed.), *The Homeric Hymns: Interpretative Essays*, Oxford: 206–31.
Gantz, T. 1993, *Early Greek Myth: A Guide to Literary and Artistic Sources*, Baltimore.
Georgiadou, A. and Larmour, D. 1998, *Lucian's Science Fiction Novel* True Histories: *Interpretation and Commentary*, Leiden.
Graver, M. 1995, 'Dog-Helen and Homeric insult', *ClAnt* 14: 41–61.
Gray, J. 2006, *Watching with The Simpsons: Television, Parody, and Intertextuality*, New York/London.
Gumpert, M. 2001, *Grafting Helen: The Abduction of the Classical Past*, Madison.
Harmon, A. 1921, *Lucian*, vol. 3, Cambridge MA.
Householder, F. 1941, *Literary Quotation and Allusion in Lucian*, New York.
Kim, L. 2010, *Homer between History and Fiction in Imperial Greek Literature*, Cambridge.
Korenjak, M. 2000, *Publikum und Redner: Ihre Interaktion in der sophistischen Rhetorik der Kaiserzeit*, Munich.
Kossatz-Diessmann, A. 1994, 'Paridis iudicium', in *Lexicon Iconographicum Mythologiae Classicae*, vol. 7, Zurich: 176–88.
Machacek, G. 2007, 'Allusion', *Publications of the Modern Language Association* 122: 522–36.
Mackie, C. J. 2013, '*Iliad* 24 and the Judgement of Paris', *CQ* 63: 1–16.
MacLeod, M. D. 1991, *Lucian: A Selection*, Warminster.
Ní Mheallaigh, K. 2014, *Reading Fiction with Lucian: Fakes, Freaks and Hyperreality*, Cambridge.
Nünlist, R. 2009, *The Ancient Critic at Work*, Cambridge.
Reinhardt, K. 1938, *Das Parisurteil*. Wissenschaft und Gegenwart, vol. 11, Frankfurt.
Richardson, N. J. 1993, *The Iliad: A Commentary*, vol. 6, *Books 21–24*, Cambridge.
Richter, D. S. 2017, 'Lucian of Samosata', in Richter, D. S. and Johnson, W. A. (eds), *The Oxford Handbook of the Second Sophistic*, New York: 327–44.
Schironi, F. 2018, *The Best of the Grammarians: Aristarchus of Samothrace on the Iliad*, Ann Arbor.
Sistakou, E. 2011, 'Mock epic in the *Greek Anthology*', in *Homère revisité: parodie et humour dans les réécritures homériques*, Acosta-Hughes, B., Cusset, C., Durbec, Y. and Pralon, D. (eds), Besançon: 193–210.
Stewart, S. 2006, 'The "blues" of Aratus' in *Beyond the Canon*, Harder, A., Regtuit, R. and Wakker, G. (eds), Leuven: 319–44.
van Thiel, H. 2014, *Scholia D in Iliadem. Proecdosis aucta et correctior 2014. Secundum codices manu scriptos*, Cologne.
West, M. L. 2003 (ed.), *Greek Epic Fragments*, Cambridge MA.
Wright, M. 2007, 'Comedy and the Trojan War', *CQ* 57: 412–31.

6

Helen Was Never Abducted, Paris Abducted Her Because He Was Bored: Two Ways of Rewriting Homer in Dio Chrysostom (Orr. 11 and 20)

Sara Tirrito

Homer lied:[1] Troy was never destroyed, Hera had no need to prove her beauty with a vanity-fuelled dispute,[2] Helen was never abducted by Paris but married him;[3] clear evidence shows that Paris' judgement of the goddesses did not actually happen: it was invented by Homer in order to justify the falsehoods he told about the defeat of the Trojans. That is what the so-called *Trojan* discourse (Orr. 11) by Dio Chrysostom tells the listeners, supposed to be the inhabitants of the New Ilion.[4] Among the messages it delivers to modern scholars, the *Trojan* discourse, recently studied because of its relevance to the Second Sophistic and the poetic past,[5] shows that the epic element, in Homer as well as in the epic cycle, can be manipulated in different ways to the point that Homer could be directly contradicted even by those authors who see him as the Supreme Poet and the incontestable source for the Trojan War.[6]

In this context, little attention has been given to an important passage of oration 20, *On the Subject of Anachoretic Life*, also known as *On Retirement*.[7] Focused on contempt for the Epicurean principle of isolation as a cause of wellness, this discourse tries to advise the philosopher about the best practices in ἀναχώρησις. Moreover, it gives an unusual reinterpretation of the myth of Paris,[8] which contrasts with the one given in the *Trojan* discourse. Paris would have come up with the idea of abducting Helen while watching cattle graze on Mount Ida, alone, at leisure. That same leisure would have suggested that he honour Aphrodite with a prize during a beauty contest, in order to obtain her help in seducing Helen.

The aim of this contribution is to enrich our understanding of the ways in which Dio manipulates the epic tradition. Starting with an introduction about Dio's view on poetry as an ethical and educational tool for kings, first the chapter shows the most common ways to learn and overturn the epos, then it focuses on a literary case study: the abduction of Helen in the epic tradition and in Dio Chrysostom. The comparison between the two versions of the myth of Paris by Dio, in particular, shows how the author acts within the tradition, rejecting it, exaggerating it, or undermining it. Moreover, by underlining the differences and inconsistencies between the two texts, a better understanding of speech 20 can be achieved. Although this speech has been long neglected, its place within Dio's corpus deserves to be reconsidered. The importance of this oration emerges from the most evident observation: it involves the author in a literary contradiction, denying what is claimed in his own works. Indeed, the *Trojan* (Orr. 11) rejects that the Judgement of Paris and the abduction of Helen could ever have taken place, and attributes these stories to political interests in Greece and Asia. On the contrary, *On the Subject of Anachoretic Life* (Orr. 20) confirms that those episodes not only took place, but even led to the Trojan War, which is held to have been definitely caused by Paris' idleness.

Idleness and kingship: why Homer is the one and only poet for leaders

'Not all poetry, any more than every style of dress, is appropriate to a king, as it seems to me. (…) The poetry of Homer, however, I look upon as alone truly noble and lofty and suited to a king, worthy of the attention of a real man, particularly if he expects to rule over all the peoples of the earth' (D. Chr. *On Kingship 2*, Orr. 2.4–6).[9] In Dio's second speech *On Kingship* – which is written in the form of an imaginary dialogue between Philip of Macedon and his son after the battle of Chaeronea (338 BC) – the future Alexander the Great clarifies which readings best fit a king.[10] The dialogue starts with Philip asking his son why he is so infatuated with Homer that he devotes himself to him alone, even though the other poets are wise too (Orr. 2.3–4). Alexander replies that some poets are made for banquets, others for love or laughter like Archilochus, some others could even be defined as 'popular', like Phocylides and Theognis, who give advice to the masses, but none of them – according to Alexander – could suit someone who 'aspires to be the master, over all to domineer'. Alexander's explanation seems to point to a denial of the ethical and educational value of lyric poetry on Dio's part.[11] For to sing Sappho, Anacreon, Stesichorus or Pindar is not appropriate for a future leader such as Alexander the Great. On the contrary, Homeric poetry could even be performed in war contexts, provided it be accompanied by powerful musical instruments, like the trumpet exhorting to battle, not the one for retreat. Indeed, Alexander adds that Homer should not be sung by a chorus of women or maids, but rather by a phalanx in arms (Orr. 2.28–29). Alexander provides other limitations concerning the performance of lyric poetry: for example, he is convinced that a king must banish as much as possible lustful and voluptuous songs from his soul, as well as licentious language or dance (Orr. 2.55–6). Only military dances are allowed on condition that they are sober. Lastly a king should sing only songs appropriate to Ares, the God of War, which are strenuous, forceful and tough.

As emerges from the second speech *On Kingship*, only epic and dramatic poetry are edifying for someone who aspires to be a leader.[12] For them 'no feeling of delight or languidness' is allowed (Orr. 2.57) in any kind of poetry. This position is even clearer in or. 18.8, where Dio addresses, in letter format,[13] a man of high position who wants to improve his rhetorical skills. On the model of Dionysius of Halicarnassus and Quintilian, Dio gives him a list of authors that he should know in order to be a good ruler, and he clarifies that 'lyric and elegiac poetry too, and iambics and dithyrambs are very valuable for the man of leisure, but the man who intends to have a public career (. . .) will have no time for them'. Although the speech does not provide definitive evidence as to the date of its composition and the identity of the addressee, it is probable that it dates to the first years of Trajan's reign,[14] and that it was written for him.[15] The same is likely true of speech 2.[16] The Emperor is not named explicitly, but he is presented as an aged man (he is said to be in the flourishing of his age in 18.1: τὸ γὰρ ἡλικίας τε ἐν τῷ ἀκμαιοτάτῳ ὄντα), a wealthy and well-established politician (18.2 and 5: πολιτικὸς ἀνήρ), who already has a cultural education (18.4: παιδείας ἐπὶ πλεῖστον ἥκοντι), with experience in public affairs but who aspires to become a statesman (18.9: τὰ κοινὰ πράττειν) and is asking for training in public speaking. He is supposed to know ancient Greek, but his knowledge of Greek culture does not seem very deep, because Dio advises him to study Homer first.

Ὅμηρος δὲ καὶ πρῶτος καὶ μέσος καὶ ὕστατος παντὶ παιδὶ καὶ ἀνδρὶ καὶ γέροντι, τοσοῦτον ἀφ' αὑτοῦ διδοὺς ὅσον ἕκαστος δύναται λαβεῖν.

But Homer comes first and in the middle and last, in that he gives of himself to every boy and adult and old man just as much as each of them can take.

Dio Chrysostom, 18.1

Dio often shows a clear predilection for Homer in his work, both literary and political. On the one hand, this fondness is certainly related to a widespread cultural tendency that saw in the Homeric poems an educational encyclopedia of ethical and behavioural paradigms, which had to be emulated in order to recover the dignity of the Hellenic tradition.[17] On the other hand, Dio seems to have his own particular way of appropriating Homer, especially as regards the poet's way of narrating historical facts (as in the *Trojan*, or. 11), and with the concepts of power, kingship and aristocracy (as in *On Kingship* 1 and 2, and the speech *On Training*, or. 18). As we have seen, in or. 2 Dio denies that all kinds of poetry are suitable for a king, and he especially condemns literature which could encourage leisure or idleness. Indeed, this seems to be the reason why Homer is considered as sufficient for a leader's education in poetry. In his introduction to the edition of *On the Good King According to Homer*, apparently composed by Philodemus of Gadara, Dorandi notes that Homer is just an ἀφορμή for the ancient authors,[18] i.e. nothing more than a starting point for handling every subject in a way which was neither too simple nor too deep. For the Homeric poems were approached by other writers as a collection of examples, which they could adapt to their own purposes regardless of their actual admiration for the works.

In the context of Dio's production, what deserves special attention is the fact that Homer is often mentioned in speeches concerning kings and power. Moreover, he is always presented as an authority on ethics, behaviour and culture for the aristocracy. While this might seem obvious at first glance, on closer inspection it reveals Dio's ingenuity, since even when Dio overturns some Homeric episodes (like the Trojan War in or. 11 or Helen's abduction in or. 20), he still does it to give to his message a sort of Homeric strength. This is the reason why when Dio starts to present the king in the first speech about *Kingship*, he says that according to Homer the king should not even sleep all night 'through as having no leisure for idleness' (1.14: ὡς οὐκ οὖσαν αὐτῷ σχολὴν ῥᾳθυμεῖν). The sentence, almost a quotation of Agamemnon's words in the *Iliad* (Hom. *Il.* 2.24–5), is presented as true and Homeric, but in fact it embodies the Dionean ideal. Dio's appropriation of the Homeric model is further emphasized by his speaking of the king 'as Homer conceives him, of him who is in very truth a king' (Orr. 1.15). As emerges from the foregoing consideration, Dio seems to use Homer especially when he either talks about royal power or addresses it directly. This is particularly evident in or. 11 and 20 in which Dio pretends to debunk two Homeric episodes but he is actually condemning an example of wrongful human behaviour.

Manipulation of Epos in the Second Sophistic: techniques and intents

Knowledge not only of Homer, but also of the epic genre as a whole, was a must for the identity of the elite. Since epic presented ethical models and anti-models, it was a fundamental part of the education of young rhetors who aimed to become philosophers, politicians, intellectuals or rulers. That is why being able to play with the most sacred plots was part of the orator's training. This is particularly clear in Dio's discourses 11 and 20. As the *Trojan* shows, Homeric plots and verses were always questioned and exploited for rhetorical purposes. Scholars have remarked that while refuting the Trojan War story, Dio Chrysostom adopts a personal reconstruction of the myth, using a soft approach and philosophical observations.[19] In a study of the intertextual references to Homer within a corpus of Imperial age προγυμνάσματα, Robert asked whether Homeric poetry was taught to orators at school.[20] By analysing the exercises for young orators, he found six ways of quoting Homer: literal quotes (with a direct or adjectival mention of the author), paraphrases, textual hints, metadiscursive quotes (namely, mentions of Homer to explain his technique), mentions of Homer's name and, lastly, epic legends presented as 'Homeric subjects'. He found that in προγυμνάσματα Homer is considered a true model for the delineation of a character (the ἠθοποιία) – in some exercises Homer is the most mentioned author after Demosthenes, Isocrates and Thucydides – but he is an anti-model in terms of style (that is, his vocabulary and use of rhythm were distant from rhetorical canons). It is interesting to underline that, according to Robert, orators used to engage with Homeric verses from very early on: they frequently memorized and manipulated Homeric poems and considered them a treasure-chest of entwined myths and themes that could inspire their work.

Favreau-Linder lists three main ways of referring to Homer in a rhetorical work: first, by borrowing some expressions from Homer and integrating them into a Sophist's speech; second, with oral quotes dealing with the rhetoric of homage and blame; and third, through poetic loans from Homer used to describe the art of a Sophist.[21] It is hard to say to which category the speeches 11 and 20 belong – perhaps the second, considering the theory according to which Dio's works were conceived as open texts that were continuously adapted and only in part survived in their written forms.[22] It is simpler to admit that mentioning Homeric tradition in a rhetorical work is something that has happened automatically in every age and Dio Chrysostom is not immune to this custom.[23]

Moreover, a Sophist never mentions Homer just to show his own poetic culture, but each allusion is part of a strategy based on the καιρός of both the speech and the context. Furthermore, this causes the listeners to identify with the discourse and learn from it. Despite the triumph of rhetor, during the Imperial age poetry is still fundamental and Homer is often mentioned as 'the Supreme Poet'. Nevertheless, in some speeches (for example or. 11 and indirectly in or. 20), Dio accuses Homer of lying.

Kindstrand thinks that there is a contradiction in the ways in which Dio refers to Homer: he theorizes a poetic use that is both pedagogic and hedonistic.[24] This view seems to have become stronger by the end of the 1970s, when Desideri observed that Dio draws from the Homeric archive as if it were an 'encyclopaedia of behaviour models', with the aim of educating his interlocutor.[25] Even when Dio denounces Homer's falsehoods, the orator is actually trying to teach his listeners when the circumstances allow overturning the truth. This is what happens in or. 11: while speaking to the inhabitants of New Ilion, Dio defends and justifies Homer's lies.

> βούλομαι δὲ καὶ περὶ Ὁμήρου ἀπολογήσασθαι, ὡς οὐκ ἀνάξιον ὁμολογεῖν αὐτῷ ψευδομένῳ. πρῶτον μὲν γὰρ πολὺ ἐλάττω τὰ ψεύσματά ἐστι τῶν περὶ τοὺς θεούς· ἔπειτα ὠφέλειάν τινα εἶχε τοῖς τότε Ἕλλησιν, ὅπως μὴ θορυβηθῶσιν, ἐὰν γένηται πόλεμος αὐτοῖς πρὸς τοὺς ἐκ τῆς Ἀσίας, ὥσπερ καὶ προσεδοκᾶτο. ἀνεμέσητον δὲ Ἕλληνα ὄντα τοὺς ἑαυτοῦ πάντα τρόπον ὠφελεῖν.

> But I wish to offer a defence on behalf of Homer by saying that there is nothing wrong in accepting his fictions. First, they are much less serious than the falsehoods told about the gods. Second, there was some advantage in them for the Greeks of those days, since they saved them from being alarmed in case war, as was expected, arose between them and the people of Asia. We can pardon one who, being a Greek, used every means to aid his countrymen.
>
> Dio Chrysostom, 11.147

Dio's double approach to this myth is inspired by his precursors. The habit of demolishing and praising Homer owes much to Plato.[26] Indeed, Dio dismantles the *Iliad* point by point: first its mythological content, and then the plot, characters and moral themes, and at the end he presents a speech that is a serious attempt at rewriting the Homeric text.[27] In this sense, the *Trojan* was intended as the result of a process of deconstruction and re-construction (as suggested by Scafoglio 2020). According to this theory, the first part of the process would consist in 1–37, where Dio confutes every passage of the *Iliad* and makes Homer appear to be ridiculous. The reconstruction occupies 38–154 and rehabilitates the author with a positive reading of his poetry. According to Hunter, the whole discourse is 'a distortion of a recurrent theme of ancient Homeric criticism'.[28] However, another evident philosophical model is Aristotle. As Scafoglio underlined, Dio applies the Aristotelian logic of syllogism. First, he premises that beggars are known to be liars, and then specifies that Homer admitted being a beggar, and so he concludes that Homer lies (contrary to popular belief).[29]

In the past, it has been said that this was just a divertissement, a school exercise and a way to practise virtuosity of the rhetorical art through paradox.[30] Nevertheless, the reasons behind this rewriting are still unknown and seem to go beyond virtuosity. In fact, between the nineteenth and the twentieth century, critics tended to apply standard criteria for interpretation, and rhetoric was viewed as a temporary training that was abandoned at a certain point of life by the cultivated. Dio's need to train his ability through προγυμνάσματα has been discussed for a long time and there are those who refuse altogether to read discourse 11 as an exercise made with the intent of producing a paradox.[31] Moreover, since the 1970s and beyond, academics have considered paradoxical rewriting an exercise to improve the rhetorical art but, at least in the *Trojan*, there must be a philosophical aim too.[32] As a result, in the 1990s, Desideri and Swain opposed each other: according to Desideri, Dio wanted to celebrate the Romans through the victory of their ancestors, the Trojans and Aeneas' descendants, while Swain (though admitting that Dio is talking to the inhabitants of New Ilion) disagreed with Desideri's interpretation because Dio's speech is supposed to have been first delivered in front of an international public who wanted to be 'converted' to philosophy and politics.[33] The two interpretations do not exclude each other. Indeed, thanks to the turning point given by Desideri to the hermeneutics of Dio's texts, today it is almost certain that the discourses were composed for a diverse audience.[34] In other words, they were probably conceived for an international public, but sometimes readapted to a local context or a specific occasion.

Concerning Dio's praxis of citing Homer in the *Trojan*, Scafoglio classifies different kinds of quotes.[35] The simplest is the textual one, but it is not always easy to identify it in the text and often requires comparison between the two different contexts of *Iliad* and *Odyssey*. We may also observe that, in the *Trojan* as well as in other discourses, Dio usually speaks as if Homer were the best and original source for this episode, a technique that was common among Alexandrian philologists.[36] This attitude has been called 'pan-Homerism' by scholars and consists of seeing Homer as the primary source for the myth of Troy. This occurs in the *Trojan* with the myth of the Judgement of Paris, which is considered by Homer even though it belongs to the *Cypria*. Scafoglio underlines how the prejudice of pan-Homerism influenced the narration of the episode, especially when the orator declares that he does not believe in the destruction of Troy or in the goddesses' dispute.

> ἐγὼ δὲ οὔθ' ὑμῖν χαριζόμενος οὔθ' Ὁμήρῳ διαφερόμενος οὐδὲ τῆς δόξης φθονῶν ἐκείνῳ, πειράσομαι δεικνύειν ὅσα μοι δοκεῖ ψευδῆ εἰρηκέναι περὶ τῶν ἐνθάδε πραγμάτων, οὐκ ἄλλοθέν ποθεν, ἀλλ' ἐξ αὐτῆς τῆς ποιήσεως ἐλέγχων, τῷ τε ἀληθεῖ βοηθῶν (...) (12) (...) δεινὸν γὰρ τὴν μὲν τῷ Διὶ συνοῦσαν μὴ νομίσαι κριτὸν ἱκανὸν τοῦ αὐτῆς εἴδους, εἰ μὴ ἀρέσει καὶ τῶν ἐν Ἴδῃ βουκόλων ἑνί, τὴν δὲ ἀρχὴν ὑπὲρ κάλλους ἐρίζειν τῇ Ἀφροδίτῃ, πρεσβυτάτην φάσκουσαν εἶναι τῶν Κρόνου (13) παίδων, ὡς αὐτὸς Ὅμηρος ἀπήγγειλε ποιήσας.

> But as for me, desiring neither to gain your favour nor to quarrel with Homer, much less to rob him of his fame, I shall try to show all the false statements I think he has made with regard to the events which happened here, and I shall use no other means of refuting him than his own poetry. In this I am simply defending the truth (...) (12) (...) For it is passing strange that the consort of Zeus did not consider him a competent judge of her beauty unless it should be pleasing to one of the shepherds of Ida also, and that she had any contest at all with Aphrodite for the prize of beauty, she who asserted that she was the eldest of the children of Cronus, (13) as Homer himself has expressed it in the verse.
> Dio Chrysostom, 11.11–13

However, a pan-Homeric mindset is also clear in the way he explains Paris' choice to abduct Helen. In or. 11.55–6, Dio denies she could have arrived and stayed in Troy with Priam and Hector's complicity because both Hector and his father would have condemned the abduction of Helen had they known about it. Dio Chrysostom's position about the truth of Helen's abduction is not coherent, first because it contrasts with a tradition, the Homeric one, which Dio supports. Second, it does not agree with other passages of his own corpus, in which the abduction of Helen is taken for granted. This is what comes to light in the speech *Diogenes* or *On Tyranny* (Orr. 6.17–18) when Paris' cupidity is considered the cause of the Trojan War. In addition, it is evident in the *Euboic* when Dio refers to the arrival of Paris at Menelaus' house (Orr. 7.93–5). In this passage, when the author explains the dangers of being envious and having many possessions, he talks about Paris' visit to Sparta as an example of bad hospitality. Indeed, although he was welcomed as a guest, he turned against Menaelaus, and robbed him of his wife, daughter and riches.

ἀκολάστους δὲ καὶ τυραννικοὺς οὔτ' ἂν οἶμαι δύναιντο θεραπεύειν (94) ἱκανῶς ξένους οὔτ' ἂν ἴσως προσδέοιντο τοιαύτης ξενίας. οὐδὲ γὰρ τῷ Μενέλεῳ δήπουθεν ἀπέβη πρὸς τὸ λῷον, ὅτι ἠδύνατο δέξασθαι τὸν πλουσιώτατον ἐκ τῆς Ἀσίας ξένον, ἄλλος δὲ οὐδεὶς ἱκανὸς ἦν ἐν τῇ Σπάρτῃ τὸν Πριάμου τοῦ βασιλέως υἱὸν ὑποδέξασθαι. (95) τοιγάρτοι ἐρημώσας αὐτοῦ τὴν οἰκίαν καὶ πρὸς τοῖς χρήμασι τὴν γυναῖκα προσλαβών, τὴν δὲ θυγατέρα ὀρφανὴν τῆς μητρὸς ἐάσας, ᾤχετο ἀποπλέων.

But guests that are dissolute and tyrannical they would neither be able, I suppose, to serve acceptably nor, perhaps, would they care to extend such hospitality. For it surely did not turn out any better for Menelaus, that he was able to receive the wealthiest prince of Asia as a guest and that nobody else in Sparta was equal to entertaining the son of King Priam. For, mark you, that prince despoiled his home, appropriated his wife as well as his treasures, left the daughter motherless and sailed away.

Dio Chrysostom, 7.94–5

The Judgement of Paris and the Abduction of Helen in the ancient texts

Although the Judgement of Paris is fundamental to the plots of both canonical Homeric poems, and for Western literature more generally, the only allusion to it in the *Iliad* is at the end of the poem, when we are told that Hera feels some resentment towards sacred Ilion, as well as against Priam and his people, because of Alexander, who offended Hera and Athena but honoured Aphrodite in order to abduct Helen.[37]

25 ἔνθ' ἄλλοις μὲν πᾶσιν ἑήνδανεν, οὐδέ ποθ' Ἥρῃ
    οὐδὲ Ποσειδάων' οὐδὲ γλαυκώπιδι κούρῃ,
    ἀλλ' ἔχον ὥς σφιν πρῶτον ἀπήχθετο Ἴλιος ἱρὴ
    καὶ Πρίαμος καὶ λαὸς Ἀλεξάνδρου ἕνεκ' ἄτης,
    ὃς νείκεσσε θεὰς ὅτε οἱ μέσσαυλον ἵκοντο,
30 τὴν δ' ᾔνησ' ἥ οἱ πόρε μαχλοσύνην ἀλεγεινήν.

And the thing was pleasing unto all the rest, yet not unto Hera or Poseidon or the flashing-eyed maiden, but they continued even as when at first sacred Ilios became hateful in their eyes and Priam and his folk, by reason of the sin of Alexander, for that he put reproach upon those goddesses when they came to his steading, and gave precedence to her who furthered his fatal lustfulness. (Transl. Murray)

Iliad, 24.25–30

By talking about Alexander's responsibilities without detailing how the events evolved,[38] here Homer does not give any evidence of the goddesses' contest, nor does he explain why Paris was chosen to be the judge. This omission led commentators to suspect that it was not part of the original myth, or at least it was not part of the version that Homer knew.[39]

The myth is presented for the first time in the *Cypria*, one of the lost poems of the so-called Epic Cycle. Eris, troubled at having been left out of the wedding of Peleus and Thetis, started a beauty dispute between Hera, Athena and Aphrodite. Zeus, not wanting to hurt any of the goddesses, named Paris as judge. Paris gave the victory to Aphrodite, and the goddess gave him Helen as a reward.

> Ζεὺς βουλεύεται μετὰ τῆς Θέμιδος περὶ τοῦ Τρωϊκοῦ πολέμου. (85) παραγενομένη δὲ Ἔρις εὐωχουμένων τῶν θεῶν ἐν τοῖς Πηλέως γάμοις νεῖκος περὶ κάλλους ἀνίστησιν Ἀθηνᾷ, Ἥρᾳ καὶ Ἀφροδίτῃ αἳ πρὸς Ἀλέξανδρον ἐν Ἴδῃ κατὰ Διὸς προσταγὴν ὑφ' Ἑρμοῦ πρὸς τὴν κρίσιν ἄγονται· καὶ προκρίνει τὴν Ἀφροδίτην ἐπαρθεὶς τοῖς Ἑλένης γάμοις Ἀλέξανδρος. (90) ἔπειτα δὲ Ἀφροδίτης ὑποθεμένης ναυπηγεῖται, καὶ Ἕλενος περὶ τῶν μελλόντων αὐτοῖς προθεσπίζει, καὶ ἡ Ἀφροδίτη Αἰνείαν συμπλεῖν αὐτῷ κελεύει. καὶ Κασσάνδρα περὶ τῶν μελλόντων προδηλοῖ.

> Zeus confers with Themis about the Trojan War. As the gods are feasting at the wedding of Peleus, Strife appears and causes a dispute about beauty among Athena, Hera and Aphrodite. On Zeus' instruction Hermes conducts them to Alexander on Ida for adjudication. Alexander, excited by the prospect of union with Helen, chooses Aphrodite. After that, at Aphrodite's instigation, ships are built, Helenus prophesies what will happen to them. Aphrodite tells Aeneas to sail with Alexander. And Cassandra reveals what will happen. (Transl. West)

Cypria, *Argumentum* 1–2

The story continues with the abduction of the princess, which is also scarcely documented. Among others, Stinton underlined the total silence of the poets when it came to describing the episode.[40] Indeed, except for the few lines by Proclus and the fragments of the *Cypria*, Ovid provides a leading account of the Judgement of Paris and its consequences. Apart from Ovid and also before him, several versions of the myth, starting from Stesichorus' *Palinode*,[41] became a model not only in poetry but in historiography,[42] philosophy[43] and theatre too. Sometimes the text was overturned in a paradoxical way, and other times it became a political artifice. Many different examples can be given of texts written to absolve Helen or Paris from the charge of causing the Trojan War (such as the *Encomium of Helen* by Gorgias),⁴⁴ while other works affirm that the war was the fault of Paris' dream. This is what Dio said in or. 20, but also what is told in one of the main texts about the fall of Troy: *The History of the Fall of Troy* by Dares Phrygius. This controversial prose work is a Latin version of the Trojan conflict – presumably a translation from an original Greek, allegedly attributed to Dares, a Trojan priest of Hephaestus in the *Iliad*. It is a short text in Latin, decidedly as pro-Trojan as Dio's or. 11, and it recounts a situation vaguely similar to or. 20 about the Judgement of Paris.

> Alexander cohortari coepit (…) de Graecia domum rediturum esse (…) Nam sibi in Ida sylva cum venatum abisset, in somnis Mercurium adduxisse Junonem, Venerem, Minervam, ut inter eas de specie judicaret. Et tunc sibi Venerem pollicitam esse, si suam speciem meliorem harum specie judicaret, daturam se ei uxorem, quae in Graecia speciosior videretur: ubi ita audisset, optimam facie Venerem judicasse: unde sperare debere Priamum, Venerem adjutricem Alexandro futuram.

> Then Alexander began to exhort them (…) and return from Greece (…) while hunting in the woods on Mount Ida, he had fallen asleep and dreamt as follows: Mercury brought Juno, Venus, and Minerva to him to judge of their beauty. Then Venus promised, if he judged her most beautiful, to give him in marriage whoever was deemed the loveliest woman in Greece. Thus, finally, on hearing Venus' promise, he judged her the most beautiful. This dream inspired Priam with the hope that Venus would aid Alexander. (Transl. Frazer)
>
> Dares Phrygius, *The History of the Fall of Troy* 7

Both Dio and Dares Phrygius state that Paris came up with the abduction of Helen when they were in *otium*. But if Dares' version seems like a dream, that of Dio is more like a fantasy, strategically used by the author to achieve a moral warning. It is surprising to discover that the main modern commentators on orations 11 and 20 do not compare the two versions of the myth.⁴⁵ The only references to this parallelism are in Gangloff and Jouan,⁴⁶ but nobody has made a thorough comparison between the two passages from Dio's corpus dealing with the Judgement of Paris. Indeed, the episode is just a detail in the huge and complex oeuvre of Dio Chrysostom, but it could be a valuable element to add to Dio's views about the epic past.

It would be inappropriate to talk at length about the spread in antiquity of one of the best-known myths. It suffices to remember that it influenced all ancient literature, from *Cypria* to Collutus (400 AD) and beyond, and it was so widespread that it was continuously manipulated.[47]

The Judgement of Paris and the Abduction of Helen in or. 11 (*Trojan*)

The *Trojan* is perhaps one of the most interesting discourses for examining the mythical influences on Dio Chrysostom's production. Kindstrand considered this speech 'Respektlosigkeit', as representing a lack of respect towards Homer, and he set it in the framework of typically cynic behaviour.[48] Later, Desideri defined the text as 'an ideological manifesto', programmatic for the spread of the political ideas that Dio expressed and realized by putting the ideological truth before the historical one.[49] Apart from its literary and philosophical aims, the fundamental contribution of this work consists in delivering a new message to Dio's contemporaries. Indeed, by telling a sort of 'strategical' version of the myth, a version where the socio-historical paradigm is changed and the war ends with an armistice between the Trojans and Achaeans (and the consequent colonization of the Romans by the Phrygians), the *Trojan* is revolutionary. The impact of this text has to be evaluated beyond the way in which it rewrites the epos; moreover, its interpretation should privilege an overall philo-Roman point of view. This means that the text – probably addressed to the inhabitants of the New Ilion – wants to transmit the superiority of the Trojans (now winners) over the Greeks (now defeated). Furthermore, it would probably feel the need to connect the two communities and put a sentiment of Trojan *fides* at the basis of the Roman one.[50] Nevertheless, when considering the aims of the speech, it cannot be ignored that Dio starts his confutation of the Trojan War myth from the declared cause of the conflict: the abduction of Helen. Neither can it be neglected that Dio criticizes the Trojans' hatred of the daughter of Tyndareus (69) and their belief that she is responsible for the war. It is unfair, because she is Paris' lawfully wedded wife (119).[51] Dio seems surprised that Homer did not open his poem with this episode, but rather told it 'incidentally and shortly' (26: παρέργως καὶ βραχέως).[52] The poet talked that way even if he knew he was telling the contrary of the truth on an essential point of the story (27–8).[53] So, according to speech 11, the Judgement of Paris seems to be invented *a posteriori* in order to justify the foolishness of Helen's abduction. Moreover, the fact that Homer keeps silent about the development of the events means that the public did not feel any sympathy towards the Trojans. Therefore, the omission of the episode in the *Iliad* is the proof that Homer lies.

The Judgement of Paris and the Abduction of Helen in or. 20 *On the Subject of Anachoretic Life*

If speeches 6 and 7 present just an allusion to the abduction of Helen,[54] too weak to be compared to the open denialism of the *Trojan*, the inconsistency becomes more evident in speech 20. Neglected for a long time, perhaps because it is poor in elements that are useful for establishing its historical context, *On the Subject of Anachoretic Life* is interesting first of all for its philosophical and literary dimension. The speech takes the form of a diatribe and is probably addressed to a public of aspiring philosophers. Dio reflects with them about the philosopher's need to be able to think in any circumstances. It was probably composed in the same period of the so-called 'Bithynians' (the group of orations 38–51), which are traditionally set in the decade after Domitian's death in 96 AD. Desideri claimed that the speech was Dio's strongest attack on the Epicurean tenet that philosophy required isolation.[55] Indeed, in this text Dio reflects on the widespread meaning of ἀναχώρησις as the habit of avoiding duties: he spares his public an account of its bad consequences but if the author strictly affirms that there cannot be any excuse or indulgence for *otium* and retirement,[56] he soon makes it clear that, on the contrary, σχολή is allowed in case of meaningless matters. In general, the author is clearly against the conception of philosophy as a sort of personal refinement that could only be reached through loneliness and detachment from reality. He provides some examples from Classical Athens with the complicity of his public, knowledgeable in fifth- and fourth-century Greece. An Athenian who does not fight with Spartans or Macedonians, but who escapes to Megara or Aegina, for example, is not practising ἀναχώρησις; nor is someone who, being rich, decides to go far from his town to avoid financing liturgies. This is not ἀναχώρησις but escaping from responsibilities (1). For a large part of the oration, Dio faces, together with his interlocutors, the challenge of finding a definition of ἀναχώρησις. After a series of examples useful in defining what ἀναχώρησις is and is not, he explains that a philosopher must follow λόγος in all circumstances, and never distract himself from fulfilling his duties.

> (9) ἰδεῖν τε ἔστι καὶ ἐν τῷ πάνυ πολλῷ θορύβῳ τε καὶ πλήθει οὐ κωλυόμενον πράττειν ἕκαστον τὸ αὑτοῦ ἔργον ἀλλ' ὅ τε (…) διδάσκων αὐλεῖν τοῦτο ποιεῖ

πολλάκις ἐπ' αὐτῆς τῆς ὁδοῦ τὸ διδασκαλεῖον αὐλεῖν τοῦτο ποιεῖ πολλάκις ἐπ' αὐτῆς τῆς ὁδοῦ τὸ διδασκαλεῖον ἔχων καὶ οὐδὲν αὐτὸν ἐξίστησι τὸ πλῆθος οὐδὲ ὁ θόρυβος τῶν παριόντων.

And we often seee how even in the midst of a very great turmoil and throng the individual is not hampered in carrying on his own occupation; but, on the contrary (...) is (...) teaching a pupil to play it devotes himself to that often holding school in the very street, and the crowd does not distract him at all, nor the din made by the passers-by.

Dio Chrysostom, 20.9

Just like a flute teacher holding school in the street, the philosopher must learn how to think in the presence of noise (9: ἐν τῷ πάνυ πολλῷ θορύβῳ) and even fear loneliness because it harbours strange and inappropriate thoughts. That happened to Paris who was relaxing on Mount Ida when he felt the desire to have the most beautiful woman:

(19) (...) οἷον δὴ ἐγὼ οἶμαι τὸν Ἀλέξανδρον, ὡς ἐτύγχανε σχολὴν ἄγων ἐν τῇ Ἴδῃ περὶ τὰ βουκόλια, τοιαύτης ἐννοίας καὶ ἐπιθυμίας αὐτῷ γενομένης ὡς ἄρα εὔδαιμόν τε καὶ μακάριον τὸ τὴν πασῶν καλλίστην γυναῖκα ἔχειν.

(19) I may cite Alexander as an instance: I fancy that, when he happened to be enjoying a respite from his herdsman's duties on Mount Ida, the thought and with it the desire came to him, what a fortunate and blissful thing it would be to have the most beautiful woman in the whole world to wife.

Dio Chrysostom, 20.19

Wondering who she could be and where she could live, he found out that she was Helen, Tyndareus' daughter, Menelaus' wife, Castor and Pollux's sister. He suddenly realized that it would be impossible to conquer her without the favour of a god. As Paris' desire increased, he figured out a plan to turn his dream into reality. First, he realized that only Aphrodite, the goddess of love and marriage, could help him:

(21) (...) εἰ δὲ θεός τις ὑπόσχοιτο καὶ δοίη, τάχ'ἂν γενέσθαι τὸ τοιοῦτον. καὶ τίνα δὴ θεὸν ἄλλην εἰκὸς τὰς τοιαύτας χαρίζεσθαι χάριτας ἢ τὴν κρατοῦσάν τε καὶ ἄρχουσαν τῶν περὶ τοὺς γάμους τε καὶ ἔρωτας;

If some god should promise and give her, so wild an ambition might perhaps be realized. What goddess, then, he asked himself, was likely to grant favours of this kind other than she who held authority and ruled over all that pertained to marriage and to love?

Dio Chrysostom, 20.21

Then Paris decides that a good strategy to honour Aphrodite would be to give her a prize during a beauty competition against the most beautiful goddesses. Reporting Paris' thoughts, Dio writes:

> (22) νικᾶν δὲ καὶ προκρίνεσθαι κατὰ τοῦτο τίνος ἄν ποτε ἀξιώσειεν ἢ θεῶν τῶν πρώτων καὶ μεγίστων, Ἀθηνᾶς τε καὶ Ἥρας;
>
> (...) over what divinity, he asked himself would she think she could afford to prevail except over the foremost and greatest of them Athena and Hera?
>
> Dio Chrysostom, 20.22

The idleness of a clever man has caused the Trojan War: inactivity allowed Paris to elaborate a plan and abduct Helen, and made him follow his dream until it became dangerous. Dio is rewriting the epic tradition again.

> (...) οὕτω δὴ διελθών τε καὶ ἐξεργασάμενος τὴν αὑτοῦ δόξαν καὶ ἐπίνοιαν, οἷον ψυχῆς ἐν ὕπνῳ φαντασίαις καὶ δόξαις ἐπακολουθούσης καὶ μακρόν τι καὶ συντεταγμένον ὑφαινούσης ὄναρ, κριτής τε ὑπὸ τοῦ Διὸς γίγνεται τῶν θεῶν.
>
> So after canvassing the matter in this way and elaborating his own imagining and conceit, like a soul which in its sleep follows out its phantasies and imaginings and spins out some long and coherent dream, he is appointed by Zeus, he fancies, umpire over the goddesses.
>
> Dio Chrysostom, 20.22

He then continues to talk about the safe thoughts, desires and ambitions of ordinary men compared with the dreams of the rulers, monarchs or those who possess power or wealth:

> (24) (...) οὕτως αἱ μὲν ἰδιωτικῆς καὶ ἀδυνάτου ψυχῆς ἔννοιαί τε καὶ ἐπιθυμίαι ὑπηνέμιοί τε καὶ ἀδρανεῖς, καὶ οὐδὲν ἀπ' αὐτῶν γίγνεται χαλεπόν (...) τὰ δὲ τῶν μοναρχῶν ἢ πλουσίων ἢ ἄλλην τινὰ ἐχόντων δύναμιν ἐπὶ πέρας ἀφικνεῖται πολλάκις χαλεπόν τε καὶ (25) φοβερόν.
>
> Thus, whereas the thoughts and desires of the soul of a man in private station and without influence are wind-begotten and ineffectual, and no difficulty arises from them (...) yet those of monarchs, on the other hand, or of men of wealth or of those who possess some other power, quite often reach a fulfilment that is both grievous and (25) terrible.
>
> Dio Chrysostom, 20.24–5

Paris dreams of being called by Zeus to judge the goddesses, honouring Aphrodite in order to marry Helen. Now, if Paris – says Dio – was an everyman, his imagination would have not led to any consequences. Unfortunately, he was a μόναρχος: he gathered his crew and went to the house of Menelaus and Helen 'bringing into Troy the beginning of many grievous troubles and disasters'. A mind at leisure had the idea that led to the war. Moreover, contrary to what the *Trojan* says, the Trojan War started because of the goddesses' beauty contest, where Alexander was called to be the judge. Then comes the abduction of Helen, which was possible thanks to Aphrodite's complicity, since in a relaxing moment Paris imagined she could help him.

> (26) εἴρηται δέ μοι πάντα ταῦτα ἀπ' ἐκείνης τῆς ἀρχῆς καὶ ἐκτροπῆς, ὅτι δεῖ τὴν ψυχὴν ἐθίζεσθαι τὰ δέοντα πράττειν καὶ διανοεῖσθαι πανταχοῦ τε καὶ ἐν ἅπαντι θορύβῳ καὶ ἐν ἁπάσῃ ἡσυχίᾳ. εἰ δὲ μή, τὸ τῆς ἐρημίας τε καὶ ἡσυχίας οὐδὲν μεῖζον καὶ ἀσφαλέστερον τοῖς ἀνοήτοις τῶν ἀνθρώπων πρὸς τὸ μὴ πολλὰ καὶ ἄτοπα διανοεῖσθαί τε καὶ ἁμαρτάνειν.

All that I have said follows from that initial digressive remark that the mind should accustom itself to do and think what is essential to it everywhere, even in a perfect din as well as in perfect quiet. Otherwise seclusion and quiet offer no advantage and no greater safeguard, for men who are fools, to keep them from conceiving and committing many strange and wicked deeds.

Dio Chrysostom, 20.26

Conclusion

The comparison between speeches 11 and 20 does not suggest that there could be any similarity in the circumstances of composition of the two texts. Nowadays scholars agree that speech 11, which has been studied more than speech 20, is political. It probably belongs to the period when Dio managed Trajan's affairs in the Asian provinces. First it aims to emphasize the Roman lineage from Troy and perhaps to bring a message of peace and union inside the Empire.[57] It also probably aims to encourage the inhabitants of New Ilion to lay claim to their role as winners, in contrast with the Homeric tradition that labelled them as losers.[58] Speech 20, on the other hand, appears as a philosophical text, oriented towards a Cynic and Stoic view aiming to remind philosophers, and maybe next politicians, of their duties. At the same time, it would condemn the foolish behaviour of powerful rulers like Paris, who is first called τύραννος καὶ δυνάστης (23), and then considered a μόναρχος καὶ πλούσιος (24).

> (23) (…) εἰ μὲν οὖν αὐτὸ τοῦτο βουκόλος καὶ ἰδιώτης ἔτυχεν ὤν, οὐδὲν ἂν πρᾶγμα ἀπήντησεν ἐκ τοῦ τοιούτου ὀνείρατος. νῦν δὲ ἐπειδὴ τύραννος καὶ

δυνάστης ἦν καὶ πλούτῳ τε ἰσχύων καὶ ἀρχῇ πόλεως τῆς τότε μεγίστης (…) ἧκεν ἄγων εἰς Τροίαν πολλῶν καὶ χαλεπῶν πραγμάτων καὶ (24) συμφορῶν ἀρχήν.

If, then, he had been nothing more than a herdsman and a commoner in rank, no trouble would have come to him from that ambitious dream. But as it was, since he was of kingly blood and a mighty prince, and of great influence owing to his wealth and the dominion over the greatest city of those days (…) he returned to his home, bringing into Troy the beginning of many grievous troubles and disasters.

Dio Chrysostom, 20.23–4

Even with their diversity of intents, style and arguments, speeches 11 and 20 present some similarities in methods. In both cases, the Homeric encyclopaedia provides the pretext to παιδεία. In the *Trojan*, this pretext is represented by the final moment of the Homeric myth, while in speech 20 it is enclosed in the starting point, i.e. the cause of the war. Second, both orations probably reflect a civic dimension: speech 11 by having the inhabitants of New Ilion as the audience, and speech 20 by talking to the future ruling class (perhaps Bithynian), probably philosophers engaged in politics. Finally, even with different arguments, both orations transmit the same message: the Trojan war was a mistake. Trapp considers the manipulation of the myth in or. 11 as the task of Dio as an 'ideological evangelist for Roman Imperial values',[59] and this is true even for or. 20. Indeed, even with the differences between the rewritings of the story (in or. 11 by showing that the Trojans won, or in or. 20 by emphasizing that the war started on a whim), Dio shows that the Imperial age is the historical moment when philosophers had to engage themselves in building long-lasting peace for their community.

Notes

1   D.Chr. 11.17.
2   D.Chr. 11.12.
3   D.Chr. 11.37–74: 61.
4   At least in the written text we have received.
5   Cf. Vagnone 2003, Gangloff 2006, Minon 2012, Scafoglio 2014, 2015, 2016. For a brief summary of the plot, see also Brodersen's contribution in this volume (Chapter 7).
6   There are several references to Homer in Dio's production, especially in *On Homer* (Orr. 53), *On Homer and Socrates* (Orr. 55) and probably in the lost work *On Homer's Defense against Plato*, that the Suda attributes to Dio.

7 It is not easy to choose a good translation for oration 20's title Περὶ τῆς ἀναχωρήσεως because of the influence Christianity played in the diffusion of the term ἀναχώρησις. In this chapter, it should be taken to mean a temporary way to express leisure and detachment from political life and social duties.
8 D.Chr. 20.19–25.
9 Here and below, the English translations of Dio Chrysostom's extracts in this chapter are always by Cohoon 1932–1940. The Greek text is by Arnim 1893–1896, which is still the most complete edition of Dio Chrysostom that is available. For an overview of the dionean theory about kingship see Desideri 2019: 239–85.
10 In this speech Alexander the Great probably represents Trajan. For an interesting perspective about the *imitatio Alexandri* in Trajan see Gangloff 2009.
11 Whereas lyric poetry seems to be allowed in religious and encomiastic contexts (see *On Kingship* 2).
12 More precisely, according to Dio's Alexander, Hesiodic epic is only fit 'for shepherds, carpenters, and farmers' (Orr. 2.8), not for men who want to rule.
13 Bost Pouderon 2008: 37–47.
14 The speech *On Training* (Orr. 18) is currently part of my PhD project; at present, the most complete study about the possible chronology and addressee of the speech is Amato 2014, especially 97–118.
15 This hypothesis was proposed for the first time by Amato and summarized in a five-point argumentation in Amato 2014: 107–8.
16 Vagnone 2012: 7–21 and Desideri 2019: 239–49.
17 This topic has been widely studied, see among others Alden in Finkelberg 2012 s.v. 'Paradigms', in *The Homer Encyclopedia*, 2, 624–6.
18 Dorandi 1982: 19 and 34.
19 Cf. Gangloff 2006: 120.
20 Cf. Robert 2015: 73–86.
21 Favreau-Linder 2013: 375–97.
22 Cf. Desideri 1991 and Desideri 2019: 75–126.
23 Consider *On Homer* (Orr. 53), for example, but also *On Homer and Socrates* (Orr. 55), *Agamemnon or On Kingship* (Orr. 56), *Nestor* (Orr. 57), *Achilles* (Orr. 58), *Chryseïs* (Orr. 61) and several other mentions of Homeric mythological episodes in Dio's corpus.
24 Kindstrand 1973: 141–62.
25 Desideri 1978: 480–2.
26 But also to the historians, see Scafoglio 2016: 457–8.
27 Vagnone 2014: 181–4.
28 Hunter 2009: 43
29 Cf. Scafoglio 2020: 16–17.
30 Olivieri 1898: 586–607.

31 I refer here to the controversy between Arnim and Hirzel concerning the literary genre of Dio's discourses. See Panzeri 2011: 57–60.
32 See, for example, Kindstrand 1973.
33 Swain 1996: 188.
34 Desideri 1991 and Desideri 2019: 75–126.
35 Scafoglio 2016: 441.
36 Gentili 2006: 98.
37 For Aphrodite's gifts see *Il.* 3.52–5. In *Il.* 3.70 Homer explicitly talks about Helen's possessions, supposedly stolen by Paris during the abduction.
38 The words Ἀλεξάνδρου ἕνεκ' ἄτης have been interpreted in different ways. For a detailed study of the term ἄτη in the *Odyssey* see Scafoglio 2015: 136.
39 Aristarchus athetized the verses *Il.* 24.28–30 as not Homeric. He thought that Homer would have narrated the episode in a better way, had he known about it. Several points are obscure. For example, why does Helen never refer to the Judgement of Paris even if she often talks about her abduction? Furthermore, even admitting that the contest did happen, why would Priam blame the conflict on the gods, and not on Paris (*Il.* 3.164)? Moreover, Homer would have never let Hera, whom he calls 'mother', join a beauty competition. Walcot 1977: 31–9 rejected Aristarchus' position. For the study of Aristarchus' scholia see Severyns 1928: 261–4; for an in-depth study of the scholia about the Trojan War see Schironi 2018: 662–5. Even accepting the verses, it is still hard to understand what Alexander's ἄτη is.
40 Stinton 1990: 17. On Helen in Latin literature see Carbonero 1989: 378–91.
41 Page 1962, fr. 15.
42 Cf. Hdt. 2.118–19.
43 Plato, one of the most recognized models for Dio Chrysostom, also believed that Helen went to Egypt. In *Rep.* 9, 586c Socrates talks to Glaucon about the pleasures that compromise the capacity of seeing the truth, so he refers to Stesichorus' *Palinode* and underlines that Helen's εἴδωλον has been at the centre of a contest due to ignorance of the truth. Plato might mean that Greeks and Trojans, misled by the desire of pleasure, fought a bloody conflict without understanding that they were fighting for a false cause. In the *Phaedrus*, too, Plato refers to Stesichorus when Socrates remembers the poet's blindness as a punishment reserved for those who make mistakes in matters of mythology (243a: τοῖς ἁμαρτάνουσι περὶ μυθολογίαν).
44 See Ioli's contribution in this volume (Chapter 1).
45 See e.g. Cohoon/Crosby 1932–1940, Calderón 1988–2000, Vagnone 2003.
46 See Jouan's PhD thesis, unpublished: 162–3 and Gangloff 2006, 244.
47 For a detailed overview of the use and reuse of Helen's myth, see Calame 2009: 645–61. For Helen's abduction, see Gumpert 2002.
48 Kindstrand 1973: 149.
49 Desideri 1978: 431–3.

50 Cf. Saïd 2000: 178.
51 Apart from the text, see also Minon 2012: 95 n. 152.
52 The passage has many *loci paralleli*, but it is useful to remember that Dio's criticism to Homer's omission comes from *schol.* b. ad *Il.* 2,494, I, 288 Erbse (cf. Vagnone 2016: 430 with n. 21).
53 Dio probably knows the Aristotelian theory (*Poet.* 1459a) that considers the Homeric choice of telling the story ἕν μέρος a good one. Indeed, Aristotle compared the Homeric version of the Trojan War with that of the Epic Cycle, concluding that Homer's version was stronger and more appealing because it was shorter and more coherent. On the contrary, the narration of the entire war would inevitably become heavy and fragmentary. Even if in speech 11 Dio criticizes the story's incompleteness, he admires the decision of focusing on just one moment of a long tale (cf. Scafoglio 2020: 18–19).
54 Or. 6, 17–18 and or. 7, 93–5: cf. above, *Manipulation of Epos in the Second Sophistic: Techniques and Intents.*
55 Desideri 1978: 377.
56 Cf. or. 20.2–3.
57 The aim of pacifism is often recognized in several texts and contexts of Dio's corpus, due both to his political role and his personal experience. A strong pacifism appears for example in or. 12 (*Olympic Speech: Or, on Man's First Conception of God*), which probably dates back to the 97 AD (Ventrella 2017: 1). Here Dio seems to laud the Getae's fighting for freedom and their patriotism in opposition to the Roman covetousness for power (see Desideri 2013; Ventrella 2014: 153–70; Ventrella 2017: 1–13, 3–4; Desideri 2019: 217–24).
58 For the aims of speech 11 see Vagnone 2003: 17–20.
59 *Troy and the True Story of the Trojan War*, the contribution is unpublished but available online, p. 17.

References

Amato, E. 2014, *Traiani praeceptor: studi su biografia, cronologia e fortuna di Dione Crisostomo*, Besançon.

Arnim, von, J. 1893-6, *Dionis Prusaensis quem vocant Chrysostomum quae extant omnia, edidit apparatu critico instruxit J. De Arnim edidit apparatu critico instruxit J. de Arnim*, Berlin.

Bost-Pouderon, C. 2008, 'Dion Chrysostome et le genre épistolaire: à propos du Περι λόγου ἀσκήσεως (Orr. XVIII), le seul "discours" de Dion rédigé sous la forme épistolaire: un traité ou une lettre?', in Laurence, P. and Guillaumont, F. (eds), *Epistulae antiquae 5. Actes du Ve colloque international "L'épistolaire antique et ses prolongements européens" (Université François-Rabelais, Tours, 6-7-8 septembre 2006)*, Leuven: 37–47.

Calame, C. 2009, 'The abduction of Helen and the Greek poetic tradition: politics, reinterpretations and controversies', in Dill, U. and Walde, C. (eds), *Antike Mythen, Medien, Transformationen und Konstruktionen*, Berlin/New York.

Calderón, G. Morocho Gayo-G. Del Cerro, 1988–2000, *Dion de Prusa. Discursos, traducción, introducciones y notas, I–IV*, vol. I, Madrid.

Carbonero, O. 1989, 'La figura di Elena di Troia nei poeti latini da Lucrezio ad Ovidio', *Orpheus* 10, 2: 378–91.

Cohoon, J. and Crosby, H. L. (eds) 1932–51, *Dio Chrysostom, with an English Translation*, 5 vols, London.

Desideri, P. 1978, *Dione di Prusa: Un intellettuale greco nell'impero romano*, Messina/Firenze.

Desideri, P. 1991, 'Tipologia e varietà di funzione comunicativa degli scritti dionei', *Aufstieg und Niedergang der römischen Welt (ANRW)* 2.33.5, Berlin: 3903–59.

Desideri, P. 2013, 'Lo Zeus di Olimpia emblema di pace secondo Dione di Prusa', *Antigüedad, Religiones y Sociedades (ARYS)* 11: 239–47.

Desideri, P. 2019, *Ellenismo imperiale. Nuovi studi su Dione di Prusa*, Pisa.

Dorandi, T. 1982, *Filodemo. Il buon re secondo Omero; edizione, traduzione e commento*, Naples.

Favreau-Linder, A. 2013, 'Citations poétiques et stratégies rhétoriques: la parole poétique comme instrument de mise en scène du sophiste', in Vial, H. (ed.), *Poètes et orateurs dans l'antiquité: mises en scène réciproques*, Clermont-Ferrand: 375–97.

Gangloff, A. 2006, *Dion Chrysostome et les mythes. Hellénisme, communication et philosophie politique*, Grenoble.

Gangloff, A. 2009, 'Le sophiste Dion de Pruse, le bon roi et l'empereur'. *Revue Historique*, 133, 1: 3–38.

Gentili, B. 2006, *Poesia e pubblico nella Grecia antica. Da Omero al V secolo*, Milan.

Gumpert, M. 2002, *Grafting Helen. The Abduction of the Classical Past*, Madison, WI.

Hunter, R.. 2009, 'The *Trojan Oration* of Dio Chrysostom and ancient Homeric criticism', in Grethlein, J. and Rengakos, A. (eds), *Narratology and Interpretation: The Content of Narrative Form in Ancient Literature*, Berlin-New York: 43-61.

Jouan, F. 1966, *Dion Chrysostom. Discours Troyen (XI: Qu'Ilion n'a pas été prise)*, PhD thesis, I–II, Université Paris IV.

Kindstrand, J. 1973, *Homer in der Zweiten Sophistik*, Uppsala.

Minon, S. 2012, *Dion de Pruse, Ilion n'a pas été prise, discours 'Troyen' 11*, Paris.

Olivieri, A. 1898, 'Gli studi omerici di Dione Crisostomo', *RFIC* 26: 586–607.

Page, D. 1962, *Poetae melici Graeci*, Oxford.

Panzeri, A. 2011, *Dione di Prusa. Su libertà e schiavitù; Sugli schiavi: discorsi 14 e 15*, Pisa/Rome.

Robert, F. 2015, *La présence d'Homère dans les Progymnasmata d'époque impériale*, in Dubel, S. (ed.), *À l'école d'Homère. La culture des orateurs et des sophistes*, Paris: 73–86.

Saïd, S. 2000, 'Dio's use of mythology', in Swain, S. (ed.), *Dio Chrysostom: Politics, Letters and Philosophy*, Oxford: 161–86.

Scafoglio, G. 2014, 'Introduction. An Epic Cycle revival', *Philologia Antiqua* 7: 11–13.

Scafoglio, G. 2015, 'I due volti di Elena. Sopravvivenze della tradizione orale *nell'Odissea*', *Gaia* 18: 133–44.

Scafoglio, G. 2016, 'Il riuso del testo omerico e del ciclo epico nel *Troiano* di Dione. Osservazioni metodologiche ed esemplificazione', in *Dion de Pruse: l'homme, son oeuvre et sa postérité. Actes du Colloque international de Nantes (21–23 mai 2015)*, Hildesheim: 435–63.

Scafoglio, G. 2017–18, 'Dione vs Omero. Decostruzione e rielaborazione della leggenda di Troia', *RET Supplément* 5: 333–82.

Scafoglio, G. 2020, 'Criticism and rework of Homeric narrative in Dio's Trojan Discourse', *Classica et Mediaevalia* 68: 15–36.

Schironi, F. 2018, *The Best of the Grammarians. Aristarchus of Samothrace on the Iliad*, Ann Arbor MI.

Severyns, A. 1928, *Le cicyle épique dans l'école d'Aristarque*, Liège.

Stinton, T. C. W. 1990, *Collected Papers on Greek Tragedy*, Oxford.

Swain, S. 1996, *Hellenism and Empire. Language, Classicism and Power in Greek World, A. D. 50–250*, Oxford.

Trapp, M. 2010, *Troy and the True Story of the Trojan War*: unpublished paper delivered to the Oxford Ancient History Seminar, available online.

Vagnone, G. 2003, *Dione di Prusa, Troiano: Or. 11. Edizione critica, traduzione e commento*, Rome.

Vagnone, G. 2012, *Dione di Prusa, Orazioni I, II, III, IV ('Sulla regalità'), Orazione LXII ('Sulla regalità e sulla tirannide'), edizione critica, traduzione e commento (con una introduzione di Paolo Desideri)*, Rome.

Vagnone, G. 2014, 'Per una storia della fortuna dell'or. XI di Dione di Prusa (Troiano, ovvero sul fatto che Ilio non è stata presa) in età moderna: da Ursinus (1679) a Krayer (1687) in Germania, a Sieben (1727) in Olanda', *QUCC* 106: 181–4.

Vagnone, G. 2016, 'L'esegesi omerica di Dione di Prusa: metodi e modelli', in Amato, E. et al. (eds), *Dion de Pruse: l'homme, son oeuvre et sa postérité. Actes du Colloque international de Nantes (21–23 mai 2015)*, Hildesheim: 421–33.

Ventrella, G. 2014, 'Appendice. Sulla presenza di Dione nel *castrum* di *Viminacium* alla morte di Domiziano', in Amato, E. (ed.), *Traiani praeceptor: studi su biografia, cronologia e fortuna di Dione Crisostomo*, Besançon: 153–70.

Ventrella, G. 2017, *Dion de Pruse dit Dion Chrysostome. Oeuvres: [Or. 12–13]*, Paris.

Walcot, P. 1977, 'The Judgement of Paris', *G&R* 24: 31–9.

7

Homer's Lies and Dio's Truth? Subverting the Epic Past in Dio Chrysostom's *Trojan Oration*

Isidor Brodersen

Introduction

> Ὅμηρος δὲ καὶ πρῶτος καὶ μέσος καὶ ὕστατος παντὶ παιδὶ καὶ ἀνδρὶ καὶ γέροντι, τοσοῦτον ἀφ' αὑτοῦ διδοὺς ὅσον ἕκαστος δύναται λαβεῖν.
>
> But Homer is first and in the middle and last for every child, adult and old man, because he gives of himself just as much as each of them can take.[1]
>
> Dio Chrysostom, 18.8

This sentiment, expressed by Dio Chrysostom in his eighteenth oration *On Training for Public Speaking*, is what one would expect from a successful orator of the period we know as the Second Sophistic: Homer is the ultimate guiding star in all human endeavours and central to a Sophist's παιδεία. There are many instances in Dio's surviving orations that feature Homer as the highest role model.[2] This in itself is hardly surprising and is in keeping with the Sophistic self-presentation which can be found not only in Dio, but in many other authors of the period as well.[3] The classicism of πεπαιδευμένοι in the first three centuries AD, in style as well as in content, has been much remarked upon, and texts from this period are rich in allusions to and quotations from Homer. These routinely show the author's erudition, and by associating himself with the greatest poet, a πεπαιδευμένος can show his own status as a member of the educated elite.

All the more interesting, then, are those instances within the Second Sophistic where Homer's prime position is contested or even flat-out denied. One of these texts, Dio Chrysostom's eleventh or Trojan oration, is the focus of this chapter. The story presented in the text goes like this: some time in the late first or early second century AD, Dio visited the Roman town of Ilium, where the ancient city of Troy used to be, and gave a speech to the local citizens. As was customary, the speech he gave was meant as a token of goodwill towards his audience. To achieve this, Dio set out on an interesting venture: he claimed that Troy had never fallen, and that Homer's account of its downfall was not to be trusted. Thus, since their ancestors were never actually defeated, the present-day Ilians should find solace in their late rehabilitation. Within the framework of a *captatio benevolentiae* and a speech aimed at this particular audience, contradicting Homer is the obvious thing to do – Dio's audience at Ilium will be more pleased with him than anyone elsewhere. This is made explicit near the beginning of the speech:

εἰ μὲν οὖν παρ' Ἀργείοις ἐτόλμων ἀντιλέγειν Ὁμήρῳ, καὶ τὴν ποίησιν αὐτοῦ δεικνύναι ψευδῆ περὶ τὰ μέγιστα, τυχὸν ἂν εἰκότως ἤχθοντό μοι καὶ τῆς πόλεως ἐξέβαλλον εἰ τὴν παρ' ἐκείνων δόξαν ἐφαινόμην ἀφανίζων καὶ καθαιρῶν· ὑμᾶς δὲ δίκαιόν ἐστί μοι χάριν εἰδέναι καὶ ἀκροᾶσθαι προθύμως· ὑπὲρ γὰρ τῶν ὑμετέρων προγόνων ἐσπούδακα.

Now if I ventured to contradict Homer in front of the Argives, and to show his poetry as false regarding the most important things, perhaps it would be only reasonable for them to be angry at me and drive me out of town, if I seemed to obliterate and clear up their (under-)standing derived from these things: but it is only right that you should be grateful and eager to hear me, because I have always been backing your ancestors.

Dio Chrysostom, 11.5

At least, this is the story that the narrator of the Trojan oration would have his audience believe. This chapter seeks to argue that not only is this not necessarily what happened, but rather that this charming picture undercuts the whole point of the speech.[4] In his Trojan oration, Dio has no interest in flattering anyone, but rather invites his audience to join him on a thought experiment which is meant to entertain, but certainly has a deeper point: in following Dio's preposterous claims and analysing them, the audience can show their own παιδεία.

In order to make this point, there will follow a brief summary of the eleventh oration. In a second step, Dio's criticisms of Homer that can be found in the speech have to be examined: what arguments does the speaker bring forward against the central authority figure, and what alternatives are there to be found? In this light, it is interesting to look at possible interpretations of theme and execution which have been brought forward in modern scholarship – and why some of these might not quite suffice in explaining the oration's agenda. Instead, it will be argued that there is much to be gained by understanding the speech not only as an oration for a special occasion such as a performance in Troy, but also as a text which invites its readers to engage with it in a meaningful way. This is not merely a speech to be heard, but rather a text to be read and re-read many times. The focus in this section is not only on the arguments Dio makes against Homer's version of events, but especially on the way he frames them. This can help in a better and deeper understanding of the text.

There have been many attempts, since the nineteenth century, to identify the precise date of the Trojan oration.[5] These endeavours, while certainly worthwhile, are not central to the argument of this chapter. It is impossible to ascertain the historical veracity of a possible visit by Dio to Ilium; such a visit is certainly plausible, but there can be no definitive proof. But if we understand the Trojan oration as a literary text meant for wider circulation, any attempt at rooting it in a particular time or place becomes not only unnecessary, but rather a hindrance in interpreting it. The central argument here is that, like most of Dio's texts, the speech is not confined to one single situation, but transcends the genre of rhetoric for one occasion. Instead, it is eminently literary in character. This is not to say that a performance of the piece by Dio or others is completely out of the question: the text is rich in rhetorical flourish and would certainly make for a good show anywhere in the Graeco-Roman world. But even such a performance is, of course, by no means confined to the specific occasion invoked by the text itself – and in many ways would struggle to do justice to the many layers of the speech, as will be shown. It is also quite a difficult hypothesis to try to reconstruct an ancient author's life merely from his own statements, as has often been tried with Dio.[6] Little can be said about him with certainty, and constructing 'phases' in his extant work is bound to be circular reasoning.[7] If, however, we engage with the text in and of itself, these matters become less important. In this vein, one more caveat: it is important to distinguish between Dio, the historical person and author of the text, and his narrative first-person voice in the eleventh oration. These two should not be considered the same, and any reference to 'Dio' as the narrator must be interpreted with this in mind.[8]

Dio's Trojan oration: a brief summary

Even if the Trojan oration is one of Dio's best-known and most discussed pieces, a very brief look at its contents and main points will help the following argument. The speech starts out by making a general observation (chapters 1–3): it is far easier, and therefore far more popular, to believe in a convenient lie than to face an inconvenient truth. This is even more true of lies that have been around for some time: the older a tale, the more believable it is. The narrator wants to tackle this phenomenon by arguing that Homer did not tell the truth about the Trojan War, especially with respect to two plot points: Helen and her abduction by (or marriage to) Paris, and Achilles and his death. The narrator's aim is to achieve this using only Homer's own texts as the basis for his argument[9] – a point that distinguishes him from, for example, Gorgias, who pays little attention to Homer in his own defence of Helen.[10] The true version of events, as the narrator tells it, comes from an Egyptian priest he supposedly met, who told him all this in great detail. The figure of this priest will be of interest later on. According to him, Paris did not abduct Helen,[11] but their liaison was the result of political manoeuvres.[12] Helen's marriage to Paris of Troy had been approved by her father and her brothers alike, and it was just Agamemnon's political anxiety that led to violent conflict.[13] Homer's version of the story is therefore plainly ridiculous: the Judgement of Paris obviously cannot be true, and the involvement of Gods and Goddesses is pure Homeric fiction. Accordingly, Homer is accused of his worst lies when he paraphrases the divine conversations: how could he possibly know what Zeus and Hera say to each other in their private chats?[14] This is straightforward enough, and in keeping with common Homeric criticism.

The argument concerning Achilles and his death is rather complex – one might even say sophistic. It is too complex to reproduce here in greater detail, but the story goes something like this: in Homer's version of events, as recorded in the *Iliad* from book 16 onwards, Hector and the Trojans attack the Greek camp and drive the Greeks back to the ships. Achilles, who is famously moping in his tent, has to send out Patroclus in his own armour to save the day. Patroclus, of course, is killed by Hector who takes Achilles' armour. After that, Thetis supplies Achilles with a fresh set of arms made by Hephaestus so he can rejoin the fight. He does, and he kills Hector, as everyone who has ever read or heard Homer is well aware. All this, according to Dio, is nonsense. The truth is that in the battle by the ships, it was Achilles, not Patroclus, who was killed by Hector. Everything that happens after this point in Homer's narration (i.e. everything after book 16) is pure fiction, cooked up on the fly by Homer in order to please the Greeks of his day. The lies pile on so much that, in the end, Homer apparently gives up and does not even bother narrating the end of his story: the sack of Troy. This argument is especially interesting since of course, in Dio's version of events, the city was never sacked anyway. Thus, Dio claims:

εἰς τοῦτο δὲ προελθὼν ἀπεῖπε λοιπόν, οὐκ ἔχων ὅ τι χρήσηται τῇ ποιήσει καὶ τοῖς ψεύσμασι δυσχεραίνων ἀγῶνά τινα προσθεὶς ἐπιτάφιον, καὶ τοῦτο πάνυ γελοίως, καὶ τὴν Πριάμου βασιλέως εἰς τὸ στρατόπεδον ἄφιξιν παρὰ τὸν Ἀχιλλέα, μηδενὸς αἰσθομένου τῶν Ἀχαιῶν, καὶ τὰ λύτρα τοῦ Ἕκτορος. καὶ οὔτε τὴν τοῦ Μέμνονος βοήθειαν οὔτε τὴν τῶν Ἀμαζόνων, οὕτως θαυμαστὰ καὶ μεγάλα, ἐτόλμησεν εἰπεῖν, οὔτε τὸν τοῦ Ἀχιλλέως θάνατον οὔτε τὴν ἅλωσιν τῆς Τροίας.

When [Homer] reached this point [i.e. his narrative dead end after having Achilles, who in Dio's reality is already dead, kill Hector], he gave up on the rest, not knowing what he should use in his poem and disgusted at his own lies, adding some sort of funeral games, a perfectly ridiculous thing, and king Priam's arrival in the [Greek] camp and his visit to Achilles, without anyone of the Greeks noticing, and the ransom of Hector. And neither of Memnon's help or of that by the Amazons, such remarkable and great things, did he venture to speak, nor of Achilles' death or of the sack of Troy.

Dio Chrysostom, 11.109

As can be seen from this excerpt, the criticism of Homer employed in the speech is twofold. On the one hand, Homer is wilfully distorting the truth and telling lies. On the other hand, his lies do not even make too much sense. Not only is Homer consciously lying to his audience, but he is supremely bad at it. Homer is not just bad at recording the truth, which would be a grievous fault in and of itself – a 'bad historian', so to speak; he is also bad at organizing and telling his fictitious version of events and arranging it according to the rules of which every πεπαιδευμένος is well aware. In other words he is even, regardless of truth, a bad storyteller![15] Therefore, it is worth looking at two separate questions: what makes Dio a better truth-teller than Homer, and what makes him a better story-teller? Of course, the distinction is not always easy to make in antiquity, but for the sake of the argument, one will be examined after the other. First, the narrator's criticism with regard to content.

Homer's lies and Dio's truth

Homer's telling of the Trojan War, especially towards the end of the *Iliad*, is well known, and was well known in antiquity. But instead of his telling of Patroclus' death and Achilles' ensuing revenge, it is now time to examine Dio's version of events. Here, the initial caveat about 'Dio' being the narrator of the Trojan oration, rather than the historical person, is complicated even further: as mentioned briefly earlier, most of the Trojan oration is not even the narrator himself, but rather his account of a conversation he had with an Egyptian priest, whose first appearance in the speech is in chapter 37:

ἐγὼ οὖν ὡς ἐπυθόμην παρὰ τῶν ἐν Αἰγύπτῳ ἱερέων ἑνὸς εὖ μάλα γέροντος ἐν τῇ Ὀνούφι, ἄλλα τε πολλὰ τῶν Ἑλλήνων καταγελῶντος ὡς οὐθὲν εἰδότων ἀληθὲς περὶ τῶν πλείστων, καὶ μάλιστα δὴ τεκμηρίῳ τούτῳ χρωμένου ὅτι Τροίαν τέ εἰσι πεπεισμένοι ὡς ἁλοῦσαν ὑπὸ Ἀγαμέμνονος καὶ ὅτι Ἑλένη συνοικοῦσα Μενελάῳ ἠράσθη Ἀλεξάνδρου· καὶ ταῦτα οὕτως ἄγαν πεπεισμένοι εἰσὶν ὑφ' ἑνὸς ἀνδρὸς ἐξαπατηθέντες ὥστε καὶ ὀμόσαι ἕκαστος.

So I will tell it as I learned it from one of the priests in Egypt, a very old man in Onuphis, who often derided the Greeks in many respects, because he thought they didn't know anything true about most matters, but he especially used this as proof: they are convinced that Troy was sacked by Agamemnon and that Helen fell in love with Paris while she was living with Menelaus. And they are so completely convinced of this, duped by one single man, that every one of them swears to its truth.

Dio Chrysostom, 11.37

This introduction (or rather lack thereof) for a trusted source for what is to follow is quite remarkable.[16] Not only does the priest remain unnamed, there is very little detail about him. The narrator does not give any names (not even his own), nor any circumstances of their meeting or any further information. Even the name of the priest's supposed hometown poses a host of problems – modern texts give it as Onuphis, since that is the closest to the mysterious ὄνυχι of the manuscripts, but this is nothing but conjecture. The figure of the priest, therefore, is highly elusive and apparently less trustworthy than one might wish. This need not be a huge problem, and a solution might not be strictly necessary: the vague nature of this Egyptian authority figure is certainly intentional, and it is clear that the reader is not meant to be able to ground him in reality. Indeed, virtually everyone agrees he is probably a figment of Dio's imagination.[17] The implications of this will be discussed shortly. As can be expected of an author of the Second Sophistic, there is of course precedent: a knowing nod to Herodotus and his 'Egyptian' version of the events surrounding Helen is highly likely.[18] But not only does the narrator introduce his mysterious Egyptian friend, the reader is even told about the sources for their story:

ἔφη δὲ πᾶσαν τὴν πρότερον ἱστορίαν γεγράφθαι παρ' αὐτοῖς, τὴν μὲν ἐν τοῖς ἱεροῖς, τὴν δ' ἐν στήλαις τισί, τὰ δὲ μνημονεύεσθαι μόνον ὑπ' ὀλίγων, τῶν στηλῶν διαφθαρεισῶν, πολλὰ δὲ καὶ ἀγνοεῖσθαι τῶν ἐν ταῖς στήλαις γεγραμμένων διὰ τὴν ἀμαθίαν τε καὶ ἀμέλειαν τῶν ἐπιγιγνομένων· εἶναι δὲ καὶ ταῦτα ἐν τοῖς νεωτάτοις τὰ περὶ τὴν Τροίαν· τὸν γὰρ Μενέλαον ἀφικέσθαι παρ᾽ αὐτοὺς καὶ διηγήσασθαι ἅπαντα ὡς ἐγένετο.

He told me that in their culture, all history of earlier times is written down, some of it in the temples, some of it on certain columns, and some things are remembered only by a few people as the columns have been destroyed; but much of what is written on the columns is disbelieved because of the ignorance and indifference of later generations. But these stories about Troy are among the most recent records: because Menelaus came to them and told them everything, just as it happened.

Dio Chrysostom, 11.38

This is an obvious nod to the beginning of the speech: even if the truth used to be visible to all, and parts of it still are, it has no power over the ignorance of the masses. This is highly ironic: Dio cannot present any concrete evidence for the Egyptian's claims, but asks his audience to believe him even without the sources to back him up. Homer, even though he is as good a source as any, is discounted on the thin basis that Dio holds the Egyptian to be more believable. This is at the same time underscored and undercut by the priest's disappearance. Even more vague than his introduction is the way this Egyptian priest fades out of the oration. In the Greek text, it becomes unclear who is speaking by chapter 110:[19] it might still be the Egyptian, it might be the narrator. The lines begin to blur.[20] This argument relies rather heavily on the aforementioned supposition that the text is meant to be read. Having a physical version in front of themselves, the ancient πεπαιδευμένος (and, by extension, the modern scholar) is able to trace this blur and make sense of it. In the event of a performance, which might plausibly last several hours, it might be doubtful whether the priest's disappearance is all that noteworthy. Only a close and repeated engagement with the text can reveal such hints which are, as will be argued later, laid on purpose by Dio.

The Egyptian's reconstruction of the story of Helen is surprisingly unsentimental about political necessities, political alliances and the resulting forces of conflict. Gods (or even Paris' bored day-dreams, as discussed in the twentieth oration – cf. Sara Tirrito's contribution in this volume, Chapter 6) have no part in it; instead it all boils down to 'an explosive cocktail of patriotism, wounded male pride and commercial calculation'.[21] These are rationalist objections to Homer's myth, as they have been brought forward by Homeric critics of all times.[22] The resulting tale of Helen and Paris could even be read as a historiographical account.[23] The truth about Achilles is far less clear-cut. Dio does have the true version of events, of course, but as mentioned earlier, it is unclear whether this comes from his Egyptian informant or somewhere else. One might question whether (and if so, why) the Egyptian columns mentioned in chapter 38 go so far as to contain the impressive deeds of Hector and the other Trojans, but that is beside the point. Because the narrator's real objection to Homer's telling of Patroclus' and Hector's death lies elsewhere, it does not make sense as a narrative.

The Egyptian can only help the narrator so much. He is invaluable in setting the historical record straight and exposing Homer's most obvious lies. However, as touched upon before, the narrator's main focus in almost all of his attacks on Homer is not historical, but literary.[24] He is not so much rewriting history as rewriting the story. He is, as Richard Hunter puts it, 'concerned not just with whether or not Homer "got his facts right", but with how elaborated poetic versions of "history" arise'.[25] In this vein, let us turn to Homer the bad storyteller.

Homer the bad storyteller

In presenting all this, Dio obviously has his tongue planted rather firmly in his cheek. Nevertheless, leaving aside all the polemics and rhetorical flashes, the version of events laid out in the Trojan oration is rather compelling. In laying out the 'true' history of the Trojan War, the narrator elegantly explains some of the most vexing problems in Homeric studies. In fact, as Gustav Adolf Seeck puts it, Dio seems to be anticipating modern analysis of Homer, as it was practised in the nineteenth and early twentieth centuries.[26] This is quite far removed from the question of historical truth. Of course, the 'truth' that Hector really killed Achilles matters, but Dio's focus is less on the events than on how to tell them. Seeck claims it 'looks like engaging with the *Iliad* has become an end in itself for Dio, and he lets his philological and literary interest run free'.[27] What is of interest in this context, then, is the way that Dio frames his criticism of Homer. Of course, part of this is the 'authentication apparatus' which is employed in the oration, from insisting on telling the truth to introducing the Egyptian priest.[28] The more interesting part, however, is the larger frame at work. In this case, the word 'frame' can be taken quite literally to mean the very beginning and the very end of the oration, i.e. roughly chapters 1–37 and 147–54. For example, in the beginning, even if Homer's preposterous story of Paris and Helen were true, the narrator takes issue with how it is presented – or rather, not presented:

ἢ πόθεν μᾶλλον ἄρξασθαι ἔπρεπεν ἢ ἀπ' αὐτοῦ τοῦ ἀδικήματος καὶ τῆς ὕβρεως τοῦ Ἀλεξάνδρου, δι' ἣν συνέστη ὁ πόλεμος, ἐπειδὴ συνωργίζοντο ἂν πάντες οἱ τῇ ποιήσει ἐντυγχάνοντες καὶ συνεφιλονίκουν ὑπὲρ τοῦ τέλους καὶ μηδεὶς ἠλέει τοὺς Τρῶας ἐφ᾽ οἷς ἔπασχον· οὕτω γὰρ εὐνούστερον καὶ προθυμότερον ἕξειν ἔμελλε τὸν ἀκροατήν.

Or where would it have been more appropriate to start, if not with this injustice and Paris' insolence, which caused the war, since then everyone who chanced upon the poem would have been outraged and would have been eager for the end, and nobody would have pitied the Trojans for what they suffered? In that way, he would have a more sympathetic and more interested audience.

Dio Chrysostom, 11.28

Similarly, Homer's decision not to recount Troy's fall and the human suffering involved is criticized. Even though it did not really happen in his version of events, the narrator cannot resist painting a vivid picture:

εἰ δ᾽ αὖ ἐβούλετο τὰ μέγιστα καὶ φοβερώτατα εἰπεῖν καὶ πάθη παντοδαπὰ καὶ συμφοράς, ἔτι δὲ ὃ πάντων μάλιστα ἕκαστος ἐπόθει ἀκοῦσαι, τί μεῖζον ἢ δεινότερον εἶχεν εἰπεῖν τῆς ἁλώσεως; οὔτε ἀνθρώπους πλείους ἀποθνήσκοντας οὐδὲ οἰκτρότερον τοὺς μὲν ἐπὶ τοὺς βωμοὺς τῶν θεῶν καταφεύγοντας, τοὺς δὲ ἀμυνομένους ὑπὲρ τῶν τέκνων καὶ τῶν γυναικῶν, οὔτε γυναῖκας ἢ παρθένους ἄλλοτε ἀγομένας βασιλίδας ἐπὶ δουλείᾳ τε καὶ αἰσχύνῃ, τὰς μὲν ἀνδρῶν, τὰς δὲ πατέρων, τὰς δὲ ἀδελφῶν ἀποσπωμένας, τὰς δέ τινας αὐτῶν τῶν ἀγαλμάτων, ὁρώσας μὲν τοὺς φιλτάτους ἄνδρας ἐν φόνῳ κειμένους καὶ μὴ δυναμένας ἀσπάσασθαι μηδὲ καθελεῖν τοὺς ὀφθαλμούς, ὁρώσας δὲ τὰ νήπια βρέφη πρὸς τῇ γῇ παιόμενα ὠμῶς, οὔτε ἱερὰ πορθούμενα θεῶν οὔτε χρημάτων πλῆθος ἁρπαζόμενον οὔτε κατ᾽ ἄκρας ὅλην ἐμπιμπραμένην τὴν πόλιν οὔτε μείζονα βοὴν ἢ κτύπον χαλκοῦ τε καὶ πυρὸς τῶν μὲν φθειρομένων, τῶν δὲ ῥιπτουμένων.

If, on the other hand, he wanted to tell of the greatest and most terrible things and of all sorts of suffering and calamities, and that which everybody wanted to hear above all else, what greater or more awe-inspiring subject would there have been to tell than the sack of the city? He could not find an occasion where more people met their death; where more pitifully some men sought refuge at the altars of their gods, while others tried to save their children and wives; never at another time were women and maidens dragged away, even royals, into slavery and disgrace, some torn from their husbands, others from their fathers or their brothers, some even from the statues of their gods, watching their beloved husbands lying in their death, unable to embrace them or to avert their eyes, and watching their infant babies thrown cruelly to the ground; never at another time were sanctuaries of the gods desecrated, or such an amount of wealth plundered, or the whole city burnt to the ground, never was there greater mourning or clash of bronze and fire, as some were perishing, others were being hurled upon the fire.

Dio Chrysostom, 11.29–30

This is a very effective rhetorical flourish (even more so in Greek, and it is quite difficult to translate) – especially considering that, as the narrator will go on to show, none of this ever happened. It can clearly be seen here that truth may just be a vehicle for the narrator, and his true intention lies elsewhere. Of course, Homer does not tell his audience any of this because this is where he has most to hide,[29] but the argument here is quite detached from that. It has far more to do with aesthetical considerations.[30] In Dio's telling, Homer was making his poem up as he was going along, which explains how he arrived at a narrative dead end and had to cobble together an unsatisfactory ending (see above). The orality of his presentation seems to be one of the larger problems – had Homer known where he was going from the beginning or not decided to change the story in order to please his Greek audience, his poem might have ended up being better. Besides the aesthetical point, therefore, this criticism already hints at the fact that Homer's ultimate aim in his lies is not too far from the narrator's own considerations as mentioned in chapter 5 of the oration, which was quoted at the beginning: it is to please his audience, and to tell a version of the story that is fit for his own day. This is made explicit near the end of the speech:

βούλομαι δὲ καὶ περὶ Ὁμήρου ἀπολογήσασθαι, ὡς οὐκ ἀνάξιον ὁμολογεῖν αὐτῷ ψευδομένῳ. πρῶτον μὲν γὰρ πολὺ ἐλάττω τὰ ψεύσματά ἐστι τῶν περὶ τοὺς θεούς· ἔπειτα ὠφέλειάν τινα εἶχε τοῖς τότε Ἕλλησιν, ὅπως μὴ θορυβηθῶσιν, ἐὰν γένηται πόλεμος αὐτοῖς πρὸς τοὺς ἐκ τῆς Ἀσίας, ὥσπερ καὶ προσεδοκᾶτο. ἀνεμέσητον δὲ Ἕλληνα ὄντα τοὺς ἑαυτοῦ πάντα τρόπον ὠφελεῖν. τοῦτο δὲ τὸ στρατήγημα παρὰ πολλοῖς ἐστιν.

But I want to offer a defence on Homer's behalf, in that it is not unseemly to agree with him in his lies. First, these lies are far less serious than those about the gods; secondly, they had a certain advantage for the Greeks of those days, so that they would not be alarmed if war came upon them against the people of Asia, as was expected. It is also quite fit and proper that one who is Greek helps his people in every possible way. This is a very common device.

Dio Chrysostom, 11.147–8

Dio (in this case meaning the narrator of the oration as well as Dio Chrysostom as its author) clearly understands that 'poetic myth is a recollection of "real events" but told for particular purposes and with a particular spin aimed at particular contemporary audiences'.[31] And as the narrator admits in the closing moments of his speech, there is nothing wrong with that – his point is just that Homer is not doing *enough* to please the Greeks, not distorting the truth far enough, and not fully embracing his aim. Implicitly, this is of course true for the narrator as well. So what is his audience to make of his claims that he is trying to please the Ilians on the one hand, but strictly adhering to the truth on the other? In order to find an answer, there will follow an overview of several distinct interpretations of the Trojan discourse by the scholarship of the last century or so.

Interpretations in scholarship so far

There has been much debate as to how seriously one should take the whole speech. Often, this has been connected with the question of its date and its place in Dio's curriculum vitae: if it is taken to be an early work from what is often called Dio's 'Sophistic' period, scholars argue that the Trojan Oration is a purely rhetorical exercise, an ἀνασκευή, without further meaning. But, in the words of the Loeb translation's introduction: 'others feel that in view of the self-assurance of the speaker and the skill with which he presents his arguments, the speech belongs to Dio's riper years and that he had some serious purpose in delivering it.'[32] As has been argued in this chapter so far, Dio did indeed have 'some serious purpose in delivering it', but this does not mean it has to be the work of an old and wise man. Nor does it mean it has to be an early piece – as stated in the beginning, it is neither necessary nor possible to pinpoint a date or the exact circumstances under which the speech was composed (and maybe delivered). The main positions on the Trojan Discourse can be divided into three categories: that it is purely rhetorical, that it is in fact a piece of pro-Roman propaganda, and that it has the aforementioned other 'serious purpose'. In going through these interpretations, it will be shown that the 'serious purpose' can be pinpointed quite well.

ἀνασκευή

The first position, that the Trojan discourse is a rhetorical showpiece, is the oldest, dating back to the twelfth century, when the Byzantine scholar Eustathius, in his *scholia* on the *Iliad*, declared that Dio 'had undertaken to perform an ἀνασκευή of the story of Troy' (καὶ ὁ Δίων ἐπηγωνίσατο ἀνασκευάσαι τὰ Τρωικά). An ἀνασκευή is roughly defined as 'the overturning of any given subject' and taken to be a regular exercise for young orators.[33] This was picked up by Hans von Arnim in the late nineteenth century.³⁴ Von Arnim and subsequent scholars like Wilhelm Kroll and Josef Mesk in the early twentieth century expanded on this argument. Using ancient rhetorical textbooks like that by Aphthonius,³⁵ they diligently tracked everything that the Trojan oration had in common with a blueprint version of the perfect ἀνασκευή. This included trying to find all the textbook modes of attack (such as the matter in question being ἀπίθανον 'unbelievable', ἀπρεπές 'improper', ἄλογον 'illogical' etc.), and if that was impossible, arguing that even diverging from textbook practice was textbook practice. As Mesk put it in 1920: 'According to the sensible provisions of the theorists, it was neither necessary to use every *topos* in every ἀνασκευή, nor was their order fixed'.³⁶ To the modern eye, however, this approach seems over-structured. It seems that rather than engaging with the speech in its entirety, scholars were concentrating on ticking off all the rhetorical boxes. But in ticking off the boxes, it is easy to lose sight of everything else that is going on. Rather than just refuting Homer, the narrator paints a vivid picture of his own (or rather the Egyptian priest's) truth, which would not be necessary in an ἀνασκευή, and he does so in remarkable fashion: by introducing a trusted source, by setting the speech in Ilium, and by expanding massively on the scope of his subject. The aforementioned German scholars do not factor this into their interpretations at all, and even in the twenty-first century, the Egyptian priest is still relegated to a footnote in papers that focus on the rhetorical side of the Trojan discourse.³⁷

Pro-Roman propaganda

In 1973, Jan Fredrik Kindstrand proposed a different reading of the Trojan oration, and for the first time expanded on the idea that there was indeed a serious purpose behind it. In his dissertation on Homer in the Second Sophistic, he proposes that Dio's real aim in making the speech is to flatter not the citizens of Ilium, but rather Rome and its empire: it is to be read, at least in part, as a piece of pro-Roman propaganda.³⁸ This interpretation was picked up and expanded upon by Paolo Desideri a few years later.³⁹ It relies heavily on the account of events after the war in the oration, in chapters 137–44. Here, the narrator presents the fates of Greek and Trojan leaders after the war as proof that Troy was indeed victorious. While the Greek leaders suffered discontent from the troops, shipwreck, discord among themselves and some of them were exiled or even killed once they got home,⁴⁰ the Trojans' actions after the war are those of victorious people: they send out parties to colonize Thessaly and Italy, headed by Helenus and Aeneas respectively. In this context, the narrator calls the city founded by Aeneas, i.e. Rome, obviously, πόλιν τὴν μεγίστην πασῶν, 'the largest city of all'. Of course, it is not impossible to translate this as 'the greatest city of all' (as the Loeb translation does), but this is far from definite. Furthermore, apart from this it is difficult to find any real praise of Rome or its empire. The closest might be chapter 150 near the very end:

ἴσως ἂν οὖν εἴποι τις ἀνήκοος, Οὐκ ὀρθῶς Ἕλληνας καθαιρεῖς. ἀλλ᾽ οὐδὲν ἔστιν ἔτι τοιοῦτον, οὐδὲ ἔστι δέος μή ποτε ἐπιστρατεύσωνται ἐπὶ τὴν Ἑλλάδα τῶν ἐκ τῆς Ἀσίας τινές· ἥ τε γὰρ Ἑλλὰς ὑφ᾽ ἑτέροις ἐστὶν ἥ τε Ἀσία. τὸ δὲ ἀληθὲς οὐκ ὀλίγου ἄξιον.

Now, perhaps someone who didn't listen might say, it is not proper how you disparage the Greeks. But this is no longer the case, and there is no more fear that someone out of Asia would wage war against Greece: For Greece is subject to others, and so is Asia. But the truth is worth a great deal.

Dio Chrysostom, 11.150

To read this as an encomium of *pax romana*, however, seems far-fetched. It comes in the context of the narrator's defence of Homer: just before the cited passage, he discusses how the Persian wars are commemorated in Persia. While the great victories at Marathon and Salamis are, of course, central to Greek identity, we are told that the Persians frame their expeditions in equal parts as unimportant and successful for themselves. The narrator presents this as understandable: within a certain political climate, it is wise to tell one's own version of events (an argument that hearkens back to the beginning of the speech, as discussed). Therefore, neither is Dio disparaging the Greeks nor is it surprising that Homer would want to please them. The argument then would be that reassuring a Greek audience about a possible Persian invasion (or vice versa) is unnecessary within Roman world domination. But to read the passage like this is to put rather too much weight on the first part of the quotation, and rather too little on the last sentence: what the speech purports to be about is truth, in all its situational forms, not Rome. If there was indeed a deeper point in the speech, wanting to praise Rome as guardian of free speech, one might reasonably expect more than this.[41] These two mentions in passing are 'hardly lavish praise',[42] and nowhere in the speech is Rome even mentioned by name. If Dio wanted to acclaim Rome and Roman power, this is surely a very subtle way of doing it. Of course, this is not the only point that Kindstrand believes the speech is meant to make. Rather, there is also a moral and educational aim at work, namely to fight imaginary knowledge and unjustified pride.[43] This point is indeed worth thinking about: what exactly is Dio's way of fighting ignorance, apart from ripping into it and blasting it rhetorically? Is there, in other words, a constructive aim to be found, a manual as to how to fight ignorance? There might be, but the audience have to think and play along, as will be discussed shortly.

'Lügenerzählung'

One last noteworthy interpretation of the Trojan discourse is that it could be a 'Lügenerzählung' or 'lying narrative', as proposed by Elfriede Fuchs in 1996. This would root the speech not in rhetorical or political culture, but rather in the context of literary narratives of, for example, the ancient novel. In this interpretation, much is made of Dio's 'lie signals',[44] such as the introduction of the Egyptian priest as a source, the insistence on telling the truth, and the attacks on Homer that differ from his treatment in other texts by Dio. The merit in this approach is that it takes the whole text, rather than only a small portion of it, and tries to make sense of it all. However, the resulting interpretation is rather thin and might even be considered a step back compared with Kindstrand. Fuchs merely states that Dio's argument is flawed and his objections to Homer are rather feeble.[45] Dio's criticism is taken seriously, but his argument is seen as too weak to be convincing. However, the way Dio presents this argument is paid less attention. Fuchs does detect the 'lie signals' Dio has put in place, which is important for a conclusive reading of the text, but does not ask why they are there. In the end, the speech as a whole is, again, not taken seriously: the aim, as Fuchs puts it, is just to ridicule the gullibility of the masses and to show that with appropriate hairsplitting, even the clearest facts can be denied.[46] This is certainly one way of interpreting the Trojan oration, and if we take it as a text that the audience is merely meant to take in, but not to interact with, it seems conclusive. But within the Second Sophistic, relegating the audience to so passive a role seems shortsighted. Even if Fuchs agrees that the speech was not necessarily held at Ilium, her argument is not quite going far enough. As concerns his immediate audience, as listeners in Ilium or as readers anywhere, the narrator is certainly not trying to ridicule their gullibility. Rather, he wants them in on the joke.[47]

Trust no one: framing Homer, framing Dio

So what is at work here then? Is it 'an earnest intervention into contemporary literary critical debates, a Cynic polemic against ignorance and popular opinion, or a devastating parody of the excesses of Homeric criticism'?[48] All these factors might well be at play here; but above all, much is to be gained by reading the oration as an invitation to the audience to join in, and to work out for themselves that Dio is pulling everyone's legs: the cynics', the critics', and the sophists' – and by extension, maybe even his own. The first clue to this is given very early in the speech, right after the narrator's announcement that the citizens of Ilium will enjoy his speech more than others, which was quoted at the beginning of this chapter. The narrator goes on to say:

προλέγω δὲ ὑμῖν ὅτι τοὺς λόγους τούτους ἀνάγκη καὶ παρ' ἑτέροις ῥηθῆναι καὶ πολλοὺς πυθέσθαι· τούτων δὲ οἱ μέν τινες οὐ συνήσουσιν, οἱ δὲ προσποιήσονται καταφρονεῖν, οὐ καταφρονοῦντες αὐτῶν, οἱ δέ τινες ἐπιχειρήσουσιν ἐξελέγχειν, μάλιστα δὲ οἶμαι τοὺς κακοδαίμονας σοφιστάς.

I will tell you upfront: it is inevitable that these words will also be spoken to other people, and that many will notice them. Of these, some will not understand them, others will pretend to sneer at them, although they don't really, and others again will try to refute them, especially, I guess, those wretched sophists.

Dio Chrysostom, 11.6

Not only is this a strong indication that the speech is indeed not confined to the city of Ilium, but the narrator actually invites criticism of his argument. Putting too much weight on the expression 'wretched sophists', as has been done in the past, can cloud the passage. Here, the narrator clearly presents his thoughts to the whole οἰκουμένη of πεπαιδευμένοι, and his expectation of his audience is clear: some might not get it – but of course, the individual reader or listener would never list themselves among these. Nor would anyone count themselves among those who pretend not to care – after all, one has taken the time and effort to engage with the speech. Rather, this is to be read as an invitation, if somewhat tongue-in-cheek, to join the 'wretched sophists' in refuting Dio, as he is refuting Homer.[49] As has been shown, he has given these critics ample material to work with:[50] he criticizes Homer for making things up as he goes along, while at the same time being sloppy himself introducing and maintaining the façade of an Egyptian priest. And while he announces very clearly that his own oration is to be heard in many places, he chides Homer for doing the same:

ἐνταῦθα δὲ γενόμενος Ὅμηρος οὐδὲν ἔτι τἀληθοῦς ἐφρόντισεν, ἀλλ' εἰς ἅπαν ἧκεν ἀναισχυντίας καὶ πάντα τὰ πράγματα ἁπλῶς ἀνέτρεψε καὶ μετέστησεν εἰς τοὐναντίον, καταπεφρονηκὼς μὲν τῶν ἀνθρώπων, ὅτι καὶ τἆλλα ἑώρα πάνυ ῥᾳδίως πειθομένους αὐτούς καὶ περὶ τῶν θεῶν, οὐκ ὄντων δὲ ἑτέρων ποιητῶν οὐδὲ συγγραφέων, παρ' οἷς ἐλέγετο τἀληθές, ἀλλ' αὐτὸς πρῶτος ἐπιθέμενος ὑπὲρ τούτων γράφειν, γενεαῖς δὲ ὕστερον ξυνθεὶς πολλαῖς, τῶν εἰδότων αὐτὰ ἠφανισμένων καὶ τῶν ἐξ ἐκείνων ἔτι, ἀμαυρᾶς δὲ καὶ ἀσθενοῦς ἔτι φήμης ἀπολειπομένης, ὡς εἰκὸς περὶ τῶν σφόδρα παλαιῶν, ἔτι δὲ πρὸς τοὺς πολλοὺς καὶ ἰδιώτας μέλλων διηγεῖσθαι τὰ ἔπη, καὶ ταῦτα βελτίω ποιῶν τὰ τῶν Ἑλλήνων, ὡς μηδὲ τοὺς γιγνώσκοντας ἐξελέγχειν. οὕτως δὴ ἐτόλμησε τἀναντία τοῖς γενομένοις.

But reaching this point [i.e. the Trojan attack on the Greek camp, before Achilles' intervention], Homer had no more concern for the truth, but instead came into complete shamelessness and simply turned everything upside down and reversed things to their opposite, because he held the people in contempt, since he saw that they were very easily convinced of the other things, even about the gods; because there were no other poets or authors from whom he could read the truth, but he was the first who set about writing about these things, collecting them many generations later, after those who had known the facts had perished, and their offspring as well, so that only an obscure and uncertain tradition was left, as it is very probable with the distant past; and because he wanted to recite his epics to the masses and the common people, and he made these epics more favourable toward the Greeks, so that even those in the know could not refute him. Thus he even went so far as to tell the opposite of what had happened.

Dio Chrysostom, 11.92

The parallels between Homer and the narrator are very clear: they both speak many generations after the events (as mentioned in the beginning of the speech, when the narrator tells his audience that older lies are even more convincing than new ones, see above), and they both have an audience in mind whom they want to please. There is, however, an important distinction between the narrator and his ancient counterpart: Homer is aiming to please not only the Greek elite of his day, but τοὺς πολλοὺς καὶ ἰδιώτας, 'the masses and the common people'. This is not the world in which the narrator (and, by extension, Dio as the author) puts himself. He will have to cope with 'wretched sophists', but commoners will not be engaging with his speech. While Homer fools the masses, Dio's objective is more focused: he wants his audience to be part of the educated few, the sophists, rhetoricians and πεπαιδευμένοι. In analysing the Trojan oration, these peers of his, the γιγνώσκοντες, 'those in the know' can indeed refute him, and he invites them to do so. Homer in hand, they can see that it is very possible indeed to accuse the narrator of 'overstating the achievements of the Trojans', in order to please his imaginary audience of Ilians. We have seen that Dio does not mind storytelling or poetry being a 'momentary opportunistic creation'.[51] It becomes increasingly clear, then, that for all his assurances that his own goal is truth alone, he surely does protest too much. And it is not only modern scholars who can detect this; the contemporary audience themselves can, too. Dio himself, quite apart from what his narrator states in the beginning of the speech, is certainly not trying to court the favour of Ilians or Romans – he is trying to show that by engaging with the speech, his readers can prove themselves worthy members of the knowing few, the πεπαιδευμένοι. And it does not hurt if there is amusement along the way.[52]

Conclusion

The aim of this chapter has been, among others, to show that it is worth reading and re-reading the Trojan oration from time to time. Its focus is less on actually refuting Homer or on making some political point, but in a display of παιδεία. This is not just Dio's own erudition: he relies on the audience to be as educated as he is, and to use their own education to set themselves apart from 'the masses and the common people'. It is worth stressing that this reading of the text does not need to be exclusive. Surely not everyone reading or hearing the Trojan oration can be trusted to follow the hints as laid out in this chapter, and there is indeed much enjoyment to be had just reading (or hearing) the oration as a bit of friendly fun at Homer's expense or a rhetorical tour de force that does indeed seek to convince its audience of its own veracity. If we take the notion of stratifying audiences and playing to more than one crowd seriously, nothing need stand in the way of other forms of reception. But, as I hope to have shown, the text does lend itself strongly towards an audience that perceives themselves as elite and are able to prove this status by following the argument and criticizing it.[53]

One of the narrator's main critiques of Homer is that he muddled his story in telling it orally, which explains his narrative shortcomings;[54] the oral tradition is 'systematically presented as an imperfect reflection of a written text'.[55] Especially by presenting his own argument in the form of a speech, rather than some other form of treatise (as he well might have done – consider Plutarch's *De Herodoti malignitate*), Dio makes it clear that the audience is meant to read him exactly as he reads Homer: as an unreliable oral presenter of a situational truth. In the end, since the Trojan oration encourages its audience not just to listen, but to engage with it, to play along in the game, the clear distinction between author and reader becomes blurred. This is why questions about Dio's life or the precise date of the oration are not as vital to its understanding as one might think: as long as you are a πεπαιδευμένος, able to engage with the text and work with it, it is always up to date. It not only transcends Dio Chrysostom as its author, it might even transcend the Second Sophistic as its cultural background – after all, we are still reading and discussing it today.

Notes

1 The translation is the author's own, as are all that follow within this chapter unless otherwise specified.
2 E.g. D.Chr. 2.6, 44.1, 53.11, 55.19; cf. Kindstrand 1973: 113–38.
3 Cf. Drules 1998: 59–63. Other authors include Aelius Aristides as well as Lucian, who, of course, does not always take Homer too seriously and, in his *True Stories*, praises him for inventing stories in quite the same way as Dio does in his eleventh oration (Luc. *VH* 2.20). For further similarities between these two writers cf. Swain 1996.
4 This is not to say that a possible performance at Troy/Ilium is completely out of the question – there is simply no way of knowing. The arguments in favour, however, are few, and there is little reference in the speech to the Trojan setting; some details are even questionable or wrong, cf. Kim 2010: 93 and Trachsel 2002: 49–52. For a different view, cf. Jones 1978: 17, Szarmach 1978: 197, Trapp 2016. For a view exploring the rhetorical setting at Ilium and its implications, see Sara Tirrito's contribution in this volume (Chapter 6).
5 Cf. the concise summary in Kindstrand 1973: 143.
6 The latest attempt is Bekker-Nielsen 2008: 119–46; cf. also Moles 1978. For a critical assessment similar to the present argument, see Sidebottom 1996, Swain 1996: 188–90.
7 Cf. Krause 2003: 3.
8 Cf. Krause 2003, Bolonyai 2001: 27 for the practice of ἠθοποιία.
9 D.Chr. 11.11 – echoing rather closely that sentiment of Aristarchus, Ὅμηρον ἐξ Ὁμήρου σαφηνίζειν, cf. Saïd 2000: 181; Kim 2010: 85.
10 Cf. Kim 2010: 86. See also Roberta Ioli's contribution in this volume (Chapter 1).
11 Cf. Sara Tirrito's contribution in this volume (Chapter 6).
12 Cf. Anderson 2000: 152.
13 D.Chr. 11.62; cf. Hunter 2009: 47.
14 D.Chr. 11.18–20; cf. Fornaro 2002: 553.
15 Cf. Fornaro 2002: 555–6.
16 Cf. Kim 2010: 108.
17 For this kind of 'pseudo-documentarism', see among others Prosperi 2013: 10.
18 Hdt. 2.112–20. Cf. Fornaro 2002: 557, Kim 2010: 109–12. Plato's *Timaeus* is also very prominently present, cf. Fuchs 1996: 134, Jackson 2017: 228 with further literature.

19 Cf. Seeck 1990: 98 n. 5, Fuchs 1996: 133: 'so können spätere Erwähnungen eines Ich-Sprechers nicht mehr eindeutig dem Priester zugeordnet werden (110; 116)'. The Loeb translation by Cohoon inserts phrases like 'so the Egyptian claimed' (93), but these have no basis in the Greek text.
20 Cf. Szarmach 1978: 196.
21 Hunter 2009: 47–8.
22 Seeck 1990: 99.
23 Cf. Jackson 2017: 228.
24 Cf. Billault 2006: 14–15: 'Dion est un lecteur et un interprète des textes. [...] Il ne pratique pas la critique historique, mais la critique littéraire.'
25 Hunter 2009: 45.
26 Seeck 1990: 98; cf. Hunter 2009: 44.
27 Seeck 1990: 97: 'Es sieht eher so aus, als ob für Dion die Beschäftigung mit der Ilias zum Selbstzweck geworden ist und er seinem philologisch-literarischen Interesse freien Lauf lässt.'
28 Fuchs 1996: 133: 'Beglaubigungsapparat'.
29 Cf. Kim 2010: 102.
30 For a different view, see Fornaro 2002: 557. The argument that Dio is borrowing heavily from forensic speeches (cf. Seeck 1990: 106, Hunter 2009: 54, Kim 2010: 100) is interesting, but space does not allow for this discussion here.
31 Hunter 2009: 45.
32 Cohoon/Crosby 1932: vol. I, 445.
33 Cf. e.g. Bolonyai 2001: 28–30, Kindstrand 1973: 154.
34 Arnim 1898: 166–71. The work remains a seminal study, even though some of its arguments have not aged well.
35 Cf. Bolonyai 2001: 26.
36 Mesk 1920: 117: 'Somit brauchten nach der vernünftigen Vorschrift der Theoretiker weder in jeder Anaskeue alle Topoi verwendet zu werden noch war deren Reihenfolge eine feste.' See also 119–20: 'Dio hat somit in der Troiana fast alle üblichen Topoi der Anaskeue (bzw. Kataskeue) angewandt, u. zw. ganz im Sinne der Schule weder alle im gleichen Umfange noch in bestimmter Reihenfolge, sondern hat allein das Bedürfnis maßgebend sein lassen. Er hält sich damit wie in seinen übrigen Reden fern von aufdringlichem schematischen Aufbau.'
37 Bolonyai 2001 only mentions the priest at p. 33 n. 41.
38 Kindstrand 1973: 158–62.
39 Desideri 1978: 431–4.
40 Dio mentions Diomedes and Neoptolemus as being exiled; Agamemnon is killed and replaced as King by Aegisthus, cf. D.Chr. 11.132–3.
41 Cf. Kim 2010: 89: The notion of a pro-Roman stance is based on 'what after all is a relatively small stretch of text'; for a different view, cf. Fornaro 2002: 549.

42 Swain 1996: 211.
43 Kindstrand 1973: 150: 'Dion hat offenbar ein moralisch-pädagogisches Ziel und will was die Mythen betrifft eingebildetes Wissen und unberechtigten Stolz bekämpfen.' Cf. the summary at p. 162: 'Zusammenfassend möchte ich sagen, dass wir in der 11. Rede eine philosophisch-literaturkritische Schrift mit einem ethischen und politischen Zweck haben, die eine sehr unterhaltende Form hat.'
44 Fuchs 1996: 129–30.
45 Fuchs 1996: 131: 'Allerdings sind Dions Einwände oft reichlich dünn.'
46 Fuchs 1996: 136: 'So macht er sich in seiner 11. Rede über die Leichtgläubigkeit der Menschen lustig und beweist, dass mit entsprechender Spitzfindigkeit und überzeugendem Aplomb auch die klarsten Tatsachen auf den Kopf gestellt werden können.'
47 For a similar game played with different strata of the educated audience, see Nicholas Wilshere's contribution on Lucian's *Judgement of the Goddesses* in this volume (Chapter 5).
48 Kim 2010: 88.
49 Cf. Hunter 2009: 51: 'One aspect of Dio as a new (and anti-)Homer, and of Dio's appropriation of the tradition of epic criticism, to which there is space here merely to allude, is the possibility that Dio has composed the Trojan Oration in such a way as to make it open to some of the same modes of criticism as the Homeric poems themselves.' See also Moles 1978: 90–1.
50 Cf. Hunter 2009: 52.
51 Kim 2010: 136.
52 Cf. Hunter 2009: 51.
53 Cf. also Nicholas Wilshere's contribution in this volume (Chapter 5).
54 Cf. Kim 2010: 130: 'Dio's innovation in the *Trojan oration* lies in his decision to read Homer's text as the written transcription of an oral, improvisatory, testimonial narrative.'
55 Saïd 2000: 177.

References

Anderson, G. 2000, 'Some uses of storytelling in Dio', in Swain, S. (ed.), *Dio Chrysostom. Politics, Letters, and Philosophy*, Oxford: 143–60.

Arnim, von, J. 1898, *Leben und Werke des Dio von Prusa. Mit einer Einleitung: Sophistik, Rhetorik, Philosophie in ihrem Kampf um die Jugendbildung*, Berlin.

Bekker-Nielsen, T. 2008, *Urban Life and Local Politics in Roman Bithynia. The Small World of Dion Chrysostomos*, Aarhus.

Billault, A. 2006, 'Rhétorique et herméneutique dans le *Discours troyen* (XI) de Dion Chrysostome', *Papers on Rhetoric* 7: 1–16.

Bolonyai, G. 2001, 'The uses of Progymnasmata: the case of "Refutations" and Dio's *Trojan Oration*', *AAntHung* 41: 25–34.
Cohoon, J. and Crosby, H. L. 1932–51 (eds), *Dio Chrysostom, with an English Translation*, 5 vols, London.
Desideri, P. 1978, *Dione di Prusa. Un intellettuale greco nell'impero romano*, Florence.
Drules, P. 1998, 'Dion de Pruse lecteur d'Homère', *Gaia* 3: 59–79.
Fornaro, S. 2002, 'Omero cattivo storico: l'orazione XI di Dione Crisostomo', in Montanari, F. (ed.), *Omero tremila anni dopo*, Rome: 547–60.
Fuchs, E. 1996, 'Die 11. Rede des Dion Chrysostomos als Lügenerzählung', *Lexis* 14: 125–36.
Hunter, R. 2009, 'The "Trojan Oration" of Dio Chrysostom and ancient Homeric criticism', in Grethlein, J. and Rengakos, A. (eds), *Narratology and Interpretation: The Content of Narrative Form in Ancient Literature*, Berlin: 43–61.
Jackson, C. 2017, 'Dio Chrysostom', in Richter, D. and Johnson, W. (eds), *The Oxford Handbook of the Second Sophistic*, Oxford: 217–32.
Jones, C. 1978, *The Roman World of Dio Chrysostom*, London.
Kim, L. 2010, *Homer between History and Fiction in Imperial Greek Literature*, Cambridge.
Kindstrand, J. 1973, *Homer in der Zweiten Sophistik. Studien zu der Homerlektüre und dem Homerbild bei Dion von Prusa, Maximos von Tyros und Ailios Aristeides*, Uppsala.
Krause, C. 2003, *Strategie der Selbstinszenierung. Das rhetorische Ich in den Reden Dions von Prusa*, Wiesbaden.
Kroll, W. 1915, 'Randbemerkungen', *RhM* 70, 591–610.
Mesk, J. 1920, 'Zur elften Rede des Dio von Prusa', *WS* 42: 115–24.
Moles, J. 1978, 'The career and conversion of Dio Chrysostom', *JHS* 98: 79–100.
Prosperi, V. 2013, *Omero sconfitto. Ricerche sul mito di Troia dall'antichità al rinascimento*, Rome.
Saïd, S. 2000, 'Dio's Use of Mythology', in Swain, S. (ed.), *Dio Chrysostom. Politics, Letters, and Philosophy*, Oxford: 161–86.
Seeck, G. 1990, 'Dion Chrysostomos als Homerkritiker (or. 11)', *RhM* 133: 97–107.
Sidebottom, H. 1996, 'Dio of Prusa and the Flavian Dynasty', *CQ* 46: 447–56.
Swain, S. 1996, *Hellenism and Empire. Language, Classicism, and Power in the Greek World AD 50–250*, Oxford.
Szarmach, M. 1978, 'Le Discours troyen de Dion de Pruse', *Eos* 66: 195–202.
Trachsel, A. 2002, 'La Troade: entre espace littéraire et paysage historique', *ARF* 4: 41–53.
Trapp, M. 2016, 'Philostratus, Aristides and the Geography of Declamation', in Poignault, R. and Schneider, C. (eds), *Fabrique de la déclamation antique (controverses et suasoires)*, Lyon 197–210.

8

A Rhetorical Trojan War: Philostratus' *Heroicus*, the Power of Language and the Construction of the Truth[1]

Valentin Decloquement

What kind of truth?

The expressed aim of Philostratus' *Heroicus* is to reach the truth about the Trojan War. Written in the first half of the third century AD, this text is a fictional dialogue between a winemaker and a Phoenician merchant who have just met: the former reveals that he became a friend of Protesilaus, the first hero who died at Troy but came back to life and told him everything he knew. Now that the winemaker has access to an eyewitness report of the legendary conflict, he can prove that Homer and the poets of the epic Cycle deliberately lied.

The status of truth in the *Heroicus* has long been the subject of discussion. From the end of the nineteenth century onwards, two possible trends can be identified. Several scholars argued that Philostratus wrote a mere rhetorical game, whose main purpose was to show off his sophistic skills to a disillusioned readership.[2] Against this sceptical vision, some researchers assumed that the text aimed at converting its audience to the traditional hero cult:[3] this is the main view of a 1929 article written by Samson Eitrem, who nonetheless admits that the sophist did not necessarily believe in what he said.[4] The current tendency is to read the *Heroicus* as a work of fiction:[5] as Peter Grossardt and Lawrence Kim showed, the *mise en scène* of an eyewitness report is a typical strategy of pseudo-documentary works of Imperial writers like Dio of Prusa, Dictys Cretensis, Dares Phrygius or Lucian.[6]

Following the latter approach, I will analyse the process of exposing that so-called 'truth'. I hope to highlight a main feature in the *Heroicus*: many episodes of its Trojan tale are introduced and supported by a rhetorical contestation of ancient poets. I will try to move beyond the dichotomy between 'serious' purposes and playful invention by using rhetorical devices as a hermeneutical tool.[7] Thus, I would like to read the dialogue as a sophistic enquiry on the power of speech. It is not an accident that Philostratus chose the heroic past of the Trojan War as the area of such an enquiry: the historicity of that event was taken for granted in Antiquity, but its content was considered to have been distorted by Homer and the Epic Cycle for poetical reasons.[8] In that sense, one of the main questions asked throughout the *Heroicus* is as follows: given that the only sources on the Trojan War are not to be trusted, how can we talk about a past that is no longer reachable?

Before getting to the heart of the matter, we can note that Protesilaus is an ambiguous source. Philostratus could have written a direct dialogue between the winemaker and the ghost. Instead, the dead hero only appears in the main interlocutor's speeches, and his testimony is often reported in indirect speech (i.e. through infinitive subordinate clauses), as we will see later. Therefore, it is sometimes hard to determine who the author of an idea is:[9] are we hearing Protesilaus' tale or the winemaker's personal commentary on this tale? Added to that, one may wonder why Philostratus chose this particular hero to propose an eyewitness report on the Trojan War. The Phoenician's objections encourage the readership to maintain a critical attitude, referring to a tradition already mentioned in the Iliadic Catalogue of Ships.[10]

> Φ.: Τὸν γὰρ πόλεμον ὃς περὶ τῇ Τροίᾳ ἐγένετο, πῶς ἂν διηγοῖτο μήτε διαπολεμήσας αὐτόν ἀποθανών τε πρῶτος τοῦ Ἑλληνικοῦ παντὸς, ἐν αὐτῇ, φασί, τῇ ἀποβάσει;
>
> Phoenician: Indeed, the war that took place for Troy, how could he [i.e. Protesilaus] possibly outline it although he did not even carry this war through, but was the first from the whole Greek army who died, as they say, during the very landing?
>
> Philostratus, *Heroicus* 7.2[11]

The repetition of the preverb δια- highlights the paradoxical nature of Protesilaus: this absent eyewitness cannot go through the war in words (διηγοῖτο), since he did not go through it in deeds (διαπολεμήσας), a bit like the absent author of the *Iliad* and the *Odyssey*.[12] The dramatic situation of the *Heroicus* would have been less ambiguous if Philostratus had chosen another hero to support its claim to truth: as we will see in the conclusion, the sophist actually did so in the *Life of Apollonius of Tyana*, where another 'real' Trojan War is told by the ghost of Achilles.[13]

The Phoenician's counterargument is dismissed by the winemaker, who solves the problem by reminding him of the real nature of δαίμονες:

Ἀ.: Εὔηθες τουτί σοι, ξένε. Ψυχαῖς γὰρ θείαις οὕτω καὶ μακαρίαις ἀρχὴ βίου τὸ καθαρεῦσαι τοῦ σώματος· θεούς τε γὰρ ὧν ὀπαδοί εἰσι γινώσκουσι τότε, οὐκ ἀγάλματα θεραπεύουσαι καὶ ὑπονοίας, ἀλλὰ ξυνουσίας φανερὰς πρὸς αὐτοὺς ποιούμεναι, τά τε τῶν ἀνθρώπων ὁρῶσιν ἐλεύθεραι νόσων τε καὶ σώματος, ὅτε δὴ καὶ μαντικῆς σοφίας ἐμφοροῦνται καὶ τὸ χρησμῶδες αὐταῖς προσβακχεύει.

Winemaker: How silly of you, foreigner! For souls that are so godly and blessed, to be pure from the body is indeed the beginning of life: then they know the gods, of whom they are the attendants, since they do not worship statues and speculations any more, but consort with them openly, and they watch human affairs free from diseases and the body, especially when they are filled full of prophetic wisdom and the oracular knowledge sends Bacchic inspiration upon them.

Philostratus, *Heroicus* 7.3

Passages like this one have been interpreted as the expression of Philostratus' belief in the Pythagorean demonology or an heroic aretalogy.[14] To my mind, we cannot infer from it any personal belief:[15] within this specific extract, there is no clue that the sophist had any particular faith or was sceptical since no ironic twist can be identified here. At least, it can be taken for granted that the winemaker's answer plays an important part in the argumentative structure of the *Heroicus*: from now on, the readership knows that the 'truth' will not be grounded in some Herodotean Egyptian priest, in contrast to Dio's *Trojan Oration* (see Isidor Brodersen in this volume, Chapter 7);[16] nor will it be based on a record written by an autoptic witness, like those of Dictys and Dares.[17] Maybe this supernatural source competes with the previous revisionist tradition: in a way, a hero who shares divine knowledge can be thought of as more reliable than a human.[18]

Be that as it may, within the text, this demonological argument is not enough to persuade the Phoenician: telling of Protesilaus' fount of wisdom does not prove that he exists, after all. The winemaker must still convince his guest of another paradox: that he has become the friend of an absent ghost. In ancient texts, ghosts appear just once at particularly dramatic moments (for instance, Patroclus in the *Iliad* or Darius in Aeschylus' *Persians*), but no friendly relationship is recorded elsewhere.[19] That may be why the foreigner remains sceptical at this point:

Φ.: Φημὶ γὰρ ἀπίστως διακεῖσθαι πρὸς τὰ μυθώδη. Τὸ δὲ αἴτιον· οὐδενί πω ἑωρακότι αὐτὰ ξυγγέγονα, ἀλλ' ὁ μὲν ἑτέρου ἀκηκοέναι φησίν, ὁ δὲ οἴεσθαι, τὸν δὲ ποιητὴς ἐπαίρει.

Phoenician: I claim that I am inclined to disbelieve in fabulous tales. Here is the reason: I have never been in contact with anyone who has seen these; on the contrary, one claims that he has heard it from someone else, another one that he thinks he knows, while a poet excites leads on still another one.

Philostratus, *Heroicus* 7.9

The sceptical Phoenician uses the term μυθώδη in accordance with the definition current in the Imperial era. According to Sextus Empiricus and a bT scholium to the *Iliad*, the grammarians used to analyse narrative following a tripartite typology.[20] In Sextus' words, ἱστορία is the statement of real facts; πλάσμα relates unreal but credible deeds that could possibly have happened; μῦθος is about unreal and impossible deeds that contradict the laws of nature (chimeras, centaurs and the like): here, the Phoenician is referring to ghost stories. At the same time, the winemaker is included in the first category of credulous persons, those who 'claim that they have heard it from someone else': everything he knows comes from an intermediate source, even if we admit that Protesilaus actually saw the Trojan War.

So how does the winemaker make his guest change his mind? The turning point is a long catalogue of giants that were rediscovered around the known world. At first sight, we finally hold the archaeological proof that heroes of the past were much taller than the present men, which means that these stories are not mere μῦθοι. However, what seems to be a statement of facts remains ambiguous. Most of the winemaker's reports are not proper counterarguments. First, he did not see the ten-cubit tall skeleton of Ajax he first mentions: he just records what his own grandfather saw and allows his addressee to retain his scepticism.[21] He also claims that Orestes' body was discovered in Nemea, but a reader of Herodotus knows that his bones were unearthed in Tegea:[22] since Herodotus was a canonical writer,[23] the literate readership of the *Heroicus* may begin to distrust the winemaker's authority.[24] Finally, of the fourteen giants he talks about, he admits that he observed two: one on Sigeion and another one on Lemnos.[25] The text remains unclear about the others. For instance, when the winemaker describes a giant found at Cape Naulokhos on Imbros, he says: 'if you don't believe it, let's sail there' (8.12: κἂν ἀπιστῇς, πλεύσωμεν), but he does not specify whether he went there or not. Moreover, the toponym Naulokhos is not mentioned elsewhere, which may lead the reader to question the existence of this place.[26] The 'conversion' of the Phoenician himself is questionable. Although he previously criticized people who had heard μῦθοι from someone else (7.9: ὁ μὲν ἑτέρου ἀκηκοέναι φησίν), a few lines later he believes in the stories of giants he has heard from the winemaker.²⁷ Maybe this contradiction incited the readers to disengage from the foreigner's belief and keep a critical mind, just as they did by following the Phoenician until now. In sum, when the introductory section of the *Heroicus* comes to an end, we have no evidence that would support the winemaker's claim to truth.

As we will see, the winemaker's story is never presented as a mere fact: it is based on a whole rhetorical process and grounded in possibility, credibility and non-contradiction. To fully understand the devices used by Philostratus, it is necessary to take his own education into account. During the whole Imperial period, teenagers were trained by practising exercises known to us as the Προγυμνάσματα.²⁸ One of them will be of use here: contestation (ἀνασκευή) of mythical and heroic tales.²⁹ Theon's treatise provides one example: 'It is not likely that Medea killed her children.'³⁰ Others can be found in some late handbooks that nevertheless reflect the current practices of Imperial period³¹ – for instance, Aphthonius' model refutation: 'It is not likely that Apollo fell in love with Daphne.'³² Similarly, Libanius provides other models: 'The accusations [of rape] against Locrian Ajax are not likely'.³³ The same rhetorical pattern can also be used to defend the credibility of a tale through a confirmation (κατασκευή): such a training shows the plasticity of Imperial education.³⁴ As we will see, although the *Heroicus* cannot be read as a mere school exercise, it was clearly written by a sophist who depends on these practices. Indeed, Philostratus' chapter dedicated to Locrian Ajax proves that he did not rape Cassandra.³⁵

More precisely, three main *topoi* of contestation outlined in the Προγυμνάσματα will be relevant for us: the impossible according to the laws of nature (ἀδύνατον), the improbable (ἀπίθανον) and the contradictory (μαχόμενον). According to Theon, one should start by demonstrating that the story is impossible:

> ἀπὸ τοῦ ἀδυνάτου ἐπιχειρήσομεν, δεικνύντες ὅτι ἀδύνατον τὸ πρᾶγμα οὕτω γενέσθαι ὥς φησιν ὁ συγγραφεὺς ἤτοι διὰ τὸ μηδ' ὅλως πεφυκέναι γίνεσθαι, ἢ διὰ τὸ μὴ κατὰ τὸν αὐτὸν χρόνον εἶναι τὰ ἱστορούμενα.

> We will argue from the topic of the impossible, showing that it is impossible for the thing to have happened as the writer says, either because it does not naturally exist at all or because the parts of the story did not happen at the same time.
>
> Theon, *Progymnasmata* 93.16–20

If the story is physically and chronologically possible, then we will prove that it is not probable: 'The improbable is what could possibly happen or be said, though we do not believe that it happened or was said' (Theon, *Prog.* 76.34–77.9: τὸ δὲ ἀπίθανόν ἐστι τὸ δυνατὸν μὲν γενέσθαι ἢ λελέχθαι, ἀπιστούμενον δὲ εἰ γέγονεν ἢ εἴρηται). The demonstration is based on the six 'journalistic' questions pupils still learn today in schools: who (πρόσωπον), what (πρᾶγμα), where (τόπος), when (χρόνος), how (τρόπος) and why (αἰτία). The comparison between the two definitions shows that the impossible is grounded in natural laws while the improbable is a question of belief: the latter does not contradict the rules of reality, but it does not gain the conviction of the audience, for it does not correspond to what is likely (εἰκός). The πιθανόν thus corresponds to the effect of the speech on the readership, while the εἰκός coincides with the discursive devices used to achieve this effect.[36] In the case of a chronological impossibility, somebody cannot be in two different places at the same moment. As for chronological improbability, it is unlikely that the person in question could have behaved in this way at that particular moment: Medea could possibly have killed her children when Jason was a powerful king, but this is improbable since, at that moment, she had no power at all to resist him.[37] Lastly, contradiction is an intradiegetic tool and gives an inner analysis of the speech in its structure. Here is Theon's definition of how to contest a fable (μῦθος): 'The topic of the contradictory is as follows: when we show that the writer of fable contradicts himself' (ὁ δὲ ἐκ τοῦ μαχομένου τόπος τοιοῦτός ἐστιν, ὅταν δείξωμεν αὐτὸν ἑαυτῷ μαχόμενον τὸν μυθογράφον).[38] Now we shall turn to the use of these argumentative strategies in the *Heroicus*.

How to contest the Mysian tradition

I would like to start by analysing the introduction of the Mysian tale reported in chapter 23 of the *Heroicus*.[39] According to the different versions of that episode, while sailing to Troy, the Achaeans landed in Mysia, to the north of Troy. In their ignorance, they attacked the city, believing it was Troy.

> Ὡς μὲν δὴ τὴν Μυσίαν οἱ Ἀχαιοὶ πρὸ Τροίας ἐπόρθησαν ἐπὶ Τηλέφῳ τότε οὔσαν, καὶ ὡς ὁ Τήλεφος ὑπὲρ τῶν ἑαυτοῦ μαχόμενος, ἐτρώθη ὑπὸ Ἀχιλλέως, ἔστι σοι καὶ ποιητῶν ἀκούειν – οὐ γὰρ ἐκλέλειπται αὐτοῖς ταῦτα.

> Of course, that before Troy the Achaeans plundered Mysia, which at that time was in the power of Telephus, and that he was injured by Achilles, you can hear it even from the poets – for these tales have not been omitted by them.
>
> Philostratus, *Heroicus* 23.4

The indistinct 'poets' the winemaker talks about refer to a whole tradition from the *Cypria* to Pindar or the tragedians, not forgetting the Hesiodic poems.[40] The pattern used is similar to that of a contestation: as defined by Aphthonius, the exercise must be introduced by an accusation of the previous authors, as put into practice by Libanius in his models.[41]

In the *Heroicus*, the contestation does not consist in questioning the Mysian episode as a fact, but rather the way it happened and its cause: it is unlikely that the Achaeans fought through plain ignorance.

> ...τὸ δὲ πιστεύειν ὡς ἀγνοήσαντες οἱ Ἀχαιοὶ τὴν χώραν τὰ τοῦ Πριάμου ἄγειν τε καὶ φέρειν ᾤοντο, διαβάλλει τὸν Ὁμήρου λόγον ὃν περὶ Κάλχαντος ᾄδει τοῦ μάντεως. Εἰ γὰρ ἐπὶ μαντικῇ ἔπλεον καὶ τὴν τέχνην ἡγεμόνα ἐποιοῦντο, πῶς ἂν ἄκοντες ἐκεῖ καθωρμίσθησαν;
>
> ...but to be convinced that the Achaeans, through ignorance of the country, believed they were pillaging Priam's wealth, is inconsistent with the tale that Homer sings about Calchas the diviner. For if they sailed while relying upon divination and used this art as their leader, how could they have anchored there unintentionally?
>
> Philostratus, *Heroicus* 23.5

The verb πιστεύειν makes the forthcoming approach clear enough: the following demonstration will be grounded in the improbable. Paragraph 5 is built on different topics. First, the 'art' of Calchas (τέχνη) corresponds to one attribute of the person (πρόσωπον) defined in many rhetorical treatises, i.e. education (παιδεία) and art (τέχνη).[42] This characterization of the prophet is based on an explicit reference to *Iliad* 1, which allows the winemaker to reconstruct how the Achaeans might credibly have behaved: asking him where to sail.[43] Thanks to this likely scenario, he identifies a contradiction in the course of the Mysian tale, but unlike the definitions outlined in the Προγυμνάσματα, this contradiction is not an internal one. According to the Iliadic scholia, the νεώτεροι and among them the poet of the *Cypria* gave Calchas no part in showing the way to Troy, attributing this instead to Telephus.[44] Thus, the authority of the Iliadic version is used against the νεώτεροι to show that their tales would be contradictory if we take Homer into account. The strategy consists of organizing all the poetic material about the heroic past into a continuous story.

This first argument is not enough: we could object that the poet of the *Iliad* does not know the *Cypria*'s version. This is maybe the reason why the winemaker introduces a second argument that is independent of Calchas.

Πῶς δ' ἂν καθορμισθέντες ἠγνόησαν ὅτι μὴ ἐς Τροίαν ἥκουσι, καὶ ταῦτα πολλοῖς μὲν βουκόλοις ἐντετυχηκότες, πολλοῖς δὲ αὖ ποιμέσι; Νέμεταί τε γὰρ ἡ χώρα μέχρι θαλάσσης καὶ τοὔνομα ἐρωτᾶν τῆς ξένης ξύνηθες, οἶμαι, τοῖς καταπλέουσιν.

And how, once they had anchored, could they have failed to realize that they had not arrived at Troy, even though they came across many cowherds and many shepherds as well? For the countryside is inhabited as far as the sea, and it is customary to ask the name of the foreign land, I think, when we come ashore.

Philostratus, *Heroicus* 23.6

The second part of the contestation is grounded in the place (τόπος). This brief description of the Mysian landscape and inhabitants refers to its actual reality, since Strabo records that this region is densely populated.[45] As it seems, Philostratus reinvents what might have been its geography in the past: he combines his own contemporary world and an imagined local image of 'cowherds and shepherds', which may remind us of Thucydides' account of Agamemnon's primitive army.[46] This reconstruction allows the text to go one step further: in such a place, what would have been the usual way to behave for the Greek heroes? The answer is given in *Odyssey* 13, when Odysseus arrives back in Ithaca and asks the first person he meets: 'What is your country (τίς γῆ)? What is your people (τίς δῆμος)? Who are your parents (τίνες ἀνέρες ἐγγεγάασιν);'[47] Here again, Homeric poetry supports a reconstitution of customs belonging to the past. This practice is also connected to προσωποποιία: the pupil performed the speech of mythical or historical persons and, as Theon says, had to consider the circumstances (καιρός), the place (τόπος) and the conditions (τύχη) of the discourse.[48]

Third, the winemaker must prevent a potential objection: what if the Achaeans had not met anyone? This counterargument/response structure is another legacy of contestation that prevails in Libanius' models.[49]

Εἰ δὲ καὶ μηδενὶ τούτων ἐνέτυχον, μηδὲ ἤροντο τῶν τοιούτων οὐδέν, ἀλλ' Ὀδυσσεύς γε καὶ Μενέλεως ἐς Τροίαν ἤδη ἀφιγμένω τε καὶ πεπρεσβευκότε καὶ τὰ κρήδεμνα τοῦ Ἰλίου εἰδότε οὐκ ἄν μοι δοκοῦσι περιιδεῖν ταῦτα, οὐδ' ἂν ξυγχωρῆσαι τῷ στρατῷ διαμαρτάνοντι τῆς πολεμίας.

But even if they had come across none of them and had not asked any question of this kind, at least it seems to me that Odysseus and Menelaus, who both had already visited Troy, had served as ambassadors and had seen the battlements that crowned Ilion, would not have overlooked that and allowed the army to miss the enemy's land completely.

Philostratus, *Heroicus* 23.7

This final argument is based on time (χρόνος): chronologically speaking, the Mysian episode happens after the embassy to Troy led by Odysseus and Menelaus, which is depicted in *Iliad* 3.[50] Again, Homer is used as an authoritative version, although there were others that could contradict the winemaker: according to Apollodorus and Proclus' summary of the *Cypria*, the embassy took place *after* the battle of Mysia.[51]

It is highly likely that these rhetorical failures did not escape the attention of some readers, since they obtained a very precise mythographic knowledge from their education.[52] It would mean that, if we adopt a critical attitude towards the winemaker's demonstration, his claim to possess the truth is not supported by a perfect argumentative system, which leads us to wonder: is he telling the truth at all?

In any case, this demonstration supports a very 'geopolitical' approach to the Mysian episode.

Ἑκόντες μὲν δὴ οἱ Ἀχαιοὶ τοὺς Μυσοὺς ἐληΐζοντο, λόγου ἐς αὐτοὺς ἥκοντος ὡς ἄριστα ἠπειρωτῶν πράττοιεν, καί πη καὶ δεδιότες μὴ πρόσοικοι τῷ Ἰλίῳ ὄντες ἐς κοινωνίαν τῶν κινδύνων μετακληθῶσι.

No, for sure, the Achaeans looted the Mysians intentionally, because the rumour had reached them that they were the richest inhabitants of the mainland, and perhaps also because they feared that, as the neighbours of Ilion, these men would be summoned to share the dangers of war.

Philostratus, *Heroicus* 23.8

The first argument recalls Thucydides' but also Dio's accounts, that the Trojan War was caused by Asian wealth – we will go back to it later.[53] The second is based on Homer himself, especially the Trojan Catalogue of *Iliad* 2 where the Mysian soldiers are presented as allies.[54] In fact, such a device is metaleptic: it is as if the Achaeans of the *Heroicus* had read the *Iliad* and had drawn strategical consequences for their battle plan.

'Helen was not in Troy': from historiography to sophistic

Now, I would like to turn to chapter 25, where the winemaker shows that Helen was in Egypt, not in Troy.[55]

[μέμφεται] εἶτα ὅτι σαφῶς γιγνώσκων ὡς ἐν Αἰγύπτῳ ἡ Ἑλένη ἐγένετο, ἀπενεχθεῖσα ὑπὸ ἀνέμων ὁμοῦ τῷ Πάριδι, ὅδε ἄγει αὐτὴν ἐπὶ τὸ τοῦ Ἰλίου τεῖχος ὀψομένην τὰ ἐν τῷ πεδίῳ κακά, ἥν εἰκός, εἰ καὶ δι' ἑτέραν γυναῖκα ταῦτα ἐγίνετο, ξυγκαλύπτεσθαί τε καὶ μὴ ὁρᾶν αὐτά, διαβεβλημένου τοῦ γένους.

Next [Protesilaus blames Homer] because, while he clearly knew that Helen was in Egypt – she had been carried away by the winds together with Paris –, he leads her to the battlements of Ilion, making her watch the woes on the plain, although it was likely that, if these events had happened because of any other woman, she would have veiled herself and would not have watched it, since her sex had been slandered.

Philostratus, *Heroicus* 25.10

In contrast to the treatment of the Mysian battle which Philostratus is alone in contesting, he borrows this one from Herodotus.[56] Nonetheless, the whole story told in the *Histories* is summed up here in one formula: ἐν Αἰγύπτῳ ἡ Ἑλένη ἐγένετο, ἀπενεχθεῖσα ὑπὸ ἀνέμων.[57] The only part of Herodotus' discussion that is preserved here is the one we could retroactively call 'sophistic', i.e. paragraph 120 where he lays out the arguments for believing his source.[58] Protesilaus clearly defines his own approach, εἰκός, which also takes us back to the question of τὸ πρέπον:[59] his arguments are founded on character (πρόσωπον) and consist in proving that it would have not been fitting (ἀπρεπές) for Helen, Hector and Priam to behave as they do in *Iliad* 3.

The first argument does not come from Herodotus. Helen's sex (γένος) is an attribute of the character which belongs to her nature (φύσις): a woman will not talk or behave in the same way as a man does.[60] This gendered prerequisite explains the following concession: 'if any other woman had caused such things'. In other words, shame would have been the natural behaviour of *any* person of the female sex, who should have covered herself (ξυγκαλύπτεσθαι). This very visual detail subverts Helen's attitude in *Iliad* 3: she comes up onto the Trojan wall veiled (καλυψαμένη).[61] The Homeric motif is thus taken out of its original context and subverted to prove that Helen's shame in the poem is not proportionate to the catastrophic situation she allegedly caused.

Then Protesilaus follows Herodotus' arguments, but he changes their order and their content slightly:[62]

Ἐπαινουμένου δὲ οὐδὲ ἐν αὐτῇ τῇ Τροίᾳ Πάριδος ἐπὶ τῇ ἁρπαγῇ τῆς Ἑλένης, οὔτ' ἂν Ἕκτορα τὸν σωφρονέστατον καρτερῆσαι φησι τὸ μὴ οὐκ ἀποδοῦναι αὐτὴν τῷ Μενέλεῳ ἐν Ἰλίῳ οὖσαν, οὔτ' ἂν Πρίαμον ξυγχωρῆσαι τῷ Πάριδι τρυφᾶν πολλῶν ἤδη ἀπολωλότων αὐτῷ παίδων, οὔτ' ἂν τὴν Ἑλένην διαφυγεῖν τὸ μὴ οὐκ ἀποθανεῖν ὑπὸ τῶν Τρωάδων ὁπόσων ἤδη ἄνδρες ἀπωλώλεσαν καὶ ἀδελφοὶ καὶ παῖδες· ἴσως δ' ἂν καὶ ἀποδρᾶναι αὐτὴν παρὰ τὸν Μενέλεων διὰ τὸ ἐν τῇ Τροίᾳ μῖσος.

Furthermore, since Paris was not praised even in Troy itself for the abduction of Helen, Hector, such a reasonable man – Protesilaus says – would not have tolerated the failure to return her to Menelaus if she had been in Ilion, nor would Priam have allowed Paris to live so luxuriously when many of his own children had already perished, nor would Helen have avoided being killed by all these Trojan women whose husbands and brothers and children had already perished; perhaps she would even have run away to Menelaus because of the hatred against her in Troy.

Philostratus, *Heroicus* 25.11

In the *Histories*, Hector is older (πρεσβύτερος) and is destined to be king.[63] These are two attributes of the character that tend to be defined as the age (ἡλικία) and condition (τύχη) by the rhetorical treatises.[64] Here, Protesilaus chooses another attribute grounded in nature (φύσις): temperance (σωφροσύνη), which belongs to the natural 'virtues of soul' in Theon's terminology and corresponds to a topical way to characterize the prince in Imperial literature.[65] As for Priam, the representation of an afflicted father is directly borrowed from Herodotus.[66] The death of his sons, which determines his emotional response to Paris, matches what will be called περιστάσεις, circumstances, in the Imperial handbooks.[67] These same circumstances are used to infer that the Trojan women would have killed Helen, a motif that does not occur in the *Histories* but is already present in the *Iliad* and is developed in Euripides' tragedies.[68] Then, Protesilaus can turn back to Helen through a variation on his own rhetorical devices: first, he argued that she would have been *naturally* ashamed (φύσις); now, she would have *pragmatically* fled from Troy given the περιστάσεις. This *a fortiori* argument gives strength to the whole system: even if Helen did not respect her natural female modesty (she was free not to follow it after all), she was bound to flee.

This Herodotean demonstration paradoxically ends up with an implicit contestation of Herodotus himself.

Ἐξῃρήσθω δὴ ὁ ἀγὼν ὅν φησιν Ὅμηρος ἀγωνίσασθαι τῷ Μενελέῳ τὸν Πάριν ἐπὶ σπονδαῖς τοῦ πολέμου· κατ' Αἴγυπτόν τε γὰρ τὴν Ἑλένην εἶναι καὶ τοὺς Ἀχαιοὺς πάλαι τοῦτο γινώσκοντας, ἐκείνη μὲν ἐρρῶσθαι φράζειν, μάχεσθαι δὲ ὑπὲρ τοῦ ἐν Τροίᾳ πλούτου.

Thus, let us delete the duel to which Homer says Paris challenged Menelaus during a truce; for Helen was in Egypt and the Achaeans, who had known this for a long time, had did not care about her but were fighting for Troy's wealth.

Philostratus, *Heroicus* 25.12

In the *Histories*, the Achaeans do not know that Helen is in Egypt, and the war begins with a misunderstanding.[69] By contrast, the Greeks of the *Heroicus* are aware of her location. The Herodotean arguments culminate with a Thucydidean 'geopolitical' approach and the same conclusion as in the Mysian battle:[70] the whole Trojan War is coherently attributed to a single cause (αἰτία).

Finally, it is highly possible that this palimpsest of references is also a way for Philostratus to compete with the *Trojan Oration* by Dio, one of his sophistic models.[71] In this discourse, the orator proves that Helen was the legitimate spouse of Paris. He grounds his own rhetorical demonstration on the same Herodotean intertext,[72] and refers to the same Thucydidean idea, that the Achaeans were fighting for the wealth of Troy.[73] Both Dio and Philostratus rework the two historians in a very similar way, reaching the same conclusion that Homer is a liar, but they lead to opposite counterfactuals: the same rhetorical devices can prove that Helen was *and* was not at Troy according to their respective choices.[74]

The fiction of the Scamander: from sophistic to historiography

My final example is chapter 48, which belongs to the last part of the *Heroicus*, dedicated to Achilles. The winemaker questions the story of the combat between the hero and the river Scamander in *Iliad* 21 (139–204).

> μήτε γὰρ τῷ Ἀχιλλεῖ τηλικούτῳ ὄντι ἄπορον ἂν γενέσθαι τὸν Σκάμανδρον καὶ ταῦτα ἥττω ἢ οἱ μεγάλοι τῶν ποταμῶν ὄντα.

> For a man who was as tall as Achilles, the Scamander would not have been impassable, even more since it was smaller than the wide rivers.
> Philostratus, *Heroicus* 48.12

Here, the river is called by its human name – Scamander – although it is known as Xanthos by the gods.[75] Thus, this extract adopts the point of view of heroes as human beings. In this regard, the perspective of the *Heroicus* is very different from the *Imagines*, where the sophist uses the divine name Xanthos to say that, thanks to Homer, it will become the son of Zeus.[76] The choice of the name Scamander allows the winemaker to talk about the *real* river free from any poetic transformation. Claiming that it is 'not as big as the great rivers' plainly contradicts its Iliadic depiction as 'deep-eddying' and 'huge' (μέγας ποταμὸς βαθυδίνης),[77] as 'divine' (δῖος τε Σκάμανδρος)[78] and descended from Zeus (ὃν ἀθάνατος τέκετο Ζεύς).[79] Here again, the contestation is based on a geographical reality. For instance,

Strabo highlights Homer's topographical lack of knowledge by reminding his readers that the Scamander has one source and not two, and that the biggest river in the region is the Aesepus.[80] This allusion to the real river rather than to its poetic description substantiates an implicit argument based on natural impossibility (ἀδύνατον): if we compare Achilles' great size to the Scamander's smallness, the hero would have been physically able to cross it. It is worth noting that, unlike the river, Achilles is described in accordance with *Iliad* 18.26, μέγας μεγαλωστί. The rhetorical strategy is effective only if we take Achilles' depiction for granted, and the winemaker never explains why he follows Homer with respect to him.

The second argument of the contestation is a concession to the first one.

> ... μήτ' ἂν τὸν Ἀχιλλέα ἐς μάχην τῷ ποταμῷ ὁρμῆσαι· εἰ γὰρ καὶ σφόδρα ἐπ' αὐτὸν ἐμόρμυρεν, ἤλυξεν ἂν ἐκκλίνων καὶ μὴ ὁμόσε χωρῶν τῷ ὕδατι.
>
> ... nor would Achilles have thrown himself into a fight against a river: even if it had rushed up to him with a vehement roar, he would have avoided it by turning away without getting close to the water.
>
> Philostratus, *Heroicus* 48.12

As we have seen, the previous argument consisted of comparing the fictional world of the *Iliad* to the geographical reality of the Scamander. Now, the winemaker immerses himself in that poetic universe as if it were real and uses the very words of the poet himself: the verb ἐμόρμυρεν is a quasi-quotation (μορμύρων).[81] By so doing, he shows that, apart from any reality, the tale of the poet is not credible (πιθανόν), for it is unlikely that Achilles behaved as Homer claims. Such an argument is grounded in what Theon calls 'the manner of the action' (τρόπος τῆς πράξεως).[82] What is contradicted here is the idea that Achilles willingly chose to face the divine Scamander (μὴ ὁμόσε χωρῶν τῷ ὕδατι), not the fact that he avoided the river (ἤλυξεν ἂν ἐκκλίνων), which he does in the poem (Πηλεΐδης δ' ἀπόρουσεν).[83]

This demonstration serves another tale which is not presented as 'true', but as 'more credible'.

> Πιθανώτερα δὲ τούτων ἐκεῖνα, οἶμαι, δίεισι. Ξυνελαθῆναι μὲν ἐς τὸν ποταμὸν τοὺς Τρῶας καὶ πλείους ἀπολέσθαι σφῶν ἢ ἐν ἅπαντι τῷ πολέμῳ ἀπώλοντο· οὐ μὴν μόνῳ γε Ἀχιλλεῖ πεπρᾶχθαι ταῦτα, ἀλλὰ θαρσήσαντας ἤδη παρ' αὐτοῦ τοὺς Ἕλληνας ἐπικαταβαίνειν καὶ τοὺς ἐν τῷ ποταμῷ σφάττειν.
>
> More credible than that are, I believe, the following explanations [given by Protesilaus]. The Trojans had been pushed back to the river and more of them

perished than in the whole war; for sure, these actions were not accomplished by Achilles alone; on the contrary, having now gained confidence from him, the Hellenes pursued them down to the river and slayed those who were in it.

Philostratus, *Heroicus* 48.13

This counterfactual story is very similar to those we can find in the *Troika* written by historians and to Dictys' account in the *Ephemeris belli troiani*.[84] The main difference here is that the tale is not given as a mere fact, but as the consequence of the rhetorical process of reasoning we have analysed. Again, Dio's and Philostratus' techniques of argumentation are very much alike: the speaker of the *Trojan Oration* blames Homer for depicting 'wonders' in *Iliad* 21 (λέγειν τι θαυμαστόν); this first step allows him to claim that Achilles was tired after having crossed the river and was then killed by Hector.[85] Again, the *Heroicus* can be read as an answer to the demonstration given by Dio: as the winemaker will explain in the following paragraphs, Achilles will kill Asteropaeus and Hector precisely because he did not have to fight first against the Scamander and was not tired at all.[86]

The adjective πιθανώτερα deserves a final analysis. The use of the comparative seems to indicate that the winemaker's speech gradually moves away from its original claim to truth. In the first half of the *Heroicus*, Protesilaus was described as a 'lover of truth' (7.8 φιλαλήθης):[87] whenever he confirmed a poetic tale, he praised it as 'true' (ἀληθής).[88] As the text progresses, this veracity is less and less definitive: first, the tale becomes 'more in keeping with truth' (ἀληθέστερα), then 'more credible and more in keeping with truth' (πιθανώτερα καὶ ἀληθέστερα).[89] Now, at the end of the dialogue, the rhetorical category has superseded the truth, which leaves room for doubt: if the winemaker's version is more credible than the *Iliad*, is it truthful after all?

A plausible Trojan War amongst other rhetorical possibilities

At first sight, the three rhetorical contestations we have analysed are intended to support the *Heroicus*' report of the Trojan War. Nonetheless, their authorship remains unclear. In the case of Helen, the eyewitness (i.e. Protesilaus), and not the narrator (i.e. the winemaker), seems to be the author of the Herodotean ἀνασκευή since it is introduced by ὅτι and infinitive subordinate clauses.[90] Thus, the pattern is different from the *Histories*, where Herodotus (the narrator) gives personal arguments to show that the Egyptian priest (his eyewitness) is convincing. As for the Mysian battle and the Scamander, we may wonder whether we are reading the winemaker's own comment on the tale that he knows from Protesilaus:[91] given that he considers this story as more credible than epic (πιθανώτερα), is he behaving like Herodotus? Perhaps this ambiguity is not meant to be resolved: in the absence of clear authorship, what is left is the argumentative process of the speech itself, which tends to achieve self-sufficiency.

Second, this rhetorical confirmation of Protesilaus' account does not mean that his truth is definitive. If we compare the *Heroicus* with the whole corpus of Philostratus, we can see that the sophist explores different versions of the Trojan War, which are sometimes contradictory.[92] For instance, the Herodotean argument that Helen was in Egypt is another motif he deals with in the *Life of Apollonius of Tyana*. At the beginning of book 4, Apollonius encounters the ghost of Achilles, just as the winemaker meets with Protesilaus. He asks five questions that have already been compared with the content of the *Heroicus*.[93] At first glance, the third one seems to provide the same information as chapter 25.

τρίτον ἠρόμην· 'ἡ Ἑλένη, ὦ Ἀχιλλεῦ, ἐς Τροίαν ἦλθεν ἢ Ὁμήρῳ ἔδοξεν ὑποθέσθαι ταῦτα;' 'πολὺν' ἔφη 'χρόνον ἐξηπατώμεθα πρεσβευόμενοί τε παρὰ τοὺς Τρῶας καὶ ποιούμενοι τὰς ὑπὲρ αὐτῆς μάχας, ὡς ἐν τῷ Ἰλίῳ οὔσης, ἡ δ' Αἴγυπτόν τε ᾤκει καὶ τὸν Πρωτέως οἶκον ἁρπασθεῖσα ὑπὸ τοῦ Πάριδος. ἐπεὶ δὲ ἐπιστεύθη τοῦτο, ὑπὲρ αὐτῆς τῆς Τροίας λοιπὸν ἐμαχόμεθα, ὡς μὴ αἰσχρῶς ἀπέλθοιμεν.'

Thirdly I asked: 'What about Helen, Achilles? Did she go to Troy or did it seem good to Homer to compose that as a fiction?' – 'For a long time, he said, we were led astray and sent ambassadors to the Trojans and fought battles over her, as if she were in Ilion, but she was dwelling in Egypt at the house of Proteus, after she had been kidnapped by Paris. But once we were convinced of this, we began to fight over Troy for the rest of the time, to avoid returning home covered in shame.'

Philostratus, *Life of Apollonius of Tyana* 4.16

Apart from the similarities, I would like to underline the fact that Protesilaus and Achilles ascribe two different causes to the Trojan War: gold in the *Heroicus* (ὑπὲρ τοῦ ἐν Τροίᾳ πλούτου); Helen and honour in the *Life of Apollonius* (ὑπὲρ αὐτῆς). Contrary to the *Heroicus*, the *Life* re-enacts Herodotus and his tale of the misunderstanding, with just one difference: here, the Achaeans discover their mistake *during* the Trojan War and not after. There is also something odd in the discovery itself. Achilles simply confesses that the Hellenes were convinced of it (ἐπιστεύθη τοῦτο), but does not reveal how they realized that they were wrong and if they really did find out the truth. Then, they behave as if they had read the Herodotean version or some sophistic demonstration. Within the story itself, the rhetorical categories precede any factual reality: this *mise-en-abime* is the mirror of Achilles' own strategies of persuasion.

Similarly, the 'real' Scamander described by the winemaker has nothing to do with the poetic one depicted at the beginning of the *Imagines*.[94] There, the narrator portrays the divine fight between Hephaestus and the river, which is never mentioned in the *Heroicus*.[95] This difference can be explained by the points of view they respectively adopt. The *Imagines* provide a textual interpretation of a visual interpretation of Homer.[96] The winemaker's contestations, by contrast, can be read interpreted as rhetorical interpretations of Protesilaus' 'true' report. Thus, the *Heroicus* is just one element in the whole *corpus Philostrateum* that builds a plausible Trojan War among other possibilities.

Third, within the dialogue, we cannot find any extra-textual evidence that would reinforce the winemaker's claim to know the truth, apart from the giants' bones that are ambiguous as evidence. Philostratus could have used archaeological discoveries like those presented by Pausanias, who claims to have seen the real spear of Achilles in a sanctuary of Athena at Phalesis.[97] Here, by contrast, the so-called real Trojan War has no existence outside the rhetorical devices that confirm it: even though the geographical allusions recall topographical enquiries like those of Strabo,[98] they serve entirely as arguments based on τόπος. Finally, the *Heroicus* works in the same way as Gorgias' *Defence of Palamedes*. In that discourse, although Palamedes knows that he is innocent, he cannot provide any technical support and grounds all his speech on rhetorical devices, ἀδύνατον, εἰκός, ἀσύμφορον (the inconvenient) and ἄπορον (the difficult).[99] In addition, he uses five of the six 'journalistic' questions defined in Imperial and late handbooks: who, what, when, how and why.[100] The lack of any extra-textual proof is used to show that, even when we know the truth, it is not accessible to humans or at least not communicable: it has to be built through speech.[101] This comparison with Gorgias' techniques is all the more effective since Philostratus himself praises Gorgias in a letter and argues that he is the very founder of the Sophistic movement in the *Lives of the Sophists*.[102] The *Heroicus* seems to put the theoretical texts of the *corpus Philostrateum* into practice: it re-enacts Gorgianic views on the Trojan War. Like the encomium of Helen, it can be read as a rhetorical game (παίγνιον) that Philostratus might have written for himself, but it happens to be a very serious game that says something about the heroic past:[103] there is no clear way to reach the truth; what is left to human beings is to construct it through the power of rhetoric.

Notes

1. I am grateful to Ruth Webb for correcting my English and making valuable remarks on this chapter. I would also like to thank Paola Bassino and Nicolò Benzi for organizing the wonderful conference in Winchester.
2. Bourquin 1884: 100–1, Bonner 1937: 132–4, Farnell 1921: 294, Nilsson 1950: 540–1. Von Wilamowitz-Möllendorff 1931–2 (II): 522 goes further by arguing that Philostratus' readership was so uneducated that they believed in his 'ghost stories' ('Spukgeschichten').
3. Münscher 1907: 505–8, Radet 1925: 9, Bourquin 1884: 112–38 already defined a middle ground between these two perspectives: nourishing a nostalgia for the past, the sophist crafted a 'fake truth' to support the hero cult.
4. Eitrem 1929: 48, followed by Mantero 1966: 13–14, 17–18 and 21–46, and more prudently by Aitken and Maclean 2004: xxi–xxiv.
5. The fictional devices of Philostratus have been read as the reinvention of the whole Greek literary tradition, mixed with local and folkloric tales: Anderson 1986: 249–54, Billault 2000: 32–4 and 37–9, Mestre 2004: 133–40, Rusten 2004: 147–57, Follet 2017: xxxvi–lxvii.
6. Grossardt 2006 (I): 59–61, Kim 2010: 108–12, 162–8 and 185–9.
7. In this I follow de Temmerman 2010. This method has been primarily applied to the *ekphrasis* in the *Heroicus*: see Grossardt 2006 (I): 123–4, Mestre 2007: 539–42.
8. Kim 2010.
9. As already noted by Billault 2000: 57.
10. Hom. *Il.* 2.695–702, Apollod. *Epit.* 3.30, Hyg. *Fab.* 103.1.
11. All translations are mine.
12. The winemaker will explain that Homer did not attend the Trojan War and lived 160 years later: cf. Philostr. *Her.* 43.7–8.
13. Philostr. *VA* 4.16. Maybe this is reminiscent of the counterfactual stories told in the *Nekyia*: see Gazis 2018, especially pp. 102–8.
14. See Mantero 1966: 75–83 and 195–7, Betz 2004: 31–3, Maclean 2004: 255–6.
15. See the discussion of Platt 2011: 240–52, and of Follet 2017: cxxvi–cxxix with further bibliography. The apparition of ghosts can also be interpreted as a fictional treatment of *ekphrasis*: the winemaker provides vivid descriptions that turn the reader into a spectator of the dead heroes in communication between past and present times. See Zeitlin 2001: 213–16 and 255–66, Whitmarsh 2009: 219–21 and 225–9.
16. D. Chr. *Or.* 11.37.
17. Dict. prol. Dar. prol. Huhn and Bethe 1917: 618–19 argued that the *Heroicus* competed with Dictys' *Ephemeris*. For more recent discussions, see Dowden 2009: 162, Rusten and König 2014: 29–30.

18 Protesilaus is even more reliable than Homer since the winegrower shows that the poet is not divinely inspired: cf. Philostr. *Her.* 43.6.
19 Hom. *Il.* 23.65–108, Aesch. *Pers.* 609–851.
20 Sext.Emp. *Math.* 1.263–4. Scholium bT *Il.* 14.342–51. On the *muthos*, see Saïd 2010: 77–95. This typology is not intended to define literary genres, since the three can occur in the same text: Bréchet 2013: 24.
21 Philostr. *Her.* 8.1–2.
22 Philostr. *Her.* 8.3 = Hdt. 1.68.
23 On the use of Herodotus in the rhetorical education, see Gibson 2004: 116–17.
24 This confusion is not a unique case: see Grossardt 2006 (I): 75–7, Rusten in Rusten and König 2014: 37–8, Miles 2018: 48–52.
25 Philostr. *Her.* 8.6, 8.11. As Rusten 2004: 147–58 shows, literary references and allusions to uncertain local observations intertwine in the whole passage.
26 Follet 2004: 226–7 however notes that this name 'sounds authentic'.
27 Philostr. *Her.* 8.18.
28 On the traditional curriculum of an educated man (πεπαιδευμένος), see Webb 2017: 141–50.
29 For a comprehensive definition of the contestation, see Berardi 2017: 51–62.
30 Theon, *Prog.* 94.17–33. According to the *opinio communis*, Theon's Προγυμνάσματα date from the first or second centuries AD. However, Heath 2002–2003: 141–58 argues that the text was written in the fourth or fifth centuries, *contra* Patillon 1997: viii–xvi.
31 See the rhetorical analysis of Dio's sixty-first oration by Kim 2008: 617–20.
32 Aphth. *Prog.* 5.3–10.
33 Lib. *Ref.* 2, edited by Gibson 2008. See Webb 2010: 147–8.
34 Aphth. *Prog.* 6.3–9: 'It is likely that Apollo felt in love with Daphne.' Lib. *Conf.* 3: 'The accusations against Locrian Ajax are likely.'
35 Philostr. *Her.* 31.4–6.
36 Berardi 2017: 225.
37 Theon, *Prog.* 94.17–94.33.
38 Theon, *Prog.* 77.19–24. What he calls μαχόμενον will be named ἀνακόλουθον and ἐναντίον by the late handbooks: Ps.-Hermog. *Prog.* 5.3, Aphth. *Prog.* 5.1, cf. Lib. *Ref.* 2.1.
39 Previous scholars persuasively argued that the whole chapter 23 of the *Heroicus* is an alternative Epic Cycle by itself: see Mantero 1966: 172–7, Beschorner 1999: 175–8, Grossardt 2006 (II): 463–87.
40 Hes. fr. 165 MW, *Cypr.* fr. 22.1 = scholium A *Il.* 1.59, Apollod. *Epit.* 3.17, Procl. *Chrest.* 125 (Severyns). Cf. Pi. *O.* 9.70–5, *I.* 5.41–2, 8.59–60, A. *TrGF* 3.143–5, S. *TrGF.* 4.409–18, E. *TrGF* 5.2.696–727c. See Gantz 1993: 576–7.
41 Aphth. *Prog.* 5.2, cf. Lib. *Ref.* 2.1: see Schouler 1984: 94, Webb 2010: 136.

42 Cf. Cic. *Inv.* 1.35 (*artes* and *artifices*), Theon, *Prog.* 110.2–11 (παιδεία), Hermog. *Stat.* 3.8 (παίδευσις), Aphth. *Prog.* 8.3 (ἀναστροφή, divided into ἐπιτηδεύματα, τέχνη and νόμοι). On the attributes of the character, see Pernot 1993: 140–2, de Temmerman 2010: 24–8.
43 Hom. *Il.* 1.69–71.
44 Scholium A *Il.* I, 59 (Dindorf) = *Cypr.* fr. 22.1 (Bernabé), scholium A *Il.* I, 71a, cf. Apollod. *Epit.* 3.20.
45 Str. 12.8.4.
46 Th. 1.8. On the local geography in the *Heroicus*, see Follet 2004: 221–36.
47 Hom. *Od.* 13.233, cf. 24.258–60.
48 Theon, *Prog.* 115.23–116.6. For a comprehensive definition of this exercise, see Berardi 2017: 154–66.
49 Cf. Lib. *Ref.* 2.3.
50 Hom. *Il.* 3.203–24, cf. 9.138–42.
51 Apollod. *Epit.* 3.28–9, Procl. *Chrest.* 125–8, 152–4 (Severyns).
52 See Cribiore 2001: 225–30, 2007: 159–65, Webb 2001: 307–10, 2010: 132–3.
53 Th. 1.8, D. Chr. *Or.* 11.63–4.
54 Hom. *Il.* 2.858–61, cf. 14.513, *Od.* 11.516–20.
55 For other sophistic views of Helen, see Roberta Ioli on Gorgias (Chapter 1) and Sara Tirrito on Dio (especially 'The Judgement of Paris and the Abduction of *Helen* in *Or.* 11 (*Trojan*)'; Chapter 6) in this volume.
56 Hdt. 2.113–20. See Blondell 2013: 142–63.
57 Hdt. 2.114: ὑπὸ ἀνέμων ... ἀπενειχθείς. See Grossardt 2006 (II): 500.
58 Cf. Thomas 2000: 271: 'This manner is reminiscent of the sophistic arguments produced for and against Helen (...).'
59 Cf. Theon, *Prog.* 77.10. On the porosity of likeliness and convenience, see Berardi 2017: 226.
60 Cf. Cic. *Inv.* 1.35, Theon, *Prog.* 116.1–2.
61 Hom. *Il.* 3.141; cf. 419.
62 Grossardt 2006 (II): 500–2.
63 Hdt. 2.120.4.
64 Theon, *Prog.* 78.25–7, 115.23–116.1, cf. Cic. *Inv.* 1.35,
65 Theon, *Prog.* 110.7–11. Cf. Plu. *Mor.* 34e–f, 73e, Max. Tyr. 26.6.
66 Hdt. 2.120.3.
67 Cf. Cic. *Inv.* 1.36, Theon. *Prog.* 77.10. On περιστάσεις, see Patillon 1997: xcvi and 37, n. 197, Berardi 2017: 223–4.
68 Hom. *Il.* 3.411–12, 6.407–39, 24.768–72, Eur. *Andr.* 91–116, *Hel.* 367–9, *Tr.* 132, *Or.* 56–60, 102.
69 Hdt. 2.118.4.
70 Th. 1.8. On the Thucydidean tale as counterfactual, see Tordoff 2014: 101–21.

71 Cf. Philostr. *VS* 1.7.486-8.
72 D. Chr. *Or.* 11.55. Scholars generally comment on the *Trojan Oration* and the *Heroicus* in a comparative approach: Grossardt 2006 (I): 70, Bär 2018: 160-3. However, there is no reason to doubt that Philostratus knew Dio's discourse: Kim 2010: 178, n. 8.
73 D. Chr. *Or.* 11.63-4.
74 Their opposing versions thus correspond to confirmation and refutation.
75 Hom. *Il.* 20.73.
76 Philostr. *Im.* 2.8.6. This text can be read as a metapoetic enquiry on the discursive power of epics: Lambin 2011: 73-5.
77 Hom. *Il.* 20.73; 21.329.
78 Hom. *Il.* 12.21.
79 Hom. *Il.* 14.434, 21.2, 24.693.
80 Str. 13.1.43 = Hom. *Il.* 22.147-8. For another geographical reconstruction of this kind, cf. scholium T *Il.* 22.147a^1.
81 Grossardt (II): 691. See Hom. *Il.* 21.324-5, cf. 237, 261.
82 Theon, *Prog.* 76.34-77.9.
83 Hom. *Il.* 21.251.
84 Cf. Hellanic. *FGrHist* 4 F 128, Serv. *FGrHist* 47 F 1, Dict. 3.14. On the historiographers, see Grossardt (I): 57-8 and 690, Trachsel 2007: 159-63. On Dictys' use of a wide historiographical and exegetical tradition, see my previous analysis: Decloquement 2018: 183-90.
85 D. Chr. *Or.* 11.32, 95.
86 Philostr. *Her.* 48.14-18.
87 Hodkinson 2011: 54-5 compares this depiction with the Socratic philosopher of Plato: cf. Pl. *Phdr.* 278c-d.
88 Philostr. *Her.* 26.3, 28.3, 33.47.
89 Philostr. *Her.* 43.8, 46.1.
90 Philostr. *Her.* 25.10-11.
91 Rusten and König 2014: 31-2 and 172, n. 71. On interpretative instances in the *Heroicus*, see Miles 2018, especially pp. 31-8 and 48-55.
92 In line with the general trend, I think that the main texts of the *corpus Philostrateum* were written by the same Philostratus: see the convincing demonstration by de Lannoy 1997: 2362-449.
93 See Grossardt 2009, especially pp. 86-8 on Helen.
94 Philostr. *Im.* 1.1.
95 Hom. *Il.* 21.324-82.
96 See Miles 2018: 81-120. On the Scamander in the *Imagines*, see Dubel 2010: 32, Webb 2015: 212-13, Sophie Schoess ('Introducing Homeric Authority: *Imagines* 1.1') in Chapter 9 of this volume.

97 Paus. 3.3.8.
98 See Kim 2010: 47–84, Bouchard 2016: 123–32.
99 Gorg. *Pal.* 6–10.
100 Gorg. *Pal.* 11–21. See Fornieles Sánchez 2015: 131–8, Paola Bassino, 'Gorgias' Apology of Palamedes' in Chapter 2 of this volume.
101 Cassin 1997: 23–4.
102 Philostr. *Ep.* 73, *VS* 1.481–4, 1.9.492–4. See Demoen/Praet 2012: 436–9.
103 Gorg. *Hel.* 21.

References

Aitken, E. B. and Maclean, J. (eds) 2004, *Philostratus' Heroicus: Religion and Cultural Identity in the Third Century* CE, Leiden.
Anderson, G. 1986, *Philostratus: Biography and Belles-Lettres in the 3rd Century* AD, London.
Bär, S. 2018, 'Diktys und Dares vor dem Hintergrund des zweitsophistichen Homerrevisionismus', in Brescia, G., Lentano, M., Scafoglio, G. and Zanusso, V. (eds), *Revival and Revision of the Trojan Myth: Studies on Dictys Cretensis and Dares Phrygius*, Zürich/New York: 152–76.
Beschorner, A. 1999, *Helden und Heroen, Homer und Caracalla: Übersetzung, Kommentar und Interpretationen zum Heroicus des Flavios Philostratus*, Bari.
Berardi, F. 2017, *La retorica degli esercizi preparatori: Glossario ragionato dei Progymnásmata*, Zürich/New York.
Betz, H. D. 2004, 'Hero worship and Christian beliefs: observations from the history religion on Philostratus's *Heroicus*', in Aitken, E. B. and Maclean, J. (eds), *Philostratus' Heroicus: Religion and Cultural Identity in the Third Century* CE, Leiden: 25–47.
Billault, A. 2000, *L'Univers de Philostrate*, Brussels.
Blondell, R. 2013, *Helen of Troy: Beauty, Myth, Devastation*, Oxford.
Bonner, C. 1937, 'Some phases of religious feeling in later paganism', *Harvard Theological Review* 30: 119–40.
Bouchard, E. 2016, *Du Lycée au Musée: Théorie Poétique et Critique Littéraire à l'Epoque Hellénistique*, Paris.
Bourquin, E.-J. 1884, 'Essai sur l'*Heroïque* de Philostrate', *Annuaire de l'Association pour l'encouragement des études grecques en France* 18: 95–141.
Bréchet, C. 2013, 'La place de la fiction dans l'exégèse Homérique, de Platon à Eustathe de Thessalonique', in Bréchet, C., Videau, A. and Webb, R. (eds), *Théories et Pratiques de la Fiction à l'Epoque Impériale*, Paris: 19–35.
Cassin, B. 1997, 'Procédures Sophistiques pour construire l'evidence', in Lévy, C. and Pernot, L. (eds), *Dire l'Evidence: Philosophie et Rhétorique Antiques*, Paris: 15–29.

Cribiore, R. 2001, *Gymnastics of the Mind: Greek Education in Hellenistic and Roman Egypt*, Princeton.

Cribiore, R. 2007, *The School of Libanius in Late Antique Antioch*, Princeton.

Decloquement, V. 2018, 'Feintise ludique et non pas leurre. Lire Dictys de Crète à la lumière de la παιδεία', in Brescia, G., Lentano, M., Scafoglio, G. and Zanusso, V. (eds), *Revival and Revision of the Trojan Myth: Studies on Dictys Cretensis and Dares Phrygius*, Zürich/New York: 177–97.

Demoen, K. and Praet, D. 2012, 'Philostratus, Plutarch, Gorgias and the end of Plato's "Phaedrus"', *CQ* 62, 1: 436–9.

Dowden, K. 2009, 'Reading Diktys: the discrete charm of bogosity', in Paschalis, M., Panayotakis, S. and Schmeling, G. (eds), *Readers and Writers in the Ancient Novel*, Groningen: 155–68.

Dubel, S. 2010, 'Le Livre et la pinacothèque: position générique des *Images*', in Ballestra-Puech, S., Bonhomme, B. and Marty, P. (eds), *Musées de mots: L'héritage de Philostrate dans la literature occidentale*, Genève: 25–38.

Eitrem, S. 1929, 'Zu Philostrats Heroicus', *SO* 8: 1–56.

Farnell, L. R. 1921, *Greek Hero Cults and Ideas of Immortality*, Oxford.

Follet, S. 2004, 'Philostratus's Heroicus and the regions of the Northern Aegean', in Aitken, E. B. and Maclean, J. (eds), *Philostratus' Heroicus: Religion and Cultural Identity in the Third Century* CE, Leiden: 221–36.

Follet, S. 2017, *Philostrate: Sur les Héros*, Paris.

Fornieles Sánchez, R. 2015, '¿Quién, qué, cuándo, dónde y por qué? en el *Defensa de Palamedes*: el *paradigma Gorgias*', *Ianua Classicorum* 11: 131–8.

Gantz, T. 1993, *Early Greek Myth: A Guide to Literary and Artistic Sources*, Baltimore.

Gazis, G. A. 2018, *Homer and the Poetics of Hades*, Oxford.

Gibson, C. A. 2004, 'Learning Greek history in the ancient classroom: the evidence of the treatises on Progymnasmata', *CPh* 99, 2: 103–29.

Gibson, C. A. 2008, *Libanius's Progymnasmata: Model Exercises in Greek Prose Composition and Rhetoric, Translated with an Introduction and Notes*, Atlanta.

Grossardt, P. 2006, *Einfürhung, Übersetzung und Kommentar zum Heroicus von Flavius Philostrat*, 2 vols, Basel.

Grossardt, P. 2009, 'How to become a poet? Homer and Apollonius visit the mound of Achilles', in Demoen, K. and Praet, D. (eds), *Theios Sophistes. Essays on Flavius Philostratus' Vita Apollonii*, Leiden: 75–94.

Heath, M. 2002–2003, 'Theon and the History of the Progymnasmata', *GRBS* 43, 2: 129–60.

Hodkinson, O. 2011, *Authority and Tradition in Philostratus'* Heroicus, Lecce.

Huhn, F. and Bethe, E. 1917, 'Philostrats *Heroicus* und Diktys', *Hermes* 52: 613–24.

Kennedy, G. A. 2003, *Progymnasmata: Greek Textbooks of Prose Composition and Rhetoric, Translated with Introduction and Notes*, Atlanta.

Kim, L. 2008, 'Dio of Prusa, *Or. 61, Chryseis*, or reading Homeric silence', *CQ* 58, 2 601–21.

Kim, L. 2010, *Homer between History and Fiction in Imperial Greek Literature*, Cambridge.

Lambin, G. 2011, *Le Roman d'Homère: comment naît un poète*, Rennes.

de Lannoy, L. 1997, 'Le problème des Philostrate: (Etat de la Question)', *ANRW* 2.34.3, Berlin: 2362–449.

Maclean, J. B. 2004, 'The αἶνοι of the *Heroicus* and the unfolding transformation of the Phoenician merchant', in Aitken, E. B. and Maclean, J. (eds), *Philostratus' Heroicus: Religion and Cultural Identity in the Third Century* CE, Leiden: 195–218.

Mantero, T. 1966, *Ricerche sull'*Heroicus *di Filostrato*, Genoa.

Mestre, F. 2004, 'Refuting Homer in the *Heroicus* of Philostratus', in Aitken, E. B. and Maclean, J. (eds), *Philostratus' Heroicus: Religion and Cultural Identity in the Third Century* CE, Leiden: 127–41.

Mestre, F. 2007, 'Filóstrato y los *Progymnasmata*', in Fernández Delgado, J. A., Pordomingo, F. and Stramaglia, A. (eds), *Escuela y literatura en Grecia antigua. Actas del simposio internacional, Universidad de Salamanca, 17-19 Noviembre de 2004*, Cassino: 523–56.

Miles, G. 2018, *Philostratus: Interpreters and Interpretation*, Abingdon/New York.

Münscher, K. 1907, 'Die Philostrate', *Philologus* Suppl. X: 467–558.

Nilsson, M. P. 1950, *Handbuch der Altertumswissenschaft, V. Abt., 2. Teil: Geschichte der griechischen Religion, 2: Die hellenistische und römische Zeit*, München.

Patillon, M. 1997, *Aelius Théon: Progymnasmata*, Paris.

Pernot, L. 1993, *La rhétorique de l'éloge dans le monde Gréco-Romain*, Paris.

Platt, V. 2011, *Facing the Gods. Epiphany and Representation in Graeco-Roman Art, Literature, and Religion*, Cambridge/New York.

Radet, G. 1925, 'Notes sur l'Histoire d'Alexandre. II: Les théores Thessaliens au tombeau d'Achille', *REA* 27, 2: 81–96.

Rusten, J. 2004, 'Living in the past: allusive narrative and elusive authorities in the world of the *Heroicus*', in Aitken, E. B. and Maclean, J. (eds), *Philostratus' Heroicus: Religion and Cultural Identity in the Third Century* CE, Leiden: 143–58.

Rusten, J. and König, J. (eds) 2014, *Philostratus:* Heroicus, Gymnasticus, *Discourses 1 and 2*, Cambridge.

Saïd, S. 2010, '*Muthos* et *historia* dans l'historiographie grecque des origines au début de l'Empire', in Auger, D. and Delattre, C. (eds), *Mythe et Fiction*, Nanterre: 69–96.

Schouler, B. 1984, *La tradition hellénique chez Libanios*, 2 vols, Lille/Paris.

de Temmerman, K. 2010, 'Ancient rhetoric as a hermeneutical tool for the analysis of characterization in narrative literature', *Rhetorica: A Journal of the History of Rhetoric* 18, 1: 23–51.

Thomas, R. 2000, *Herodotus in Context: Ethnography, Science and the Art of Persuasion*, Cambridge.

Tordoff, R. 2014, 'Counterfactual history and Thucydides', in Wohl, V. (ed.), *Probabilities, Hypotheticals, and Counterfactuals in Ancient Greek Thought*, Cambridge: 101–21.

Trachsel, A. 2007, *La Troade: un paysage et son héritage littéraire. Les commentaires antiques sur la Troade, leur genèse et leur influence*, Basel.

Webb, R. 2001, 'The *Progymnasmata* as practice', in Too, Y. L. (ed.), *Education in Greek and Roman Antiquity*, Leiden/Boston: 289–316.

Webb, R. 2010, 'Between poetry and rhetoric: Libanios' use of Homeric subjects in his *Progymnasmata*', *QUCC* 95: 131–52.

Webb, R. 2015, 'Homère dans les *Images* de Philostrate', in Dubel, S., Favreau-Linder, A.-M. and Oudot, E. (eds), *A l'école d'Homère. La culture des orateurs et des Sophistes*, Paris: 203–14.

Webb, R. 2017, 'Schools and *Paideia*', in Richter, D. S. and Johnson, W. A. (eds), *The Oxford Handbook of the Second Sophistic*, New York: 139–53.

Whitmarsh, T. 2009, 'Performing Heroics: language, landscape and identity in Philostratus' *Heroicus*', in Bowie, E. and Elsner, J. (eds), *Philostratus*, Cambridge/New York: 205–9.

von Wilamowitz-Möllendorff, U. 1931-2, *Der Glaube der Hellenen*, 2 vols, Berlin.

Zeitlin, F. 2001, 'Visions and revisions of Homer in the Second Sophistic', in Goldhill, S. (ed.), *Being Greek under Rome: Cultural Identity, the Second Sophistic and the Development of Empire*, Cambridge: 196–266.

Reading Homer and the Epic Cycle through *Ekphrasis*: Philostratus' Epic *Imagines*[1]

A. Sophie Schoess

Ὅστις μὴ ἀσπάζεται τὴν ζωγραφίαν, ἀδικεῖ τὴν ἀλήθειαν, ἀδικεῖ καὶ σοφίαν, ὁπόση ἐς ποιητὰς ἥκει – φορὰ γὰρ ἴση ἀμφοῖν ἐς τὰ τῶν ἡρώων ἔργα καὶ εἴδη – ξυμμετρίαν τε οὐκ ἐπαινεῖ, δι᾽ ἣν καὶ λόγου ἡ τέχνη ἅπτεται.

Whosoever scorns painting is unjust to truth; and he is also unjust to all the wisdom that has been bestowed upon poets – for poets and painters make equal contribution to our knowledge of the deeds and the looks of heroes – and he withholds his praise from symmetry of proportion, whereby art partakes of reason.

Philostratus, *Imagines*, Proem 1.1[2]

Already in this first sentence of the proem to his *Imagines*, Philostratus addresses the complicated relationship between image and text, authoritatively proclaiming painting and poetry kindred arts. That the sophist is engaging in an ongoing academic discussion is immediately clear: Philostratus puts his own views in direct opposition to those of a particular group, those who do not embrace painting, μὴ ἀσπάζεται τὴν ζωγραφίαν. In arguing that painting and poetry share in the same σοφία, Philostratus draws attention to the fact that the two media are often seen in opposition to, and competition with, one another.[3] Rather than accepting such a division, however, Philostratus underscores their similar concern with heroes, ἥρωες, and highlights painting's συμμετρία, its harmony and proportion, as signifying its sharing in λόγος.

Philostratus invokes both σοφία and ἀλήθεια to underscore the shared cultural knowledge and value of poetry and painting. His use of the term ἀλήθεια in the discussion of mimetic arts is indicative of his approach to painting, and immediately positions him in dialogue with, and in opposition to, Plato.[4] For Philostratus, painting, and narrative painting in particular, often transcends its mimetic nature, drawing narrator and audience into the world of the image and creating its own kind of reality or ἀλήθεια.[5] What Plato refers to as the painter's tricking or deceiving children and mindless adults[6] is for Philostratus part of a game that highlights the skill of painter and ekphrastic narrator simultaneously: the effect of a well-executed painting on the viewer may be a false sense of reality, but the aim of *ekphrasis* is to create through speech a vivid and convincing visual reality for the reader.[7] When Philostratus' ekphrastic narrator claims to have lost himself in the painting (e.g., *Im*. 1.4.4), it is really his readers who have lost themselves in the narrator's *ekphrasis* (e.g., *Im*. 1.28.2).[8] Indeed, Philostratus plays with Plato's conceptualization of painting's being thrice removed from ἀλήθεια by adding a further degree of removal, his *ekphrasis*.[9] Philostratus' epic *ekphraseis* in particular draw attention to the different narrative realities of text and image, as well as to the relationship between the painting and its model. Realism and reality in the *Imagines* are thus closely connected with (visual) realization and imagination.[10]

It is, however, not only his use of ἀλήθεια that marks Philostratus' first sentence as a challenge to contemporary critical art theory and as a programmatic statement for the *Imagines*. Philostratus emphasizes the skill and knowledge of artist and poet alike, and leaves his reader to ponder whether the skill of the ekphrastic narrator might rely on kindred principles. Fairbanks' translation of σοφία as 'wisdom' here leaves unacknowledged the term's connotations of technical and artistic skill,[11] something the German *Kunstverständnis*, an appreciation of and feeling for art, in Schönberger's translation conveys more successfully.[12] The translation of λόγος (or lack thereof) is telling in a similar way: Fairbanks opts for 'reason' where Schönberger retains the Greek word, leaving its inherent ambiguity.[13] Given Philostratus' interest in word play – γράφειν is often used ambiguously, potentially confusing the act of the painter's drawing and Philostratus' writing[14] – λόγος may here also be seen to refer to speech or narrative. While it is the *ekphrasis*, Philostratus' language, that ultimately imbues the painting with vivid narrative, the paintings themselves tell a story, a λόγος,[15] precisely through the proportions of and the relationships between the objects and people depicted, in other words, through συμμετρία.[16]

Of particular importance to this chapter is Philostratus' assertion that τὰ τῶν ἡρώων ἔργα καὶ εἴδη, heroes' deeds and forms, are of equal concern to both painting and poetry. The reader's attention is thus immediately drawn to the world of myth and specifically to its treatment in epic and dramatic poetry. Indeed, though Philostratus acknowledges sources of heroic myth other than literary retellings,[17] his main point of reference is poetry. The emphasis on both ἔργα and εἴδη also once again links the literary and the visual, as ἔργα are more easily associated with verbal narrative and εἴδη with visual depiction; yet both media show an interest in and treat to varying degrees both aspects of the heroic world and its characters, each according to its own principles.[18]

The reader's attention is thus, from the outset, drawn to the interplay between image and text, and specifically to the heroic subject matter shared by painting and poetry. While many of the paintings described in the *Imagines* do not actually depict epic or tragic scenes of heroic endeavours, the audience has been prepared to expect such content and the reader is primed to detect poetic, especially Homeric, allusions, references, and even quotations.[19] This expectation is further reinforced by the first *ekphrasis* of the collection, a description of the epic battle between Scamander and Hephaestus,[20] which begins and ends with invocations of Homer's *Iliad*.

Philostratus' textual references

Philostratus does not, however, limit his literary references to paintings of heroic subject matter, but rather scatters literary intrusions throughout the *Imagines*.[21] These textual references vary in scope, relevance and transparency. Philostratus, at times, draws his audience's attention to a literary passage that directly relates to, and further illuminates, the image described (e.g., *Im.* 1.1), while at others he alludes more obliquely to a literary source by providing details about his subject that are known to originate from a specific text or group of texts (e.g., *Im.* 2.10).[22] In some cases, he even directly attributes a particular phrase or sentiment to a famous author – Ὅμηρος ... φησιν (*Im.* 1.26.1) or φησὶ ... ὁ Τήιος (*Im.* 1.15.2) – or he inserts a direct quotation without alerting his audience to this literary intrusion (e.g., *Im.* 1.2.5).[23] Whatever the register of such literary references, Philostratus' audience is expected to recognize and engage with the connections drawn between the literary and the visual.

Connections between text and image are, of course, central to Philostratus' endeavour to verbalize paintings. Even without literary intrusions, his descriptions bridge, or at least appear to bridge, the obvious gap between the visual and the verbal. As noted above, however, Philostratus delights in blurring rather than simply connecting the lines between the two media. The many literary references scattered throughout the *ekphraseis* further confuse the reader's sense of text and image as distinct media, while simultaneously challenging them to examine their previous assumptions about literature, works of art, and their relationship in the rhetorical exercise, or literary device, of *ekphrasis*.

Where most other sophistic texts engage with the epic past primarily through text, be it through the epics themselves or through critical discussions thereof, Philostratus' *Imagines* introduces not only a further kind of source material and critical engagement, but also an additional degree of removal from the 'original' epic text. This chapter therefore examines the visuality of Philostratus' views of the epic past, foregrounding both his treatment of Homeric subjects and his complicated reception of narratives from the wider Epic Cycle. It discusses connections between extant and lost epic and visual traditions and Philostratus' images, and highlights how his use of Homeric vocabulary and phrases adds a learned note and, arguably, a certain vividness to his descriptions. Building on a shared cultural literacy common to ekphrasist and, certainly, the ancient audience, the *Imagines* invites the reader to recall known visual and literary traditions, and to reflect on their newly reshaped visual, textual, and performative representation.

In what follows, I briefly discuss the role of Philostratus' audience in the creation of meaning in works of art and, perhaps more importantly, their role in the *recognition* of meaning, that is to say their ability to recognize intended cultural references, visual or literary. With this in mind, I draw attention to Philostratus' choice of epic sources and discuss what these can tell us about Philostratus' expectation concerning his reader's παιδεία, and specifically concerning their familiarity with archaic Greek epic and its literary tradition. It is in this context that three distinct yet interconnected approaches to the epic past are examined: first, the ekphrasist's introduction of Homer as the quintessential epic reference (*Im.* 1.1); second, his use of Homer to explore narrative familiar from the wider cyclical tradition (*Im.* 2.7); and third, his departure from the Homeric model for the visual (*Im.* 1.7).[24] Finally, I examine the choices underlying the literary and visual framing of Philostratus' epic *ekphraseis* and discuss the cultural and educational realities these choices reflect.

Philostratus' audiences

Before discussing Philostratus' inclusion of epic subject matter and epic language in his *ekphraseis*, it is important to consider the role of the audience in the *Imagines* and their response to, and reception of, literary and, especially, epic intrusions. The narrator of the *Imagines* famously engages not only with an external audience, that is to say the reader, ancient or modern, but also with an internal audience, a young boy, παῖς, and a group of young men, μειράκια.[25]

Philostratus' ekphrastic narrator, the sophistic instructor guiding his audience through a picture gallery on the Bay of Naples, chooses as his primary addressee his host's young son, whose familiarity with the pictorial and literary discussion is evidently limited. This is done, so Philostratus tells us in his proem, in order to facilitate a lesson not only for the boy, but also for the young men, the former eager to comprehend the narratives depicted in the paintings, the latter keen to absorb lessons in rhetoric and to listen to Philostratus' μελέτας, his lectures or rhetorical exercises (*Proem* 4).[26] Given the differing pedagogical aims in this lesson, directed as it is at two distinct groups of students, it should not come as a surprise that Philostratus holds the young men to a different educational and intellectual standard than he does the young boy.[27] Where he expects the young men to be able to recognize when the *ekphrasis* diverges from its subject and exhorts them to engage with his discussion, he firmly guides the boy, highlighting the details and connections he ought to be recognizing, while supplying the ones he might not.

Philostratus' reader, ideally one adept at recognizing and following his literary and visual games, may in turn be seen to occupy a still higher place in the intellectual and educational hierarchy of audiences. Though they share with the internal audience the foundation of their παιδεία, the Homeric epics, their engagement with the texts is expected to be far more nuanced. They are to delight in the rich literary tradition embedded, adapted and purposefully used in the *Imagines*; Philostratus' reader is to enjoy the literary games, to engage with the hidden meanings, and to disentangle the literary from the visual.[28] At the same time, however, that reader is also faced with a dilemma: they are to follow Philostratus' descriptions, immersing themselves in them, and yet must not be overwhelmed and outwitted by the vividness.[29] When Philostratus' internal audience fails to remain intellectually distanced from the painting's reality, uncritically following the narrator's description, the reader is implicated in this failure, precisely because of their distance from the picture and their reliance on Philostratus' *ekphrasis* alone. For the reader, the pictures come alive through the sophist's words and, more importantly, they exist purely because of the ekphrasist; he is at once writer and painter.

As readers, we thus follow the *ekphraseis* primarily as literary passages, perhaps as rhetorical exercises turned literary work, but not as accompaniments to actual images.[30] We are necessarily bound to engage more closely with the literary elements of the text than with the paintings themselves.[31] The image, after all, depends on our ability to visualize, at times based simply on shared human experience, at times based on our familiarity with ancient visual traditions, and at times based on our knowledge of the literary tradition and its own visuality.

As modern readers of Philostratus' work we must, of course, be aware that many literary (as well as visual) allusions, including those to specific passages from the Epic Cycle, are lost to us. Some of these we may be able to reconstruct based on fragmentary evidence or on references in later authors; some we may be able to recognize as references without necessarily being able to parse them; many more, however, we have at present no hope of discerning. Even within antiquity, as various texts and traditions fell out of favour over time, audiences of different periods would have had different perspectives on intertextual references. What is of interest to the present study in this context is the question of how much of the Epic Cycle, and therefore of the archaic epic tradition, might already have been lost or at least difficult to access at the time of Philostratus' writing, and how this might be reflected in the *Imagines*.

Introducing Homeric authority: *Imagines* 1.1

While the first sentence of the proem serves to link painting and poetry with the world of heroes, the first *ekphrasis* of the collection serves to establish Homer as the literary source of epic narrative *par excellence*. Here, Homer's work is presented not simply as lying behind the visual narrative of the painting, but as essential to its existence. It is at once literary source and organizing principle of the epic scene.

The epic battle between Scamander and Hephaestus described in *Imagines* 1.1 is easily linked to Homer's narrative in *Iliad* 21 (211–384), not least because Philostratus tells us it is so.[32] The scene in both Homer and Philostratus is known for its visual detail and vividness,[33] but it is notably absent from the visual tradition.[34] It is perhaps this visual novelty that initially leads Philostratus to exhort his internal audience to turn away from the picture and toward the text:

Ἔγνως, ὦ παῖ, ταῦτα Ὁμήρου ὄντα ἢ οὐ πώποτε ἔγνωκας δηλαδὴ θαῦμα ἡγούμενος, ὅπως δήποτε ἔξῃ τὸ πῦρ ἐν τῷ ὕδατι; συμβάλωμεν οὖν ὅ τι νοεῖ, σὺ δὲ ἀπόβλεψον αὐτῶν, ὅσον ἐκεῖνα ἰδεῖν, ἀφ' ὧν ἡ γραφή. οἶσθά που τῆς Ἰλιάδος τὴν γνώμην, ἐν οἷς Ὅμηρος ἀνίστησι μὲν τὸν Ἀχιλλέα ἐπὶ τῷ Πατρόκλῳ, κινοῦνται δὲ οἱ θεοὶ πολεμεῖν ἀλλήλοις. τούτων οὖν τῶν περὶ τοὺς θεοὺς ἡ γραφὴ τὰ μὲν ἄλλα οὐκ οἶδε, τὸν δὲ Ἥφαιστον ἐμπεσεῖν φησι τῷ Σκαμάνδρῳ πολὺν καὶ ἄκρατον. 2. ὅρα δὴ πάλιν· πάντα ἐκεῖθεν. ὑψηλὴ μὲν αὕτη ἡ πόλις καὶ ταυτὶ τὰ κρήδεμνα τοῦ Ἰλίου, πεδίον δὲ τουτὶ μέγα καὶ ἀποχρῶν τὴν Ἀσίαν πρὸς τὴν Εὐρώπην ἀντιτάξαι, πῦρ δὲ τοῦτο πολὺ μὲν πλημμυρεῖ κατὰ τοῦ πεδίου, πολὺ δὲ περὶ τὰς ὄχθας ἕρπει τοῦ ποταμοῦ, ὡς μηκέτι αὐτῷ δένδρα εἶναι. τὸ δὲ ἀμφὶ τὸν Ἥφαιστον πῦρ ἐπιρρεῖ τῷ ὕδατι, καὶ ὁ ποταμὸς ἀλγεῖ καὶ ἱκετεύει τὸν Ἥφαιστον αὐτός. ἀλλ᾽ οὔτε ὁ ποταμὸς γέγραπται κομῶν ὑπὸ τοῦ περικεκαῦσθαι οὔτε χωλεύων ὁ Ἥφαιστος ὑπὸ τοῦ τρέχειν· καὶ τὸ ἄνθος τοῦ πυρὸς οὐ ξανθὸν οὐδὲ τῇ εἰθισμένῃ ὄψει, ἀλλὰ χρυσοειδὲς καὶ ἡλιῶδες. ταῦτα οὐκέτι Ὁμήρου.

Have you noticed, my boy, that the painting here is based on Homer, or have you failed to do so because you are lost in wonder as to how in the world the fire could live in the midst of the water? Well then, let us try to get at the meaning of it. Turn your eyes away from the painting itself so as to look only at the events on which it is based. Surely you are familiar with the passage in the *Iliad* where Homer makes Achilles rise up to avenge Patroclus, and the gods are moved to make battle with each other. Now of this battle of the gods the painting ignores all the rest, but it tells how Hephaestus fell upon Scamander with might and main. Now look again at the painting; it is all from Homer. Here is the lofty citadel, and here the battlements of Ilium; here is a great plain, large enough for marshalling the forces of Asia against the forces of Europe; here fire rolls mightily like a flood over the plain, and mightily it creeps along the banks of the river so that no trees are left there. The fire which envelops Hephaestus flows out on the surface of the water and the river is suffering and in person begs Hephaestus for mercy. But the river is not painted with long hair, for the hair has been burnt off; nor is Hephaestus painted as lame, for he is running; and the flames of the fire are not ruddy nor yet of the usual appearance, but they shine like gold and sunbeams. In this Homer is no longer followed.

Philostratus, *Imagines* 1.1

In their detailed study of this *ekphrasis*, Squire and Elsner demonstrate that *Imagines* 1.1 serves several programmatic purposes: it cements the didactic nature of the collection;[35] it highlights the literary indebtedness of Philostratus; and it illustrates his intricate play with image and text, as well as with the textuality of the visual and the visuality of the textual.[36] Importantly for this chapter, it serves the additional purpose of showcasing Philostratus' sophistic interest in Homer and his reception.[37]

The didactic element discussed by Squire and Elsner is closely linked with Philostratus' choice of internal audience. The young boy is the explicit addressee, as the first three words indicate, ἔγνως, ὦ παῖ. Philostratus first inquires as to whether the boy is able to recognize the underlying textual source, adding that he must surely know the corresponding passage from Homer, οἶσθά που. This implies that the subject matter is so clear and its literary source so obvious that even a child should recognize it.[38] Homer's epics are presented as forming the backbone of education, highlighting both their popularity and their perceived literary value.[39] Though the boy, as far as the reader knows, never responds to the question, the narrator's assumptions about his education have been made plain. Philostratus nonetheless elucidates the reference, providing a brief synopsis of the Iliadic episode and listing the key players. The reader is left to ponder whether this is done for the benefit of the boy who might, after all, have needed the explanation, or for that of the reader who cannot see the painting and relies entirely on the *ekphrasis*.

The reader's inability to see the actual painting forces them to rely more heavily on the Homeric texts than the internal audience. While the boy and the youths are tasked with looking exclusively, ἀπόβλεψον, at the Homeric source of the painting, αὐτῶν ... ἀφ' ὧν ἡ γραφή,[40] the reader has access only to the ancient text. The scene is declared explicitly literary, which is further reinforced by the verbal echoes of the *Iliad* scattered throughout the *ekphrasis*.[41] The reader, engrossed in the literary narrative, is no doubt expected to engage more closely than the internal audience with the various levels of Homeric reference in this *ekphrasis*.

This passage, for all its emphasis on the Homeric eminence, also illustrates the sophistic tendency to compete with the Homeric model,[42] in this case wrestling with its vividness and level of detail. In directing his audience to the text of the *Iliad*, Philostratus raises the expectation that the painting will prove to be an illustration of sorts, shaped primarily by its textual source. Initially, this expectation is not disappointed, as the scene is identified as part of the larger narrative of the battle of the gods, and details in the painting are aligned with the text, πάντα ἐκεῖθεν. Indeed, the detailed description of the landscape evokes a vivid image, while the painted figures appear animated in their actions, most prominently Scamander himself, who, it is said, 'is suffering and in person begs Hephaestus for mercy', ἀλγεῖ καὶ ἱκετεύει τὸν Ἥφαιστον αὐτός. It is at this most vivid and Homeric point of the *ekphrasis* that Philostratus introduces non-Homeric elements, ἀλλ' οὔτε ... οὔτε, details provided only by the picture, such as the real consequences of the river's burning and Hephaestus' agility, impossible to reconcile with his Homeric limp. This part of the description culminates in a final declarative statement, ταῦτα οὐκέτι Ὁμήρου. It highlights simultaneously the limits of the Homeric account and its authority, and the independence of the medium of painting.[43] Artist and ekphrasist have the final word, and it is not Homeric.

The competition with Homer, as Squire and Elsner argue, is played out both in the painting itself and in the *ekphrasis*.[44] The aforementioned lack of a visual tradition to support readers in visualizing the described painting leads them to engage more closely with the visuality of the words, both of the Homeric poem and of the Philostratean description. The visuality of Homer's description is initially reflected in the detail of the painting: text has become image, and the visual quality of the former has found its expression in the medium of the latter. As Squire and Elsner highlight, however, this translation from one medium to another happens unseen by the reader, and can be traced only in Philostratus' *ekphrasis*. Yet, the visualization transforms the Homeric source, creating a new narrative path for Philostratus to follow and explore. *Imagines* 1.1 thus serves not only to introduce Homer as a literary source, but also to illustrate the ways in which text and image may be related, but are ultimately independent in their epic treatments.

It is with this programmatic *ekphrasis*, then, that Philostratus introduces us into both his *Imagines* and his epic world. Following this first painting, however, Homeric narratives are seldom referred to directly, though the poems continue to be invoked and evoked. While we encounter numerous Homeric heroes in the *Imagines*, their painted exploits typically take place outside the frames of *Iliad* and *Odyssey*, and are literarily linked either with tragedy or with other poems of the Epic Cycle. The deaths of Antilochus and Memnon, fixed components of the larger Trojan War narrative, are not told of by Homer, though in modern scholarship these are often argued to be closely linked with the deaths of Patroclus and Hector.[45] While Philostratus does not invoke Homer in his treatment of Memnon's death (*Im.* 1.7), he does draw the connection between Antilochus' role in the *Iliad* and his death in the *Aethiopis*, explicitly invoking only the former (*Im.* 2.7).[46]

Homer and the Epic Cycle: *Imagines* 2.7

Philostratus begins his treatment of Antilochus' death with a clear statement, once again expressing his expectation that the boy's education has led to his familiarity with the world of Homeric epic, πεφώρακας οἶμαι παρ' Ὁμήρῳ. Indeed, the introduction to the *ekphrasis* is entirely based on Homeric narrative, though the painting itself is not:[47]

Τὸν Ἀχιλλέα ἐρᾶν τοῦ Ἀντιλόχου πεφώρακας οἶμαι παρ' Ὁμήρῳ, νεώτατον τοῦ Ἑλληνικοῦ ὁρῶν τὸν Ἀντίλοχον καὶ τὸ ἡμιτάλαντον τοῦ χρυσοῦ ἐννοῶν τὸ ἐπὶ τῷ ἀγῶνι. καὶ ἀπαγγέλλει τῷ Ἀχιλλεῖ κεῖσθαι τὸν Πάτροκλον, σοφισαμένου τοῦ

Μενέλεω παραμυθίαν ὁμοῦ τῇ ἀγγελίᾳ, μεταβλέψαντος Ἀχιλλέως εἰς παιδικά, καὶ θρηνεῖ ἐρωμένου ἐπὶ τῷ πένθει καὶ συνέχει τὼ χεῖρε, μὴ ἀποκτείνῃ ἑαυτόν, ὁ δ᾽ οἶμαι καὶ ἁπτομένῳ χαίρει καὶ δακρύοντι.

That Achilles loved Antilochus you must have discovered in Homer, seeing Antilochus to be the youngest man in the Greek host and considering the half talent of gold that was given him after the contest. And it is he who brings word to Achilles that Patroclus has fallen, for Menelaüs cleverly devised this as a consolation to accompany the announcement, since Achilles' eyes were thus diverted to his loved one; and Antilochus laments in grief for his friend and restrains his hands lest he take his own life, while Achilles no doubt rejoices at the touch of the youth's hand and at the tears he sheds.

Philostratus, *Imagines* 2.7.1

Philostratus asserts here that Homer describes the relationship between Achilles and Antilochus as one of love, ἐρᾶν, and that this detail ought to be familiar to the boy. He again refers to specific details that characterize Antilochus in the *Iliad*, such as his youth (*Il.* 15.569), his role in the chariot race at Patroclus' funeral games (*Il.* 23.796) and his delivering the news of Patroclus' death (*Il.* 18.1–34). The Greeks' despair at Patroclus' death and their calling on Antilochus to tell Achilles (*Il.* 17.682–761) is here framed as part of a tragic love story.[48] Both Antilochus' tears, δακρύοντι, and his touch, ἁπτομένῳ, are eroticized, setting the tone for the actual *ekphrasis*.

With these epic and erotic expectations raised, Philostratus announces that there is a difference to be observed between the Homeric narrative, αὗται μὲν οὖν Ὁμήρου γραφαί, and the painting itself, τὸ δὲ τοῦ ζωγράφου δρᾶμα (*Im.* 2.7.2). The former is a text, γραφαί, fixed in form and narrative, while the latter is a vivid, moving, and living δρᾶμα.[49] Once again, we witness the competition with Homer playing out between genre and medium, as the δρᾶμα of the painter is animated by the words of Philostratus.

When Philostratus finally turns to the painted scene, his silence on the actual literary sources behind the painting is marked. Based on the paradigm set by *Imagines* 1.1 the reader might expect the artist to have strayed from the Homeric narrative in details, but finds instead an entirely different narrative represented. Still, Homeric verbal echoes abound once more, anchoring the scene in a particular literary tradition:[50]

ὁ Μέμνων ἐξ Αἰθιοπίας ἀφικόμενος κτείνει τὸν Ἀντίλοχον προβεβλημένον τοῦ πατρὸς καὶ τοὺς Ἀχαιοὺς οἷον δεῖμα ἐκπλήττει – πρὸ γὰρ τοῦ Μέμνονος μῦθος οἱ μέλανες – κρατοῦντες δὲ οἱ Ἀχαιοὶ τοῦ σώματος ὀδύρονται τὸν Ἀντίλοχον οἱ

Ἀτρεῖδαι καὶ ὁ ἐκ τῆς Ἰθάκης καὶ ὁ τοῦ Τυδέως καὶ οἱ ὁμώνυμοι. ἐπίδηλος δὲ ὁ μὲν Ἰθακήσιος ἀπὸ τοῦ στρυφνοῦ καὶ ἐγρηγορότος, ὁ δὲ Μενέλεως ἀπὸ τοῦ ἡμέρου, ὁ δὲ Ἀγαμέμνων ἀπὸ τοῦ ἐνθέου, τὸν δὲ τοῦ Τυδέως ἡ ἐλευθερία γράφει, γνωρίζοις δ᾽ ἂν καὶ τὸν Τελαμώνιον ἀπὸ τοῦ βλοσυροῦ καὶ τὸν Λοκρὸν ἀπὸ τοῦ ἑτοίμου. 3. Καὶ ἡ στρατιὰ πενθεῖ τὸ μειράκιον περιεστῶτες αὐτῷ θρήνῳ ἅμα, πήξαντες δὲ τὰς αἰχμὰς εἰς τοὔδαφος ἐναλλάττουσι τὼ πόδε καὶ στηρίζονται ἐπὶ τῶν αἰχμῶν ἀπερείσαντες οἱ πλεῖστοι δυσφορούσας τὰς κεφαλὰς τῷ ἄχει. 4. Τὸν Ἀχιλλέα μὴ ἀπὸ τῆς κόμης – οἴχεται γὰρ τοῦτο αὐτῷ μετὰ τὸν Πάτροκλον – ἀλλὰ τὸ εἶδος αὐτὸν ἐνδεικνύτω καὶ τὸ μέγεθος καὶ αὐτὸ τὸ μὴ κομᾶν. θρηνεῖ δὲ προσκείμενος τοῖς στέρνοις τοῦ Ἀντιλόχου, καὶ πυρὰν οἶμαι ἐπαγγέλλεται καὶ τὰ ἐς αὐτὴν καὶ τὰ ὅπλα ἴσως καὶ τὴν κεφαλὴν τοῦ Μέμνονος· ἀποτεῖσαι γὰρ καὶ τὸν Μέμνονα ὅσα τὸν Ἕκτορα, ὡς μηδὲ ταῦτα ὁ Ἀντίλοχος ἔλαττον τοῦ Πατρόκλου ἔχοι. ὁ δ᾽ ἐν τῷ τῶν Αἰθιόπων στρατῷ δεινὸς ἕστηκεν ἔχων αἰχμὴν καὶ λεοντῆν ἐνημμένος καὶ σεσηρὼς ἐς τὸν Ἀχιλλέα.

Memnon coming from Ethiopia slays Antilochus who had thrown himself in front of his father, and he seems to strike terror among the Achaeans – for before Memnon's time black men were but a subject for story – and the Achaeans, gaining possession of the body, lament Antilochus, both the sons of Atreus and the Ithacan and the son of Tydeus and the two heroes of the same name. The Ithacan is made known by his austere and vigilant look, Menelaus by his gentleness, Agamemnon by his god-like mien, while the son of Tydeus is marked by his nobility, and you would recognize the Telamonian Ajax by his grimness and the Locrian by his alertness. And the army mourns the youth, standing about him in lamentation; and, their spears fixed in the ground and their legs crossed, they stand, most of them in their grief bowing their sorrowing heads on their spears. You are not to recognize Achilles by his long hair, for that is gone since the death of Patroclus, but let his beauty make him known to you, and his stature, aye, and the very fact that he does not wear long hair. He laments, throwing himself on the breast of Antilochus, and he seems to be promising him a funeral pyre and the offerings to be placed upon it and perchance the arms and head of Memnon; for he proposes that Memnon shall pay all the penalties Hector paid, that in this respect also Antilochus may have no less honour than Patroclus had. Memnon stands, terrible to look upon, in the army of the Ethiopians, holding a spear and wearing a lion's skin and sneering at Achilles.

Philostratus, *Imagines* 2.7.2–4

Despite the Homeric introduction to Antilochus, the *ekphrasis* foregrounds first Memnon as he kills Antilochus, and then the other Achaeans as they mourn his fate. Indeed, Philostratus treats his audience to a series of descriptions of his protagonists' defining features, beginning with Memnon and his army. In many ways, this *ekphrasis* resembles Homer's *teichoscopia* in *Iliad* 3, where Helen identifies the Achaean heroes for Priam, who marvels at their physical strength.[51] Here, however, we hear only the voice of Philostratus as he enlivens the scene of mourning. It is when Achilles moves into focus that the narrative of the *Iliad* returns to the fore. The death of Patroclus, used earlier to introduce Antilochus, here serves to explain Achilles' physical appearance; it has left a mark that profoundly alters him.[52]

In Achilles' physical response to Antilochus' death, Philostratus sees a repetition of Patroclus' end. He gives voice to Achilles' promises to Antilochus, which not only echo, but actively invoke, those made to Patroclus: ὡς μηδὲ ταῦτα ὁ Ἀντίλοχος ἔλαττον τοῦ Πατρόκλου ἔχοι. Memnon is but a second Hector, one who overstepped his bounds and is to be punished for his ὕβρις toward a beloved of Achilles.[53] Indeed, the visual path, too, takes us back to Memnon and his Ethiopians as they watch the Achaeans' mourning.

Only once these living heroes have been examined does Philostratus call our attention back to the lifeless figure of Antilochus himself:

Σκεψώμεθα οὖν καὶ τὸν Ἀντίλοχον· ἡβάσκει μὲν ὑπήνης πρόσω, κομᾷ δὲ ἐν ἡλιώσῃ κόμῃ. κοῦφος ἡ κνήμη καὶ τὸ σῶμα σύμμετρον ἐς ῥαστώνην τοῦ δρόμου καὶ τὸ αἷμα οἷον ἐπ᾽ ἐλέφαντι χρῶμα ἤνθηκεν ἐμπεσούσης αὐτῷ κατὰ τοῦ στέρνου τῆς αἰχμῆς. κεῖται δὲ οὐ κατηφὲς τὸ μειράκιον οὐδὲ νεκρῷ εἰκάσαι, φαιδρὸν δ᾽ ἔτι καὶ μειδιῶν· τὴν γὰρ οἶμαι χαρὰν τὴν ἐπὶ τῷ τὸν πατέρα σῶσαι φέρων ἐν τῷ εἴδει ὁ Ἀντίλοχος ἀπώλετο ὑπὸ τῆς αἰχμῆς, καὶ τὸ πρόσωπον ἡ ψυχὴ κατέλιπεν οὐχ ὡς ἤλγησεν, ἀλλ᾽ ὡς ἐπεκράτησε τὸ εὐφραῖνον.

Let us next look at Antilochus. He is in the prime of youth, just beyond the period of downy beard, and his bright hair is his pride. His leg is slender and his body proportioned for running with ease, and his blood shines red, like colour on ivory, where the spear-point penetrated his breast. The youth lies there, not sad of aspect nor yet like a corpse, but still joyous and smiling; for it was with a look of joy on his face (because, I fancy, he had saved his father's life) that Antilochus died from the spear-thrust, and the soul left his countenance, not when he was in pain, but when gladness prevailed.

Philostratus, *Imagines* 2.7.5

Where the description of the heroes evoked the Homeric beginning to the *ekphrasis*, this last part evokes its erotic overtones, as the youthful body of Antilochus is scanned, σκεψώμεθα, by viewer, narrator and reader alike.[54] His youthful vigour is described with reference to his Homeric victories,[55] and his wounds are visualized evoking a Homeric simile.[56] Yet, while Antilochus is presented as a devoted son in the *Iliad*, it is Diomedes who saves Nestor's life there (*Il.* 8.78–112), while Antilochus' self-sacrifice for his father is a detail associated with the *Aethiopis*. In this final Philostratean assertion, then, Homer is no longer followed, but replaced by a literary source adumbrated but never explicitly invoked.

The Epic Cycle and visual culture: *Imagines* 1.7

Philostratus' description of Memnon's death, in turn, does not draw on a Homeric model, narratively or verbally. Instead, it focuses on visual details that are, so Philostratus tells us, combined in a coherent and easily recognizable visual treatment of the famous epic narrative:

> Ἡ μὲν στρατιὰ Μέμνονος, τὰ ὅπλα δὲ αὐτοῖς ἀπόκειται καὶ προτίθενται τὸν μέγιστον αὐτῶν ἐπὶ θρήνῳ, βέβληται δὲ κατὰ τὸ στέρνον ἐμοὶ δοκεῖν ὑπὸ τῆς μελίας. εὑρὼν γὰρ πεδίον εὐρὺ καὶ σκηνὰς καὶ τεῖχος ἐν στρατοπέδῳ καὶ πόλιν συμπεφραγμένην τείχεσιν οὐκ οἶδ' ὅπως οὐκ Αἰθίοπες οὗτοι καὶ Τροία ταῦτα, θρηνεῖται δὲ Μέμνων ὁ τῆς Ἠοῦς. τοῦτον ἀφικόμενον ἀμῦναι τῇ Τροίᾳ κτείνει, φασίν, ὁ τοῦ Πηλέως μέγαν ἥκοντα καὶ οὐδὲν ἂν αὐτοῦ μείω.

> This is the army of Memnon; their arms have been laid aside, and they are laying out the body of their chief for mourning; he has been struck in the breast, I think, by the ashen spear. For when I find a broad plain and tents and an entrenched camp and a city fenced in with walls, I feel sure that these are Ethiopians and that this city is Troy and that it is Memnon, the son of Eos, who is being mourned. When he came to the defence of Troy, the son of Peleus, they say, slew him, mighty though he was and likely to be no whit inferior to his opponent.
>
> Philostratus, Imagines 1.7.1

The fallen Memnon and his army are purportedly identified on the basis of the wide plain on which they are encamped, its wall, and the walled city looming in the background. These elements are seemingly so distinct that Philostratus can imagine reading the scene no other way, οὐκ οἶδ' ὅπως οὐκ.[57] According to this rationalization, it is the scenery, not the people in it, that signals the narrative episode, though later in the *ekphrasis* Philostratus makes clear that the painted figures contribute considerably to his ability to identify the scene. The fallen Memnon, for instance, is characterized by both his size and the colour of his skin:

σκόπει γάρ, ὅσος μὲν κεῖται κατὰ τῆς γῆς, ὅσος δὲ ὁ τῶν βοστρύχων ἄσταχυς, οὓς οἶμαι Νείλῳ ἔτρεφε· Νείλου γὰρ Αἰγύπτιοι μὲν ἔχουσι τὰς ἐκβολάς, Αἰθίοπες δὲ τὰς πηγάς. ὅρα τὸ εἶδος, ὡς ἔρρωται καὶ τῶν ὀφθαλμῶν ἀπολωλότων, ὅρα τὸν ἴουλον ὡς καθ᾽ ἡλικίαν τῷ κτείναντι. οὐδ᾽ ἂν μέλανα φαίης τὸν Μέμνονα· τὸ γὰρ ἀκράτως ἐν αὐτῷ μέλαν ὑποφαίνει τι ἄνθους.

Notice to what huge length he lies on the ground, and how long is the crop of curls, which he grew, no doubt, that he might dedicate them to the Nile; for while the mouth of the Nile belongs to Egypt, the sources of it belong to Ethiopia. See his form, how strong it is, even though the light has gone from his eyes; see his downy beard, how it matches his age with that of his youthful slayer. You would not say that Memnon's skin is really black, for the pure black of it shows a trace of ruddiness.

Philostratus, *Imagines* 1.7.2

The detail of Memnon's long curl, ὁ τῶν βοστρύχων ἄσταχυς, is put in the cultural context of the veneration of the Nile and in the geographical context of the Nile's origins, τὰς πηγάς, in Ethiopia. A reader familiar with the *Imagines* as a whole might notice the contrast between Achilles' shorn hair (*Im.* 2.7.4),[58] a symbol of his loyalty to Patroclus, and Memnon's long curl, a symbol of his enduring devotion to the Nile, a devotion that unlike Achilles' can now never come to its natural conclusion.[59] While Achilles is not explicitly named here – he is referred to as Memnon's slayer, ὁ κτεῖνας – his presence looms and the comparison between him and Memnon is drawn explicitly in the detail of their shared youth: ὅρα τὸν ἴουλον ὡς καθ᾽ ἡλικίαν τῷ κτείναντι. More important for this *ekphrasis* as a whole, however, is Philostratus' explicit interest in the historical rather than the mythological aspects of the narrative. In *Imagines* 2.7, Philostratus shows a similar, though far less explicit, interest in the Ethiopians, commenting on the darkness of their skin with a statement that, in broad strokes, contrasts myth and history: πρὸ γὰρ τοῦ Μέμνονος μῦθος οἱ μέλανες (*Im.* 2.7.2).[60] The Greek encounter with Memnon's Ethiopians is presented as changing the way the Greeks think about τοὺς μέλανας: they have become part of Greek reality. In *Imagines* 1.7, it is the homeland of the Ethiopians that is explored:

αἱ δὲ μετέωροι δαίμονες Ἠὼς ἐπὶ τῷ παιδὶ πενθοῦσα κατηφῆ ποιεῖ τὸν Ἥλιον καὶ δεῖται τῆς Νυκτὸς ἀφικέσθαι πρὸ καιροῦ καὶ τὸ στρατόπεδον ἐπισχεῖν, ἵνα ἐγγένηταί οἱ κλέψαι τὸν υἱόν, Διός που ταῦτα νεύσαντος. καὶ ἰδοὺ ἐκκέκλεπται καὶ ἔστιν ἐπὶ τέρμασι τῆς γραφῆς. ποῦ δὴ καὶ κατὰ τί τῆς γῆς; τάφος οὐδαμοῦ Μέμνονος, ὁ δὲ Μέμνων ἐν Αἰθιοπίᾳ μεταβεβληκὼς εἰς λίθον μέλανα. καὶ τὸ σχῆμα καθημένου, τὸ δὲ εἶδος ἐκείνου, οἶμαι, καὶ προσβάλλει τῷ ἀγάλματι ἡ ἀκτὶς τοῦ Ἡλίου. δοκεῖ γὰρ ὁ Ἥλιος οἱονεὶ πλῆκτρον κατὰ στόμα ἐμπίπτων τῷ Μέμνονι ἐκκαλεῖσθαι φωνὴν ἐκεῖθεν καὶ λαλοῦντι σοφίσματι παραμυθεῖσθαι τὴν Ἡμέραν.

As for the deities in the sky, Eos mourning over her son causes the Sun to be downcast and begs Night to come prematurely and check the hostile army, that she may be able to steal away her son, no doubt with the consent of Zeus. And look! Memnon has been stolen away and is at the edge of the painting. Where is he? In what part of the earth? No tomb of Memnon is anywhere to be seen but in Ethiopia he himself has been transformed into a statue of black marble. The attitude is that of a seated person, but the figure is that of Memnon yonder, if I mistake not, and the ray of the sun falls on the statue. For the sun, striking the lips of Memnon as a plectrum strikes the lyre, seems to summon a voice from them, and by this speech-producing artifice consoles the Goddess of the Day.

Philostratus, Imagines 1.7.3

Eos' divine intervention and her support from Nyx and Zeus initially draw the audience back into the mythical world,[61] but they primarily serve to link two parts of the painting, both depicting Memnon: his corpse, discussed above, and his statue, the result of his transformation, μεταβεβληκώς. The transformation, however, seems secondary to Philostratus' *ekphrasis*, as he first ponders, ποῦ δὴ καὶ κατὰ τί τῆς γῆς; and then asserts the statue's location, ἐν Αἰθιοπίᾳ. The reader has moved not only from one part of the painting to another, ἐπὶ τέρμασι τῆς γραφῆς, but from one part of the world, the Trojan plain, to another, Ethiopia. In the spirit of this movement, Philostratus provides a detail familiar from contemporary travel narratives: the story of Memnon's statue.[62] In addition to linking epic past and geographical realities, Philostratus here brings together different artistic media: sculpture and painting. By Philostratus' time, Memnon's story has become immortalized in the visual arts and wider cultural heritage, while the literary narrative has faded into the background, and this, it seems, is reflected in Philostratus' writings, too.

Homer, the Epic Cycle and the independence of painting

In the three *ekphraseis* discussed here, Philostratus illustrates the very relationship between painting and poetry he introduced in his proem. The two media's interest in τὰ τῶν ἡρώων ἔργα καὶ εἴδη is examined alongside the 'languages' in which each medium tells its narrative. Philostratus' *ekphraseis*, straddling the divide between literary and visual, follow at times more literary paths and at others more visual ones. In *Imagines* 1.1, the divide between these two paths is explored as each is taken in turn, though their intersection, too, is highlighted. The painting itself, depicting a Homeric scene, is already deeply connected with its literary source, but it is only through Philostratus' explicit identification of this source and his inclusion of Homeric verbal echoes in his *ekphrasis* that the painting's own narrative, its λόγος, so to speak, is subordinated to that of the text. In the un-Homeric details, however, the painting's independence becomes evident: it depicts the ἔργα of the Homeric texts, but does so by means of its own visualization of the εἴδη.

The lines between the visual and the verbal are most blurred in *Imagines* 2.7, the description of Antilochus' death. The *Iliad* is once again presented as the main source, but this time it cannot elucidate the painted scene itself, only provide its backstory. Again, Philostratus includes Homeric verbal and narrative echoes, but the narrative is distinctly not Homeric. Since Philostratus does not alert his audience to the painting's real literary source, Arctinus' *Aethiopis*, the painting's own narrative is foregrounded: it is a scene of mourning, characterized by the various heroes' relationships with the fallen Antilochus.[63] Once these heroic figures have been identified, their εἴδη are perused, the countenance of each is described, followed by the observation that most are bowing their heads in mourning.[64] While Philostratus' words create a narrative around the central figures of the mourning Achilles and the fallen Antilochus, it is the painting's own language, expressed through its συμμετρία, that allows for the ekphrastic narrator's elaboration.

The epic past in *Imagines* 1.7, in turn, is treated in predominantly visual terms, as Philostratus again neglects the literary link with the *Aethiopis*. The painting is decoded according to its visual principles, its συμμετρία, as first the painted objects and later the painted figures are discussed in relation to one another: their arrangement creates a meaningful narrative whole, as Philostratus illustrates immediately. It is, moreover, worth noting that the epic scene of Memnon's death on the battlefield at Troy is visually linked with a tourist site popular in the Imperial period, the talking statue of Memnon. Painting and sculpture together obscure the lingering poetic authority. Philostratus embraces this split from the poetic source, drawing more heavily on travel literature or history in this *ekphrasis*, though without superimposing it onto the image. Both painting and *ekphrasis* are testament to the independence of the visual tradition of the

Memnon episode and its aftermath, and the prominence of this tradition in the cultural framework within which Philostratus and his ancient audience operate.

This cultural framework, influenced by contemporary and earlier literary and artistic tastes, is made up of various artistic media and influenced by sociopolitical and religious contexts. Philostratus shows great awareness of how differently the narratives of *Imagines* 1.1, 1.7 and 2.7 are represented within this cultural framework, highlighting the predominantly literary reception of Scamander's battle with Hephaestus and the, in his time, primarily visual transmission of Memnon's death. The continued oral tradition, that is to say, the oral transmission of heroic narratives from one generation to the next, of course plays an important part in keeping the narratives alive and the visual tradition meaningful to its audience. Philostratus, however, does not seek out oral traditions as sources for his paintings, not considering them part of the artistic tradition with which he engages. As a sophistic instructor his narrator seeks to test and strengthen his audience's literary and artistic παιδεία, not their familiarity with folktales.[65]

Homer's epics are clearly presented as forming the backbone of this παιδεία, while the ability to 'read' and interpret images is a skill to be learned from teachers, such as Philostratus' ekphrastic narrator. The narratives told by the other poems of the Epic Cycle are preserved in cultural memory, even once the poems themselves are lost.[66] In many ways, Philostratus' silence about the poet of the *Aethiopis* and his work does not lessen the scholarly uncertainty about the circumstances of the loss of the Epic Cycle in antiquity. An easy explanation for this silence would be the contention that Philostratus could not rely on his audience's familiarity with Arctinus' poem, even if he himself had read it. Yet a number of things unrelated to the question of contemporary access to the cyclic poems could account for Philostratus' choice not to mention Arctinus' name or poem.[67] Indeed, the literary reception of the cyclic poems as inferior to the *Iliad* and *Odyssey* may well have influenced Philostratus' literary choices. Ultimately, whatever lies behind the literary silences in the *Imagines*, it tells us something about the cultural landscape of his time that Philostratus places such emphasis on the Homeric background to the scene of Antilochus' death, not a popular subject in classical art,[68] and simultaneously focuses so heavily on the visuality of Memnon's, a scene widely represented in the visual arts of classical antiquity.[69] In this, the sophistic instructor can be seen to guide his audience not only in how to examine a painting depicting the epic past, but also in how to relate it to the cultural traditions in which it most prominently features.

Conclusion

From the first sentence of his proem, Philostratus draws close connections between painting, epic poetry, and heroic narrative. The three *ekphraseis* discussed here illustrate these connections through their varied sources: the Homeric epics; the narratives of the Epic Cycle, though likely not the cyclic poems themselves; and the visual tradition. Philostratus highlights the pre-eminence of Homer as literary source for epic narrative, even while drawing on narratives told in other poems. That he discusses the depiction of Memnon's death in purely visual rather than literary terms suggests that, by Philostratus' time, the most common point of reference for this particular narrative was the visual rather than the textual tradition.

Philostratus' engagement with the epic past thus gives us a sense of the cultural landscape of epic narrative in his time, as well as of the reception of the Epic Cycle, including the Homeric epics, and of the value attached to the individual poems. Though it is impossible to know whether Philostratus might have included direct quotations or specific references to the *Aethiopis* in his descriptions of the deaths of Memnon and Antilochus, his choice to discuss these heroes with explicit reference to the visual tradition and to Homer only is telling. It contributes to a view of a cultural landscape that preserved epic narratives in different forms and media: literary, oral, and visual. In viewing the epic past from such different perspectives, Philostratus draws attention to the diverse artistic traditions that play a part in the transmission of heroic narrative, and demonstrates his own skill in adapting and re-inventing them.

Notes

1 I wish to thank Paola Bassino and Nicolò Benzi for organizing a stimulating conference and the audience for their helpful questions and comments. I also wish to express my gratitude to Jaś Elsner, Jason König and the anonymous reviewers for their comments on this chapter.
2 Text and translation throughout this chapter: Fairbanks 1931.
3 See Squire 2013: 106–7 on the conceptual and linguistic games Philostratus plays here.
4 In Book 10 of the *Republic*, Plato argues that mimetic arts, including poetry and painting, are, by multiple degrees, removed from truth (595c–602c, esp. 602c: τὸ δὲ δὴ μιμεῖσθαι τοῦτο [οὐ] περὶ τρίτον μέν τί ἐστιν ἀπὸ τῆς ἀληθείας; ἦ γάρ;). On

Plato's approach to painting, poetry and truth, as well as on the difficulties inherent in the study of the subject, see, e.g., Demand 1975; Halliwell 2000; Keuls 1974; Morgan 2011. Philostratus' choice to claim ἀλήθεια for both poetry and painting, and his explicit positioning of this choice in opposition to the rejection of painting, places him firmly within the ancient debate on the value and contribution of mimetic arts; see, e.g., Squire/Elsner 2016: 72; cf. Blanchard 1978: 238–43.

5   On the reception of mimesis in Greek literature of the Roman period, see Whitmarsh 2001: 41–89. Cf. Elsner 1995: 28–39 on Philostratus' sense of realism.
6   E.g., *Republic* 598c: ἀλλ' ὅμως παῖδάς γε καὶ ἄφρονας ἀνθρώπους, εἰ ἀγαθὸς εἴη ζωγράφος, γράψας ἂν τέκτονα καὶ πόρρωθεν ἐπιδεικνὺς ἐξαπατῷ ἂν τῷ δοκεῖν ὡς ἀληθῶς τέκτονα εἶναι.
7   See Webb 2006 on Philostratus' creation of ekphrastic reality.
8   See Newby 2009: 323, 334–40 for discussion of Philostratus' movement between absorption and intellectual detachment; see also Elsner 1995: 23–39.
9   See n. 4; cf. Thein 2002 on the invention of painting in Philostratus.
10 See Squire 2013 for a detailed discussion of Philostratus' understanding of the relationship between image and text, and his play with realism in the wider philosophical and critical context of Classical and Late Antiquity. See Webb 2015 on Homeric images and visuality in Philostratus.
11 In the context of art, σοφία is often linked with ἔντεχνος to convey cleverness or skill, and is associated with Athena and Hephaestus as gods of artistic and crafting skills (*LSJ* s.v. 'σοφία'). Cf. Newby 2009: 324–6.
12 Schönberger 1968: 85. For a detailed discussion of Philostratus' use of painterly and poetic σοφία, see Michel 1974.
13 Schönberger 1968: 85.
14 See, e.g., Squire/Elsner 2016: 80.
15 Cf. Michel's use of '*Bildsprache*' in this context (Michel 1974: 462–6).
16 See Bachmann 2015: 28–31 on the usage of συμμετρία in the Second Sophistic and Baumann 2011: 166–73 on συμμετρία in the *Imagines*; cf. König 2014: 378–82 on the use of συμμετρία to discuss the athletic body and the art of training in Philostratus' *Gymnasticus*. See, e.g., Bal/Bryson 1991 for a detailed discussion of how the linguistic and literary concepts of semiotics can be applied to the visual arts, highlighting the narrative capacity of the non-verbal medium.
17 See, e.g., *Im.* 1.15.1, where Philostratus dismisses the accounts of nurses (τίτθαι) as old-wives' tales.
18 Cf. Webb 2013, esp. 23–4.
19 On Homeric subject matter in the *Imagines*, see Webb 2015.
20 For a detailed discussion of this *ekphrasis*, see Squire/Elsner 2016.
21 See Squire 2013: 107–10

22 Here, without explicitly invoking Homer or Aeschylus, Philostratus describes the murder of Agamemnon and Clytemnestra. In his language and in the details, he plays with his epic and tragic models; he finally teases his reader with the acknowledgement that a δρᾶμα τετραγῴδηται, and hints that the painting has itself more to offer than the texts alone (*Im.* 2.10.1); see Elsner 2007: 329–37 and Webb 2015: 206–11 for discussion.
23 Here, a particular turn of phrase from Euripides' *Bacchae* (836, 852) is used, θῆλυν ἐνδῦναι στολήν, to illustrate aspects of the revelry of Comus (*Im.* 1.2.1: δαίμων ὁ Κῶμος).
24 In discussing the three images in this order, I do not follow the order of Philostratus' *Imagines* to illustrate the different degrees of textual and visual engagement in the *Imagines* and to highlight the narrative independence of the visual arts more clearly. It is worth noting that Philostratus himself disregards the narrative order of the Epic Cycle in his *Imagines* indicating that, despite their indebtedness to literary sources, the paintings and their *ekphraseis* follow their own narrative and organizational paradigms; cf. Miles 2018: 85.
25 See Webb 2006: 123–8 for further discussion.
26 Cf. Newby 2009: 323–4.
27 On the importance of Homer for the educational curriculum, from initial instruction to advanced rhetorical training, see, e.g., Tirrito (Chapter 6) and Brodersen (Chapter 7) in this volume. On παιδεία and Greek identity in the Roman period, see Whitmarsh 2001: 90–130.
28 See Squire 2013 on the ideal reader's awareness of theories about image and text in dialogue.
29 On the relationship between narrator and audience, see Baumann 2011: 145–52; cf. Squire 2013: 110–17.
30 See Shaffer 1998 for a discussion of Philostratus' *ekphrasis*, rhetoric and acts of viewing. See Squire/Elsner 2016: 76–80 on Philostratus' play with meta-*ekphrasis* and his audience's acts of viewing.
31 For discussion of the scholarly interest in reproducing and authenticating the paintings behind Philostratus' *ekphraseis*, see, e.g., Lehmann-Hartleben 1941: 16–17 and Squire/Elsner 2016: 72–4.
32 Cf. Decloquement (Chapter 8) in this volume on Philostratus' treatment of another part of the Homeric Scamander narrative in Philostratus' *Heroicus*.
33 On ancient discussions of Homeric visuality, see, e.g., Létoublon 2018; Snodgrass 1998; Squire/Elsner 2016: 60–1.
34 See Squire/Elsner 2016: 64–9.
35 See Baumann 2011: 22–5 for a detailed discussion of the instructive use of hermeneutic analysis in this *ekphrasis*.
36 Squire/Elsner 2016. See also Boeder 1996: 149–53.
37 See Squire/Elsner 2016: 60.

38 Compare *Im.* 1.15, where the boy is also expected to be familiar with the narrative, though this time not because of his literary education, but because of his exposure to an oral culture, the stories told by nurses, τίτθαι; cf. Philostr., *Her.* 7.9–10. See below, n. 65.
39 See Finkelberg 2003: 91–6; Lamberton 1997: 41–8.
40 See Newby 2009: 326–7 on the idea of text as a corrective to θαῦμα.
41 Fairbanks notes similarities between, e.g., τὰ κρήδεμνα τοῦ Ἰλίου and the Homeric Τροίης ἱερὰ κρήδεμνα at *Il.* 16.100 (Fairbanks 1931: 8–9).
42 See Blanchard 1978: 238–43 for a detailed discussion of the various levels of Philostratus' engagement with Homer's poems through text and image. On the competitive responses to Homer in the literature of the Second Sophistic more generally, see, e.g., Brodersen (Chapter 7), Decloquement (Chapter 8), Tirrito (Chapter 6), and Wilshere (Chapter 5) in this volume. Cf. Bär/Baumbach 2007 and Bär 2010 on how this sophistic tendency influenced Quintus Smyrnaeus' epic reception of Homer and the Epic Cycle in his *Posthomerica*.
43 See Dubel 2009: 313 on the importance of colour in this shift from text to image.
44 Squire/Elsner 2016: 76–80.
45 See, e.g., Allan 2005; Burgess 1997; Kullmann 2005; Sammons 2013; West 2003; cf. Miles 2018: 85.
46 See Miles 2018: 83–6 on the explicit and implicit links between the two images.
47 See Newby 2009: 330–1 for the suggestion that Philostratus may here be commenting on his contemporaries' tendency to seek out Homeric sources even in inappropriate contexts; cf. Squire/Elsner 2016: 60.
48 See Webb 2015: 205–6; cf. Newby 2009: 328–9. Cf. Philostr., *Her.* 26.6–20.
49 On Philostratus' play with painted δρᾶμα, see Beall 1993: 351–3 and Elsner 2007.
50 See Webb 2015: 206–9 on the Homeric echoes in the paintings surrounding *Im.* 2.7.
51 While the Homeric and Philostratean scenes foreground a number of the same heroes, Philostratus neither keeps the Homeric order nor uses the Homeric descriptors to identify the figures.
52 Τὸν Ἀχιλλέα μὴ ἀπὸ τῆς κόμης – οἴχεται γὰρ τοῦτο αὐτῷ μετὰ τὸν Πάτροκλον – ἀλλὰ τὸ εἶδος αὐτὸν ἐνδεικνύτω καὶ τὸ μέγεθος καὶ αὐτὸ τὸ μὴ κομᾶν; cf. *Il.* 23.141–2: στὰς ἀπάνευθε πυρῆς ξανθὴν ἀπεκείρατο χαίτην / τήν ῥα Σπερχειῷ ποταμῷ τρέφε τηλεθόωσαν. Cf. Philostr., *Her.* 19.5.
53 See Burgess 1997 for a discussion of the vengeance motif in *Iliad* and *Aethiopis*.
54 Compare Philostratus' treatment of Hippolytus in *Im.* 2.4; see Elsner 2007: 321–3 for discussion. See König 2005: 337–44 on the treatment of the athletic male body in Philostratus' *oeuvre* more generally.
55 τὸ σῶμα σύμμετρον ἐς ῥαστώνην τοῦ δρόμου; cf. *Il.* 23.756: ὃ γὰρ αὖτε νέους ποσὶ πάντας ἐνίκα.

56 τὸ αἷμα οἷον ἐπ' ἐλέφαντι χρῶμα ἤνθηκεν ἐμπεσούσης αὐτῷ κατὰ τοῦ στέρνου τῆς αἰχμῆς; cf. *Il.* 4.140–2: αὐτίκα δ' ἔρρεεν αἷμα κελαινεφὲς ἐξ ὠτειλῆς. / ὡς δ' ὅτε τίς τ' ἐλέφαντα γυνὴ φοίνικι μιήνῃ / Μῃονὶς ἠὲ Κάειρα, παρήϊον ἔμμεναι ἵππων.

57 Michel argues that the most recognizable element of the painting might well be the statue mentioned only toward the end of the *ekphrasis* (Michel 1974: 458).

58 Compare also Scamander's short hair in *Im.* 1.1; see Elsner/Squire 2016: 75–6 for discussion.

59 The intertextual relationship with the *Iliad* is, of course, still more complex, as Achilles' lock was intended as an offering to the river Sperchius, but became a symbol not only of Achilles' devotion to Patroclus, but also of his acceptance of an early death as a result; see Miles 2018: 85–6 for further discussion.

60 It is worth noting that, in *Im.* 1.7, Philostratus qualifies the darkness of Memnon's skin as differing from that of the other Ethiopians: οὐδ' ἂν μέλανα φαίης τὸν Μέμνονα· τὸ γὰρ ἀκράτως ἐν αὐτῷ μέλαν ὑποφαίνει τι ἄνθους; see Schönberger 1968: 288 and 395–7, and Miles 2018: 84 for discussion. While the meaning of ἄνθος is somewhat obscure here, it can be translated as either yellow or, more generally, brightness or brilliancy, hence Fairbanks' 'ruddiness'. It is also possible to read the detail of Memnon's skin colour as a narrative nod to the hero's divine parentage (McGrath 1992: 11 n. 63); cf. Dubel 2009: 311: 'Philostratus' uses of colour appear at times to be more literary than pictorial'. See McGrath 1992: 2 on Memnon's changing skin colour in the visual arts of Classical and Late Antiquity. Compare *Im.* 1.29.3, where Andromeda's whiteness is highlighted, despite her Ethiopian origins; see McGrath 1992, esp. 1–3 for discussion of Andromeda's skin colour in ancient texts and its reception in later periods.

61 Eos' intervention in the death of Memnon is well attested in the visual arts, see *LIMC* s.v. 'Memnon'.

62 Compare the description of Memnon's statue in Philostratus' *Apollonius of Tyana* 6.4, discussed by Platt 2009: 136–45. Cf. Strabo 17.1.46; Pausanias 1.42.3. On the statue itself and its association with the story of Memnon, see, e.g., Bowersock 1984; Griffith 1998.

63 See Hodge/Kress 1988: 37–78 for a discussion of the semiotics of spatial context.

64 *Im.* 2.7.3: καὶ στηρίζονται ἐπὶ τῶν αἰχμῶν ἀπερείσαντες οἱ πλεῖστοι δυσφορούσας τὰς κεφαλὰς τῷ ἄχει.

65 See Heath 2011 for a discussion of popular transmissions of heroic narrative and the dismissal of its female storytellers. Cf. Hansen 1997 on oral retellings of modern folk- or fairytales.

66 See West 2013: 47–50 for a detailed discussion of the reception of the Epic Cycle in the late Hellenistic and early Roman Periods.

67 On the question of when the poems of the Epic Cycle were lost and its implications for the discussion of the relationship between Imperial literature and the Epic Cycle, see, e.g., Bär/Baumbach 2015: 604–6; Maciver 2012: 8–9.

68 *LIMC* s.v. 'Antilochus'. Only one image is listed as showing the mourning of Antilochus' death ('Antilochus' 35), and this is in fact a circular reference to the 'nicht erhaltene Wandgemälde' described by Philostratus. The scene of *Im.* 2.7 is thus, much like that described in *Im.* 1.1, visually unattested outside of Philostratus' *ekphraseis*.
69 *LIMC* s.v. 'Memnon'.

References

Allan, W. 2005, 'Arms and the man: Euphorbus, Hector, and the death of Patroclus', *CQ* 55: 1–16.
Bachmann, C. 2015, *Wenn man die Welt als Gemälde betrachtet: Studien zu den* Eikones *Philostrats des Älteren*, Heidelberg.
Bal, M. and Bryson, N. 1991, 'Semiotics and art history', *The Art Bulletin* 73: 174–208.
Bär, S. 2010, 'Quintus of Smyrna and the Second Sophistic', *HSPh* 105: 287–316.
Bär, S. and Baumbach, M. 2007, *Quintus Smyrnaeus: Transforming Homer in Second Sophistic Epic*, Berlin.
Bär, S. and Baumbach, M. 2015, 'The Epic Cycle and Imperial Greek Epic', in Fantuzzi, M. and Tsagalis, C. (eds), *The Greek Epic Cycle and Its Ancient Reception. A Companion*, Cambridge: 604–22.
Baumann, M. 2011, *Bilder schreiben: virtuose Ekphrasis in Philostrats 'Eikones'*, Berlin.
Beall, S. 1993, 'Word-painting in the *Imagines* of the Elder Philostratus', *Hermes* 121: 350–63.
Blanchard, J. M. 1978, 'The eye of the beholder: on the semiotic status of paranarratives', *Semiotica* 22: 235–68.
Boeder, M. 1996, *Visa est Vox: Sprache und Bild in der spätantiken Literatur*, Frankfurt am Main.
Bowersock, G. 1984, 'The miracle of Memnon', *The Bulletin of the American Society of Papyrologists* 21: 21–32.
Burgess, J. 1997, 'Beyond Neo-Analysis: problems with the vengeance theory', *AJPh* 118: 1–19.
Demand, N. 1975, 'Plato and the painters', *Phoenix* 29: 1–20.
Dubel, S. 2009, 'Colour in Philostratus' *Imagines*', in Bowie, E. and Elsner, J. (eds), *Philostratus*, Cambridge: 309–21.
Elsner, J. 1995, *Art and the Roman Viewer: The Transformation of Art from the Pagan World to Christianity*, Cambridge.
Elsner, J. 2007, 'Philostratus visualizes the tragic: some ekphrastic and pictorial receptions of Greek tragedy in the Roman era', in Kraus, C., Goldhill S., Foley, H. and Elsner, J. (eds), *Visualizing the Tragic. Drama, Myth, and Ritual in Greek Art and Literature. Essays in Honour of Froma Zeitlin*, Oxford: 309–37.
Fairbanks, A. 1931, *Elder Philostratus,* Imagines; *Younger Philostratus,* Imagines; *Callistratus,* Descriptions *(edited and translated by Arthur Fairbanks)*, Cambridge MA.

Finkelberg, M. 2003, 'Homer as a foundation text', in Finkelberg, M. and Stroumsa, G. (eds), *Homer, the Bible, and Beyond: Literary and Religious Canons in the Ancient World*, Leiden: 75–96.

Griffith, R. 1998, 'The origin of Memnon', *ClAnt* 17: 212–34.

Halliwell, F. S. 2000, 'Plato and painting', in Rutter, K. and Sparkes, B. (eds), *Word and Image in Ancient Greece*, Edinburgh: 99–116.

Hansen, W. 1997, 'Homer and the Folktale', in Morris, I. and Powell, B. (eds), *A New Companion to Homer*, Leiden: 442–62.

Heath, J. 2011, 'Women's work: female transmission of mythical narrative', *TAPhA* 141: 69–104.

Hodge, R. and Kress, G. 1988, *Social Semiotics*, Oxford.

Keuls, E. 1974, 'Plato on painting', *AJPh* 95: 100–27.

König, J. 2005, *Athletics and Literature in the Roman Empire*, Cambridge.

König, J. 2014, 'Introduction (*Gymnasticus*)', in Rusten, J. and König, J. (eds), *Philostratus, Heroicus; Gymnasticus; Discourses 1 and 2 (edited and translated by Jeffrey Rusten, Jason König)*, Cambridge, MA: 333–85.

Kullmann, W. 2005, '*Ilias* und *Aithiopis*', *Hermes* 133: 9–28.

Lamberton, R. 1997, 'Homer in antiquity', in Morris, I. and Powell, B. (eds), *A New Companion to Homer*, Leiden: 33–54.

Lehmann-Hartleben, K. 1941, 'The *Imagines* of the Elder Philostratus', *The Art Bulletin* 23: 16–44.

Létoublon, F. 2018, 'War as spectacle', in Kampakoglou, A. and Novokhatho, A. (eds), *Gaze, Vision, and Visuality in Ancient Greek Literature*, Berlin: 4–32.

LIMC = Ackermann, H.C. and Gisler, J.-R. et al. (eds) 1981–1999; Suppl. 2009, *Lexicon Iconographicum Mythologiae Classicae*, 18 vols. Zurich/Munich.

LSJ = Liddell, H.G., Scott, R., Jones, H.S. 1996, *A Greek-English Lexicon*, with a Revised Supplement edited by Glare, P.G.W., with the assistance of Thompson, A.A. Oxford.

Maciver, C. 2012, *Quintus Smyrnaeus' Posthomerica: Engaging Homer in Late Antiquity*, Leiden.

McGrath E. 1992, 'The Black Andromeda', *JWI* 55: 1–18.

Michel, C. 1974, 'Die 'Weisheit' der Maler und Dichter in den "Bildern" des Älteren Philostrat', *Hermes* 102: 457–66.

Miles, G. 2018, *Philostratus: Interpreters and Interpretation*, Oxford.

Morgan, M. 2011, 'Plato, inquiry, and painting', *Apeiron* 23: 121–45.

Newby, Z. 2009, 'Absorption and erudition in Philostratus' *Imagines*', in Bowie, E. and Elsner, J. (eds), *Philostratus*, Cambridge: 322–42.

Platt, V. 2009, 'Virtual visions: *Phantasia* and the perception of the divine in *The Life of Apollonius of Tyana*', in Bowie, E. and Elsner, J. (eds), *Philostratus*, Cambridge: 131–54.

Sammons, B. 2013, 'Narrative doublets in the *Epic Cycle*', *AJPh* 134: 529–56.

Schönberger, O. 1968, *Philostratos, Die Bilder. Griechisch und deutsch. Nach Vorarbeiten von Ernst Kalinka herausgegeben, übersetzt und erläutert*, Berlin.

Shaffer, D. 1998, '*Ekphrasis* and the rhetoric of viewing in Philostratus' Imaginary Museum', *Philosophy & Rhetoric* 31: 303–16.

Snodgrass, A. 1998, *Homer and the Artists: Text and Picture in Early Greek Art*, Cambridge.

Squire, M. 2013, 'Apparitions apparent: ekphrasis and the parameters of vision in the Elder Philostratus' *Imagines*', *Helios* 40: 97–140.

Squire, M. and Elsner, J. 2016, 'Homer and the ekphrasists: text and picture in the Elder Philostratus' 'Scamander' (*Imagines* I.1)', in Bintliff, J. and Rutter, N. (eds), *The Archaeology of Greece and Rome: Studies In Honour of Anthony Snodgrass*, Edinburgh: 57–99.

Thein, K. 2002, 'Gods and painters: Philostratus the Elder, Stoic Phantasia and the strategy of describing', *Ramus* 31: 136–45.

Webb, R. 2006, 'The *Imagines* as a fictional text: *ekphrasis, apatē* and illusion', in Costantini, M., Graziani, F. and Rolet, S. (eds), *Le défi de l'art: Philostrate, Callistrate et l'image sophistique*, Rennes: 113–36.

Webb, R. 2013, 'Les *Images* de Philostrate: une narration éclatée', in Briand, M. (ed.), *La trame et le tableau: poétiques et rhétoriques du récit et de la description dans l'antiquité grecque et latine*, Rennes: 19–33.

Webb, R. 2015, 'Homère dans les *Images* de Philostrate', in Dubel, S., Favreau-Linder, A.-M. and Oudot, E. (eds), *À l'école d'Homère: la culture des orateurs et des sophistes*, Paris: 203–14.

West, M. L. 2003, '*Iliad* and *Aethiopis*', *CQ* 53: 1–14.

West, M. L. 2013, *The Epic Cycle: A Commentary on the Lost Troy Epics*, Oxford.

Whitmarsh, T. 2001, *Greek Literature and the Roman Empire*, Oxford.

Index

Page numbers: Notes are given as [page number]n.[note number]

Achaean women 23, 123
Achaeans
   Ajax versus Odysseus 66–8, 72, 79
   Antilochus' death 221
   Judgement of Paris 154
   Mysian tradition 192–5
   Priam and 222
   Trojan War 198, 201
Achilles 27, 171–2, 201–2
   Antilochus and 220, 222
   death of 168, 200
   epithets 122, 124
   in mythological role-play 92–3, 101
   Patroclus and 224, 232n.59
   Scamander tale 198–200
Achilles' arms 65–8, 73–4, 79, 106, 168
Adrastus 101–2
aedic performance 21, 24–5
Aeneas 149, 176–7
Aeschines 13n.19
Aeschylus 31
   Judgement of the Arms 68
   Palamedes 43
   Persians 189
Aesepus river 199
aesthetics in Homer 174
afterthought theme 105
Agamemnon 122, 146
   Achilles' arms 68
   murder of 230n.22
   Trojan War 41, 168, 194
Ajax
   Achilles and 122
   Antisthenes on 109n.38
   contestation topics 191–2
   as a giant 190
   in mythological role-play 100, 106
   Odysseus and 3, 7, 65–88, 101
   shield 72, 78–9, 84n.48
   speech 65, 70–2, 90

Alcidamas 3, 95–6, 100
   Odysseus or On the Treachery of
      Palamedes 6, 41, 52–7, 60n.32,
      82n.3, 90
   On the Sophists 54, 57
Alcman and Odysseus 69
Alexander the Great 144–5, 151–3, 158,
   160n.10, 160n.12
Andromeda 232n.60
anger 75–7, 85n.65
Antilochus
   Achilles and 220, 222
   death of 219, 221, 226–7, 233n.68
Antiphon 94, 102
Antisthenes 3, 7, 65–6, 90, 101,
   109n.38
   Ajax 41
   cynicism 65, 74, 81
   Homeric criticism 11
   Judgement of the Arms 67–70, 72–3
   mythological role-play 100
   Odysseus 41, 75–7, 82n.8
   referentiality 71
   similes 81, 87n.89
Anubis 122, 138n.21
Aphrodite 116–17, 122–7, 133, 135, 143,
   151–2, 156–8
Aphthonius 176, 191, 193
Apollo 24–5, 36n.42, 92
Apollodorus 195
Apollonius 106, 201
Archilochus 69, 144
Arctinus, *Aethiopis* 219, 223, 226, 227
Ares, songs to 145
argumentation 30, 32, 105, 200
Argus and Hermes 127
Aristarchus
   Homer's epics 118, 120–1, 126,
      161n.38
   Judgement of Paris 127, 137n.13

Aristophanes
  Birds 91
  Clouds 12n.11
  Frogs 58n.19, 97, 105
  Knights 82n.15
  Women at the Thesmophoriae 58n.18
Aristotle 27, 29, 31, 37n.51
  heroes' principles 69–70
  Homeric criticism 149, 162n.52
  technical skills 36n.44
art
  Athena/Hephaestus 229n.11
  object of 21
  products of 28–9
artistic media, cultural framework 227
Asian wealth 195
asses, references to 80–1, 86n.85
Ast, F. 102
Asteropaeus 200
Astydamas, *Palamedes* 58n.18
Athena 229n.11
  Judgement of the Arms 67, 68, 82n.15
  Judgement of Paris 118, 122–3, 125–8, 151–2
Athens
  language's power 43
  legal practice 47, 97
  rhetorical skill 2, 4
Athetesis 115–41
audience involvement
  Dio 179–80
  Philostratus 214–17

Barrett, James 97, 100, 101
Bartley, A. 133
Bassino, Paola 6, 10
beauty 28, 133
Bellerophon 129
'Bithynians' 155
blame theme 68, 76
Blondell, Ruby 92–3
Bouquiaux-Simon, O. 119
bravery/courage 70, 73
  see also excellence
Brodersen, Isidor 8, 10
Burton, R. 70

Calchas 193
Callicles 105

Calypso and Odysseus 66, 82n.7
Cassandra and Ajax 191
Cassin, Barbara 26
Castor 156
Chaeronea battle 144
chronological possibility 191–2, 195
Clader, Linda 20
Classical age, rhapsodes 10–11
Cleon 91, 105, 107
Cleopatra 27–8
cleverness 49, 55–6, 57
Clytemnestra 230n.22
Colluthus 138n.27
colour, use of 125, 232n.60
comedy 105, 107
  see also humour
Comus 230n.23
Contest of Homer and Hesiod 70, 83n.36
contestation exercises 191–5, 198–9
contradictory topic, contestation 191–2
Coulter, James 99–100
courage/bravery 70, 73
cowardice 71, 73, 76, 78
credibility
  Protesilaus' tales 201
  Scamander tale 199–200
'critical moment' concept 52–3
cultural framework 227
  see also visual culture
Cyclops and Odysseus 66
Cynicism
  Antisthenes 65, 74, 81
  Homer/Dio 178
  Lucian 115
  Nestor 106
  Odysseus' prediction 75
Cypria (epic poem) 42–3, 116–18, 125, 150, 152, 154, 193, 195

Danaans 66, 131
Dares Phrygius 189
  The History of the Fall of Troy 153
deception 22–3, 44
  see also lies
Decloquement, Valentin 8, 10
Deliades, ministers of Apollo 24–5
Delphi, Neoptolemus' death at 92
democracy 46
Demodocus 25

Demoen, Kristoffel 106
demonology 189
Dentith, S. 134–5
Desideri, Paolo 148–9, 154–5, 176
Dictys 189
   Ephemeris belli troiani 200
Dio Chrysostom 143–64, 195
   Diogenes 150
   Euboic 150
   mythological role-play 106
   On Kingship 144–6
   On the Philosopher 93
   On the Subject of Anachoretic Life 8, 10, 143–4, 147–8, 153, 155–9
   On Training 146, 160n.14, 165
   On Tyranny 150
   Trojan Oration 8–10, 143–4, 146–50, 153–5, 158–9, 165–85, 189, 198, 200, 206n.72
   truth 165–85
Diogenes and Odysseus 74
Diomedes 223
Dionysus 97
direct quotations 119
Domitian, death of 155
Dorandi, T. 146
double identity in role-play 106
Dušanić, Slobodan 95, 102

educational authority 218
educational standards 215
Egyptian characters 170–2, 176, 178–9, 200
Egyptian stories 98–9, 195–6, 201
Eileithyia 123
Eitrem, Samson 187
eikos 9, 20–3, 31–3, 33n. 8, 34n.11, n.18, 37n.52, n.55, n.56, 47, 59n.24, 98, 124, 156, 180, 192, 196, 202
ekphrasis, Homer/Epic Cycle 211–35
Eleatic Palamedes 95–6
Elsner, J. 217–19
embroidering, art of 20–1
emotions 27–8, 31
empathy 31
enchantment 25–6
Eos 225

epic
   approaches to 2–3
   evolution of 19
epic characters, manipulations of 6
Epic Cycle
   ekphrasis 211–35
   Homer and 219–23, 225–7
   Judgement of the Arms 66
   Judgement of Paris 152
   Palladium's theft 71
   Second Sophistic 143
   Trojan War 162n.52, 188
   visual culture 223–5
epic poetry
   authority 216
   speech and 28
   see also poetry
Epicurean principles 143, 155
epideixis, Hippias 92–3
Epimetheus and Prometheus 102–3, 105
epithets 119–20, 122, 124, 126
Epos, manipulation of 147–51, 154
Eris 152
ethical matters 65–6
ethical uses, mythology 29
Ethiopians 224–5, 232n.60
Euripides 105
   Andromache 92
   Bacchae 230n.23
   death of 45
   epithets 124
   Helen 19, 33n.1
   Herodotus and 197
   Iphigenia at Aulis 58n.18
   Odysseus in 69
   Orestes 58n.18
   Palamedes 97–8
   Philoctetes 43–4
   Trojan Women 19, 44
Eustathius 175
excellence 70, 73, 76, 79, 81, 104–5
exegesis, Homer 115–41
eyewitness reports 187, 200–1

fables, contesting 192
Fairbanks, A. 212
falsehoods 148
   see also lies
Favreau-Linder, A. 147

fiction
    ekphrasis as 203n.15
    Heroicus as 187
    as reinvention 203n.5
First Sophistic 5–7, 9
    Ajax versus Odysseus 65–88
    Helen's power 19–40
    mythological role-play 89–112
    Palamedes 41–63
forethought theme 104–5, 110n.44
'frame', use of term 172
Freud, Sigmund, *Der Dichter und das Phantasieren* 29
Fuchs, Elfriede 178

games–poetry analogy 29
Gangloff, A. 153
Ganymede 128, 139n.44
Gargaron 138n.37
gendered perspectives 196
geographical reality 198–9
ghost stories 189–90, 201, 203n.15
giants 190–1, 202
Glaucon 161n.42
gods, forms assumed by 34n.18
Gorgias 9–10, 36n.41, 92, 95, 97
    Apology of Palamedes 3, 6, 41, 46–52, 74, 82n.3
    clothing 11, 14n.34
    Defence of Palamedes 32, 60n.29, 60n.32, 90, 96–9, 202
    Encomium of Helen 3, 6, 19–20, 26–32, 35n.28, 36n.38, 37n.51, 37n.53, 47, 51, 60n.29, 85n.63, 153
    Helen in 19–20, 25–32, 51, 82n.1, 168
    historical themes 13n.19
    mythological role-play 100, 101
    Nestor identification 94
    On the Non-Being 47, 52, 60n.31
    On Non-Existence 60n.29
    On What Is Not 97–8
Greek culture
    epic tradition 1
    poetry 3, 6
    rhetoric 4
    Roman rule 4
Greek heroes 23, 42, 194
    see also heroes
Greek identity 177

Greek imagination
    Homer's lies 174–5
    Odysseus and Ajax 69–70
Greek leaders, Trojan War 176
guilt 36n.41
Gyselinck, Wannes 106

Hades *see* Underworld
Harmon, A. 126
harmony 21, 28
Hector
    Achilles and 122, 168, 200
    Ajax and 86n.72, 101
    death of 126, 172, 219, 222
    Helen and 150, 196–7
    Judgement of Paris 127–8
    Odysseus and 77
Helen 10, 200, 222
    abduction 143–64, 168
    Egyptian stories 170–1, 195–6, 201
    in Gorgias 19–20, 25–32, 51, 82n.1, 85n.63, 168
    historiography 195–8
    in Homer 19–25, 26–30, 35n.23, 172
    in Lucian 135, 137n.14
    as storyteller 6, 9
Helenus 176
the Hellenes 201–2
Hellenic tradition, Homer 146
Hephaestus 202, 213, 216–18, 227, 229n.11
Hera
    in Homer 143, 151–2, 161n.38, 168
    Judgement of Paris 118, 120, 122–5, 127, 137n.14
Heracles 3
Hermes 102, 106, 117, 121, 123, 126–9, 132–3
Hermogenes, *On Issues* 89
hero cult 187, 203n.3
Herodotus 33n.1, 170, 196–8, 201–2
    Histories 196–8, 200
heroes 22, 41–63, 96, 100, 189
    ekphrasis 222
    ethical models 66
    as giants 190
    as mythological characters 7, 108
    painting 212, 216
    poetry 25, 212, 216
    principles of 69–70

rhetoric 101
shields 72, 78–9, 84n.48
styles of 90
writing 129
heroic narratives 227
Hesiod 43, 70, 83n.36, 160n.12, 193
   Theogony 22
hexameter poetry 43
Hippias 2–3, 91–5, 101, 103
   clothing 11, 14n.34
   epideixis 92–3
   Trojan Dialogue 91–3
Hippocrates 104
historiography
   Helen's story 195–8
   Scamander 198–200
history
   mythology contrast 224–5
   rewriting 172
Homer 7–8, 33n.9
   Ajax in 69–71, 73, 86n.85
   Antisthenes' interest 65–6
   authority 216–19
   Cypria 97
   in Dio Chrysostom 143–64
   ekphrasis 211–35
   Epic Cycle and 219–23, 225–7
   exegesis 115–41
   Helen in 19–25, 26–30, 35n.23
   Hesiod and 70, 83n.36
   Hippias' *epideixis* 92–3
   Iliad 2–3, 5, 12n.12, 14n.33, 24, 41–2, 61n.38, 71–2, 77–8, 101, 118–20, 123–5, 129–31, 146, 148–9, 151, 153, 155, 168–9, 172, 188–90, 193, 195–200, 213, 216, 218–20, 222–3, 226–7, 232n.59
   lies 165–85, 198
   Nestor in 106
   Odysseus' speech 75–9, 80–1
   Odyssey 2–3, 5, 21–2, 34n.18, 35n.23, 41, 61n.38, 66, 68, 85n.62, 149, 188, 194, 219, 227
   rhapsodes 11
   rhetoric 47, 89
   similes 81, 87n.89
   storytelling 9–10, 169, 172–5
   Trojan War 8–10, 20–1, 168–9, 172–4, 188, 202

Homeric criticism
   Antisthenes 11
   Aristotle 149, 162n.52
   Dio 166, 168, 171–3
   parody 178
Homeric Hymns 123–5, 139n.39
Householder, F. 119, 124
humour 115–16, 124, 133, 138n.24, 140n.54
   see also comedy
Hunter, Richard 93, 149, 172

idleness 144–6, 157
ignorance 73–6, 79, 177–8
Ilium/Troy
   Dio at 165–7, 182n.4
   Homer at 179–80
image
   cultural framework 227
   text relationship 211–15, 217, 219
imitation 23–5
Imperial Age
   Homer 7–8
   rhetoric 148, 191
   sculpture 226
Imperial audiences, typology 134–5
impossible topic, contestation 191–2, 199
improbable topic, contestation 191–3
improvisation 53
indirect speech 188
Ioli, Roberta 6, 9, 69
Ion rhapsode 11
Iris 123
irony 109n.19, 126, 171
Isocrates 52, 57
Italy, colonization 176–7

Jason and Medea 192
Jebb, R. 69
Jouan, F. 153
Judgement of the Arms 65–70, 72–3, 82n.15
Judgement of Paris 115–41, 149–58, 168
justice, Palamedes 47–8

Kim, L. 116
Kindstrand, Jan Fredrik 148, 154, 176, 177–8

kingship 144-6
Kirk, G. 69
knowledge
   claim to 86n.73
   opinion distinction 47-9
   truth 51, 70
Knudsen, Rachel 3, 47, 90
Koning, Hugo 7, 11, 101
Korenjak, M. 134
krisis tradition 71
Kroll, Wilhelm 176
Kunstverständnis 212

Laertius, Diogenes 65
Laks, Andrew 1-2, 3
language
   power of 43, 187-210
   referentiality 71
legal practice 47, 97
Libanius 191, 193, 194
'lie signals' 178
lies 165-85, 198
   see also deception; falsehoods
literary tradition
   Odysseus 75
   visual depictions 212-13, 215-16
Loeb edition
   Homer's epics 118-19
   Trojan Oration 175, 183n.19
loneliness 155-6
Lucian
   Against the Ignorant Book Collector 115
   Judgement of the Goddesses 7-8, 11, 116, 118, 120, 122-5, 129-31, 134-5, 136n.5, 184n.47
   Judgement of Paris 115-41
   Parliament of the Gods 117, 122
   Phalaris speeches 115
   Prometheus es 115
   Pseudologistes 135
   To One Who Said 'You're a Prometheus in Words' 106-7
   True Histories 134, 136n.6, 139n.41
   True Stories 182n.3
   Tyrannicide 115
   Zeus the Tragedian 117
'Lügenerzählung' (lying narrative) 178
lyric poetry 145, 160n.11

McCoy, M. B. 46, 53
Marathon 177
Medea 191-2
Meleager myth 27
Memnon
   Antilochus' death 221
   death of 219, 222-6, 227
   skin colour 224, 232n.60
Menelaus
   Helen's tale 21, 23, 25, 150-1, 156, 158
   Trojan War 41, 195
Menippus 131-2, 136n.2
Mesk, Josef 176
mimetic arts 211, 228n.4
mimetic skills 23, 25
Momus 117, 122, 136n.9
Montiglio, S. 74
Morgan, Kathryn 3, 7, 10, 41-2, 46, 51
Most, Glenn 1-2, 3
Muses 22, 24, 37n.46
Mysian tradition 192-5, 200
mythological characters 5, 90
   humour 115
   nicknames 91, 97
   role-playing 89-112
   speech 7, 10
mythological role-play 89-112
mythology
   ethical uses 29
   history contrast 224-5
   painting/poetry 212-13
   reuse of 2-5
   speech 10
   storytelling 9, 174

narrative first-person voice 167
narrative painting 211
narrative reality, text/image 212
narrative skills, Helen 21-2
narratives
   painting 215, 218, 220, 226-7
   poetry 21
nature
   attributes of 197
   laws of 191-2
Naulokhos 190
Nauplius and Palamedes 43
Neoptolemus 91-2

Nestor
  Diomedes and 223
  in role-play 90, 91–5, 101, 103, 105–6
New Ilion 158–9
Ní Mheallaigh, Karen 107
nicknames, mythological characters 91, 97
Nightingale, Andrea W. 44, 98
Nigrinus 117, 136n.9
Nile, veneration of 224
Nireus 130–2
nudity 120–1
Nyx 225

Odysseus
  Ajax and 3, 7, 65–88, 101, 109n.38
  Antisthenes' admiration 11
  contestation 194–5
  Helen and 21, 23–4
  Palamedes and 6, 41–4, 52–7, 59n.19, 70, 96–8, 100
  in role-play 90–1, 92–3, 95, 103–4, 106
  speech 65, 72–9, 80–1, 90
  storytelling 22
Olson, S. 91
Onuphis town 170
opinion–knowledge distinction 47–9
oral tradition 174, 227
  see also verbal narrative
oration 52–3, 147
Orestes 190
Orpheus and Protagoras 103–4
Ovid
  Ajax versus Odysseus 83n.16
  Judgement of Paris 152
oxen, references to 80–1, 87n.87

pacifism 162n.56
painting
  independence of 225–7
  narratives 215, 218, 220, 226–7
  poetry relationship 211–13, 216–17, 225–6
  reality 212, 215
  scenes 223
  text as image 219
Palamedes 9, 41–63
  archaic/classical traditions 42–6
  argumentation 32
  Euripides as 105

Gorgias' speeches 82n.1, 202
Odysseus and 6, 70, 96–8, 100
Sophists' use of 10, 90, 95–101, 106
Palladium, theft of 71, 73
'pan-Homerism' 149–50
Paneides 83n.36
Panope 133
paradox–rhetoric relationship 149
Paris
  abduction of Helen 143–64, 168
  Herodotus on 197–8
  Homeric criticism 171, 172–3
  Judgement of 115–41, 149–58, 168
parody 118, 133–5, 140n.54, 178
Patroclus
  Achilles' loyalty 224, 232n.59
  death of 101, 168, 172, 219–20, 222
  Trojan Horse 23
Pausanias 89, 202
  Cypria summary 42–3
Penelope 22, 23, 35n.23
Pericles 91, 101–2, 103
Persian wars 177
Phaedrus 94–5, 99
Phemius 25
Philip of Macedon 144
Philodemus, *On the Good King According to Homer* 146
philosophy and rhetoric 53
Philostratus 10, 115
  Gymnasticus 229n.16
  Heroicus 8, 10, 187–210
  Imagines 8–9, 11, 198, 202, 211–35
  Life of Apollonius of Tyana 106, 188, 201, 232n.62
  Lives of the Sophists 4, 94, 202
  textual references 213–14
Phocylides 144
Pindar
  Ajax in 69, 73
  Antisthenes and 81
  Mysian tradition 193
  Nemean Odes 67–8, 92
Plato 1, 61n.39
  Antisthenes and 65
  Apology of Socrates 45–6, 59n.19, 99–101, 104
  Cratylus 96
  Hippias Major 91, 101

Hippias Minor 13n.13, 92–3, 101, 103
Homer's reconstruction 148–9
mythological role-play 91
Odysseus and 69
painting 211–12
Parmenides 95
Phaedrus 10, 36n.43, 59n.19, 60n.32, 94–6, 98–9, 100–2, 161n.42
Protagoras 89–91, 102–6
Republic 228n.4
Socrates and 11, 45–6
Sophistai 110n.44
teachers' roles 92
Timaeus 182n.18
plurality of elements 34n.21
Plutarch, *De Herodoti* 181
poetic myth 174
poetic rhetoric 27
poetry 2–3, 5, 6, 31
 definition 27
 Deliades 25
 Dio's view 180
 games analogy 29
 Gorgias' views 19–20, 30
 for kings 144–6
 Muses 37n.46
 narratives 21
 painting relationship 211–13, 216–17, 225–6
 Palamedes 43
 power of 26
 speech and 28
 theory of use 148
 value of 22
 voice similarity 24
Pollux 156
Porphyry 66, 77
praise theme 68
Priam
 Achaeans and 222
 Helen's abduction 150–1
 Herodotus on 196–7
 Judgement of Paris 137n.14
 Neoptolemus' death 92
Prince, Susan 73–4, 78, 101
pro-Roman propaganda 175–8, 183n.41
probability arguments 47
Proclus, *Cypria* summary 42, 195
Prodicus 3
Prometheus 90, 102–7, 110n.44, 110n.45

Protagoras 2
 Greet Speech 102
 Homeric language 11, 12n.12, 14n.33
 mythological role-play 89–91, 102–6
 nicknames 91
Protesilaus 187–90, 196–7, 200–2, 204n.18

Quintilian, *Institutio oratoria* 95–6
Quintus, *Posthomerica* 14n.27, 231n.42
quotations
 classification 149
 Homer's epics 119, 147

Radermacher, L. 89
Rankin, H. 78–9
reading 115, 129–30, 133–4
realism 212
reality
 appearance relationship 22
 painting 212, 215
recusatio 34n.10
referentiality of language 71
Reinhardt, K. 123
rhapsodes 10–11
rhetoric 2, 4, 9
 aims of 56–7
 defining 94–5
 Dio 175–6
 educational standard 215
 Gorgias 26–7, 29, 47, 51–2, 95
 heroes 7, 101
 Imperial Age 148
 mythological characters 89, 101–2
 Odysseus 80–1
 through paradox 149
 philosophy and 53
 poetry's relationship 5, 19
 quotations 147
 speech and 28, 46, 98
 Trojan War 187–210
 truth 174
Robert, F. 147
Rohde, N. F. M. 4
Roman Empire 175
Roman lineage, in Troy 149, 158
Roman propaganda, *Trojan Oration* 175–8, 183n.41
Roman rule, Greece 4
Rome city 177

Rowe, Christopher 100
Rufinus 121
rusticity, Paris 127

Salamis 177
satire 44, 115, 117
Scafoglio, G. 149–50
Scamander 198–200, 213, 216–18, 227
Schoess, Sophie 8–9, 11
Schönberger, O. 212
Scopelian, *Gigantias* 14n.27
sculpture 225, 226, 232n.62
Second Sophistic 4–5, 7
    abduction of Helen 143–64
    Dio Chrysostom 143–64, 165–85
    ekphrasis 211–35
    Epos manipulation 147–51
    Homeric *exegesis* 115–41
    mythological role-play 106–7
    Trojan War 187–210
Seeck, Gustav Adolf 172
Sextus Empiricus 190
shields, heroes 72, 78–9, 84n.48
silence 72–3
similes 81, 87n.89
singing
    Deliades 25
    Helen 20–1
    Homeric poetry 145
    Muses 24
Sirens 24, 34n.19
Sistakou, E. 121
Sisyphus and Odysseus 68, 100
Sisyphus (satyr drama) 44
Socrates
    Achilles' similarity 101
    Antisthenes and 65
    Egyptian stories 98–9
    Glaucon and 161n.42
    irony 109n.19
    mythological role-play 90–3, 103–5, 110n.44, 110n.45
    Palamedes' similarity 44–6, 59n.19, 96, 100
    rhapsodes 11
    rhetorical skill 2, 94–5
    Sophistic traits 12n.11
Sophist
    mythological character conflation 90
    terminology 1

Sophistic, terminology 1
Sophocles 73, 75
    Ajax 69–71
    The madness of Odysseus 43
    Palamedes 43–4
    Philoctetes 69
speech
    adapting 56–7
    early arts of 96, 98
    improvisation 53
    mythological characters 7, 10, 97
    poetry as 27
    positive/negative effects 55
    power of 2, 8, 26, 46, 188
    truth 50–2, 60n.30, 202
    wisdom connection 44, 49
Squire, M. 217–19
Stanford, W. 69
statues *see* sculpture
Stesichorus
    on Palamedes 43
    Palinode 19, 33n.1, 152, 161n.42
Stinton, T. C. W. 152
Stoic view, anger 85n.65
storytelling
    Dio's view 180
    Homeric epics 9–10, 20, 22, 30, 169, 172–5
    mythic function 6
Strabo 194, 199, 202
Strauss Clay, J. 69
superlatives 130, 132–3
Swain, S. 149

teachers' roles 92
Telemachus and Helen 25, 34n.13
Telephus 193
text
    image relationship 211–15, 217, 219
    painting's independence from 226
textual references, Philostratus 213–14
Theban War 136n.10
Theodorus 95
Theognis 69, 144
Theon 191–2, 194, 197, 199, 204n.30
    Progymnasmata 191
Thersites 131–2
Thessaly, colonization 176
Thetis and Achilles 168
Theuth and Palamedes 98–9

thinking, value of 74
Thrasymachus 95
Thucydides 194–5, 198
Tirrito, Sara 8, 10
Tisias 32
tragedy 19, 26–8, 97, 100
Trajan 145, 160n.10
transcendence 73, 75, 77, 79–81
Trapp, M. 159
Triphiodorus, *The Sack of Troy* 23
Troika 200
Trojan Horse 23, 25
Trojan leaders 176
Trojan War 187–210
    Ajax versus Odysseus 74, 76, 79–80
    Dio Chrysostom on 147, 150, 153
    Homer on 8, 9–10, 20–1, 143, 162n.52, 168–9, 172–4, 188, 202
    Judgement of Paris 137n.11, 154, 158
    Palamedes' role 41–2, 98
    Paris' idleness 144, 157
Trojans as Roman ancestors 149, 158
Troy/Ilium
    Dio at 165–7, 182n.4
    Homer at 179–80
trust 178–81
truth 23, 32
    construction of 187–210
    Dio Chrysostom 165–85
    knowledge 47–8, 70
    poetry 22, 30
    rhetoric 174
    speech 50–2, 60n.30, 202
Tyndareus 154, 156
Typhon 100
Tyrtaeus 102

Underworld
    Odysseus in 66, 72, 104
    Socrates in 100

verbal narrative 213, 226
    see also oral tradition

virtue 71, 74
visual culture 223–5, 226–7
visual depictions 212–13, 215–16, 226
    see also painting
visual reality 212
visuality
    Homer 219
    Philostratus 214, 216
voice 23–5
von Arnim, Hans 176

warfare, art of 71, 78, 80
weapons
    mastery of 79
    as 'sign' 84n.42
weaving 20–1
Wilshere, Nicholas 7–8, 11
wisdom 1, 44, 49, 212
word play 212
Worman, Nancy 90
writing
    dangers of 98
    inferiority of 54–5, 61n.38
    'signs' 129
    support for 57

Xanthos (Scamander) 198
Xenophanes 124
Xenophon 69
    Apology of Socrates 59n.19

Zeno of Elea 95, 97
Zenodotus 131–2
Zeus
    Eos and 225
    Homeric criticism 168
    Paris and 116–17, 119, 127–9, 132–3, 137n.14, 152, 157
    Prometheus and 102–3
    Scamander and 198
    Theban War 136n.10
Zeus' altar, Priam's death 92

www.ingramcontent.com/pod-product-compliance
Lightning Source LLC
Chambersburg PA
CBHW062136300426
44115CB00012BA/1949